berlin

TRAVELER

berlin

Damien Simonis
photography by Pierre Adenis

National Geographic
Washington, D.C.

CONTENTS

TRAVELING WITH EYES OPEN 6

CHARTING YOUR TRIP 8

History & Culture 13
Berlin Today **14–21**   History of Berlin **22–37**
Food & Drink **38–39**   The Arts **40–50**

Unter den Linden & Potsdamer Platz 51
Introduction & Map **52–53**   A Walk Around Wilhelmstrasse & Old
Regierungsviertel **70–73**   Feature: The Berlin Wall, Then & Now **78–79**

Central Berlin 81
Introduction & Map **82–83**   A Walk Around Red Berlin **100–101**
Feature: Berlin's Jewish Community, Past & Present **112–113**

Tiergarten & Around 115
Introduction & Map **116–117**   Feature: The Shock of the New **122–123**

Charlottenburg 133
Introduction & Map **134–135**   Walk: Strolling Around the
Ku'damm **138–139**   Feature: Berlin's Brightest Christmas Lights **146–147**

Prenzlauer Berg, Friedrichshain, & the East 155
Introduction & Map **156–157**   Walk: A Prenzlauer Promenade **158–159**
Feature: Berlin Design **164**

Schöneberg to Kreuzberg 175
Introduction & Map **176–177**   Feature: Marvelous Marlene **182**

Spandau, Dahlem, & the West 187
Introduction & Map **188–189**   Feature: The Strange Story of Rudolf
Hess **194–195**

Excursions 207
Introduction & Map **208–209**   Mecklenburg Lake District Drive **218–219**

TRAVELWISE 233
Planning Your Trip **234**   Hotels & Restaurants **241**   Shopping **256**
Entertainment **260**   Language Guide & Menu Reader **265**

INDEX 266   CREDITS 270

Pages 2–3: All that glitters at the entrance to Schloss Charlottenburg
Left: The green space of the Volkspark Friedrichshain offers respite to local high-rise residents.

TRAVELING WITH EYES OPEN

Alert travelers go with a purpose and leave with a benefit. If you travel responsibly, you can help support wildlife conservation, historic preservation, and cultural enrichment in the places you visit. You can enrich your own travel experience as well.

To be a geo-savvy traveler:

- Recognize that your presence has an impact on the places you visit.

- Spend your time and money in ways that sustain local character. (Besides, it's more interesting that way.)

- Value the destination's natural and cultural heritage.

- Respect the local customs and traditions.

- Express appreciation to local people about things you find interesting and unique to the place: its nature, scenery, music or food, historic villages, and buildings.

- Vote with your wallet: Support the people who support the place, patronizing businesses that make an effort to celebrate and protect what's special there. Seek out shops, local restaurants, inns, and tour operators who love their home—who love taking care of it and showing it off. Avoid businesses that detract from the character of the place.

- Enrich yourself, taking home more memories and stories to tell, knowing that you have contributed to the preservation and enhancement of the destination.

That is the type of travel now called geotourism, defined as "tourism that sustains or enhances the geographical character of a place—its environment, culture, aesthetics, heritage, and the well-being of its residents." To learn more, visit National Geographic's Center for Sustainable Destinations at *www.nationalgeographic.com/travel/sustainable*.

berlin

ABOUT THE AUTHORS & PHOTOGRAPHER

Damien Simonis, raised in Sydney, Australia, has had a little trouble settling down since he took a one-way flight to Cairo in 1989. In his baggage was a degree in languages and seven years' experience on some of Australia's leading dailies, including the *Australian* and the *Age*. Since landing in the Egyptian capital, Simonis has lived, studied, and worked all over Europe and the Middle East. In 1992, he started writing guidebooks and travel articles for publications in Australia, the U.K., and North America. He hasn't stopped since. His wanderings have taken him from Ukraine to Sudan, from the Alps to the Red Sea. Even before that flight to Cairo, Simonis had had his first taste of foreign travel in Germany in the 1980s. Repeated study trips brought him back and he frequently visited Berlin at the height of the Cold War. Although he now lives in the warmer climes of Barcelona, Spain, his affection for Germany, and Berlin in particular, has never waned. He'll be back again soon.

Photographer **Pierre Adenis,** born in Toulon, France, studied in Nice, Lille, and Paris before moving permanently to Berlin in 1987. In 1990, he began his career as a press photographer and became the Berlin correspondent for Paris Sipa Press photo agency. He became a partner in Berlin's GAFF agency in 1992 and has been represented worldwide by LAIF since 2000. In addition to his work in his current home country of Germany, Adenis has traveled to and photographed the United States, France, Russia, the Middle East, and Greece. He has been published in numerous books and magazines, mostly in France and Germany.

Jeremy Gray wrote the original Travelwise and updates and sidebars for this edition. Born of English parents in Louisiana, Gray grew up with an equal affinity for crumpets and fried chicken. After a university scholarship took him to Europe, he worked as a journalist and author in Amsterdam, Frankfurt, and London, contributing to newspapers, magazines, wire services, and more than 20 travel guides for leading publishers. Since 2004, Gray has lived in a converted butter factory in Berlin's humming Mitte district.

Charting Your Trip

Though Berlin is nine times the size of Paris, the "poor but sexy" capital (the mayor's catchphrase) is easy to get your head around. Superb public transportation gets you where you want to go in a hurry, squeezing the most out of your precious moments.

It's impossible to resist Berlin's relentless dynamism—a spirit that transformed Potsdamer Platz from a Cold War zombie into a forest of glinting skyscrapers, and the Berlin Wall into a bicycle trail. But where to start?

After communism got the boot, Berlin's center returned to its 19th-century heart in the Mitte district, where its Prussian jewels are being fastidiously restored. The once grungy, former working-class areas of Prenzlauer Berg and Friedrichshain are now gentrifying darlings of the party set. South across the Spree, multicultural Kreuzberg and its crunchy cousin Neukölln add to the cosmopolitan brio. Since the *Wende* (the "turning point" of reunification), these neighborhoods generate the most creative sparks for the arts, gastronomy, and nightlife, not to mention droves of quirky hole-in-the-wall shops and clothing boutiques. The magic is spreading north to Pankow, the dormitory suburb of GDR (German Democratic Republic, or East Germany) appa-ratchiks, and to parts of Treptow, an old Soviet stronghold on the city's eastern fringe.

Affluent western Berlin exudes a sedate charm in gracious, old-money districts like Charlottenburg, Wilmersdorf, or villa-studded Zehlendorf. But wealth doesn't inure its residents to fun; on the contrary, their brand of cheeky humor can crack a smile on the most hardened cynic. Schöneberg still has the bohemian flair that captivated *Goodbye to Berlin* author Christopher Isherwood, whose colorful experiences inspired the movie *Cabaret*.

For a major metropolis, Berlin is surprisingly green and wreathed in natural playgrounds. To the west, lush forests, lakes, and sandy beaches beckon around the Havel River network, and to the east, in Köpenick.

How to Get Around

Until the costly, delay-plagued Berlin-Brandenburg Airport (BER) opens, the city will continue to be served by two airports, Tegel and Schönefeld. From Tegel, buses X9 and 109 connect to Zoologischer Garten, while bus TXL heads to the main train station (Hauptbahnhof) and Alexanderplatz. From Schönefeld (and later from BER), take Deutsche Bahn's RE Airport

Berlin's coat of arms

Express (around 30 minutes) or the S-Bahn into town. A taxi will cost €20 to €35 ($25–$45) but usually, you needn't bother.

Fast and efficient, Berlin's public transportation system whisks you around town in no time flat. Transit authority BVG runs a tightly woven network of bus, tram, and commuter rail (consult the map on the rear flap of this book, and the journey planner at www.bvg.de). Fares are based on three zones: Zone A for central Berlin, zone B to the edge of the suburbs, and zone C for Potsdam and Schönefeld Airport/BER. The basic A+B ticket gets you to most destinations in town. You can buy tickets from BVG machines at stations, or on buses, trams, and ferries. There are no turnstiles, but validate your ticket in a time-stamping machine or risk a fine by plainclothes inspectors.

Berlin is rather vast to be fully explored on foot, but its sight-filled bits can be surprisingly compact. Places too far to walk are a cinch on two wheels, as this environmentally minded city is laced with bicycle paths. You might consider renting a car for excursions farther afield, although trains and buses do the trick.

NOT TO BE MISSED:

Ascending the dome of the Reichstag building 55

The Brandenburger Tor, Germany's eternal portal 58–59

The sobering displays of the Holocaust Monument 60–61

Taking in the artistic treasures of Museum Island 84–96

Strolling through former communist East Berlin 100–101

Queen Sophie's opulent Schloss Charlottenburg 140–145

Nightlife in Prenzlauer Berg & Friedrichshain 158–160

Touring Frederick the Great's palaces at Potsdam 210–216

If You Have Only a Week

Lovers of history, urban culture, and fine architecture should logically begin their visit in Mitte in central Berlin, where 10 of the city's top 25 attractions lie within a half hour's stroll of one another. On **Day 1,** take a tour of Germany's phoenix, the Reichstag building, and enjoy the panorama from its transparent visitor dome. Admire the iconic Brandenburger Tor and wander past historic buildings on Unter den Linden, showcase avenue of Prussian kings. View the ecclesiastical riches and royal crypt of the Berliner Dom, court church of the Hohenzollerns. Enjoy the world-class collections of Museum Island on **Day 2,** perhaps starting with the ancient treasures of the Pergamonmuseum or the bust of Queen Nefertiti in the Neues Museum. Take the elevator to the top of the Fernsehturm—Germany's tallest structure—and dine in its rotating cloud-level café. Float along Berlin's waterways on a boat tour, and cool your heels at Strandbar Mitte.

Visitor Information

The city's visitor service, **Berlin Tourism and Marketing** (www.berlin-tourist-information.de and www.visitberlin.de), runs well-organized Infostores at outlets including the main train station, the Alexa shopping mall on Alexanderplatz, inside Brandenburg Gate, and at the airport.

You can book tickets for events and sightseeing tours, and make hotel reservations for a small fee. For entertainment listings in English, check out www.bangbangberlin.com; more details are available in German from magazines *Tip, Zitty,* and *Prinz* (see Travelwise p. 239).

Discount Cards

Available at ticket offices and hotels, the **Welcome Card** *(www .berlin-welcomecard.de)* is the city's premier saver pass. Valid for up to five days on buses, trams, and trains, the card also gives you free or reduced entry to guided tours, museums, theaters, and other leisure facilities. The three-day **Museum Pass** *(www.visitberlin.de)* opens doors at 55 state-run galleries, including those of Museum Island. An exceptional value is the **Berlin Scheckheft** *(www.berlin scheckheft.de)*, sold at newsstands from May to August and giving you hefty discounts not available with the other two passes.

Explore the thicket of skyscrapers and stores in the former no-man's-land on Potsdamer Platz and take in a movie at the Filmmuseum on **Day 3.** Sample the tasty snacks at the nearby Winterfeldtplatz farmers' market in Schöneberg. Spend **Day 4** poking around the gorgeous interiors of Schloss Charlottenburg and its sprawling, folly-filled gardens, and browse for unusual souvenirs in the Gipsformerei (statue replica workshop).

Head for the east on **Day 5** and sharpen your sense of Berlin style in Prenzlauer Berg or Friedrichshain, whose shops, cafés, and nightclubs set standards for hipness. In nearby Lichtenberg, learn about the surveillance society at the Stasi Museum. Make your way back toward the center on **Day 6** and relive the Cold War's nail-biting confrontations at the Checkpoint Charlie Museum. Take a self-guided walking tour of the old government district along Wilhelmstrasse, and spend time in the sobering Holocaust Monument. Treat yourself to a culinary extravaganza at Restaurant Tim Raue in Kreuzberg.

On **Day 7,** jump on the RegionalExpress train from Berlin's main station and venture outside the city to see Frederick the Great's palatial treasures at Potsdam (a 25-minute journey), or frolic with the small fry on the beaches of Wannsee (only 15 minutes away). But before you say *tschüß,* let it all hang out at one of Berlin's delightful street festivals (see Travelwise pp. 234–235; view a full festival calendar online at *www.visitberlin.de/en* under "Event Highlights").

If You Have More Time

Longer stays will allow you to explore in depth and venture into the countryside. Spend more time in West Berlin, starting with the city's war-torn symbol, the Kaiser-Wilhelm-Gedächtniskirche. Stroll down the shopping boulevard Kurfürstendamm, and fill up on exotic delicacies at KaDeWe. Take the kids to see the latest adorable offspring at the Berlin Zoo and Aquarium. Linger in the

Sights on the Move

An excellent way to tour Berlin is on board a public double-decker bus. Lines 100 and 200 of the BVG, the city's transport authority, run past major landmarks of the city center for €2.40 ($3.12), the price of a single fare. Bus 100 runs a half hour from Bahnhof Zoo to Alexanderplatz, taking in the Gedächt-

niskirche, Tiergarten, Victory Column, Reichstag building, Brandenburg Gate, and Unter den Linden. Line 200 also starts at Bahnhof Zoo, but plies a more southerly route.

Pick up a brochure with descriptions from the BVG's information booth at Bahnhof Zoo.

German soccer fans celebrate at Brandenburger Tor after a win against the Netherlands.

stands of the 1930s Olympiastadion, where sprinter Jesse Owens dashed Hitler's theories of Aryan superiority, and take a stroll through the leafy Grunewald.

In the second week, admit the folly of ambition, regroup, and gobble up the cultural nuggets you missed earlier. Explore the singular Egyptian finds of the Altes Museum or Casper David Friedrich's otherworldly landscapes at the Alte National-galerie, both in historic Mitte. Nearby, a WWII air-raid shelter is reborn as art gallery Sammlung Boros, as hip as anything you'll find in the bohemian fringe. Stick with civil defense and hop north to Wedding district for a creepy Berlin Underworlds tour of Nazi-era bunkers. In cross-cultural Kreuzberg, absorb the twists and turns of Germany's Jewry in the zigzag Jüdisches Museum. Take in a concert at the world-renowned Berliner Philharmoniker by Potsdamer Platz, or at neoclassical Gendarmenmarkt, a blink from the blue-blooded Prussian boulevard Unter den Linden.

If you get restless in town, Berlin has terrific excursions within easy striking distance. Visit the unspoiled nature reserves of the Mecklenburg Lake District, about 80 miles (130 km) northeast of Berlin, and cycle around the glittering Müritzsee, Germany's largest lake. Or head to the punt-filled canals of the UNESCO-protected Spreewald beginning at Lübben, 53 miles (85 km) to the southeast. The Saxon city of Leipzig, located some 118 miles (190 km) southwest of the capital, is known for its musical traditions. This fun-loving destination works as a day trip thanks to a superb train connection, but just a few miles farther south, the richly stocked museums, restored baroque gems, and pretty Elbe valley setting of Dresden can easily fill a weekend.

Tipping

By law, sales tax and a service charge are included in your restaurant bill, but it is customary to add a gratuity of 5 to 10 percent if you are happy with the service. Tips in taxis vary widely—some people round up, while others pay an extra 5 to 10 percent. Bellhops get €1 ($1.30) per bag in top-end hotels.

History & Culture

Berlin Today   14–21

Experience: Beach Bar Craze   20

History of Berlin   22–37

Experience: Do You Tango?   29

Food & Drink   38–39

Experience: Underground Supper Clubs   39

The Arts   40–50

Experience: Silent Cinema   48

Elegant Pariser Platz has been rebuilt since World War II. Opposite: Saint George fights a dragon in front of the Nikolaikirche.

Berlin Today

"It is Berlin's destiny never to be, but always to be in the process of becoming."
The phrase from art historian Karl Scheffler (1869–1951) is as true today as
when he wrote it in the 1920s. Berlin is the most changeable city in Europe. Its
physical face has been repeatedly reassembled, and its restless populace is as
fickle as it is creative. A city of paradoxes, it exerts a charm that few can resist.

Munich may be richer and Hamburg more of a commercial powerhouse, but
neither attracts the attention Berlin does. A colorful army of *Zuzügler* (newcomers)
from all over the world and all walks of life has come and seems unable to leave.

Berlin's skyline includes the Sony Center, Bahntower, and Kollhoff buildings at Potsdamer Platz.

The number of tourists visiting the city has rocketed since 2000, placing Berlin in third place in Europe after London and Paris. More than 10 million overnight visitors were registered in 2012.

Berlin has something for everyone. In few places is the drama and tragedy of 20th-century European history so deeply etched into the fabric of a city. Berlin's grand galleries are world class and the cultural calendar is jammed. With three opera houses, the Berlin Philharmoniker, and a thriving local gallery scene, Berlin is busy year-round.

Night owls have myriad opportunities to test their staying power in the restaurants, bars, and clubs of different districts. Even working-class Friedrichshain, once a dour East German neighborhood, now has its own lively scene to rival the well-established nocturnal offerings of the Kreuzberg

The city had to sew its two halves together, which meant creating citywide transportation, telecommunications, and utilities.

and Prenzlauer Berg areas. As local party animals will tell you, it is virtually impossible to keep up with the clubs that open and close across a city where there is no regulated closing time. And Berlin is one of the continent's gay magnets, drawing over a million revelers for the summer Christopher Street Day parade.

The Phoenix Rises

Bombed to the ground in World War II and divided in two on the Cold War front lines for 40 years, this indomitable phoenix continues to rise from its ashes. The scars of war, cold or otherwise, have yet to be completely healed, but progress has been breathtaking. Lack of money and simple neglect had left much of East Berlin in decay. Infrastructure was poor (few East Berlin households had telephones), and the no-man's-land on both sides of the Berlin Wall had left vast tracts of the city center as wasteland.

But from 1990 on, Berlin became one of the biggest construction sites in the world. The city had to sew its two halves together, which meant creating citywide transportation, telecommunications, and utilities. A bevy of international architects flocked to the city to fill the gaps with imaginative new buildings, many of which constitute sights in their own right in 21st-century Berlin. Potsdamer Platz, one of the busiest squares of prewar Germany and a desert from 1945 to 1990, is again a bustling nerve center.

Much of the city disappeared in the 1940s bombings and postwar demolition, but the solution hasn't simply been to build from scratch. Many of Berlin's grandest buildings have been restored to their former glory. Some are an exciting mix of old and new. The remodeling of the Reichstag, once again the seat of Germany's national parliament, is perhaps the most startling architectural symbol of this attempt to marry the city's (at times) glorious past with an optimistic look into the future.

Controversy is never far away. Now, as decades ago, arguments rage over what should be restored, demolished, replaced, or rebuilt from scratch. Icons of western Berlin, such as Schloss Charlottenburg and the ruined Kaiser-Wilhelm-Gedächtniskirche, were due to be finished off by the wrecking ball in the 1950s, but have now been saved. On the east side, the damaged but intact Berliner Schloss, onetime residence of Germany's emperors, was destroyed in a cynical demonstration of ideological willfulness. To the communists, it had been a symbol of German imperialism. Its successor, the Palast der Republik, the East German parliament building, was torn down in 2008. To many Germans, it was a symbol of dictatorship. To others, however, it was a piece of history and should have been left in place. Why, they cried, should this building go when so many erected under Adolf Hitler's regime (such as the former Aviation and Propaganda ministries and Tempelhof airport) have been left standing? After a lengthy debate, the authorities are pressing ahead on the reconstruction of the original Berliner Schloss, although funds for the €600 million ($780 million) project have not been fully secured.

A Cultural Crucible

Berlin's value as a tourist destination was long restricted to the curiosity of the Berlin Wall, the fortified ideological frontier that separated West from East. Indeed, in the early 1990s, tourism to the city collapsed. With the same tenacity that distinguished Berliners as they rebuilt their city after World War II, the city's residents set about rebuilding their reputation as a destination for art lovers.

The extraordinarily costly business of restoring the central Museumsinsel (Museum Island) to its former glory and turning it into one of the world's biggest and most modern museum complexes is symbolic of the city's efforts to renew itself. Much has already been done, but in the coming years all of Berlin's collections of antiquities as well as much of its European art through the 19th century will be housed here.

So many of [Berlin's] buildings, monuments, streets, and districts are redolent of the events of the 20th century.

The Kulturforum, which arose in West Berlin in the 1960s as a new pole of the arts, is also undergoing change, but it will remain home to such major collections as the Neue Nationalgalerie (20th-century art) and Kunstgewerbemuseum (applied arts). Schloss Charlottenburg, along with its surrounding museums, and the Dahlem Museen complex in the city's southwest are further cultural magnets.

Other signal museums have emerged from nothing. A once glorious—and then bombed out—railway station is now at the core of the Deutsches Technikmuseum (German Museum of Technology), one of the world's great homages to human creativity. Nearby, a daring design has given life to the Jüdisches Museum, dedicated to German Jewry. The Berlinische Galerie has established itself as a major stop on the modern and contemporary art circuit. Another former railway station, Hamburger Bahnhof, is now an enormous contemporary art gallery. In all, the city counts around 200 museums.

Young Berliners enjoy sound and light at the Sage Club in Mitte.

History Hounds

For many, though, the fascination of Berlin lies in its historical resonance. So many of its buildings, monuments, streets, and districts are redolent of the events of the 20th century. Those seeking to come to grips with the horrors of the Nazi period can try to do so in countless ways. The Denkmal für die ermordeten Juden Europas, a controversial site in the heart of the city, is a broad, open-air monument dedicated to the memory of the Jews killed under Hitler. The Sachsenhausen concentration camp just outside Berlin is enveloped in a terrifying quiet on a cold winter's day. A stroll around the Scheunenviertel, the main Jewish quarter in prewar Berlin, has an eerie quality. Similarly, a walk around Wilhelmstrasse, the old government district, will bring back memories of the Nazi era, especially in the Topographie des Terrors, on the site of the former SS (Schutzstaffel) headquarters.

Berlin's history has many other layers, however. Parts of the wall that cut the city in two from 1961 to 1989 are still in place. Checkpoint Charlie continues to be visible. On the eastern side of the city, you can visit the former Ministry for State Security (Stasi) and its horrifying jail. In Karlshorst, you can visit a museum dedicated to the fighting on the Eastern Front that's housed in the former Soviet military headquarters in Berlin. Soviet war memorials, especially in Treptower Park, recall not only the huge sacrifices made by the Soviet Union during World War II but also the imposition of Soviet control on East Germany.

Schloss Charlottenburg, Berliner Dom (Berlin Cathedral), the Brandenburg Gate, and Gendarmenmarkt, all heavily restored, evoke seemingly more innocent times under the kings of Prussia and emperors of the German Reich from 1871. Unter den Linden, Potsdamer Platz, and Alexanderplatz, however altered down the years, are still powerfully evocative of times before the Nazi nightmare.

East Meets West

Berlin and its people manage the neat trick of living with the city's often painful history without allowing themselves to be dragged down by it. Time, however, will be needed to heal all the wounds. In spite of the frantic pace of reconstruction, the city's western and eastern halves have yet to fully blend.

Catch the U1 train from Uhlandstrasse, in the west of the city, to Warschauer Strasse in the east and observe the subtle changes as you travel. At early stops, you will see locals reading the *Berliner Morgenpost* or western German dailies such as the *Frankfurter Allgemeine Zeitung.* By the time you reach Warschauer Strasse, most will be reading East Berlin's *Berliner Zeitung.* A few may even be flipping through *Neues Deutschland,* the old Communist Party organ. On your way through Kottbusser Tor, you may hear more Turkish spoken than German, and by the end of the line it might well be Russian. The city's central districts (such as Mitte, Prenzlauer Berg, and Kreuzberg) have largely been taken over by Germans from other parts of the country and by foreigners. Berliners stick to the periphery. East Berliners prefer Pankow or Karlshorst. West Berliners congregate in Charlottenburg, Wilmersdorf, and beyond. It would hardly occur to them to move east, just as an East Berliner would feel like a fish out of water in, say, Dahlem.

The division manifests itself in other ways. While West Berlin is for the most part solidly bourgeois, the eastern half exerts an ongoing fascination for a younger, alternative set. Much of what is thought to be hip happens on the east side, and young

Art looks at art in Kreuzberg's Berlinische Galerie, one of a phalanx of world-class galleries in Berlin.

Gentrification Blues

"Currywurst, not Spätzle." The banner hanging from a Kreuzberg balcony isn't extolling the virtues of Berlin curried sausage over rolled Swabian noodles. This is an oblique protest against gentrification, a process that pits city planners, real estate brokers, and affluent newcomers against the lower classes and Berlin's billowing community of cash-poor creatives. After the Wall came down in 1989, grungy-chic Berlin became a magnet for bohemian artists and musicians. They showed up in droves as underground galleries, bars, and nightclubs emerged in abandoned bunkers and disused industrial buildings.

That era, however, seems to be ending despite vocal opposition by Berlin's alternative community. Everywhere you look, critics complain, the wealthy seem to be getting the upper hand. Swanky condos are springing up across former East Berlin, driving up rents and forcing small shops, nightclubs, and poorer tenants out of the center. In Mitte, Kunsthaus Tacheles, a legendary graffiti-strewn artists' squat in a ruined department store, has been cleared to make way for new investors. Construction of Mediaspree, a giant swath of offices, residential lofts, and hotels on the riverbank, has gone ahead despite stiff resistance from locals in Friedrichshain, a rough-edged hub of nightlife.

Critics fear a fate similar to what happened in New York's Greenwich Village: Where the lure of a cool, creative atmosphere and lifestyle attracts the well-to-do, they, in turn, extinguish the spark that drew them there in the first place.

Berliners will tell you that 90 percent of the best bars, clubs, and entertainment venues lie east of the former Berlin Wall—quite a change from the years before 1989.

The Spirit of Berlin

Locals are known for their *Schnauze,* the Berlin version of attitude. Yes, Berliners can have a curt and grouchy side, pretty much like any big-city folk. They also have a limitless sense of humor and self-deprecation. Berliners will be the first to smile and admit that they forever *meckern* (grumble) about almost everything (another big-city malady).

One thing that attracts so many other Germans to Berlin is that the city is, well, so un-German. To many, it is a mysterious East European city, far removed from the center of things and having more in common with Warsaw or Moscow than with the former capital, Bonn, or the banking city of Frankfurt.

It can be untidy and easygoing. Berlin in the 1920s was an anything-goes town, and so it is today. Nowhere else in Germany will police turn such a blind eye to minor infractions such as jaywalking. The trains and trams don't always run exactly on time. The city can seem grubby and shabby in places. And the myriad bohemian taverns look like they would be more at home in Madrid or Barcelona.

Berlin is the biggest college town in Germany, with three universities, various other higher education centers, and more than 140,000 students. The city's mostly left-leaning governments pour money into the arts. Although prices are on the rise, Berlin remains one of the cheapest cities in the country for renting, dining, or entertaining yourself. All of this has contributed to the energized feeling in Berlin. Art galleries and alternative theater thrive. And Berlin has gotten itself firmly on the map as a design center, from fashion to interiors. In January 2006, UNESCO named Berlin a Design City, praising it as a crossroads of creativity in building, the arts, interior design, fashion, and other applied arts.

Nearly one-quarter of the city's population of 3.3 million are either immigrants or foreign citizens. Leading the major groups are the Turks—the largest single community in mainland Europe, last estimated at about 103,000—followed by around 40,000 Poles. Australians, who number about 2,000, bring up the rear. These immigrant groups have added still more color to the cityscape and variety to local eating habits.

The Tough Get Going

Not all is well, however. Berlin's vitality and creativity are palpable, but the city's present is as rich in tension and contrast as its past.

Berlin is a city, but is also at the heart of a tiny *Land* (federal state), not unlike Washington, D.C. Covering 343 square miles (889 sq km), about the area of London, Berlin is cradled by the Spree and Havel Rivers and lies 112 feet (34 m) above sea level. It was the capital of Prussia until 1945 and of the German *Reich* (empire) from 1871 to 1945. East Berlin was the capital of East Germany from 1949 to 1990. The united city was made the capital of a reunited Germany in 1990, but the Bundestag (federal parliament) and government moved from Bonn only in 1999. Under an agreement designed to protect Bonn from collapse, six ministries remained behind and various other bodies moved into the small West German town. Curiously, while Berlin continues to struggle economically—the capital, for instance, tops the German rankings for recipients of long-term unemployment—Bonn is today booming more than ever.

After reunification, many speculated on a rapid resurrection of Berlin as Germany's capital. The greatest enthusiasts dreamed of the city becoming a grand metropolis at the crossroads of Eastern and Western Europe. In the first 15 or so years after reunification, the dreamers may have been a mite too ambitious. Many real estate speculators who bought up big in Berlin in the 1990s had their fingers burned, and much of the heavy industry that had kept East Berliners employed collapsed. Federal subsidies to West Berlin dried up. Certain planners saw the new Berlin, which had been an industrial powerhouse in prewar Germany, as a sparkling government, services, and media center. Aided by a bounce in Germany's

EXPERIENCE:
Beach Bar Craze

Berlin is admittedly no Club Med, but don't worry, its professional party animals bring the seaside to you. Whenever the temperature cracks about 65°F (18°C), the beach bar season opens with unbridled gusto. In the heart of Berlin, you can sun yourself on palm-shaded lounge chairs framed by improbable expanses of pristine white sand. The best ones set up on the Spree riverbanks, where tropical huts serve beer, cocktails, and pizza (see Travelwise pp. 260–261).

At the East Side Gallery, a surviving stretch of the Berlin Wall, locals create a summer beach bar.

export-oriented economy, a recovery in those sectors has helped bring down Berlin's unemployment to under 12 percent, which however is still almost double the national average. And the Berlin state government is €62 million ($81 million) in debt.

In spite of such problems, the city continues to pour money into its own transformation. In mid-2006, the city's first central train station, the Hauptbahnhof, was opened. Spread over four levels, it is Europe's biggest rail junction; about 300,000 rail passengers pass through this hub daily, making the city of Berlin one of Europe's main transportation nerve centers.

Berlin is not out of the woods, but perhaps a corner has been turned. Recent challenges for Berlin's gay, Socialist *Regierende Bürgermeister* (governing mayor), Klaus Wowereit (in power since 2001), include a series of costly delays on the scandal-plagued construction of Berlin-Brandenburg Airport at Schönefeld. As elsewhere in Germany, disillusion with the established parties has shaken up the political landscape. Founded in Berlin only in 2006, the liberal-progressive Piratenpartei (Pirate Party) won seats in local parliament for the first time in 2011, ejecting the much older Free Democrats.

This feat served to remind how things rarely stand still in one of Europe's most inspiring cities. Its burgeoning intellectual, café, and restaurant life gives the city a unique dynamism. Berlin is gaining a Europe-wide name for design as well as cutting-edge industrial sectors. High unemployment notwithstanding, there is an unmistakable buzz in the air. And Berlin has weathered far greater storms with grit and humor. ∎

History of Berlin

Few of Europe's capitals have had such a roller-coaster ride. And few could have seemed less destined to play a significant role in world affairs in the early days of their existence. London, Paris, and Rome all had more than a thousand years of history behind them when Berlin was little more than a huddle of muddy, medieval huts on the Spree River.

On the Edge of Civilization

Chronicles from 1237 are the first to mention a settlement called Kölln on a tiny island in the Spree River. The town was in the wild and woolly territory that came to be known as the Mark Brandenburg (a *Mark*, or march, was a frontier territory).

The restored statue of the goddess of peace dominates the Brandenburg Gate.

Another settlement, called Berlin, was founded close by about the same time. The surrounding thinly populated, marshy land was hotly contested by rival Slav and German counts and princes.

Invasions from the east, including those by the Mongols in the 13th century, threatened the existence of the two communities. In 1307, Berlin and Kölln joined forces in mutual defense. Through much of the 13th and 14th centuries, no one controlled the Mark Brandenburg. Plundering robber knights roamed at will, extorting what they could from towns and country folk.

Thirty Years' War & Berlin's Rebirth

Into the Brandenburg power vacuum stepped Friedrich Hohenzollern (1371–1440), a German noble who imposed the rule of (his) law on the Mark and the entire region and became *Kurfürst* (Elector) Friedrich I in 1415. Seven electors—among them archbishops, a duke, a margrave, a count, and a king—elected the Holy Roman Emperor, who had at least nominal control over much of what is today Germany, Austria, and central Europe; he was supposed to be the secular counterpart of the pope. Berlin-Kölln was brought to heel in 1448 and then made the elector's capital.

> **Disaster befell the twin towns [of Berlin-Kölln] when they were overrun by marauding troops during the Thirty Years' War.**

After two relatively stable centuries, disaster befell the twin towns when they were overrun by marauding troops during the Thirty Years' War (1618–1648) and hit by plague, leaving them with only 7,000 inhabitants. Friedrich Wilhelm (*R.* 1640–1688), who became known as the Great Elector, made it a priority to regain control of Brandenburg and repopulate the city. Protestants expelled from Catholic Austria were welcomed, as were wealthy Jewish families ordered to leave the Austrian capital, Vienna, in 1670. Around the same time, French Protestants (Huguenots) fleeing persecution also began to arrive. Other immigrants came from Poland, Holland, Sweden, Switzerland, and Bohemia. By the end of the century, what would from 1710 be known simply as Berlin had a population of 30,000, a third of them Huguenots.

In 1701, Kurfürst Friedrich III (*R.* 1688–1713), whose territories included Prussia to the east, named himself King Friedrich I of Prussia. He opened the purse strings to embellish his now royal capital, financing the rebuilding of the central *Schloss* (palace), the creation of the Friedrichstadt quarters, the *Zeughaus* (armory), and Gendarmenmarkt square. A country palace was built for Queen Sophie Charlotte (1668–1705) and, after her death, named Charlottenburg.

His successor, King Friedrich Wilhelm I (*R.* 1713–1740), curtailed spending on construction and the arts (except for the expansion

of Potsdam into a second royal residence), concentrating instead on raising a standing army. The soldier-king was, by all accounts, a man of little humor and of odd tastes. His particular obsession was "collecting" unusually tall men *(lange Kerls)* to fill his regiments.

Frederick the Great

Friedrich Wilhelm I was not missed by ordinary Berliners, who hoped for less austere times under his son, Friedrich II (*R.* 1740–1786), later known as Friedrich der Grosse (Frederick the Great).

A philosopher-king, Friedrich II enacted a policy of religious tolerance, attracted French philosophers (such as Voltaire) and artists to his court, banned the most excessive forms of torture, and even dropped censorship for a while. Such freedoms were unheard of in 18th-century Europe.

Friedrich II, known to mouthy Berliners as Der Alte Fritz (Old Fred), was also the warrior-king of a draconian military state. The people of Prussia (and Berlin) were considered not citizens, but subjects whose duty it was to obey their superiors unquestioningly. In the army, it was policy that soldiers should fear their often brutal noncommissioned officers more than the enemy. In a series of clashes culminating in the Seven Years' War, which he came within an ace of losing, Friedrich established Prussia as a major military player in Europe.

Friedrich II sought to augment Prussia's population and modernize the state by attracting immigrants. At the end of the Seven Years' War in 1763, he expressed the wish: "May the French and Turks populate Berlin." By the time he died in 1786, Berlin had 150,000 inhabitants, a burgeoning arms industry, and a thriving cultural life.

> The people of Prussia (and Berlin) were considered not citizens, but subjects whose duty it was to obey their superiors.

Revolution & Napoleon

Three years after the death of Friedrich II, the French Revolution rocked Europe. By the time Napoleon Bonaparte (1769–1821) crowned himself emperor of France in 1804, he was at war with much of the continent. After an initial stint in a Europe-wide coalition against France, Prussia opted for neutrality. Having crushed an Austrian-Russian army at Austerlitz in December 1805, Napoleon created a Rhine Federation of occupied German states, modernizing the political and legal structure of these formerly feudal ministates.

Egged on by the military, Friedrich Wilhelm III (*R.* 1797–1840) demanded in October 1806 that Napoleon vacate southern Germany. It was just the excuse Napoleon needed. After routing the Prussians at Jena, he entered Berlin on October 27. The Berliners welcomed the French at first, though the cost of occupation proved onerous.

Napoleon allowed a shrunken Prussian state to remain, but the king had to watch as French-style reforms were pushed through. These included the (theoretical) end of rural serfdom, the creation of city councils, including one for Berlin, and the modernization of the army (though the French kept its numbers limited). Berlin's first council of deputies was elected (by limited suffrage) in 1809.

In 1810, the von Humboldt brothers, Wilhelm and Alexander, intellectuals from a Huguenot family, founded the university that would later take their name on Unter

An 18th-century engraving shows Frederick the Great in charge at the Battle of Mollwitz (1741).

den Linden. In these years of French control came the first stirrings of a pan-German nationalism. Intellectuals and the bourgeoisie began to dream openly of uniting all the German states in a single, free nation.

The dreamers would have to wait. After joining Napoleon in his ill-fated assault on Russia in 1812, Prussia switched sides and began a "war of liberation" that saw the French ousted from Berlin in 1813. With Napoleon defeated, the Congress of Vienna redrew the map of Europe. Most of the continent returned to the old order, though Prussia gained important territory in western Germany.

Restoration & Empire

In Berlin, rulers rolled back the reforms of earlier years and tightened press censorship. The city quickly developed as an industrial hub. It got its first railway line (to Potsdam) in 1838 and by 1870 counted more than a thousand factories. The working class grew just as quickly. Chronic housing shortages were solved in 1820 by the creation of *Mietskasernen* (rental barracks), high-density tenements stretching over several inner courtyards. Most of the population lived on starvation wages and conditions in the factories were appalling, so the first major working-class riots in 1830 should have come as no surprise.

In 1848, as in many other European cities, a short-lived revolt was repressed without delicacy. A Prussian parliament (Landtag) was created, but within a year a voting system was imposed that concentrated votes and power in the hands of the wealthy, conservative minority.

In 1862, King Wilhelm I (R. 1861–1888) appointed a chancellor from that parliament. He was a *Junker* (Prussian landed noble) by the name of Otto von Bismarck (1815–1898), whose motto was that the important questions in life could be settled only with "iron and blood." His ambition was a Germany united under Prussia, and he achieved this with breathtaking alacrity using a wily combination of dirty tricks and warfare (against Denmark in 1864, Austria in 1866, and France in 1870). In January 1871, in the Palace of Versailles, Bismarck dictated peace terms (involving hefty reparations payments from Paris) and announced the creation of the German *Reich* (Empire). All the hitherto independent German states came together under Prussia, with Berlin as capital. King Wilhelm I became *Kaiser* (Emperor) Wilhelm I.

Going Courting

Berlin's distinctive *Hinterhöfe* (inner courtyards) were a by-product of the city's 19th-century industrial boom. Behind the bourgeois street fronts, life teemed in courtyards strung together by narrow carriageways. Factory workshops occupied the ground floors, their laborers often living upstairs in cramped, dimly lit tenements up to six stories high.

Many such courtyards have been spruced up as real-estate showpieces, but they can still ooze atmosphere. Interesting ones to visit include the Hackesche Höfe, a riot of Art Nouveau tiles and brimming with restaurants, shops, and theaters (pp. 107–108); the gritty cultural center Regenbogenfabrik at Lausitzer Strasse 22, Kreuzberg; and the rambling Hirschhof (Stag's Courtyard) at Kastanienallee 12 in Prenzlauer Berg.

Four years later, the press took rather less notice of the founding of the Sozialistischen Arbeiterpartei Deutschlands (Socialist Workers Party, or SAP); it became the Sozialdemokratische Partei Deutschlands (SPD) in 1890. Its political program was aimed at defending the interests of the burgeoning proletariat. By the beginning of the 20th century, the SPD would be the most important party in Berlin and a major force throughout Germany.

Berlin, meanwhile, was in the grip of a boom. Now the capital of a united Germany, and with five billion gold francs in war reparations due from Paris, it grew rapidly. New factories opened, housing projects blossomed, and land speculation was rife. The first electrically powered city railway lines began to operate and electric street lighting was introduced (although most street lighting remained gas-powered until the 1930s). By the 1880s, Berlin counted 1.5 million inhabitants.

Kaiser Wilhelm II *&* World War I

The young Kaiser Wilhelm II (*R.*1888–1918) ascended the throne with big plans. He embarked on what he considered a beautification program of the city, adding dozens of monuments and more than 30 new churches in his first 20 years on the throne. One of these was the Kaiser-Wilhelm-Gedächtniskirche, dedicated to the memory of his grandfather, Kaiser Wilhelm I, which gets more attention now as a bombed-out war memorial than it ever did as a church.

The bulk of Berliners thought little of the kaiser's monuments. Their interests lay with other priorities. When one of the founding fathers of the SPD, Paul Singer, died in 1911, his funeral cortege was accompanied by almost a million red-flag-bearing mourners. For several years, Berlin's unionized workers had been campaigning and striking for improved conditions and wages, women's rights, and an end to Kaiser Wilhelm II's saber rattling.

As early as 1905, the kaiser had written to Chancellor Bernhard von Bülow: "First render the Socialists harmless, in a bloodbath if necessary, and then war abroad!" Singer's funeral and the 1912 Reichstag (national lower house of parliament) elections, in which the SPD emerged as the strongest party with 110 seats—in spite of rigged voting regulations—showed that the Socialists were far from "harmless."

On June 28, 1914, the heir to the Austrian throne, Archduke Franz Ferdinand, was assassinated. In August, the kaiser launched a war that initially pitted Germany, Austria-Hungary, and Turkey against France, the United Kingdom, and Russia. The Socialists joined the right-wing parties and voted for war credits.

At first, many Berliners enthusiastically greeted the news of war, believing firmly in a quick victory and that the boys would be home by Christmas. But it was to be more than four years of some of the most frightful slaughter humankind had ever witnessed before the war finally ended with Germany's defeat in November 1918. The kaiser abdicated and fled to Holland. Some called for the establishment of a republic; in the confusion, militants of the so-called Spartacist League (a precursor to the German Communist Party) under Karl Liebknecht (1871–1919) took virtual control of Berlin. The SPD under Friedrich Ebert (1871–1925) sent in right-wing paramilitary Freikorps (Free Corps) troops to put down the Spartacist Revolt in early 1919. The antirepublican troops went a

Kaiser Wilhelm II and Kaiserin Augusta Victoria, ca. 1914

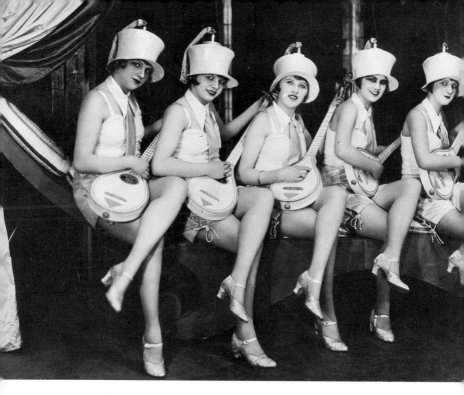

Nowhere did the '20s roar more than in the cabarets and bars of interwar Berlin.

step further, assassinating Liebknecht and the cofounder of the league, Rosa Luxemburg (1871–1919). Their deaths set the tone for the years of tit-for-tat political assassinations that would bloody the streets of Berlin in the coming years.

As Germany struggled with its internal chaos, the Allies dictated drastic peace terms at Versailles in 1919. Enormous reparations, the reduction of the armed forces to 100,000 men, huge territorial losses—in the toughness and humiliation of the peace treaty terms lay the germ of the unimaginable tragedy that would follow.

The Weimar Republic

In the quiet town of Weimar, a national parliamentary assembly came together and by August 1919 had approved Germany's first parliamentary democratic constitution. Trouble was never far away in those years. An antirepublican military coup attempt in Berlin in early 1920 was strangled by a general strike. Shortly thereafter, various communist uprisings also took place in Berlin, all bloodily put down.

In 1920, a city law was passed expanding Berlin's municipal boundaries to include independent satellite districts (such as Charlottenburg, Wilmersdorf, Spandau, and Köpenick). This action took the city's total population to just short of four million.

The sputtering German economy came close to disintegration under the weight of reparation payments to the Allies. French troops occupied the industrial Ruhr area and the currency collapsed. A U.S. dollar had bought 8.9 Reichsmarks in 1919. By November 1923, one dollar bought 4.2 billion Reichsmarks.

A coalition government under right-wing chancellor Gustav Stresemann (1878–1929) carried out a painful currency reform that wiped out most of the middle class's

savings but saved the country from implosion. Reparation payments were rescheduled, and foreign (mostly U.S.) loans pumped capital into the economy.

The Golden Twenties

To the Berliners, they were *Die Goldenen Zwanziger* (the Golden Twenties), that manic period separating the end of the nightmare of World War I, with its immediate postwar misery, and the rise of the Nazis in 1933. It was not a period of great prosperity. But after the horrors of World War I, an electric energy rippled through the city, and nothing could be like it was before 1914. With an almost utopian republican constitution in place and the worst shocks of the postwar years surmounted, the 1920s, and especially the brief period from 1924 to 1929, saw an unprecedented explosion in all fields of the arts and a flowering of social freedoms.

Artists, poets, and musicians could not accept the old order and cast everything into doubt. Satirical writing flourished as it had never before, with the acid pens of Kurt Tucholsky (1890–1935) and Erich Kästner (1899–1974), or the socially critical plays of Bertolt Brecht (1898–1956), leading the way. Max Reinhardt (1873–1943) and Erwin Piscator (1893–1966) animated Berlin's theater and cabaret world with stinging, satirical work. The dada movement and the expressionists painted and formed images of the world and society that sought to tear down ingenuous formalisms. Atonal music, seemingly trying to break free from its 19th-century bourgeois bonds, led the experimental way. German cinema lived its moment of glory.

Where the arts and the people came together most often, perhaps, was in the city's more than one hundred cabarets. Here political satire mixed with saucy entertainment in smoke-filled, steady-drinking bars that spanned the range from gin palaces along Kurfürstendamm (Ku'damm) to the less reputable spots around Friedrichstrasse.

EXPERIENCE: Do You Tango?

Berlin's cabarets of the 1920s have evolved into nightclubs today, but the capital still boasts a vibrant dance scene. Visitors can enjoy tango, swing, and salsa in venues ranging from grand old ballrooms to fancy modern salons.

Clärchens Ballhaus (*Auguststrasse 24, tel 030 282 92 95, www.ballhaus.de*) is a time-warped GDR dance hall that lives on in a pleasant state of decay. You can take beginners' courses in salsa and tango Monday and Tuesday evenings, and there is a popular restaurant and beer garden. For more of an Eastern Bloc flair, the quirky **Roter Salon** (*Linienstrasse 227, tel 030 44 04 71 95, www.roter-salon-berlin .de*) at the Volksbühne theater hosts an Electric Ballroom night once a month.

A certain social and sexual emancipation accompanied it all. Hemlines rose and men and women mixed in bars and restaurants as they never had before. That they were eating in restaurants at all was a novelty, but as the economy steadied in 1924, Berliners seemed to unload all the tension of the previous years.

Berlin soon acquired a name for itself as Europe's anything-goes pleasure palace; it became one of the continent's biggest tourism drawing cards. The city liked to sell itself as the *Stadt der Musik und des Theaters* (city of music and theater), but many came for more dubious pleasures. And come they did. Up to 180,000 foreigners, especially Americans and Britons, visited the city every month. That figure might not seem much by modern standards, but it was a veritable flood at the time.

Some came to party. Sex was no longer as taboo a subject as it had been, and Berlin was seen as a loose town. Homosexuality, while not open, was widespread. The bar scene, including drag queen shows, was particularly busy around Nollendorf-Platz. It attracted the likes of Anglo-American Christopher Isherwood (1904–1986), who lived just off the square and later wrote *Goodbye to Berlin,* the novel that would inspire the musical *Cabaret.*

Cabaret not only depicts the manic looseness and nightlife of Berlin of the twenties; it also portrays the growing presence of a dark new force in the city and across the country. The party was soon to be over.

Hitler's gift for rousing oratory helped him to power in 1933.

The Third Reich & World War II

The fragile social peace came unstuck on October 25, 1929, the day of the Wall Street crash. The effects were felt in Germany almost immediately. By 1930, the unemployed totaled a record half million in Berlin. Protests were again the norm.

In the following years, parliamentary democracy ground to a halt as the crisis led the president, Field Marshal Paul von Hindenburg (1847–1934), to intervene with emergency decrees. The atmosphere led to the rapid rise of extremist parties at both ends of the political spectrum. In Berlin, the Communist Party gained ground at the expense of the SPD. At the September 1930 elections, the previously insignificant, Bavaria-based Nazionalsozialistische Deutsche Arbeiterpartei (NSDAP, National Socialist German Workers Party—or Nazis, for short), led by an Austrian World War I corporal by the name of Adolf Hitler (1889–1945), won 107 seats. Street fighting between communist militants and the thugs of the Nazi Sturmabteilung (SA, Stormtrooper Department) increased, and Hindenburg, in an effort to bring stability, finally appointed Hitler chancellor on January 30, 1933.

> ### Stolpersteine
> Resembling cobblestones but made of shiny brass, *Stolpersteine* (literally "stumbling blocks") are simple but poignant memorials to Holocaust victims. The plaques are the brainchild of Gunther Demnig, a Cologne sculptor who has devoted his life to the project. Set in the sidewalks in front of houses and beginning with *"Hier wohnte..."* ("Here lived..."), each Stolperstein is engraved with a victim's name, year of birth, date of deportation, and place he or she died, usually a Nazi concentration camp. Since 2004, Demnig has personally laid over 32,000 plaques in 700-plus locations across Europe. Each work is commissioned, usually by a friend or relative of the victim.

The violence of the brown-shirted SA, years of virulent anti-Jewish campaigning, and the existence of Hitler's political manifesto, *Mein Kampf (My Struggle)*, were all ample signs of the antidemocratic nature of the Nazis, but few could imagine just how far Hitler was prepared to go, including his conservative and moneyed backers.

Under the cover of emergency decrees signed by Hindenburg after the Reichstag was set on fire on February 27, 1933, Hitler grabbed full power. He banned the Communist Party and so created for himself a de facto majority in parliament. Persecution of left-wing opponents began in earnest. In Köpenick alone, 91 were murdered in a week. On March 23, 1933, the Reichstag virtually voted itself out of existence with the Enabling Law, which gave dictatorial powers to Hitler.

This act opened the way for *Gleichschaltung* ("bringing into line"). In December 1933, the government banned all trade unions and all political parties except the NSDAP. On April 1, 1934, a total boycott of Jewish shops was declared and on May 10 the Nazis staged the *Bücherverbrennung* (burning of the books) in Opernplatz (Bebelplatz today) and other cities. Books by authors considered perverted or dangerous to the party and state were tossed onto enormous bonfires. On August 1, 1934, Hitler proclaimed himself *Führer* (leader) of the German state. At the same time, he brought a sense of prosperity to Germany with a massive public works program (including steady rearmament) that wiped out unemployment in just three years.

The 1935 Nuremberg race laws, which deprived German Jews of citizenship and most rights, affected about 170,000 Berlin Jews (and as many as 40,000 foreign Jews resident in the city). By 1939, about half the city's Jewish population had fled, leaving behind all their property, taken by the state as an "emigration tax." On the night of November 9, 1938, in what came to be known as *Kristallnacht* (night of broken glass), SA troopers in civilian clothing destroyed synagogues, shops, offices, houses, and other Jewish properties across the city and around Germany. In the war years to come, 50,000 Berlin Jews would be deported to concentration camps, where at least two-thirds perished. In June 1943, a report declared Berlin to be *judenfrei* (free of Jews).

Hitler's foreign policy aims were becoming clear by 1935. By the time he announced the invasion of Poland on September 1, 1939, he had already reoccupied the demilitarized Rhineland (1936), absorbed Austria and the Czech Sudetenland (1938), and occupied Prague (1939), all without having fired a shot.

Public reaction in Berlin to the start of hostilities in Poland had been muted, but the military parade beneath the Brandenburger Tor in the summer of 1940, after Hitler's lightning victories in a few short months over Denmark, Norway, Holland, Belgium, and France, was greeted with greater enthusiasm.

Until 1943, Berlin remained largely unscathed by the war. From that point on, however, Allied bombing raids increased in intensity. By the end of the war, some 50,000 civilians had died in more than 360 air raids. Starting in November 1943, the government evacuated up to a million civilians to "safe areas," some located in occupied Poland and Czechoslovakia. By the time Hitler returned to Berlin from the Eastern Front on January 16, 1945, most people could see that the war was lost. Berliners working in munitions factories around the city put in 60-hour weeks on increasingly tight rations. All the city's parks had been cleared of trees and turned into potato and cabbage fields.

The final Soviet assault on Berlin, with three armies totaling 1.5 million men, began on April 16, 1945. By April 25, the city was encircled; it finally surrendered to the Soviets two days after Hitler committed suicide in his *Führerbunker* on April 30. Soviet troops celebrated with days of raping and looting throughout the ruined city. On May 8, German forces signed an unconditional surrender in the Berlin suburb of Karlshorst, where the Soviets had set up their headquarters.

More than half of Berlin's buildings had been destroyed in the fighting, as well as a third of its industry. The population stood at about 2.5 million. In all, more than 120,000 Berliners had lost their lives in air raids and the final battle.

> As cooperation between the Soviets and western Allies faltered, so the divisions between east and west deepened.

The City Divided

Soviet-occupied Berlin was a smoldering ruin, but the Berliners were soon working to get basic services running again. The U-Bahn (*Untergrundbahn*, or subway) was running again on May 14, and six days later the first trams were operating. On May 26, the Berlin Philharmoniker gave its first free concert. On June 10, political parties with antifascist credentials were allowed to begin their activities again.

Five days earlier, the Allies had agreed to divide the country into four occupied sectors (American, British, French, and Soviet). Significantly, the Soviets picked up large tracts of eastern Germany (western Saxony, Thuringia, and Mecklenburg) in exchange for the division of Soviet-occupied Berlin into four Allied sectors. By mid-August, U.S.,

Bombs and street fighting in 1945 destroyed most of Berlin's buildings, including the Reichstag.

British, and French troops had arrived in Berlin. It is tempting to speculate that a separate East German state might never have arisen in the following years had the western Allies not ceded those territories.

At war's end, women made up as much as two-thirds of the population in Berlin. They set about clearing more than 2.6 billion cubic feet (75 million cu m) of rubble in the city center, becoming known as *Trümmerfrauen* (rubble women). Rations were scarce and considerable resources went to the occupying Soviet forces. In the western sectors, the black market flourished, with Allied soldiers exchanging supplies for anything from jewels to sex (despite an initial strict nonfraternization policy). Prostitution and street crime soared. To top it off, the winter of 1946 was one of the coldest on record.

The fighting had not finished when Walter Ulbricht (1893–1973) and other German communist comrades were flown in from Moscow to set up a German administration. In April 1946, these authorities attempted to force the two main parties in Berlin, the resurrected SPD and the Stalinist KPD (Kommunistische Partei Deutschlands) to fuse into one, the Sozialistische Einheitspartei Deutschlands (SED, German Socialist Unity Party). SPD members opposed the fusion; some were arrested and tortured for their trouble by Soviet secret police. In the first free citywide elections to be held after the war, in October 1946, the rump SPD (in the western Allied occupied sector of the city) won 48.7 percent of the vote, with the SED trailing behind with 19.8 percent.

The Soviets and western Allies were soon at loggerheads. When SPD leader Ernst Reuter (1889–1953) was elected mayor of Berlin in 1947, the Soviets opposed his nomination (he finally became mayor of West Berlin in 1948). As cooperation between the Soviets and western Allies faltered, so the divisions between east and west deepened. In 1948, the Allies introduced a new currency (the *Deutsche Mark,* DM or D-Mark) in the western zones and prepared the way for the creation of a German government in their zones. The Soviets reacted by creating an East German mark *(Ostmark)* and in late June 1948 imposed a blockade on West Berlin. The Allies circumvented this with an air bridge, ferrying in vital supplies around the clock until the blockade was lifted in May of the following year (see sidebar p. 185).

Under the circumstances, the division of Germany was inevitable. In 1949, the three western sectors became the Federal Republic of Germany (FRG), while the Soviet sector became the German Democratic Republic (GDR), headed by SED party boss Ulbricht. Fatefully for Berlin, the FRG shifted its capital to Bonn, inducing many of the city's industries to shut down and head west, too. East Berlin was worse off still. More heavily bombed than the western half of the city, it had lost virtually all its industry—dismantled and shifted to the U.S.S.R. in lieu of official reparations.

On June 17, 1953, massive strikes and violent protests in East Berlin against the communist regime were put down by Soviet tanks, costing more than 250 lives. Playwright Bertolt Brecht, who lived in East Berlin, wrote that the East German government had distributed leaflets after the June 17 rising "in which you could read that the people had lost the government's confidence . . .Would it in that case not be simpler if the government dissolved the people and elected another?"

Whether out of dislike for the Soviet-backed SED government or simply because life was clearly harder in East Germany, many East Germans streamed westward, half of them through Berlin, where it was easy to move between the Soviet and Allied sectors. West Berlin itself was becoming an attractive option. The West German government pumped billions of D-Marks into the city. From 1945 to the summer of 1961, 2.7 million Germans fled from east to west. On August 12, 1961, the East German People's Army closed all but 12 of the 80 sector crossing points and began to build what soon became

German children greet an Allied transport plane during the 1948 Soviet blockade of Berlin. During the height of the blockade, an Allied plane landed with supplies every 90 seconds.

a nearly impenetrable wall around West Berlin. Patrols had orders to shoot to kill anyone trying to cross.

West Berlin's SPD mayor from 1957 to 1964, Willy Brandt (1913–1992), kept the lines of communication open with the East Berlin authorities, procuring permission for West Berliners to make brief visits to the east side in late 1963. As West German chancellor (1969–1974), Brandt went further with his *Ostpolitik* (eastern policy), managing to sign various agreements with East Germany's Erich Honecker (1912–1994), in power since 1971, to ease travel restrictions from west to east. In the other direction, access was restricted for all but senior citizens and the disabled.

By 1980, traffic into East Berlin from West Berlin was fully regulated. Foreigners could visit on a day visa that expired at midnight. Compulsory exchange of DM25 at a one-for-one rate (the real exchange rate was more like 10 East German marks for DM1) represented a source of hard currency for the East German government.

> **On August 12, 1961, the East German People's Army...began to build what soon became a nearly impenetrable wall around West Berlin.**

The two Berlins could not have looked any different. Even in the 1980s, many of the surviving historic buildings in East Berlin had been left more or less as they were in 1945. Austere apartment buildings had gone up in much of the city. Traffic was almost nonexistent, consisting of locally produced Wartburg and Trabant cars. Soldiers patrolled quiet streets in which nightlife was anything but scintillating. It was a gray city.

The bright lights of West Berlin presented a rather different picture. The Ku'damm had become the city's center, lined with shops, restaurants, and bars. Nearby Bahnhof Zoologischer Garten won an unhappy reputation as a hangout for the city's young heroin addicts, many of whom resorted to street prostitution to survive.

Life in Berlin could be surreal. Every day, West Berlin commuters on U-Bahn lines that passed below East Berlin would glide through dimly lit "ghost stations," patrolled by heavily armed East German soldiers, on their way to work. No one could have imagined what was in the offing.

Berlin Reunited

If Honecker and his SED party pals could have done anything about it, the status quo would have remained indefinitely. But events were moving beyond their control. The rise to power of reformer Mikhail Gorbachev (born 1931) in the U.S.S.R. in 1985 marked a significant change. Poland and Hungary were also beginning to loosen their Communist Party shackles. For the GDR, the real trouble came from Hungary, which in May 1989 opened its border to Austria, allowing a limited number of East Germans to cross to the West.

The situation snowballed in the following months, with East Germans streaming into Hungary and taking refuge in West German embassies in various East European capitals. At home, a protest movement quickly gained momentum. On November 4, half a million people demonstrated against the communist government in Alexanderplatz. Overtaken by events and with no help coming from Moscow, the East German government tried to ingratiate itself with its people by announcing on November 9, 1989, that East Germans could travel freely to the West.

Incredulous, the first Berliners crossed the wall into West Berlin that evening. What started as a trickle of visitors turned into a flood, and spontaneous parties erupted at Brandenburger Tor, where West and East Berliners came together. The first breaches were hacked into the wall on November 10. On November 11 and 12, an incredible 2.7 million exit visas were issued at East Berlin checkpoints. *Die Wende* ("the change") had begun.

From the fall of the wall, it was a surprisingly short step to the collapse of the East German state. Conservative West German chancellor Helmut Kohl (born 1930 and in power 1982–1998) declared that his aim was a united Germany. As East Germans visited the western half of the country and realized how much better off their western cousins were, the idea of maintaining a separate, socialist state quickly lost attractiveness for most of them. Making what proved to be imprudent promises of a prosperous future just around the corner, Kohl moved to accelerate the process. Elections in March 1990 in East Germany brought victory for Kohl's Christian Democratic Union party. By July, both governments had agreed upon a unified currency and political union. In September, the four World War II allies ended formal occupation of Germany (with the last troops leaving Berlin in September 1994). On October 3, administrative unity in the city was restored, and the following year the German national parliament (Bundestag) decided to make Berlin the capital. The Bundestag moved to the imaginatively renovated Reichstag building in April 1999.

After the initial partying, reality set in. The huge national subsidies that had long propped up West Berlin were gradually dropped. Special unification taxes imposed on *Wessis* (West Germans) created ill feeling toward *Ossis* (East Germans). Easterners felt increasingly patronized by the better-off Westerners. They resented long-lasting differences in pay and job opportunities.

Unemployment in both sides of the city rose as heavy industry and unprofitable businesses in former East Berlin went belly up. With the wall gone, tourism to Berlin declined sharply. And people began to vote with their feet. Berlin's city administration made much of the fact that in 2005, for the first time since reunification, the city's population of 3.45 million did not decrease.

All the while, city and federal governments, together with private enterprise, have poured money into Berlin. Aside from the huge task of linking the two halves of city,

The Great GDR Sell-off

Founded a few months before German reunification, the Treuhandanstalt was a government agency charged with privatizing the GDR's state-owned enterprises. As it became obvious how woefully uncompetitive East Germany's industry was, investors hung back. By the early 1990s, more than half of four million public-sector employees had been laid off. For Ossies, the Treuhandanstalt was the face of brutish Western capitalism; West Germans saw a financial sinkhole. In April 1991, the agency's head, Detlev Rohwedder, was assassinated by terrorists of the Rote Armee Fraktion (RAF) at his home in Düsseldorf. Under his successor, Birgit Breuel, the pace of privatization picked up, as did reports of corruption by carpetbagging investors. When the Treuhandanstalt was dissolved in 1994, some 14,000 companies had been sold for around 60 billion DM (ca. $31 billion)—one-tenth of Rohwedder's estimate four years earlier.

An East German border guard greets a West Berliner atop the Berlin Wall in 1989.

billions have been spent on the restoration of old landmarks and the creation of new ones. A who's who of local and international architects has had a field day in Berlin, for years described as the biggest construction site in Europe.

In the process, the city has gone deep into the red. The unexpectedly high economic and social costs of unification have sharply dented Germany's economy since the early 1990s. Although Germany is recovering well from the recent recession, unemployment remains at about 10 percent in the former East Germany and about 13 percent in Berlin. Many of the region's disillusioned young are heading west.

On the other hand, a stream of creative people is pouring into the capital from around Germany and the rest of Europe. Drawn by Berlin's vibrant and uninhibited cultural scene, they are helping to propel the city to the forefront of European capitals. It is a rough diamond, but glittering nonetheless. ■

Food & Drink

Ask a Berliner what the city's greatest contribution to world cuisine is and you may well be told *Currywurst* (see sidebar p. 153). Germans just love a snack of *Wurst* (sausage) with *eine Portion Pommes* (a serving of fries). Berlin's specialty is this lightly spicy sausage bathed in a tangy sauce; just about any *Imbiss* (snack stand) will serve up this treat, along with a variety of other sausage options.

The ingredients for many a meal come from markets like this one at Winterfeldplatz.

You don't have to live on sausages and fries. In the days of the wall, Berlin's culinary reputation was not the stuff of Michelin stars, but things have changed. Top chefs are at work in Berlin, now home to 13 Michelin-star restaurants. Leading the way (and reestablishing a pre–World War II tradition) is the Lorenz Adlon restaurant in the resurrected Hotel Adlon on Pariser Platz, considered one of the best eateries in the capital. With thousands of options, eating in Berlin is a treat.

International cuisine abounds, servings are generous, and prices are reasonable. Of all the world cuisines on offer, the most deeply rooted in Berlin is Turkish. The big Turkish population introduced *döner* (meat slow-grilled on a vertical rotating spit) to Berlin palates in the 1970s, and filling rolls jammed with the meat, salad, and spices are nowadays as popular as wurst.

Traditional Fare

German cooking has a reputation for being heavy, and Berlin's specialties are no exception. Local food is meaty and hearty, and while you may not want to indulge daily, it is worth trying authentic dishes.

Boulette (or *Bulette*) is a kind of meatball, usually served with mixed vegetables and a shot of mustard. Order a serving of *Berliner Eisbein* (pork knuckle) and you'll be in for a shock: What seems like a whole leg of corned-beef-style meat will appear, on the bone and covered by the skin (which you don't eat). It comes with sauerkraut and, sometimes, mashed peas. *Kalbsleber Berliner Art* (calf liver, served with, say, glazed onions and oven-cooked apple) is another classic. Much beloved are the variations on veal that generally come from southern Germany. *Kalbsgeschnetzeltes* is sliced, breaded, and fried (similar to Wiener schnitzel) and best served in a hearty mush-room sauce.

Popular national dishes include *Kassler Rippen*, a feast of sliced smoked pork rib meat with a hammy flavor. Pork dominates traditional menus, but things change in mid-November when the Feast of St. Martin arrives. This means goose feasts. Such a banquet might involve goose with sauce, trimmings, and a bottle of red wine for around €50 ($65) a head.

Dessert plays a big role. You should not leave Berlin without indulging in a chunky slice of *Apfelstrudel* (apple pie), preferably drowned in vanilla sauce. Berlin's most famous pastry, a jam-filled donut, is known worldwide as a Berliner—but ask for a Berliner in Berlin and the locals will stare at you blankly, as here it is called a *Pfannkuchen* (literally "pancake").

Remember to save room for brunch. On weekends in particular, cafés and restaurants around the city feature set-price, all-you-can-eat buffet brunches over which local families will linger for hours.

Beer & Wine

Beer is the Berliner's tipple of choice. The city once teemed with breweries. Several local lagers, such as Berliner Kindl, continue to keep the after-hours conversations well oiled. The local specialty is *Berliner Weisser mit Schuss* (Berlin White with a shot); the shot is raspberry (red) or woodruff (green) syrup.

Many locals prefer a good *Weizenbier* (wheat beer that can be *Hefe*, yeasty, or *Kristall*, filtered). You can order it *hell* (light) or *dunkel* (dark). A weightier option is a *Schwarzbier*, a dark, porter-like ale. Light and refreshing is *Weinschorle*, a glass of white wine with sparkling water, or the nonal-coholic *Apfelsaftschorle* (apple juice with same).

Most restaurants offer an international wine list, but it is worthwhile to try wines from closer to home. The nearest decent winemaking area is in Saxony, Germany's smallest and most northerly wine region. Both whites and reds are produced there along the Elbe River. Output is dominated by the Müller-Thurgau (20 percent of production) and Riesling (15 percent) variet-ies. Among the reds, the dry Grauburgunder (Pinot Grigio) is popular; the fruitier Ruländer is harder to come by.

EXPERIENCE: Underground Supper Clubs

Across Berlin, hungry strangers gather in settings that carry a frisson of the forbidden: secret supper clubs. Diners are told where the next meal is through social media and food blogs that promote the monthly feasts.

The cuisine is as unconventional as the venues, treating curious palates to unusual combinations and explosions of flavors. Popular clubs include the **Good**

Stuff Supper Club (email: curlystew@hotmail.co.uk), blending the Middle East with Iberian and South American flavors; the **Shy Chef** (http://theshychef.wordpress.com), held in a different beautiful living room once a month; and **Metta Una Sera a Cena** (http://mettiunaseraacena.wordpress.com), where two visual artists serve updated Italian classics like meat carpaccio dusted with licorice.

The Arts

Berlin reached its creative apogee in the arts amid the chaos of the Weimar Republic. Today it again seethes with activity. Most visible in its daring new architecture, the artistic renaissance is equally dramatic in the city's theaters, literary circles, and art galleries. The numbers alone speak volumes: Berlin has 3 opera houses, about 150 theaters, 200 museums, and 400 to 600 art galleries.

Architecture

Until the 18th century, Berlin was rarely thought of as more than a fairly grubby, unprepossessing town. Since then, the city has shed its skin several times, most spectacularly in the energetic years since its reunification.

Berlin's annual Karneval der Kulturen (Carnival of Cultures) in Kreuzberg

Little remains to remind us of the first five centuries of Berlin's existence. Most of what you see standing in central Berlin was built after World War II. Among the oldest standing buildings in Berlin are those of the central Nikolaikirche (with tapering 19th-century twin towers) and Heilig-Geist-Kapelle, both churches built around the late 13th century. The slightly later Marienkirche and Klosterkirche (the latter left in its ruined wartime state) are also Gothic churches, typical of northern Germany. Renaissance reminders come in Spandau's Zitadelle fort and, to a lesser extent, the Jagdschloss Grunewald.

The first wave of serious building came with Great Elector Friedrich Wilhelm. His master architects embellished his capital, largely in a sober baroque style. Dutchman Johann Arnold Nering (1659–1695) designed the Zeughaus (armory) on Unter den Linden. Hamburg-born Andreas Schlüter (1660–1714) decorated its internal courtyard and designed the heart of the nearby Berliner Schloss, the central royal residence (demolished after World War II). The Swede Johann Friedrich Eosander von Göthe (1669–1728) and Parisian Huguenot Jean de Bodt (1670–1745) were among Schlüter's competitors. Eosander had a major hand in Schloss Charlottenburg and de Bodt completed the Zeughaus. Shortly after, Gendarmenmarkt was graced with the Französischer Dom and Deutscher Dom churches.

> **Little remains to remind us of the first five centuries of Berlin's existence. Most of what you see standing in central Berlin was built after World War II.**

The next building spurt came under Friedrich II, who dreamed of a rococo Forum Fridericianum along Unter den Linden. Under architect Georg Wenzeslaus von Knobelsdorff (1699–1753), various elements of Friedrich's plan were carried out, among them the Staatsoper, Altes Palais, and Sankt-Hedwig-Kathedrale. His greatest work was, however, Schloss Sanssouci, a jewel of Prussian rococo, in Potsdam. If baroque was a sensuous outgrowth of the sterner Renaissance, rococo was baroque on a sugary high, all swirls and curls.

The prolific Karl Friedrich Schinkel (1781–1841) and his students, especially Friedrich August Stüler (1800–1865) dominated the first half of the 19th century. Schinkel's Neue Wache and Altes Museum are masterpieces of neoclassicism, a more sober style. Stüler designed the temple-like Alte Nationalgalerie and Matthäuskirche. The century closed on what might be considered a fanciful note, with buildings such as the Reichstag and Berliner Dom built in grandiose (even bombastic) neo-Renaissance form.

Major undertakings were not the order of the day in the cash-strapped postwar Weimar Republic. Nevertheless, the infectiously creative spirit of the city spilled over into individual building projects, often well in advance of their time. The Shell-Haus just south of Tiergarten remains a telling example, as is the Hufeisensiedlung, a horseshoe-shaped residential project in the Neukölln District, designed in part by the city's town planner, Martin Wagner (1885–1957). Wagner attracted a flock of avant-garde architects, such as the founder of the Bauhaus movement, Berlin-born Walter Gropius (1883–1969), and Ludwig Mies van der Rohe (1886–1969), to the city. They and others dedicated most of their efforts to residential and industrial projects. Berlin's best example of Bauhaus, the Bauhaus Archiv, was built in 1976 to 1979 to a Gropius design meant for another city.

The Nazis brought a monumental approach to city architecture and, largely under the direction of Albert Speer (1905–1981), Hitler's favorite architect, added buildings designed to last centuries and make impressive ruins. They cooked up plans to tear up much of Berlin and build the *Welthauptstadt Germania* (World Capital Germania). Two axes, one east–west from the Brandenburger Tor to Charlottenburger Tor and the other north–south from the Reichstag to Tempelhof airport, would define the core of this thousand-year capital.

An imposing but austere style marked those buildings completed, especially Hitler's New Reich Chancellery. Major reminders of the Nazi period include the 1936 Olympiastadion, the former Aviation Ministry (nowadays the Finance Ministry), and Tempelhof.

> **Between its grand collections of everything from old masters to Picasso and its thriving contemporary scene, Berlin is the place to be.**

Massive destruction during World War II gave the city an unwelcome opportunity to embark on new architectural adventures. In East Berlin, Hermann Henselmann (1905–1995) dominated the scene and was responsible for the city's highest structure, the Fernsehturm (TV tower), as well as the master plan for the showcase boulevard, Stalinallee (now Karl-Marx-Allee). For much of the city's rebuilding, ugly *Plattenbau* (prefabricated concrete slabs, see sidebar p. 104) were used.

Meanwhile, West Berlin was preoccupied with residential construction, but had room for modern monuments, too. In the center, key postwar buildings are Mies van der Rohe's Neue Nationalgalerie and the Philharmonie designed by Hans Scharoun (1893–1972).

Reunification in 1989 was the starting shot for a race to sew the wounded city back together. (For a look at what has been built in recent decades and a glimpse into the future, see pp. 122–123.)

Berlin's cinematic glory years unfold before visitors at the Filmmuseum Berlin in the Sony Center.

Painting & Sculpture

Berlin was late off the blocks in the visual arts, but you would hardly know that today. Berlin is where the heart of Germany's arts scene beats loudest. Between its grand collections of everything from old masters to Picasso and its thriving contemporary scene, Berlin is the place to be.

When Prussian king Friedrich I decided to embellish his now royal city at the outset of the 18th century, Berlin was a provincial backwater. Nearby Dresden, thanks to the extravagant art acquisitions of its ruler Augustus the Strong (R. 1694–1733), was just one of many European cities that eclipsed Berlin.

Architect Andreas Schlüter was also a gifted sculptor; he created the statue (restored after World War II) of the Great Elector that now stands in front of Schloss Charlotten-burg. Friedrich I had Antoine Pesne (1683–1757) brought from France as court painter in 1711. A master of frescoes, he led Berlin's artistic development in the first half of the 18th century. Some of his paintings can be seen in the Gemäldegalerie.

Nineteenth-century Berlin was dominated by its sculptors, among them Johann Gottfried Schadow (1764–1850), known for his classicist Quadriga sculpture atop the Brandenburger Tor (which had to be remade from scratch after World War II), and Christian Daniel Rauch (1777–1857), who produced the equestrian statue of Friedrich II on Unter den Linden. Other works by both can be seen in the Friedrichwerdersche

Kirche. Reinhold Begas (1831–1911) made the statue of Friedrich Schiller in Gendarmenmarkt square and the Neptune fountain by the Marienkirche in Alexanderplatz.

In painting, Berlin failed to shake off its academic provincialism. Architect Karl Friedrich Schinkel was a capable landscape artist, and we owe a debt to Eduard Gärtner (1801–1877) for his prolific production of Berlin panoramas. Adolph Menzel (1815–1905), who tended toward realism, was a major factor in the latter half of the century. Cottbus-born Romantic painter Carl Blechen (1798–1840) concentrated on landscapes and indeed was professor of landscape painting at the Berliner Akademie.

Kaiser Wilhelm II rather fancied himself an art critic. As far as he was concerned, the work of Berliner Max Liebermann (1847–1935) or Norway's Edvard Munch (1863–1944) was "gutter art." To combat such official rejection, Liebermann, who became one of Germany's leading impressionists and head of the Prussian Art Academy in 1920 (resigning in 1933 after the Nazis came to power), launched the Berliner Secession of contemporary artists in 1898. Leading artists to join included Lovis Corinth (1858–1925) and Käthe Kollwitz (1867–1945), one of Germany's finest expressionists.

The horrors of World War I produced radical reactions in Berlin art. The first was the outlandish dada movement (which had started in Zurich). Its leading painter was Berlin's George Grosz (1893–1959), who later went on to lead the *Neue Sachlichkeit* (New Objectivity) movement and some of whose works can be seen in the Neue Nationalgalerie's collections. Dada's key message was the wholesale rejection of convention, in society and art. It favored an anarchic approach, in which collage and montage were favored and subjects were deliberately provocative.

Dada quickly fizzled, and the 1920s were dominated by expressionists, whose art was dedicated to the expression of emotion rather than strict realism. They included Otto Dix (1891–1969), who is also identified with Neue Sachlichkeit; Max Beckmann (1884–1950); and Ernst Ludwig Kirchner (1880–1938). The latter was a leading light in the Brücke art movement, to which a museum is now dedicated. They were abetted by a bevy of foreign artists, notably Wassily Kandinsky (1866–1944), Paul Klee (1879–1940), and Marc Chagall (1887–1985). The first two were leading figures of the Bauhaus movement.

To the Nazis, most of this was *entartete Kunst* (degenerate art). Their arrival in power in 1933 put an almost immediate stop to the artistic ferment in Berlin.

The post–World War II years saw realist painter Karl Hofer (1878–1955) squaring off against what he saw as the self-indulgent

A 1913 portrait of author Gerhart Hauptmann painted by Berlin artist Max Liebermann

abstract artists of the West Berlin Zone 5 group, which included Hans Thiemann (1910–1977) and Heinz Trökes (1913–1997). Werner Heldt (1904–1954) was the artist of ruined Berlin, combining realism with an expressionistic twist in, for instance, his "Berlin am Meer" ("Berlin at the Seaside") series.

East Berlin artists who managed to carve a path away from imposed socialist norms include Harald Metzkes (born 1929) and Manfred Böttcher (born 1931), part of the Berlin School. In the 1970s and 1980s, an artistic subculture evolved in semilegal galleries in Prenzlauer Berg, which showed artists whose individualistic work clashed with the ruling ideology's concepts of real socialist art. In West Berlin, the focal point of creativity, a potpourri of conflicting movements and styles shifted to Kreuzberg. The experimental sculptures of Bernhard Heiliger (1915–1995) are a feature of Berlin life. Several remain scattered around the city's public spaces today, such as his bronze "Die Flamme" ("The Flame") on Ernst-Reuter-Platz or his iron "Echo I" and "Echo II" at the Philharmonie.

Today, a dynamic contemporary scene in the reunited capital keeps a plethora of small, precarious galleries (especially in Prenzlauer Berg and Mitte) in business, with a restless local populace of artists hard at work.

The manic interwar capital was a magnet for writers, thinkers, and charlatans from all over Germany and beyond.

Literature

Berlin's literary career started with the Enlightenment. Friedrich II, who declared himself the "first servant" of the state, was attracted by the writings of French thinkers like Voltaire (1694–1778), who spent some time at the court in Berlin.

Friedrich had little time for his own subjects' writings. Towering above the rest of Berlin's writers was Gotthold Ephraim Lessing (1729–1781), whose classic play *Minna von Barnhelm* was a box office hit in Berlin theaters and despised by the king.

The Romantic period in the early 19th century that followed the Enlightenment saw myriad poets working in Berlin. They included Heinrich von Kleist (1777–1811), whose work won little favor in his lifetime and who died in a suicide pact with his lover on the Wannsee shore near Potsdam; Joachim Ludwig Achim von Arnim (1781–1831); and Clemens Brentano (1778–1842). E.T.A. Hoffmann (1776–1822) penned stories rich in fantasy.

The post-Napoleonic restoration managed to muzzle Berlin's literary scene. Alone, Adolf Glasbrenner (1810–1876), a cheeky pamphleteer, regaled Berliners with sparkling prose in his reviews and fell frequent victim to censorship. The tail end of the 19th century was dominated by two quite different figures. Theodor Fontane (1819–1898) wrote a series of grand novels (among them *Effi Briest*) depicting the strictures of bourgeois Berlin society. Gerhart Hauptmann (1862–1946) caused upheaval with his social drama, encapsulated in *Die Weber (The Weavers)*, a play about the misery of Silesian weavers; Kaiser Wilhelm II canceled his box at the Deutsches Theater when the play premiered there in 1894.

Berlin reached a peak of literary genius in the 1920s. The manic interwar capital was a magnet for writers, thinkers, and charlatans from all over Germany and beyond. Alfred Döblin (1878–1957), by trade a doctor, wrote the quintessential (if opaque) Berlin novel with *Berlin Alexanderplatz,* the story of a released jailbird, Franz Biberkopf, trying to make good. Heinrich Mann (1871–1950), Lübeck-born brother of Thomas and a diehard anti-Nazi, penned one of the most biting satires of German society, *Der Untertan (The Subject)* in 1919. Dresden-born Erich Kästner also poured forth volumes of mostly satirical poetry. He later watched as his books were burned in Opernplatz in 1933. The plays of Bertolt Brecht, who staged *Die Dreigroschenoper (Threepenny Opera)* in the 1920s, were laced with social criticism. He continued to write during a 15-year exile and became an icon in 1950s East Germany, where he founded the Berliner Ensemble theater.

Bertolt Brecht

Bavarian-born Bertolt Brecht made his name as a playwright in Berlin with his 1928 musical drama *Die Dreigroschenoper (Threepenny Opera),* a satire on capitalism. His works were marked by his Marxist beliefs and a theatrical practice he called "alienation"; he wanted his audiences to remain aware that they were watching a vehicle for social messages. In his 15-year exile from Germany beginning in 1933, Brecht wrote many of his best plays, such as *Der Kaukasische Kreidekreis (The Caucasian Chalk Circle)* and *Mutter Courage und Ihre Kinder (Mother Courage and Her Children).* Only after his return to East Berlin was he able to stage them at his Deutsches Ensemble Theater.

Brecht was the greatest figure writing in immediate postwar Berlin. On the eastern side, party control made it difficult for writers who did not toe the line to prosper. One of the best who did was Christa Wolf (1929–2011), whose novel *Der Geteilte Himmel (Divided Heaven)* was the first in a line that dealt with the hopes and realities of communist Germany. That reality was not always pleasant was demonstrated by the fate of rambunctious singer-songwriter Wolf Biermann (born 1936). In 1953, he moved to East Berlin on ideological grounds, but in 1976 he was stripped of East German citizenship because of his regime-critical lyrics.

West Berlin's literary life was long dominated by Günter Grass (born 1927). His novels include the powerful *Die Blechtrommel (The Tin Drum,* 1959). In it, the hypocrisy and horrors of the Nazi years and postwar West Germany are seen through the honest eyes of a man with the mind of a child.

Foreign writers have also used Berlin as a backdrop. A Cold War classic is John Le Carré's (born 1931) 1963 thriller *The Spy Who Came In from the Cold.* More recent is Ian McEwan's (born 1948) *The Innocent,* another twisting Cold War tale. Edinburgh-born Philip Kerr (born 1956) has written countless detective novels, among them the Berlin Noir trilogy. Early in the new century, the writer of the moment is Moscow-born Wladimir Kaminer (born 1967), whose *Russendisko, Karaoke,* and *Schönhauser Allee* are all set in the capital. The city's Turkish community is beginning to make itself heard, too, with writers like Emine Sevgi Özdamar (born 1946) and Yadé Kara (born 1965). Kara's *Selam Berlin* provides a Turkish perspective on the changes in Berlin since the wall came down.

Cinema

Had history taken another turn, the mecca of global filmmaking might have been Babelsberg. The 1920s was a period of deep political and social unrest in Germany, but in that cauldron was born some of the greatest cinema of the day. Classics from *The Blue Angel* to *Metropolis* are as admired today as they were then.

In the late 1890s, film houses began to spring up along Friedrichstrasse, but things got serious when the Deutsche Bioskop company set up film studios in Babelsberg, near Potsdam, in 1911. Taken over by Universum Film AG (UFA) after World War I, Babelsberg was Europe's leading film production center and second only to Hollywood. Stars of the 1920s included Swedish actresses Greta Garbo (1905–1990) and Zarah Leander (1907–1981), Emil Jannings (1884–1950), and the Danish-born superstar Asta Nielsen (1881–1972).

Among UFA's masterpieces was *Das Kabinett des Dr. Caligari* (*The Cabinet of Dr. Caligari,* 1920), a hallucinatory horror story by Robert Wiene that still mesmerizes audiences. Others followed, such as Ernst Lubitsch's *Madame Dubarry* (1919) and Friedrich Wilhelm Murnau's *Nosferatu* (1922) and *Der Letzte Mann* (*The Last Man,* 1924), a psychological drama. Fritz Lang's (1890–1976) futuristic fantasy *Metropolis* (1926) was UFA's biggest attempt to outdo Hollywood, with a suitably dark, German Gothic touch. It was restored, edited, and brought out with a modern soundtrack in 1987. Lang was back with plenty of twisted social and psychological drama in *M–Eine Stadt Sucht einen Mörder* (1931), a thriller known simply as *M* in English and starring the inimitable Peter Lorre. Berlin-born Marlene Dietrich (1901–1992; see p. 182) got her big break with *Der Blaue Engel* (*The Blue Angel,* 1930), based on Heinrich Mann's 1905 novel *Professor Unrat* and

2003's *Good Bye, Lenin!* takes a lighthearted look at East Berliners' adjustment to reunification.

EXPERIENCE:
Silent Cinema

Rediscover the magic of 1920s Berlin at a screening of silent films. Drawing on the archives of the German Historical Museum, the **Zeughauskino** (see Travelwise p. 262) shows such timeless masterpieces as Fritz Lang's *Metropolis* and F. W. Murnau's *Nosferatu*. Every July, the atmospheric Babylon Mitte hosts an annual **Stummfilmfestival** (Silent Film Festival, *www.babylon.de*). Watch for live piano accompaniment by Stephan von Bothmer, who composes works especially for these silver-screen classics.

For silent flicks on the move, check the video screens in every U-Bahn car during the **Going Underground** festival *(www.goingunderground .de)* each September.

directed by Josef von Sternberg (1894–1969). Dietrich plays a nightclub star who seduces and destroys a schoolteacher. Von Sternberg shot German and English versions of the film simultaneously.

The heady pre-Hitler years in Berlin—a mix of bubbling creativity, louche nightlife, and political violence—were captured years later in the film musical *Cabaret* (1972), starring Liza Minnelli (born 1946).

Moviemakers in California didn't have to deal with the economic and political chaos that assailed Germany, and in the early 1920s, talent had already started to slip away from Babelsberg. Directors Erich von Stroheim (1885–1957) and Lubitsch were among the first to flee to Hollywood, followed by Jannings, Murnau (both in 1926), and von Sternberg (1930). Dietrich packed her bags the following year. The rise of the Nazis to power in 1933 turned the trickle into a flood. Polish-born Billy Wilder (1906–2002), for instance, who had lived in Berlin since 1926, fled to Paris and then the United States. There he became known for such classics as *A Foreign Affair* (1948), which he shot amid the ruins of postwar Berlin, *The Seven Year Itch* (1955), and *Some Like It Hot* (1959).

The arrival of the Nazis sounded a sudden, if temporary, death knell for German filmmaking. Much of Babelsberg production in this period ranged from crude propaganda to technically brilliant propaganda. *Der Triumph des Willens* (*The Triumph of the Will,* 1934) and two films on the 1936 Olympic Games by Berlin-born Leni Riefenstahl (1902–2003) were masterpieces of the latter. The first captured the atmosphere of Hitler's carefully orchestrated Sixth Party Congress rallies at Nuremberg, winning the gold medal at the 1937 universal exposition in Paris. The Olympics films were also brilliantly executed and won an award from the International Olympic Committee in 1939.

The postwar division of Berlin led to a split film industry. The East Germans eventually took over Babelsberg. Under the umbrella of the DEFA film institute, they churned out a steady diet of mostly party-loyal, but occasionally good-quality, dramas. Among them was Wolfgang Staudte's (1906–1984) *Die Mörder sind unter uns* (*The Murderers Are Among Us,* 1946), Germany's first postwar film. This DEFA production tells the story of a doctor who returns home to a Berlin in ruins and encounters an officer who had ordered the execution of innocent hostages. It tackled the Nazi issue openly and predated a long phase in the 1950s and 1960s when the issue was not discussed.

In the West, the center of production migrated to Munich and Hamburg, although some of Germany's most creative directors worked in West Berlin (and in some cases continue to work in the now united city). Among them were Wim Wenders (born 1945), Rainer Werner Fassbinder (1945–1982), Volker Schlöndorff (born 1939), and Werner Herzog (born 1942). Overall, however, Berlin has struggled to get back onto the cinema map, except as host to the Berlinale, the city's prestigious annual film festival, held in February.

Postwar Berlin has been a lead player in several key films. Italy's Roberto Rossellini (1906–1977) made use of destroyed Berlin as a set for his moving *Germania, Anno Zero* (*Germany, Year Zero,* 1948), a masterpiece of black-and-white Italian neorealism. Wenders's ethereal *Der Himmel über Berlin* (*Wings of Desire,* 1987) placed, for a moment, both German cinema and the city center stage. Bruno Ganz (born 1941) and Otto Sander (born 1941) star as two good-natured angels posted to Berlin. They range across the city, listening in to the lives of mortals and, in the case of Ganz, falling in love with one of them.

A delightful farce, *Good Bye, Lenin!* (2003) by Wolfgang Becker (born 1954), managed the trick of dealing compassionately with the trials of adjustment for East Berliners at the time of reunification. Altogether different is Fatih Akin's (born 1973) *Gegen die Wand* (*Against the Wall,* 2004), a tough film about the difficulties facing Turks born in Germany (and particularly Berlin).

Bruno Ganz returned to Berlin not as an angel, but something approaching the opposite, in the lead role of *Der Untergang* (*Downfall,* 2004), written by Bernd Eichinger (1949–2011). Ganz's performance as Hitler during his last weeks in the Berlin bunker in 1945 is a tour de force that reveals a human side to the Führer, along with his unfathomable cruelty. *Das Leben der Anderen* (*The Lives of Others,* 2006), directed by Florian Henckel von Donnersmarck (born 1973), won an Oscar for its depiction of Stasi surveillance in East Berlin.

> **Berlin has struggled to get back onto the cinema map, except as host to the Berlinale, the city's prestigious annual film festival.**

The Babelsberg studios are alive and kicking. One of the most expensive European films in history, the 70-million-dollar blockbuster about the battle of Stalingrad, *Enemy at the Gates* (2001), was shot here.

Music

One name says it all: Herbert von Karajan (1908–1989). The authoritarian figure graced countless millions of record sleeves and CD covers down the decades. Von Karajan ruled the Berlin Philharmonisches Orchester (aka Berlin Philharmoniker), the city's top musical calling card, from 1955 until his death in 1989. The orchestra is one of the world's finest, but it is just the tip of the iceberg. Berlin's musical offerings range from chamber music to opera, and from jazz to "click house."

King Friedrich Wilhelm I, no music lover, cut the royal budget for court orchestras and choirs. Indeed, Berlin was long musically overshadowed by cities such as Leipzig and Vienna. Friedrich II was a different matter. In 1743, he opened Berlin's first opera house, what is today the Staatsoper, on Unter den Linden. Along with the Komische Oper and Deutsche Oper, it is one of three opera houses in the city.

The Berlin Philharmoniker came into being in 1882 with 50 musicians (today it numbers around 130). Until Wilhelm Furtwängler (1886–1954) arrived as conductor in 1922, the orchestra worked under various people, including guest conductors such as Peter Tchaikovsky, Gustav Mahler, and Richard Strauss. Alongside the classics,

Furtwängler supported experimental composers working in Berlin, including Paul Hindemith (1895–1963) and the Viennese Arnold Schönberg (1874–1951), both of whom left the capital in the 1930s. Schönberg was particularly interested in atonal music, and support of this kind of "degenerate art" got Furtwängler into hot water with the Nazis. He stayed on as artistic director but was forced to resign his other positions with the orchestra, which from 1934 on became a vehicle of Nazi propaganda. Furtwängler, after a period of "de-Nazification," resumed his position fully in 1952. His successor, von Karajan, combined genius at the podium with a sense of marketing that took him and "his" orchestra to hitherto unattained heights of world renown. In 1938, as director of the Staatskapelle, he conducted the first stereo music recording in the world. Today, the Philharmoniker is flourishing under the direction of Britain's Sir Simon Rattle (born 1955) and is one of five city orchestras (all subsidized by the state).

There was musical life in Berlin before the Philharmoniker. Carl Maria von Weber (1786–1826) premiered his opera *Der Freischütz* to acclaim in Berlin in 1821, while Berliner Felix Mendelssohn Bartholdy (1809–1847) proved a virtuoso composer and conductor from an early age. His most enduring work is the opera *A Midsummer Night's Dream* (1843). Giacomo Meyerbeer (1791–1864), made Prussian general director of music in 1842, was one of Europe's most successful opera composers. The works of Leipzig-born Richard Wagner (1813–1883), however, who wrote an anti-Semitic pamphlet against Meyerbeer, didn't get a hearing in Berlin until the 1890s.

A night at the opera is not everyone's idea of fun; in the 1920s, most Berliners could be found hanging out in cabarets and jazz clubs. Today, too, the jazz scene is humming. The annual Jazzfest Berlin in November is one of Europe's top jazz festivals. Among the big names to look for in Berlin are Ed Schuller, Till Brönner, Ernst Bier, David Friedman, and Kurt Rosenwinkel. Plenty of new talent is emerging, with outlets in venues around the city. The Berlin Voices are four divine vocalists (none from Berlin) who fuse modern jazz elements with pop and soul. M&M are a pair of Berlin-based guitarists whose band performs mostly original material in a modern jazz context.

More successful on a broader stage has been Berlin's techno scene. The city was the launchpad for European electronic music and retains its primacy today. Clubs across town pump it out late into the night and locals love it. House, hip-hop, electrojazz, R&B, breakbeat, and most other electronic variants are on Berlin's menu. ■

Hansa by the Wall

The apocalyptic chords of David Bowie's 1977 album *Heroes* were heavily influenced by Cold War Berlin, where the British pop star lived and worked for a few years in the 1970s. The tracks were laid down a stone's throw from the east–west border at Hansa Studios. Bowie, who shared a Schöneberg apartment with fellow rock agitator Iggy Pop, recalled looking out the window and seeing an East German border guard staring back through binoculars.

Others to record at "Hansa by the Wall" included Nick Cave, Brian Eno, Depeche Mode, REM, and U2, among many other major musicians. Still in operation, Hansa Studio 2 and the ballroom-like Meistersaal can be visited with **Fritz Tours** (tel 030 30 87 56 33, www.music tour-berlin.com).

The central stage for centuries of Berlin's history and the nearby Reichstag, symbol of Germany's modern political rebirth

Unter den Linden & Potsdamer Platz

Introduction & Map   52–53

Reichstag Building   54–57

Brandenburger Tor & Pariser Platz   58–59

Holocaust Monument   60–61

Along Unter den Linden   62–65

Experience: Chocolate Chefs   64

Zeughaus & Deutsches Historisches
    Museum   66–67

Gendarmenmarkt & Around   68–69

A Walk Around Wilhelmstrasse & Old
    Regierungsviertel   70–73

Potsdamer Platz   74–76

Checkpoint Charlie   77

Feature: The Berlin Wall, Then & Now   78–79

Experience: Pedaling the Wall Trail   79

More Places to Visit in Unter den Linden
    & Potsdamer Platz   80

Hotels & Restaurants   242–243

Detail of the Apollo hall in the Staatsoper

Unter den Linden & Potsdamer Platz

The most widely known boulevard in Germany, Unter den Linden is Berlin's central artery. With more than three centuries' history, this avenue "under the linden trees" has witnessed the city's greatest and most harrowing moments. Around it, signs of Berlin's past exist uneasily next to the modern creations of a city reborn.

Much of Unter den Linden and the surrounding area was destroyed in World War II, and after the wall went up, the boulevard came to an ignominious dead end at its west end, the Brandenburger Tor (Brandenburg Gate).

It is hard to appreciate any of this decay today. Many fine buildings along Unter den Linden have been restored or rebuilt. The single greatest symbol of the city's rebirth is the Reichstag building northwest of the avenue. Here a united national parliament again proudly sits in a building that combines the pomp of the past with a vision of the future.

It is a leitmotif heard all over the area. The Brandenburger Tor has been repaired and its square, Pariser Platz, restored to its former elegance. The embassies that once stood here have returned, and the ritzy Hotel Adlon has risen from its ashes.

At the opposite end of Unter den Linden, its most sumptuous edifices (such as the Altes Palais, Staatsoper, and Opernpalais) bask again in glory. Following the lead of the Reichstag, the 18th-century Zeughaus (and its German history museum) has been restored and equipped with a daring 21st-century extension.

Potsdamer Platz has been transformed by the best in international

NOT TO BE MISSED:

Peeling away layers of history at the
  Reichstag **54–57**

The impressive Brandenburg
  Gate **58–59**

The sobering displays at the
  Holocaust Monument **60–61**

Strolling the opulent royal boulevard
  Unter den Linden **62–65**

The neoclassical jewels of
  Gendarmenmarkt **68–69**

Learning about daring escapes at the
  Checkpoint Charlie museum **77**

architecture. And while the pretty Gendarmenmarkt square remains true to its origins, Friedrichstrasse has won new life as a shopping artery.

The scars and reminders of the city's troubled past also make their presence felt. Checkpoint Charlie still stands. A vast memorial to the victims of the Holocaust lies just south off Pariser Platz, and painful history is on view at the Topographie des Terrors, an open-air display and documentation center located on the site of the Gestapo's former headquarters. ■

AM WEIDENDAMM

AM KUPFERGRABEN

Museumsinsel (Museum Island)

Bahnhof
Ⓢ Friedrichstrasse
Ⓤ Friedrichstrasse

MITTE

Spree

REICHSTAGUFER

FRIEDRICHSTRASSE

DOROTHEEN STRASSE

Zeughaus &
Deutsches
Historisches
Museum

DOROTHEENSTRASSE

CHARLOTTENSTR.

Staatsbibliothek

Humboldt
Universität

Neue
Wache

Schlossbrücke

WILHELMSTRASSE

REGIERUNGS-VIERTEL

GLINKASTRASSE

UNTER DEN LINDEN

Römischer Hof

statue of
Frederick the Great

Altes Palais

UNTER DEN LINDEN

PRINZESSINNEN-GARTEN

BEBEL-PLATZ

Staatsoper

Kronprinzenpalais

NIEDERLAG STRASSE

Bauakademie site

WERDERSTR.

☆ Ⓢ Brandenburger
Ⓤ Tor

Hotel
Adlon

British Embassy

Russian
Embassy

Komische
Oper

BEHRENSTRASSE

Hotel
de Rome

Opernpalais

Friedrichswerdersche
Kirche

Akademie
der Künste

BEHRENSTRASSE

Französische
Strasse Ⓤ

FRANZÖSISCHE STR.

St.-Hedwigs-Kathedrale

CORA-BERLINER-STRASSE

MAUERSTRASSE

GLINKA STRASSE

Quartier
207

Französischer Dom
and Hugenottenmuseum

Foreign
Ministry
buildings

Jungfernbrücke

Spreekanal

OLD
REGIERUNGS-VIERTEL

Friedrichstadtpassagen

Quartier
206

GENDARMENMARKT

statue of Friedrich von Schiller

Konzerthaus

Hausvogteiplatz

KUR STRASSE

GERTRAUDEN STR.

Quartier
205

MOHRENSTRASSE

CHARLOTTENSTR.

MARKGRAFEN-

Deutscher Dom
and Historische
Ausstellung

Ⓤ Mohrenstrasse

Stadtmitte Ⓤ

STRASSE

LEIPZIGER

STRASSE

Ⓤ
Spittelmarkt

STRASSE

KRAUSEN STRASSE

LEIPZIGER

STRASSE

FRIEDRICHSTRASSE

MAUER STR.

Bundesrat

Bundesministerium
der Finanzen
(former
Luftfahrtministerium)

WILHELMSTRASSE

Museum für
Kommunikation

ZIMMERSTRASSE

Abgeordnetenhaus

NIEDERKIRCHNERSTR.

Checkpoint Charlie
site

former Berlin Wall

Mauermuseum
Museum Haus am
Checkpoint Charlie

Martin-Gropius-Bau

Hotel Prinz-Albrecht site

KOCHSTRASSE

Gestapo
headquarters
site

Topographie
des Terrors

Kochstrasse Ⓤ

Prinz-Albrecht-Palais site

To Mehringplatz,
five blocks

STRESEMANN STRASSE

ANHALTER STRASSE

STRASSE

Ⓢ Anhalter
Bahnhof

0   200 meters
0   200 yards

UNTER DEN LINDEN &
POTSDAMER PLATZ

Area of map detail

Reichstag Building

There is perhaps no more fitting way to begin an acquaintance with Berlin than at its symbolic epicenter, the national parliament building. Used by Hitler on his rise to power, bombed but not destroyed in World War II, the Reichstag building sits right next to the path of the Berlin Wall, for nearly 29 years the dividing line between East and West.

Sir Norman Foster created a people's dome for the Reichstag building, home to the parliament.

The Reichstag (Imperial Parliament) has inspired strong reactions. Kaiser Wilhelm II liked to refer to the building, completed from a design by Paul Wallot (1841–1912) in 1894, as the "imperial monkeys' cage." He worried that its apparent grandeur might overshadow that of his official Berlin residence, the Schloss, at the eastern end of Unter den Linden. In the end, he could do nothing about its dimensions and contented himself with harrumphing that it was the "height of bad taste." Wallot's daring iron-and-glass dome, however, awakened admiration

among public observers.

Although executive powers when the Reichstag was built lay with the kaiser and his ministers, in particular the chancellor, the parliament did exercise some influence over the affairs of state. One can only wonder what might have happened had it, for example, voted against war credits at the outbreak of World War I. In 1916, as that war was grinding on, the words *Dem Deutschen Volke* (To the German People) were added to the facade.

Although Hitler used the fragile interwar parliamentary system to achieve power in the early

1930s, he never entered the Reichstag building, which was seriously damaged by fire under suspicious circumstances in 1933 (see sidebar). The Nazis didn't bother to restore the building, which was further damaged in the final months of World War II. The remains of Wallot's dome were dynamited in

INSIDER TIP:

On your tour of the Reichstag building, keep an eye out for the graffiti scrawled by Russian troops who took Berlin in 1945.

—ULRICH KRATZ-WHAN
Kulturbüro Berlin tours manager

1954, but the rest of the edifice, on the west side of the Berlin Wall, was restored in the 1960s. A 1971 accord prohibited the Bonn-based West German federal parliament (Bundestag) from sitting in the Reichstag (and competing with East Germany's government).

The Renewed Building

Everything changed with reunification in 1990. The federal parliament voted in 1991 to move to Berlin, and British architect Sir Norman Foster won the bid to make over the building. He retained the grave exterior but gutted the inside. The most spectacular element is his **glass dome.** To see it, visitors should book two days in advance online or show up at least two hours beforehand to book an available time slot. An elevator whisks you up to the dome, which lies directly above parliament's plenary hall. At the center of the dome, a funnel seemingly armored with mirror plates spreads upward. Around its base you can read a little of the building's tumultuous history. Then climb the spiral ramp to the top of the dome for ever better views across central Berlin. There's a rooftop café there, as well.

Parliament moved here from Bonn in 1999. Visitors can sit in on a session of parliament and tour the **Plenarsaal** (the gray

Reichstag Building

- 🅰 Map p. 52
- ✉ Besucherdienst, Platz der Republik 1
- ☎ 030 22 73 21 52; fax 030 22 73 64 36
- 🕐 Dome 8 a.m.– midnight; last admission 11 p.m.
- 🚇 U-Bahn: Bundestag

www.bundestag.de

The Reichstag Fire

Less than a month after Hitler was sworn in as chancellor, the NSDAP found its pretext for seizing absolute power. On the night of February 27, 1933, a fire was reported in the Reichstag, and by the time firefighters arrived, the plenary hall was in flames. Police at the scene arrested Marinus van der Lubbe, a 24-year-old unemployed Dutch bricklayer and known arsonist, although many believe the Nazis started the fire themselves. The very next day, the Weimar constitution was suspended and a state of emergency declared, paving the way for the legal persecution of the Nazis' political opponents, particularly the communists. With these parliamentary seats now empty, the Nazis were able to gain an absolute majority and named Hitler dictator the following year, after President Hindenburg's death. Van der Lubbe, meanwhile, was tried in a Leipzig court and then executed for treason in January 1934.

semicircular hall, dominated by the enormous eagle that symbolizes the federal republic, where parliament sits) and other parts of the building. Most organized visits are conducted in German, but 90-minute guided tours are also available in nine more languages, including English. Details of tour days and times are available on the Bundestag's website. You can also fax or write to apply for an appointment to visit.

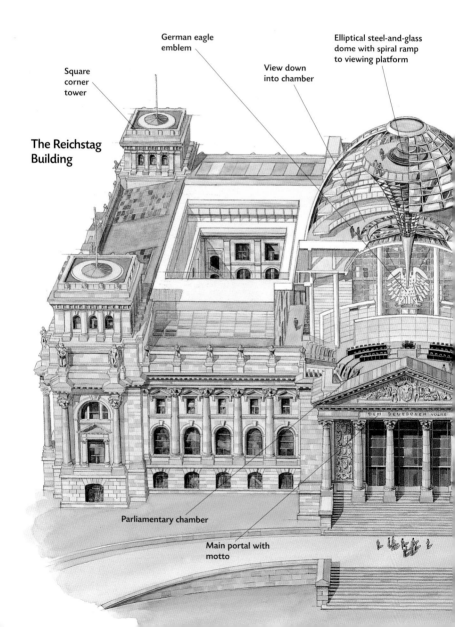

German eagle emblem

View down into chamber

Elliptical steel-and-glass dome with spiral ramp to viewing platform

Square corner tower

The Reichstag Building

Parliamentary chamber

Main portal with motto

DEM DEUTSCHEN VOLKE

Past and present dovetail in the Reichstag building, with its grand 19th-century exterior intact.

Internal courtyard

Rusticated pedestal facade

East of the Reichstag stands the **Jakob-Kaiser-Haus,** a modern complex that houses half the offices of members of parliament. It was built around 1904 as the Reichstagspräsidentenpalais, which was the office of the parliamentary president until 1933.

The bare square in front of the Reichstag was, until World War II, altogether different. Known as Königsplatz (King's Square) until the 1920s, when it became **Platz der Republik** (Republic Square), it hosted the Siegessäule, the winged golden symbol of victory that Hitler moved to its present lofty location in the Tiergarten (see pp. 120–121) in the 1930s. From 1961 until reunification, the square was the scene of frequent demonstrations demanding freedom for East Germany and the removal of the wall. ■

Brandenburger Tor & Pariser Platz

Until the Berlin Wall tumbled down in 1989, most Western visitors to the city could not mean-der beneath the grand Brandenburger Tor (Brandenburg Gate), the key prewar landmark for Berlin's weekend strollers.

The Brandenburg Gate was for a time the symbol of the division between West and East.

In the postwar decades, the pockmarked gate could be observed only across the wall. Those who made the day trip to East Berlin were generally dissuaded from getting too close by troopers patrolling Unter den Linden. The buildings around the once elegant square to its immediate east, Pariser Platz, had all been demolished after the war, allowing Unter den Linden boulevard to peter out in a desolate plain.

That was then. Since reunifica-tion, the gate has been restored to its initial splendor and the Pariser

Platz has regained much of the style it once knew.

The rectangular Pariser Platz was laid out in 1734 to cap the western end of Unter den Linden on its way from the now vanished royal Schloss (palace). It was part of a careful town-planning exercise under Philipp Gerlach (1679–1748) that included the circular Mehringplatz (then called the Rondell), completed two years earlier, and the octagonal Leipziger Platz (now reconstructed), which was also laid out in 1734.

Each square was meant to have a city gate, and in 1791 the

Brandenburger Tor was opened to public acclaim on Pariser Platz. Its designer, Carl Gotthard Langhans (1732–1808), found that "the location, in its way, is without doubt the most beautiful in the world," even if he did say so himself. A low-slung, broad affair, it is graced with simple Doric columns.

The gate was supposed to symbolize the triumph of peace. In 1795, it was topped by the 18-foot-high (5.5 m) copper **Quadriga** statue depicting the goddess of peace, Eirene (or the goddess of victory, according to other versions), riding into the city on a chariot drawn by four horses. To drive the peace message home, a sculpture of the war god, Mars, at the southern end of the gate shows him sheathing his sword.

The Quadriga was created by Johann Gottfried Schadow, a Berliner born into a tailor's family. At 20, he eloped with the daughter of a rich jeweler, who paid for his art studies in Italy. What you see now is a copy made in West Berlin in the 1960s in a rare gesture of East-West cooperation. The original was largely destroyed in World War II.

If running around central Berlin has you gasping, pop into the **Raum der Stille** (Silence Room) in the north flank of the gate *(daily 11 a.m.–4 p.m.)*. This room, with its spotlighted wall hanging and artistically situated rock, is a place in which to meditate in silence.

Since 1992, generous European Union funding has allowed Pariser Platz to be transformed into a close approximation of its former self. The grand early 20th-century **Hotel Adlon** again stands proudly on the southeast corner. New buildings also house the embassies of France, the United States, and the United Kingdom (with a playful main facade on Wilhelmstrasse) in their prewar locations. Graceful gardens, modeled on those planted in 1880, have been laid out.

Much of the glittering, glass **Akademie der Künste** (Arts Academy) building—one of two locations, the other being on the far side of the Tiergarten—is given over to archives and administration, but temporary exhibitions are also held. The academy also stages exhibitions across the square in the reconstructed **Max Liebermann building.**

Canadian-born U.S. architect Frank Gehry (born 1929) designed the **DZ Bank,** between the Akademie der Künste and the U.S. Embassy. The sober facade belies Gehry's mad interior. ∎

Tear Down This Wall!

When Ronald Reagan visited the Brandenburg Gate in 1987, he addressed the Soviet president: "General Secretary Gorbachev, if you seek peace, if you seek prosperity for the Soviet Union and Eastern Europe, if you seek liberalization: come here to this gate! Mr. Gorbachev, open this gate! Mr. Gorbachev, tear down this wall!" In 2012, a plaque was unveiled to commemorate Reagan's appeal. You'll find it embedded in the pavement on the western side. Other American presidents to make speeches here included John F. Kennedy in 1963 (the Soviets hung red banners blocking JFK's view into the East), Bill Clinton in 1994, and Barack Obama in 2013.

Hotel Adlon
- Map p. 53
- Unter den Linden 77
- Tel 030 226 10
- www.kempinski .com/adlon

Akademie der Künste
- Map p. 53
- Pariser Platz 4
- 030 20 05 70
- Exhibits Tues.–Sun.
- Free–$$
- U-Bahn & S-Bahn: Brandenburger Tor
- www.adk.de

Holocaust Monument

Berlin is not short on sites that evoke the history of Nazi persecution of the Jews. But for more than a decade, a debate raged in and out of parliament. Should a monument to Europe's murdered Jews, the six million victims of Hitler's Holocaust, be built in the heart of a newly reunited Berlin? And if so, what form should it take? Only in 1999 did the Bundestag, the federal parliament, vote in favor of a memorial. In late 2005, 15 years after the debate kicked off, the monument was a reality.

A forest of concrete pillars lies at the heart of Berlin's monument to victims of the Holocaust.

Holocaust Monument

- 🅐 Map p. 52
- ✉ Cora-Berliner-Strasse 1
- ☎ 030 26 39 43 36
- 🚫 Closed Mon.
- 🚇 U-Bahn & S-Bahn: Brandenburger Tor

www.stiftung -denkmal.de

From the country villa in Wannsee (see pp. 203–204) where the Final Solution was devised to the Sachsenhausen concentration camp outside of town (see p. 217), Berlin offers the visitor plenty of opportunity to explore this path of darkness. The debate that erupted in the 1990s, however, was about the creation of a public place of remorse and recognition in the core of the capital.

The location is itself symbolic. A stone's throw from the Reichstag, Brandenburger Tor, and course of the former Berlin Wall,

it lies at the city's center. Officially named Denkmal für die ermordeten Juden Europas (Monument to the Murdered Jews of Europe), it is silent testimony to the German people's recognition that the genocide is an inescapable part of their national history.

For all the importance of the monument's placement, no sign tells passersby what it is. And it is by no means obvious. New York architect Peter Eisenman (born 1932) designed a field of 2,711 concrete pillars, all leaning slightly off-center but otherwise different from one another only in their height—varying from 8 inches to 15 feet (0.2–4.7 m). The monument rests on an undulating and deepening field of concrete slabs. The view across this petrified forest is different from every angle. The gray stone field is sliced by a grid of paths so narrow that visitors can see only the path they are following and the ones that cross their path.

On the eastern side of the monument is the entrance to the Ort der Information *(entry recommended only to visitors 14 years and older)*, a poignant introduction to the horror of the Holocaust. Get here in good time, as lines and tight security can slow down entry considerably. The first of a series of rooms holds an overview of the persecution of the Jews from 1933 until 1945. Along a corridor, a series of texts and images provides an introduction to this unfathomable history. From here, one is led to the **Room of Dimensions,** in which victims express themselves in letters, diary entries, and last notes. Writes one journalist in his diary: "If something like this [the persecution and extermination] was possible, what else is there? For what reason is there war? For what reason hunger? For what reason the world?"

The **Room of Families** that follows uses text, pictures, movie reels, and audio to illustrate the lives and destinies of 15 Jewish families across Europe—most of whom did not survive the war. Then comes the **Room of Names.** An audio loop reads names and short biographies of murdered and missing Jews from those years. An annex allows access to data on more than three million victims from the pages of testimony held by the Yad Vashem Holocaust Memorial in Israel. The **Room of Sites,** the last, depicts (in pictures and film) some 220 locations in Europe connected to the Holocaust, from ghettos to concentration camps. ■

The Other Victims

On the edge of the Tiergarten, two memorial sites are dedicated to Holocaust victims whose recognition was long in coming. Directly opposite the main Holocaust Monument, the "Memorial to Homosexuals Persecuted by the Nazis" by artists Ingar Dragset and Michael Elmgreen consists of a single concrete slab with a screen showing a video of a same-sex couple kissing.

Between 5,000 and 15,000 gay men were interned in concentration camps by the Nazis because they were "antisocial." Something like two-thirds did not survive the ordeal. Incredibly, homosexuals were not recognized as victims of the Holocaust and were denied reparations and state pensions. Only in 2002, nearly six decades after the war ended, did the German government formally admit that their incarceration was a crime.

Even longer in the making, in 2012 a memorial to Sinti and Romany victims of the Holocaust was unveiled in a clearing of the Tiergarten, not far from the Reichstag building. The work, "Torn Heart" by Israeli artist Dani Karavan, focuses on a pond with a retractable triangular stele at its center. Lining the water's edge is a timeline of the systematic murder of these minorities during the Third Reich.

Along Unter den Linden

In 1646, the avenue was a royal road from the Berliner Schloss, home of Prussia's rulers, to their hunting grounds in what is now the Tiergarten. By the end of the 19th century, it had become Berlin's Champs-Élysées. Pounded to smithereens during World War II, neglected by the East Germans, and deprived of its central-city status by the division of Berlin, it has regained much of its former glory since reunification.

Restored to its rightful place at the heart of reunited Berlin, Unter den Linden is dotted with cafés.

Just east of Pariser Platz stretches the compound of the **Russian Embassy.** The embassy of tsarist Russia in the 19th century, what was then Unter den Linden 7 became the Soviet Embassy in 1918. Destroyed in World War II, the present structure (Nos. 63–65) was built by the Soviets in 1949–1952, and it has all the Cold War gravity of the period. Nevertheless, the building had little trouble transforming itself into the Russian Embassy to the Federal Republic of Germany when the Cold War faded in 1991.

Across Glinkastrasse is the drab **Komische Oper** (*Behrenstrasse 55–57, tel 030 47 99 74 00 for tickets, www.komische-oper-berlin .de*), whose main entrance is on Behrenstrasse. The opera house may not look like much from the outside (the result of postwar rebuilding), but it has a pedigree. A theater has stood on this site, with interruptions, since 1764.

INSIDER TIP:

Make like Marlene Dietrich and take afternoon tea at Berlin's elegant Hotel Adlon [see p. 59]; you'll feel like a movie star.

—JEANNE HORAK-DUFF
National Geographic contributor

The plush neobaroque interior of the theater was largely untouched by Allied bombs and is today a protected monument. The best way to get a look is to take in one of the shows, which range from light classics to contemporary performances.

Diagonally across the road at Unter den Linden 10 is the **Römischer Hof** shopping and office center, built into the restored shell of the former Hotel de Rome. Opened in 1867, the hotel was converted into public offices in 1910.

Directly across Charlottenstrasse is the **Staatsbibliothek.** In this central branch of the German state library, a skillful blend of old and new, lie extraordinary treasures. In its map archives, for instance, is a 1664 world atlas—the biggest in the world. The library moved here in 1914 from the Altes Palais on Bebelplatz, where it had been since 1784.

On the median strip in Unter den Linden, a proud equestrian **statue of Frederick the Great** could almost be directing traffic. He was restored to his position here only in 1981, having languished in Potsdam in the postwar decades. In late 2005, he got a fright when a bomb dropped by the Royal Air Force in World War II was found buried nearby and had to be destroyed in a controlled detonation.

Next door to the library is the seat of the **Humboldt Universität,** founded in 1810 and still a center of excellence, with buildings scattered across the city. The main edifice was raised in the 18th century as the palace of Prince Heinrich of Prussia (1726–1802) and was extended in 1920.

Directly across the road from the university is the curvaceous **Altes Palais,** also known as the

Staatsbibliothek
- Map p. 53
- Unter den Linden 8
- Tel 030 26 60
- http://staatsbiblio thek-berlin.de

Humboldt Universität
- Map p. 53
- Unter den Linden 6
- Tel 030 209 30
- www.hu-berlin.de

Burning the Books

On the night of May 10, 1933, Bebelplatz (then Opernplatz) became the site of an enormous bonfire. In front of the Altes Palais, which for more than a century had been the city's main library, thousands of books by authors considered undesirable by the Nazis were heaped onto the flames. Karl Marx, Sigmund Freud, Thomas and Heinrich Mann, and Bertolt Brecht were just a few of the writers whose works had to be "cleaned out."

The scene, organized by student associations as an "action against un-German thinking" and attended by university rectors and professors, was repeated in university cities across the country.

Under the cobblestones is a poignant memorial, "The Empty Room," by Israeli artist Mischa Ullman, showing a set of eerily vacant white bookshelves through a sheet of plexiglass.

St.-Hedwigs-Kathedrale

🗺 Map p. 53

✉ Behrenstrasse

☎ 030 203 48 10

Ⓤ U-Bahn: Französische Strasse

www.hedwigs-kathedrale.de

Alte Bibliothek, on Bebelplatz. Built in 1780 and once home to the Staatsbibliothek, it is now part of Humboldt University. Berliners, who just love to give their buildings sobriquets, dubbed this one the Kommode because it looks like an antique chest of drawers (Kommode).

EXPERIENCE:
Chocolate Chefs

A shop, café, and workshop rolled into one, **Bunte Schokowelt**—the "colorful world of chocolate" two blocks south of Unter den Linden—offers children 7 to 18 the opportunity to make chocolate bars with their chosen ingredients. While the masterpieces set, young chocolatiers can visit a Ritter Sport museum (Französische Strasse 24, tel 030 200 95 08, $$, http://schokowerkstatt-berlin.ritter-sport.de).

Facing the Altes Palais across the square is the **Staatsoper** (tel 030 20 35 45 55), built by Georg Wenzeslaus von Knobelsdorff in 1743 as Berlin's first theater, which was damaged in air raids in 1945. The stately edifice is being spruced up through 2017; meanwhile, you can catch Daniel Barenboim, the opera's famed artistic director, leading productions at Charlottenburg's Schiller Theater.

The broad copper dome at the southeast corner of Bebelplatz belongs to the city's main Catholic church, **St.-Hedwigs-Kathedrale.** The church, which was completed in 1773 by Knobelsdorff, was inspired by the Pantheon in Rome. Next door, the luxury Hotel de Rome opened in 2006

in a restored late 19th-century former bank headquarters.

Back on the main drag, Unter den Linden is graced by the **Opernpalais,** located across a park from the Staatsoper. Its opulent Operncafé and two restaurants closed for a revamp in 2011, and the future of the property is uncertain.

The park itself is occupied by several martial statues of Prussian generals who fought against Napoleon. Leading the way is Gerhard von Scharnhorst (1755–1813). Behind him line up Count Johann Yorck (1759–1830); Gebhard von Blücher (1742–1819), who led the Prussians against Napoleon at Waterloo; and August von Gneisenau (1760–1831). After World War II, the East German regime removed the statues, judging that the generals personified the imperial past of Germany and were thus politically incorrect. However, the regime changed its mind in 1963 and brought the generals back.

Next door, the restored **Kronprinzenpalais** (Unter den Linden 3) dates to the mid-17th century. Once a private residence and later an art gallery shut down by the Nazis for showing "degenerate art" (such as expressionism), it opens only occasionally for exhibitions or other events.

Anyone who visited East Berlin prior to 1990 will remember the **Neue Wache,** across Unter den Linden. Here, goose-stepping sentries would change the guard outside what had become a memorial to the victims of World War II and, in particular, of the Nazi war machine. Karl Friedrich Schinkel built it in 1818 as a barracks for the King's Watch troops. Since 1993, it has become Germany's central memorial to all victims of World War II and, pointedly, of the East German regime. Next door is the Zeughaus museum (see pp. 66–67).

Art & Architecture

Just behind the rebuilt Kronprinzenpalais rises one of the rare buildings to have survived the bombing of Berlin more or less intact. Schinkel built the **Friedrichswerdersche Kirche,** a neo-Gothic redbrick caprice topped by slender pinnacles and imitating 19th-century English retro tastes, in 1831. Since 1987, the building has housed a part of the **Alte Nationalgalerie**'s sculpture collection. In the nave you will find a selection of works by such important Berlin sculptors as Johann Gottfried Schadow and Christian Daniel Rauch. Schinkel himself is immortalized in a statue on the right as you enter, created by his friend and sculptor Friedrich Tieck (1776–1851). The architect's life and work are displayed along the upper gallery.

Just across Niederlagstrasse from the Friedrichswerdersche Kirche is, or rather isn't, yet another Schinkel effort, the **Bauakademie,** a 19th-century architecture school that Schinkel liked so much he chose to live there. It survived the war but not the East

German regime, which demolished it in 1962 to make way for its foreign office. This building was itself torn down in 1995, leaving a huge vacant lot. A private group has been campaigning to have the Bauakademie reconstructed; to lend the campaign more weight, they have created a tarpaulin imitation on the site.

The restored **Schlossbrücke** marks the end of Berlin's best known boulevard. Schinkel designed the bridge, which was completed in 1824, although the sculptures were added in 1849. Destroyed in the war, it was restored in 1950. ■

Friedrichs- werdersche Kirche

- ⚠ Map p. 53
- ✉ Werderscher Markt
- ☎ 030 266 42 42 42
- Ⓜ U-Bahn: Hausvogteiplatz

www.smb.spk-berlin .de

The Friedrichswerdersche Kirche was one of the few monuments in central Berlin to survive World War II.

Zeughaus & Deutsches Historisches Museum

In the remarkably ornate building that once held the city's armory (Zeughaus), the past, present, and future seem to flow together. Housing the Deutsches Historisches Museum (German History Museum), the building is a voyage through the nation's history; with its ultramodern extension, it symbolizes a forward-looking vision in its presentation of the past.

I. M. Pei's glass spiral stairway is part of his extension of the Deutsches Historisches Museum.

Completed in 1706, the vaguely pink-hued facade on Unter den Linden is more suggestive of a baron's mansion than a weapons depot. One of the earliest buildings to grace the boulevard, the Zeughaus has gone through repeated transformations. Only its heady facade is unchanged.

Originally designed by Johann Arnold Nering, with continued work by Andreas Schlüter and Jean de Bodt, it was finished in 1729 and served as an armory until the late 19th century. By 1829, however, some rooms had been remodeled to display the national collection of Prussian war booty (mostly weapons, ensigns, flags, and the like). By the 1880s, the entire building had been transformed into a military museum.

On entering from Unter den Linden today, you seem to travel

through time. The **entrance hall,** with its sober pillars encased in travertine marble, is a faithful restoration of the East German design of the 1950s.

From here, you proceed to the inner courtyard, commonly known as the **Schlüterhof** because of the masks of dying warriors, carved by Andreas Schlüter, that frame the windows. The gently vaulted glass ceiling, which stretches like a sheet of bubble wrap over the grand hall, was designed by Chinese-American architect I.M. Pei (born 1917). It takes its cue from the late 19th-century steel-and-glass roof destroyed in World War II. The elegantly curving stairwells in the Schlüterhof are among the few surviving details from the original baroque building.

Where Pei really went to town, however, was behind the Zeughaus. From the Schlüterhof, you proceed down escalators to the underground passage that leads to his **extension** of the museum. The building itself, as well as its exhibitions, is worth a close look. The bright limestone walls, all smooth surfaces and straight lines, transport you to a wonderfully orderly flight of fancy. Arrowhead angles and broad bow shapes combine to create a unique open space that allows visitors to observe all floors at once. Behind closed doors on each floor are generous exhibition spaces.

The Zeughaus

The museum's core exhibition is in the Zeughaus. It starts in the west wing of the upper floor,

with collections and displays taking you from the earliest days of Germanic tribal history through the Middle Ages to about 1500. You then proceed around the rest of the top floor for a look at events from the Renaissance until World War I and the collapse of the German Reich in 1918.

INSIDER TIP:

The Deutsches Historisches Museum's Zeughauskino cinema screens classic and rare movies as well as documentaries.

—JEREMY GRAY
National Geographic author

Down on the first floor, the collection picks up again with the Weimar Republic. The main following sections are devoted to the rise of Nazi Germany, World War II, and the parallel histories of East and West Germany. Another area deals with reunification and the withdrawal of wartime occupation troops from Berlin and the rest of the country. The last rooms are given over to contemporary history and change regularly.

In the Pei extension, temporary exhibitions treat specific areas related to German history or draw on the museum's massive archives. An in-house cinema, the **Zeughauskino** (see Travelwise p. 262), generally shows classic films from the early decades of moving pictures. ∎

Zeughaus & Deutsches Historisches Museum

🅰 Map p. 53
✉ Unter den Linden 2
☎ 030 20 30 40
💲 $
🚇 U-Bahn & S-Bahn: Friedrichstrasse

www.dhm.de

Gendarmenmarkt & Around

This 17th-century market square emerged as part of the city-planning effort known as Friedrichstadt, and it is arguably the prettiest such space in central Berlin. Kurfürst Friedrich III (from 1701, King of Prussia Friedrich I) commissioned the district's construction beginning in 1688. In the next decades, the square came to host the buildings that still give it beauty.

The twin churches of Gendarmenmarkt make the square one of Berlin's prettiest.

Französischer Dom

- Map p. 53
- Gendarmenmarkt 5
- 030 229 17 60
- Closed Mon.
- $
- U-Bahn: Französische Strasse

www.franzoesischer -dom.de

Gendarmenmarkt square took its name both from the regiment of *gens d'armes*—men at arms— stationed here and from the fact that it was, until the 1880s, Germany's biggest weekly produce market.

On either side of the square stand two virtually identical baroque churches. The one on the north side was raised for the city's burgeoning French Huguenot population, many of whom moved into the area in the 18th century. A simple church, the **Friedrichstadt Kirche,** built here in 1705, was modeled on the French Protestants' main church in France at

Charenton. It is overshadowed by the grand baroque tower next to it, which was completed in 1785 by Carl von Gontard (1731–1791). Capped by a dome, it came to be known as the **Französischer Dom** (French Dome), a confusing appellation as *Dom* in German also means "cathedral," which this building is not. The climb to the top of the tower is rewarded with fine views.

At the tower's base, the **Hugenottenmuseum** tells the story of the persecution of the Protestants in France, their flight into exile, and their role in the history of Berlin. The church is frequently

German Debt Clock

At the height of hyperflation during the Weimar era, a barrowful of Reichsmarks bought a loaf of bread. This memory left individual Germans with a deep aversion to debt, although the government seems to have fewer qualms. To keep tabs on obligations, the German Taxpayers Federation installed a national debt clock near the swanky shops of Friedrichstrasse. The red LCD meter, its numbers spinning day and night, was inspired by the original in New York City. In mid-2013, Germany's national debt was rising €870 ($1,137) per second and amounted to roughly €2.08 trillion ($2.72 trillion) or €25,400 ($33,200) per capita.

used for concerts and boasts a 60-bell carillon.

The town's German Lutheran community built a church in 1708 at the southern end of the square. In 1785, von Gontard raised a tower there nearly identical to the French one. It was inevitably dubbed the **Deutscher Dom** (German Dome) and was heavily damaged in World War II.

In the 1980s, the East Germans started to convert the church into an arts center. United Berlin decided to turn it into a museum **(Historische Ausstellung)** on the history of German democracy—a worthy if rather dry introduction to this subject. It starts in the basement with a look at German parliamentary democracy today and ascends through earlier history to finish with Germany's role in the European Union.

Between the two churches, the more lighthearted **Konzerthaus** (originally Schauspielhaus) was yet another Karl Friedrich Schinkel creation. Its opulent interior is the result of restoration, as the theater was gutted during World War II. The Berlin Symphony Orchestra, formerly the East German answer to the Berlin Philharmoniker, calls it home, and it is the scene of a

busy program of classical music concerts. Outside on the square stands a **statue of Friedrich von Schiller** (1759–1805), one of the giants of German literature.

One block to the west of Gendarmenmarkt runs Friedrichstrasse, one of the city's principal arteries until the end of World War II and back with a vengeance. In the early 1990s, an international team of architects created a shopping promenade, the **Friedrichstadtpassagen.** The stores, or *Quartiers,* start to the north with **Quartier 207,** designed by France's Jean Nouvel (born 1945) and home to a branch of Paris's Galeries Lafayette. This curvy glass cathedral is dominated inside by two glass funnels that pierce all floors. Next is **Quartier 206,** an angular building designed principally by U.S. architect Henry Cobb (born 1926). Cologne-based architect Oswald Mathias Ungers (1926–2007) finished the row with his cubic **Quartier 205.**

Two blocks east of the Gendarmenmarkt loom the **Foreign Ministry buildings.** The main one was the Nazi Reichsbank, and in GDR times, SED party headquarters. It has a grand, open atrium on Werderstrasse. ∎

Hugenotten-museum
- Map p. 53
- Gendarmenmarkt 5
- 030 229 17 60
- $
- U-Bahn: Französische Strasse

www.franzoesischer-dom.de

Deutscher Dom
- Map p. 53
- Gendarmenmarkt 1
- 030 22 73 04 31
- Closed Mon.
- U-Bahn: Stadtmitte

www.bundestag.de

Konzerthaus
- Map p. 53
- Gendarmenmarkt 2
- 030 203 09 23 33
- $
- U-Bahn: Stadtmitte

www.konzerthaus.de

A Walk Around Wilhelmstrasse & Old Regierungsviertel

Standing on the corner of Unter den Linden and Wilhelmstrasse, you can well believe that this area was once a center of government. Wilhelmstrasse was Germany's powerhouse, known as the Regierungsviertel (Government District), and it was lined with ministries and government offices from the early 19th century until Hitler's heyday. Today, with few exceptions, it is all gone, sucked up in the whirlwind of war. This walk is a ghost tour.

A mural at the former Aviation Ministry commemorates the 1953 uprising against the GDR.

Start at the Russian ❶ and British ❷ Embassies, which lie within a few feet of the street corner in their historic locations. Two blocks down, at No. 54 Wilhelmstrasse, which in those days was No. 64, the **Prussian State Council** ❸ had its office between World War I and the arrival of the Nazis. The then president of the

Prussian State Council and later first president of West Germany Konrad Adenauer (1876–1967) lived here in 1932–1933, until the Nazis abolished the federal states and centralized power in Berlin. The building then became the headquarters of Rudolf Hess, Hitler's deputy (see pp. 194–195), until Martin Bormann moved in to replace

NOT TO BE MISSED:

- **Luftfahrtministerium**
- **Stasi Bildungszentrum**
- **Topographie des Terrors**

him. It now houses the Berlin branch of the federal Ministry of Consumer Protection, Nutrition, and Agriculture.

Next door to the south was the **office of the Prussian prime minister ④**. When Nazi chief Hermann Göring (1893–1946) took up that position, he moved the office to Leipziger Strasse and Hess took over this building, too. Directly across the road was

the **Foreign Ministry ⑤**, run by the Nazi Joachim von Ribbentrop (1893–1946) from 1938 until the end of the war.

On the same western side of Wilhelmstrasse was the **old Reich Chancellery ⑥**, the residence and offices of the German chancellor from 1878 to 1939, when Hitler's **new Reich Chancellery ⑦** was completed on Vosstrasse. Nothing remains of either, or of the bombproof **Führerbunker ⑧**

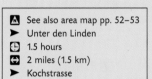

- ⓐ See also area map pp. 52–53
- ► Unter den Linden
- ⊕ 1.5 hours
- ⇄ 2 miles (1.5 km)
- ► Kochstrasse

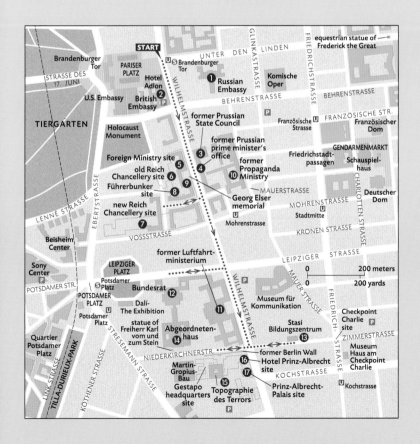

in between, in which Hitler and company cowered in the last days of the war. Although these buildings are gone, panels with information about them in German and English are scattered along Wilhelmstrasse. At the corner of An der Kolonnade towers a giant **silhouette of Nazi resister Georg Elser ❾**, a surreal squiggle of a monument. Acting alone in 1939, the Swabian carpenter hid a bomb at a Munich beer hall, intent on killing Hitler during a party gathering. The Führer left early and unharmed, while Elser was caught and executed at Dachau.

Up, Up, and Away

Fitted with a large gondola and logo of daily newspaper *Die Welt (The World)*, a tethered balloon around the corner from Checkpoint Charlie rises about 500 ft (150 m) over the capital for a 360° view. During the 15-minute ride, you can move around the gondola and cast your eyes on Checkpoint Charlie, the headquarters of publisher Axel Springer, the skyscrapers at Potsdamer Platz, and the Brandenburg Gate.

    Buy tickets on the spot or book online *(Zimmerstrasse 97, tel 030 40 05 62 60, www.air-service-berlin.de)*. The balloon operates year-round in good weather.

Opposite the original Reich Chancellery, at Wilhelmstrasse 49 (a side lane), you can see Joseph Goebbels's (1897–1945) **Propaganda Ministry ❿,** now the country's Health and Labor Ministry. It is best seen from Mauerstrasse.

Return to Wilhelmstrasse and continue south. Göring's **Luftfahrtministerium ⓫,** or Aviation Ministry, which lines Wilhelmstrasse (No. 97) between Leipziger Strasse and Niederkirchnerstrasse, was the first of the Nazis' megalomaniacal public buildings to be built (1936). It was used in the GDR's

time as the House of Ministries and was the scene of the workers' protest that launched the June 17, 1953, uprising. Today it is the federal Finance Ministry. Next door along Leipziger Strasse is the **Bundesrat ⓬,** the upper house of the federal German parliament, located in what was the upper house of the Prussian parliament until 1933.

Secrets of the Secret Police

The next stop is a handsome turn-of-the-20th-century building not far from Checkpoint Charlie, where you will find the **Stasi Bildungszentrum ⓭** *(Zimmerstrasse 91, tel 030 23 24 50, www.bstu.de)*, an information center on the secret police of communist East Germany. Through documents, photos, and interview clips (in German only), the display casts a light on the Stasi's methods and impact on daily GDR life. (The East German Ministry for State Security had 91,000 employees and 189,000 *Inoffizielle Mitarbeiter,* or civilian informants.) Personal stories of six victims are told at listening stations.

Among the more alarming objects are jars with bits of material that contain the scent of potential enemies of the state, given to dogs who would search out their presence. The center allows anyone, foreigners included, to access its archives to check for traces of personal surveillance.

Berlin is at the same time the capital city and one of 16 federal states. Its state parliament, the **Abgeordnetenhaus ⓮,** has its home in what was from 1899 to 1934 the Prussian state parliament lower house on Niederkirchnerstrasse. Standing proudly before the parliament building is a much restored 1869 **statue of Freiherr Karl vom und zum Stein** (1757–1831), a statesman who was instrumental in a wide-ranging series of reforms in Prussia in the early 1800s. These novelties were greeted with gritted teeth by the Prussian monarchy and nobility, who would later roll most of them back and prefer instead to recall the reformer's patriotism in fighting Napoleon's army.

Gestapo & SS

Virtually across Niederkirchnerstrasse from the Abgeordnetenhaus at what was once No. 8, behind a stretch of the former Berlin Wall, is a near-vacant parcel of land with a shudder-inducing history.

In 1933, the Third Reich commandeered the neobaroque building that stood on the lot and converted it into the Reichssicher-heitshauptamt, the umbrella body for Nazi Germany's police state apparatus. In the same building was lodged the scariest of Hitler's security tools, Heinrich Himmler's (1900–1945) Geheime Staatspolizei (Secret State Police), or Gestapo for short. Opponents of Hitler's regime wound up here for interrogation and torture in the cellars. Now a moving exhibition, **Topographie des Terrors** ⑮ (Niederkirchnerstrasse 8,

tel 030 254 50 90, www.topographie.de) catalogs the crimes the Nazis perpetrated in sobering detail.

Next door, in the former **Hotel Prinz-Albrecht** ⑯ at No. 9, was the SS (Schutz-staffel, a paramilitary security organization) headquarters, while the SD (Sicherheits-dienst, or Security Service), run by Reinhard Heydrich (1904–1942), moved into the **Prinz-Albrecht-Palais** ⑰, around the corner at Wilhelmstrasse 102. The buildings were heavily damaged during World War II and demolished in the 1950s.

A self-guided walking tour of the grounds of the Topographie des Terrors indicates what was where. Opened in 2010, the site's vast documentation center focuses on the Nazis' rise to power. Photos, audio, and film clips add context to displays. The site is partly given over to an open-air display, "Between Propaganda and Terror," set in exposed parts of a cellar where prisoners were kept.

The Topographie des Terrors is one of the most visited sites in Berlin.

Potsdamer Platz

One of the busiest squares in prewar Berlin, Potsdamer Platz was largely razed in World War II and then sliced off from West Berlin by the wall. It was here, close to where the sparkling Bahntower (the German railway's national headquarters) now soars above the square, that the first hammers were taken to the wall on November 10, 1989. Since then, a wasteland has been propelled into the 21st century by reconstruction that will soon be completed on adjacent Leipziger Platz.

The Sony Center Forum is a beacon in the heart of Berlin.

The most exciting project on the square is the **Sony Center,** designed by German-American architect Helmut Jahn (born 1940). Made up of eight buildings and completed in 2000, it has become a symbol of modern Berlin. The centerpiece is the oval Forum, a warren of restaurants, bars, an IMAX cinema, and offices beneath a stunning glass-and-steel big top. Lit up at night in ever changing colors, it is a beacon to Berliners (including those who gather with laptops to benefit from the free Wi-Fi hot spot).

Cunningly built into the glass structure is the old-world **Kaisersaal** *(Bellevuestrasse 1, tel 030 25 75 14 54),* a gourmet restaurant that was the only part of the once elegant late 19th-century Esplanade Hotel to survive World War II. The adjacent 26-floor **Bahntower** is the tallest building on the square.

Moving Pictures

Inside one of the angular buildings of the complex is the **Deutsche Kinemathek,** which covers the history of film and television in Germany from the early days of the fabled Babelsberg studios to contemporary

German cinema. The exhibition starts on the third floor with a marvelous mirror game. You wander along a silver-lit path past screens showing snippets of classic films and see yourself reflected to infinity in the mirrors that constitute ceiling, floor, and walls. The exhibition proper starts off with the earliest stars of the German screen, including Henny Porten (1890–1960, the "white goddess of the masses") and Danish-born Asta Nielsen.

From there, you are taken through the heady days of the Weimar Republic, an era that produced masterpieces such as Josef von Sternberg's *Der Blaue Engel* (*The Blue Angel,* with Marlene Dietrich) and Fritz Lang's landmark sci-fi film *Metropolis.* Several rooms are dedicated to Berlin-born star Dietrich (see p. 182) herself, and others to the steady exodus of German directors and actors to Hollywood in the 1920s and 1930s. The Nazi era is treated briefly, with a room on Leni Riefenstahl's *Olympia* but no film clips. The remainder of the exhibition deals with the work of Germans in the United States and German cinema to the present. The museum is part of the **Filmhaus,** which contains the Arsenal cinema, the city's film archives, and a professional film academy.

Urban Architecture

Not as immediately arresting as the spectacular Sony Center is the labyrinthine **Quartier Potsdamer Platz**

(*www.potsdamerplatz.de*) across Potsdamer Strasse to the south. The two complexes turn their backs to one another on either side of this windy canyon. Until 2007, it was called the Quartier Daimler (and before that, Quartier DaimlerChrysler) and at the time, represented the single greatest urban construction project in European history. Under the direction of Italian architect Renzo Piano (born 1937), a total of 19 new buildings, 10 streets, and 2

INSIDER TIP:

After a day at the Kulturforum, catch a movie at nearby CineStar in the Sony Center on Potsdamer Platz, where films are shown in original versions and beer is available at the snack bar.

—ELIZABETH BARRETT
National Geographic contributor

squares were created in just four years from 1994. It is a mix of office space, hotels, casino, shopping center, apartments, and entertainment center. Among the world-class architects to go to town here were Japan's Arata Isozaki (born 1931), Britain's Sir Richard Rogers (born 1933), and Spain's Rafael Moneo (born 1937), as well as several Germans. The signature building is the dark,

Deutsche Kinemathek

- Map p. 52
- Potsdamer Strasse 2
- 030 300 90 30
- Closed Mon.
- $$
- U-Bahn & S-Bahn: Potsdamer Platz

www.deutsche-kinemathek.de

Panoramapunkt

⚑ Map p. 52

✉ Potsdamer Platz 1

☎ 030 25 93 70 80

💲 $$

🚇 U-Bahn & S-Bahn: Potsdamer Platz

www.panorama punkt.de

peat-fired tiled office block at Potsdamer Platz 1, designed by Hans Kollhoff (born 1946). Reaching 338 feet (103 m) and climbing in three layers toward its peak, it has a whiff of Manhattan about it.

Inside the Kollhoff building, you can take what is said to be Europe's fastest elevator (a 20-second whoosh) to the **Panoramapunkt** on the 24th and 25th floors for some of the best views to be found in Berlin.

winery from the time it opened until well into World War II, it is now restored and again home to a fine restaurant, Diekmann (*Potsdamer Strasse 5, tel 030 25 29 75 24*). The fourth floor holds the gallery **Daimler Contemporary,** a constantly changing display of some of the carmaker's collection of more than a thousand works of contemporary minimalist and conceptual art. Scattered about inside the Quartier mini-city are eight pieces of

Best Berlin Vistas

Savor the finest views of the city at these spots:

- Through the Reichstag's sparkling glass cupola (see p. 55)
- From the Panoramapunkt observation deck over Potsdamer Platz (see above)
- On the open-air dome terrace of Berliner Dom (see p. 97)

- Atop the Sputnik-era TV tower at Alexanderplatz (see sidebar p. 103)
- Over the lush Tiergarten from the Victory Column (see pp. 120–121)
- On a Spree River boat tour past the German Chancellery (see p. 143)
- From the Viktoriapark memorial (see p. 183)

Haus Huth & Daimler Contemporary

⚑ Map p. 52

✉ Alte Potsdamer Strasse 5

☎ 030 25 94 14 20

🚇 U-Bahn & S-Bahn: Potsdamer Platz

www.sammlung .daimler.com

The third tower on the square (after the Bahntower and Kollhoff's building) is a daring work by Renzo Piano. The ocher-tinted 18-story office culminates in an acutely angled glass structure that, seen head-on, seems to be a razor-edged rocket.

The only building on the square to survive World War II intact was **Haus Huth,** a six-story building raised in 1912 by architects Conrad Heidenreich (1873–1937) and Paul Michel (1877–1938). Their decision to use a steel skeleton in construction, revolutionary at the time, gave it the strength to withstand Allied bombs. A restaurant and

street sculpture, the most striking being "*Balloon Flower*" by controversial American artist Jeff Koons (born 1955) on Marlene-Dietrich-Platz. It looks likes a series of navy blue sausage balloons twisted together to form, well, a fat flower.

The last of the three big projects on the square is the **Beisheim Center** (*www.beisheim -center.de*), rising on the triangle of land between Ebertstrasse and Bellevuestrasse. Financed by German tycoon Otto Beisheim, it comprises three top hotels, offices, and luxury apartment buildings created by local and international architects. ∎

Checkpoint Charlie

For years, most foreign day-trippers to East Berlin crossed at the U.S. Army's Checkpoint Charlie. A replica of the checkpoint was erected on the spot in 2001, along with a copy of the sign: "You Are Leaving the American Sector. " This memorial owes its existence to Rainer Hildebrandt (1914–2004), the man who started the adjacent Haus am Checkpoint Charlie museum.

A higgledy-piggledy collection begun in a building right next to the Berlin Wall in June 1963, the museum has been an organic affair, growing in haphazard fashion to document each new escape and tragedy associated with the wall.

With photos, videos, and models, the meandering museum is full of engrossing details. Several cars used to smuggle people over the border are surpassed by more astounding methods of escape. One woman was taken out of East Berlin inside a big stereo system speaker, another between two hollowed-out surfboards. The most daring escape was that undertaken by two families of four, who sailed across the border in 1979 in Europe's biggest ever handmade balloon.

Plenty of material is devoted to those who died trying to cross the East German border—but not all East German soldiers shot to kill. One photo in the collection shows a banner erected on the west side in 1971 that thanks "the many GDR border guards who had no wish and will have no wish to fire on escapees."

Nearby, that giant steel cylinder is the **Asisi Panometer** *(Friedrichstrasse 205, tel 0341 355 53 40, www.asisi.de, $$)*, a re-created 360-degree look over the wall

during the 1980s. Details are stunningly realistic: You see children playing, street artists spraying graffiti, and drunks hanging out at a Currywurst stand, while sentries patrol the death strip. The attraction is planned to run through 2014, but will likely be extended. The adjacent Black Box houses displays on the Cold War, the forerunner of a museum that should be raised here in the years ahead. ∎

Mauermuseum/ Museum Haus am Checkpoint Charlie

- Map p. 53
- Friedrichstrasse 43–45
- 030 253 72 50
- $$$
- U-Bahn: Kochstrasse or Stadtmitte

http://mauer museum.de

Checkpoint Charlie, the best known Cold War crossing point

The Berlin Wall, Then & Now

It happened around midnight. Units of the National People's Army stationed in East Berlin (the Soviet sector of the occupied city) went on alert late on August 12, 1961, and by early morning had improvised a wall of barbed wire and tank traps along the 96-mile (155 km) border with West Berlin. U-Bahn and S-Bahn transit between the two halves of the city was shut down.

With the exception of a few last pieces, the Berlin Wall is turning into a distant memory.

East Germans had been voting with their feet for years. In the first half of 1961 alone, 200,000 had left for the West. The exodus threatened to destroy the country's economy. SED party chief Walter Ulbricht had declared in June: "No one has any intention of building a wall." He was lying. In agreement with the other countries of the Soviet-controlled Warsaw Pact, East Germany decided to "settle the Berlin problem" with a physical barrier.

On the morning of August 13, hundreds of East Berliners made a last break for freedom. By the end of the day, provisional strips of brick wall were being hastily built, ditches dug, and people forcibly removed from houses overlooking the border. Of 81 crossing points, 69 were permanently shut. Until 1963, virtually no one was allowed to cross the dividing line in either direction.

In the coming years, the "Anti-Fascist Protection Wall" was perfected. In 1975, a 27-mile (43 km) concrete wall was put into place between the western and eastern halves of city. Made of 2.75-ton (2.5 tonne) prefabricated sections, it was 11.5 to 14 feet (3.5–4 m) high. It often cut through the middle of streets or houses. Behind the wall was a strip of no-man's-land, the "death strip," followed by a ditch and then a roadway for military vehicles. The remaining 69 miles (112 km) of Berlin's boundary with the state of Brandenburg were sealed off with heavily fortified fences. Along the length of the boundary were 300 watchtowers with searchlights and machine-gun openings. Then came a guard-dog run, trip wires, and, later, automatic weapons. Finally an inner fence was erected.

The wall's first fatality, Günter Litfin, fell on August 24, 1961. The last victim, Chris Gueffroy, died on February 5, 1989. About 5,000 people tried to get through the wall and more than 3,000 were arrested. Eighty would-be escapees died and 115 were wounded.

Still Standing

Berliners began to knock down the wall on November 10, 1989, and by 1991 most of it had been demolished. However, isolated strips of the wall have been left standing, including strips along Niederkirchnerstrasse on the corner with Wilhelmstrasse (see p. 73) and the Gedenkstätte Berliner Mauer (see p. 114) along Bernauer Strasse in northern Mitte. Several watchtowers have been retained, including ones at Kieler Strasse, Erna-Berger-Strasse (near Potsdamer Platz), and Am Schlesischen Busch (see p. 167).

Memorials to the wall's dead include one on the Tiergarten side of the Brandenburger Tor and another on the Spree River just north of the Reichstag.

INSIDER TIP:

In an old watchtower near the Hamburger Bahnhof art gallery, the Günther Litfin Memorial *[Kieler Strasse 2]* is an intriguing display of GDR-era documents.

—GABRIELLA LE BRETON
National Geographic author

EXPERIENCE: Pedaling the Wall Trail

Where monstrous slabs of concrete once zigzagged around West Berlin, the **Berlin Mauerweg** (Wall Trail) is now a popular hiking and biking trail some 100 miles (160 km) long. Much of the newly paved route follows roads that once were patrolled by GDR border troops or West German customs officials.

The trail is divided into 14 walkable and bikeable sections, each accessible by public transportation. (Most public transport allows you to take bicycles on board, but check in advance.) Information stations give details on the division of Germany and events at the wall by means of recorded audio, photographs, and text.

The trail alternates between scrappy, built-up areas and stretches of serene farmland and is clearly signposted with maps at regular intervals. Those who lost their lives at the wall are recalled with short biographies en route.

Berlin on Bike (*Knaackstrasse 97, tel 030 43 73 99 99, www.berlinonbike.de*) conducts an excellent four-hour tour, covering 9 miles (14 km) with stops at onetime border crossings, abandoned train stations, and one of the last remaining observation towers. Tours leave from Prenzlauer Berg (*English offered, Tues., Thurs., & Sat. at 11 a.m., April–Oct., $$$ incl. bike rental*). Reserve in advance.

More Places to Visit in
Unter den Linden & Potsdamer Platz

Martin-Gropius-Bau

A russet red noble relic from 19th-century Berlin, the Martin-Gropius-Bau was restored in the late 1970s largely at the insistence of Walter Gropius, a grandnephew of the man after whom this museum space is named. Built in 1881 by Martin Gropius as the Renaissance-style home for the Kunstgewerbemuseum, it housed various of the city's museum collections until World War II. It narrowly escaped the wrecking ball and, since its restoration, sponsors art exhibitions. *www.gropiusbau.de* 🗺 Map p. 53 ✉ Niederkirchnerstrasse 7 ☎ 030 25 48 60 🕐 Closed Tues. 💲 $$ (depends on exhibition) 🚇 U-Bahn & S-Bahn: Potsdamer Platz

---

Dalí Delights

A few steps east of Potsdamer Platz, the intriguing gallery Dalí—The Exhibition on Potsdamer Platz *(Leipziger Platz 7, www.daliberlin.de)* boasts 400-plus works of surrealist maestro Salvador Dalí. These are mostly lesser-known pieces—no dripping clocks—drawn from private collections. Highlights include his lithograph "Don Quixote," which the artist created by firing antique muskets into stone, the "Surrealist Angel" (Dalí himself), and "The Apocalypse of St. John," consisting of splattered nails and a sewing machine run over by a steam roller.

Museum für Kommunikation

The modern successor to an 1898 postal museum, this collection is spread over three floors gathered in a V around an inner courtyard, whose ceiling glows cobalt blue at night. In the entrance hall, you may be intercepted by one of three good-humored robots, although they don't seem to speak English. On the first floor, exhibits are mostly dedicated to postal history and include a collection of German post office signs, as well as an equally curious collection of mailboxes from around the world. You have probably never seen so many telephones in one exhibition room, complemented by old-time switchboards and other telecommunications paraphernalia of the not-so-distant past. The top floor focuses on radio and TV, including some of the first (huge) sets with small screens. The 1936 upright TV, whose horizontal screen was viewed through a mirror, is the most bizarre model of all. 🗺 Map p. 53 ✉ Leipziger Strasse 16 ☎ 030 20 29 40 🕐 Closed Mon. 💲 $ 🚇 U-Bahn: Stadtmitte

Palace of Tears Exhibition

After the Berlin Wall went up in August 1961, Bahnhof Friedrichstrasse became one of the most important, and surreal, of the city's border crossing points. Erected alongside, this glass-and-steel building quickly became known as the Tränenpalast (Palace of Tears). Western visitors would queue for passport control and say tearful goodbyes to their family and friends in the GDR, most of whom could not obtain a permit. One minute you were in the grim reality of communist East Berlin, the next in a U-Bahn train hurtling back to the lights of the West. A historical exhibition, Border Experience, explores the impact on lives on both sides of the wall. Gripping tales of Cold War spies and smuggled goods abound. Film clips include then GDR premier Walter Ulbricht uttering the infamous lie: "No one has any intention to build a wall." 🗺 Map p. 53 ✉ Friedrichstrasse 🚇 U-Bahn & S-Bahn: Friedrichstrasse

High culture in the Museumsinsel, the onetime showcase square of East Berlin—Alexanderplatz—and historic Jewish neighborhoods

Central Berlin

Introduction & Map   82–83

Museum Island   84–96

Experience: Long Museum Nights   90

Experience: Berlin's Trippy Tours   92

Berliner Dom & Lustgarten   97

Schlossplatz & Around   98

DDR Museum   99

A Walk Around Red Berlin   100–101

Alexanderplatz & Around   102–104

Nikolaiviertel & Around   105–106

Experience: Something's Brewing   106

Hackescher Markt & Around   107–109

Experience: Photoautomats   109

Oranienburger Tor & Around   110–111

Feature: Berlin's Jewish Community, Past & Present   112–113

More Places to Visit in Central Berlin   114

Hotels & Restaurants   243–246

Translucent sea life swims in the AquaDom.

Central Berlin

This is where Berlin started, huddled around an island in the middle of the Spree River in the 13th century. Where thatched huts of the Middle Ages once stood, proud museums built in the early 20th century house extraordinary royal and imperial art collections.

On the same island were the symbols of royal and (from 1871) imperial power. Opposite one another stood the Berliner Schloss, Berlin residence of Prussian kings and German kaisers, and the late 19th-century Berliner Dom (Berlin Cathedral), its equally impressive, if gaudy, religious counterpart. Both Schloss and Dom were severely damaged in World War II.

Prussian king Friedrich Wilhelm IV (R. 1840–1861) originally designated the area north of the Lustgarten as a "free zone for art and science." He could not have imagined how it would develop. The Museumsinsel (Museum Island) lodges five museums whose seemingly endless collections take you from the Babylonian Ishtar Gate to the French Impressionists. It was declared a UNESCO World Heritage site in 1999. Restoration and modernization work on four of the five—the Bode-Museum, Alte Nationalgalerie, Altes Museum, and Neues Museum—has been completed. The Pergamonmuseum will remain open during renovations through 2019 and will sprout a fourth wing around 2024.

NOT TO BE MISSED:

The jaw-dropping treasures of the Pergamonmuseum 85–89

Taking in the Dom's ecclesiastical riches and crypt 97

The vertiginous views from the Fernsehturm 103

Entering the glittering dome of the Neue Synagoge 109

Enjoying nightlife and art galleries around Oranienburger Tor 110–111

Things don't stop there. The neo-Renaissance Alexander-Kaserne Quartier Am Kupfergraben, formerly a barracks, will be converted into the headquarters of the Stiftung Preussischer Kulturbesitz (Prussian Cultural Heritage Foundation) beginning in 2018. A new wing will be built to create the Museumshöfe (Museum Courtyards), which will one day host the Gemäldegalerie (see pp. 126–128).

East over the Spree sprawls Alexanderplatz—"Alex" to the locals—home to the unmistakable

East Berlin TV tower as well as the rebuilt City Council building. To its south is a little corner of old Berlin. The Nikolaiviertel, largely a GDR restoration effort, is as close as World War II–battered Berlin comes to evoking its centuries-old past.

The bulk of Berlin's poorer Jewish community lived in the colorful Alexanderplatz quarter. The most obvious trace of their presence is the Neue Synagoge on Oranienburger Strasse. After a long GDR winter, the area is again exploding with life. ■

Museum Island

Sometimes called the "Prussian Acropolis" and now a World Heritage site, Berlin's central complex of five museums on Museum Island (Museumsinsel) occupies the northern tip of the island in the Spree River. Nineteenth-century Germans were pioneer archaeologists and antiquarians who unearthed the heritage of the ancient world. The incomparable spoils they brought home include the Pergamon Altar and Babylon's Ishtar Gate.

The glory that was Babylon unfolds before you with the Pergamonmuseum's Ishtar Gate.

Many of the island's buildings suffered severe damage during World War II, followed by neglect under communism. An ambitious and extremely expensive master plan is under way, aimed at restoring the built fabric and reassembling in this key location many of the city's treasures. Most of the improvements, including the fancy new James-Simon-Galerie visitors center and an "archaeological promenade" linking four of the five museums, should be completed by 2017. Take a look at *www.museumsinsel-berlin.de* to see how the Museumsinsel and surrounds may appear in 2025, including plans for an extension that may (or may not) end up being the new home of the Gemäldegalerie (pp. 126–128).

Pergamonmuseum

It was the last of the five museums to be built in the Museumsinsel (1930) and easily the most imposing. The Pergamonmuseum, Berlin's most visited, was built with the airs of a Babylonian temple and is the city's most monumental art space, in every sense. Home to three extraordinary collections, it is best known for its re-creation of ancient sites, from Babylon's Ishtar Gate to the ancient Greek Pergamon Altar after which the museum is named.

Throughout the 19th century and up until World War II, German archaeologists were busy in the Middle East digging up everything from pottery to whole buildings. You could spend hours in this treasure chest. A handful of highlights are mentioned below. In each of the museums of the Museumsinsel, an audio guide in English is available and recommended, as many of the written explanations are in German only.

The Pergamon Altar: There is no slow lead-up to the first of the big stars. With tickets in hand, you wander straight into a vast room containing the re-creation of the Pergamon Altar, a combination of original ruins shipped to Berlin, then reassembled and completed inside the museum. The mostly destroyed altar was unearthed with other parts of the Acropolis

in the Greek town of Pergamon (today Bergama) in western Turkey in the 1870s and 1880s. The most important finds were sizable chunks of the friezes that surrounded the altar.

What we see today in the hall is the re-creation of the west side of the altar, originally built around 170 B.C. The friezes from the north, south, and east sides of the altar hang on the exhibition room's walls. They depict battles pitting gods against giants—allegorical stories representing the struggle between good and evil in which the gods (the good guys) come out on top, although, like any good drama, only just.

From mid-2014 till 2019, the altar has a date with preservation staff, so expect scaffolding.

Tickets, Please

Entry to each of the museums on the Museumsinsel can be purchased separately ($$), but a *Bereichskarte* (area ticket) handily groups several collections at a discount ($$$). Better value still is the three-day Museumpass ticket ($$$$, *available from museums, tourist offices, & www.visitberlin.de*) that gives entry to a list of museums across the city, including those of the Museumsinsel. Note that in many museums entry is free to visitors under 18 years old.

Upstairs, inside what would have been the altar courtyard, is another series of friezes. These pieces tell the life story of Telephos, the mythical founder of Pergamon who, as a boy, was cast out into the desert and then led a life of adventure and warfare to wind up a hero.

Pergamonmuseum

🅰 Map p. 83
✉ Am Kupfergraben
☎ 030 20 90 55 77
🕐 Closed Mon.
💲 $$$ incl. audio guide
🚆 S-Bahn: Hackescher Markt

www.smb.museum

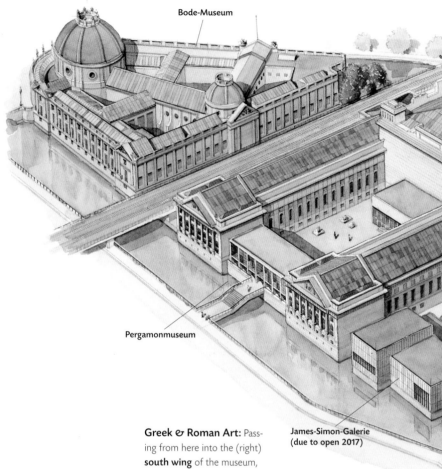

Bode-Museum

Pergamonmuseum

Greek & Roman Art: Passing from here into the (right) **south wing** of the museum, you are confronted by another enormous monumental removal job: the Roman market gate of Milet, an originally Greek town on the west coast of modern Turkey, about 50 miles (80 km) south of the city of Izmir. Built about A.D. 120, the massive gate, 95 feet (29 m) wide by almost 55 feet (17 m) high, was in fact a rather modest part of the cityscape of ancient Milet when it was a major Mediterranean trading port.

To the right of the portal, look for an advertisement of a local

James-Simon-Galerie
(due to open 2017)

hairdresser etched into the ancient stonework. Mostly destroyed by an earthquake in the Middle Ages, the gate was reconstructed by German archaeologists and then again damaged in Allied bombing raids in World War II.

Until 2019, the museum's display of Greek architecture in the north wing, including the propylon to the temple of Athena, will be closed for a facelift. A cross-section of its classical sculptures will be on show in the Altes Museum (pp. 95–96).

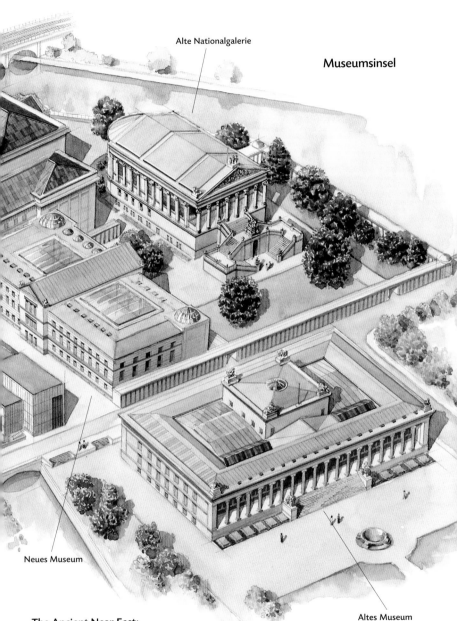

Alte Nationalgalerie

Museumsinsel

Neues Museum

Altes Museum

The Ancient Near East:
To head into another world
altogether, return to the Milet
gate and cross it into the
Vorderasiatisches Museum
(Museum of the Ancient Near
East). It could hardly begin in
a more overwhelming fash-
ion, for in this area has been

reconstructed the fabulous **Ishtar Gate** of Babylon, built in the sixth century B.C. under Nebuchadnezzar II (*R.* 605–562 B.C.). The gate is adorned with glazed blue ceramic bricks and reliefs of dragons and bulls. The central corridor leading away from it is lined by equally blue walls and adorned with images of marching lions. All the animal figures were symbolic of Babylonian gods.

far back as 2300 B.C., making them some of the earliest examples of written documents in the world. **Room 2,** at the western end of the hall, contains impressive finds from ancient Syria, including the partial re-creation of a stretch of the citadel wall, built in about the eighth century B.C.

Rooms 10 to **12** contain a welter of original and copied Assyrian reliefs. Ancient Assyria emerged as a power in northern Mesopota-

Lamassus guard a reconstructed Assyrian palace entrance in the Museum of the Ancient Near East.

There is plenty more to explore in this collection. In **Room 7,** the glazed decorative theme continues with colorful reliefs, depicting soldiers, that once graced palaces in the ancient Persian cities of Persepolis and Susa (in present-day Iran). **Room 6** contains clay tablets with texts in cuneiform script dating as

mia and took in parts of modern Syria, Turkey, Iraq, and Iran from around 2400 B.C. to the sixth century B.C.

A highlight here is a communal basin from 704–681 B.C. commissioned by Sennacherib, who ascribed to the belief that pouring water cast out demons. A populist king, Sennacherib claimed that he built more water installations than any other monarch.

Islamic Art: From the ancient Near Eastern world, you travel upstairs to the third collection, the **Museum für Islamische Kunst** (Museum of Islamic Art). **Room 4** is dominated by a stunning ceramic mihrab (prayer niche), which was removed from the Maidan Mosque in Kashan, Iran. The British consul general in Isfahan bought it in 1897 and had it sent to his family home in London. German officials then purchased it in 1927 for the Berlin museum.

Still more stunning is the 13th-century turquoise faience mihrab in **Room 5,** from the Beyhekim Mosque in Konya, Turkey.

To the right in **Room 6,** look for the Alhambra Dome, a fabulous carved ceiling taken from an observation tower of a 14th-century palace in what is now Granada, in the dying days of the Moorish empire in Spain. The mesmerizing patterns of stars, creeping ivy, books of learning, pinecones, and woven baskets you see on the dome are recurring themes in Islamic art. After a series of unlikely journeys, the dome ended up in the hands of a Berlin banker and art collector, Arthur Gwinner, in 1886 and was eventually acquired by the Pergamonmuseum.

This museum's core collection, of oriental carpets, was accumulated by the founder of what is now the Bode-Museum (see p. 90), Wilhelm von Bode. Some of the best of them, early Ottoman

see p. 90

INSIDER TIP:

Berlin's state-run museums have free lockers that, if you're not returning to your hotel, are generally roomy enough to store small suitcases and hand luggage.

—KAREN CARMICHAEL
National Geographic writer

rugs from Turkey, are on view in **Room 12.**

The Islamic art collections grew quickly from the late 19th century. The single biggest item, found in **Room 9,** was a present from the Turkish sultan Abulhamid II to Kaiser Wilhelm II in 1904. It was nothing less than the base of the facade and towers of an eighth-century prince's palace in Mshatta, about 19 miles (30 km) from Amman in present-day Jordan. It bears complex geometrical decoration within triangular fields along its length and is a stunning piece of reconstruction.

The last item of the Islamic collection is the **Aleppo Room,** a whole reception room removed from the house of a wealthy Christian businessman in the northern Syrian town of Aleppo. Reconstructed here, it is an extraordinary example of marquetry work, rich in the geometric design typical of Muslim art in the Arab world and adopted by Arab Christians.

Bode-Museum

🅰 Map p. 83

✉ Am Kupfergraben (entrance on Monbijoubrücke)

☎ 030 266 42 42 42

🕐 Closed Mon.

💲 $$$ incl. audio guide

🚉 S-Bahn: Hackescher Markt

www.smb.museum

Bode-Museum

In 2006, another major piece in Berlin's ambitious plan for museum renewal fell into place with the reopening of the Bode-Museum, home to the city's main sculpture and coin collections, as well as to a section on Byzantine art. Highlights of the Gemäldegalerie (see pp. 126–128) may soon be displayed here for several years.

EXPERIENCE:
Long Museum Nights

Twice a year, more than 70 Berlin museums and exhibition spaces open their doors from 6 p.m. to 2 a.m. These popular events draw many thousands of visitors and are accompanied by guided tours, workshops, films, and concerts. The entrance pass covers admission and transportation on shuttle buses between venues, while the exact dates (usually a Saturday night in March and August) and a map are published ahead of time at *www.lange-nacht-der-museen.de.*

Ridiculed by the local press when it opened in 1904 and dubbed the "Cul de Berlin" (Berlin's Ass), the neobaroque Kaiser-Friedrich-Museum (as it was originally called) forms the graciously curving northern bow of the Museumsinsel that splits the Spree River in two. Designed by Ernst Eberhard von Ihne (1848–1917), it lay half destroyed by the end of World War II. In 1956, the building was renamed after Wilhelm von Bode (1845–1929), long the city's most prominent museum director.

The museum's collections are spread out over several branch corridors on two floors, along with a brand-new underground level. The prime collection is the **Skulpturensammlung** (Sculpture Collection). Among the jewels of sculpture here are the 12th-century "Madonna des Presbyter Martinus" ("Father Martin's Madonna"), an archetypal Romanesque Virgin Mother and Child figure from central Italy; the 15th-century polychrome walnut "Dangolsheimer Muttergottes" statue of the Virgin and Child; and German reliefs and works by the Bavarian Ignaz Günther (1725–1775). Other works in stone and wood span a period from Byzantine times to the 18th century.

Also important is the **Museum für Byzantinische Kunst** (Museum of Byzantine Art), containing works from the dying years of the ancient world and the Byzantine Empire. Items from the latter include some remarkable mosaics, such as a late 13th-century representation of the Crucifixion of Christ, flanked by the Virgin Mary and Apostle John.

The **Münzkabinett** (Coin Cabinet), a collection of more than 500,000 coins and medallions from all historical eras, is one of the most important of its kind in the world. Most of the objects are stored in 82 cabinets with nearly 11,500 display drawers in the museum's basement.

Alte Nationalgalerie

Designed by Friedrich August Stüler, the neoclassical building that houses the Old National Gallery of 19th-century art opened in 1876. For most visitors, the highlight of its collection is the selection of French Impressionists on the third floor. The museum also has an extensive display of the works of Adolph Menzel, one of the most important Berlin artists of the century.

You reach the **second floor** by a flight of stairs from the ticket desk. The large first room is lined with 19th-century sculptures, including Johann Gottfried Schadow's "Prinzessinen Luise und Friedrike von Preussen" and a bust of Johann Wolfgang von Goethe (1749–1832), one of Germany's greatest poets.

Rooms 1.02 and **1.03** harbor a mixed group of early 19th-century realist works, mostly landscapes, by an international group including John Constable (1776–1837), Gustave Courbet (1819–1877), Eugène Delacroix (1798–1863), and even

one by the Spaniard Francisco de Goya y Lucientes (1746–1828).

Menzel, Berlin's painter and a favorite with the royal court, dominates **Rooms 1.05** to **1.12**. In **Room 1.06** are some of his bigger canvases, including "Flötenkonzert Friedrichs des Grossen in Sanssouci," which depicts Frederick the Great giving a flute concert in the Sanssouci summer palace. His smaller paintings hang in **Room 1.08** onward.

You access the **third floor** by an atrium graced with statues by Reinhold Begas (1831–1911). In **Room 2.02** and a few others are displayed works of the so-called German Romans, a group of Germans and Austrians who lived in Rome in the early 19th century.

The French Impressionists are gathered in the central hall on the third floor **(Room 2.03).** These paintings, glistening like jewels, were acquired mainly around the turn of the 20th century amid much

Alte Nationalgalerie

🅰 Map p. 83
✉ Bodestrasse 1–3
☎ 030 266 42 42 42
🕐 Closed Mon.
💲 $$$ incl. audio guide
🚉 S-Bahn: Hackescher Markt

www.smb.museum

The Alte Nationalgalerie forms an impressive backdrop for summer outdoor films.

controversy in Berlin's conservative circles, which thought little of Impressionism.

"Le Jardin d'Hiver" ("Winter Garden") by Édouard Manet (1832–1883) depicts two of the artist's friends in a florid southern French garden. Paul Cézanne (1839–1906), Auguste Renoir (1841–1919), and Claude Monet (1840–1926) are each represented with three works. Edgar Degas (1834–1917) and Camille Pissarro (1830–1903) also have works on this floor. To finish is a couple of bronzes by Auguste Rodin (1840–1917).

The other star of the third floor is Berlin's own Max Liebermann, whose large canvases **(Room 2.13)** depict realistic scenes of everyday working life.

The three figures dominating the top floor are Karl Friedrich Schinkel, Caspar David Friedrich (1774–1840), and Carl Blechen (1798–1840). Although Schinkel **(Room 3.05)** was principally active as an architect (see p. 41), he had an eye for canvas, too. His attention to architectural detail is notable.

Fine though Schinkel's paintings are, the emotions are stirred more by Friedrich **(Room 3.06)**. This Romantic painter, who worked in Dresden, evoked in his art the power, majesty, and mystery of nature, whether on land ("Der Watzmann—A Mountain Peak") or on the coast ("Zwei Männer am Meer—Two Men by the Sea").

In Blechen's works, look for the change that occurs on his voyage to Italy **(Rooms 3.07– 3.08)**. While "Felsenlandschaft mit Mönch" ("Monk by Cliffs") exudes the shadowy textures of his northern homeland, his Italian paintings such as "Fischer auf Capri" ("Fishermen on the Island of Capri") are flooded with Italian summer sunlight.

Neues Museum

Designed by Friedrich August Stüler and completed in 1855, the Neues Museum (New Museum) was one of the most

---

EXPERIENCE: Berlin's Trippy Tours

Why join a standard walking or bus tour in Berlin when you can motor in the East German commuter car, the Trabant? Here's your chance to join a convoy on a jaunt through central Berlin with **Trabi Safari** (tel 030 27 59 22 73, www .trabi-safari.de). You can also rent a street-legal go-kart, powered by an 8 to 13hp engine and capable of up to 56 mph (90 kph), by the hour or day from **Kart 4 You** (tel 0177 646 85 97, http://kart4you .de). Or downsize to two wheels on

Segways tours run by **Mindways** (tel 030 49 20 59 80, www.segway-citytour.de).

Soviet aircraft were once a familiar sight in Berlin, but not like this. Climb aboard a Russian Antonov AN-2, one of the world's largest double-decker planes, and take a 30-minute spin over the united city. Contact **Air Service Berlin** (tel 030 53 21 53 21, www.air-service-berlin.de).

Berlin is also fascinating underground. Tours of spooky Cold War and Third Reich sites are available (see sidebar p. 166).

The Egyptian Museum, holding sarcophagi and other treasures, is part of the Neues Museum.

advanced museums in the world when it was built. The restored landmark houses the acclaimed Egyptian Museum and Papyrus Collection, the Museum of Prehistory, and early history collections with artifacts going back to the dawn of civilization.

After World War II, the Neues Museum was still standing but it was in bad shape, and its collection resided in the Bode-Museum. In the early years after World War II, as most of the Museumsinsel museums were shut down, the museum's prize Egyptian treasures were moved first to Charlottenburg and later to the Altes Museum.

The building was reopened in 2009 after a six-year, €1.5 billion ($1.95 billion) revamp led by British architect David Chipperfield. Some parts were thoroughly re-created with as many original

details as possible, while others were repaired using plain concrete and wood beams. You can readily tell the old from the new, and the effect is striking even if all critics don't agree. To avoid lines, buy your ticket online, print it out, and show up for the appointed half-hour entry slot.

The ground-floor exhibition leads you through richly decorated chambers presenting the 180-year history of the museum. Preserved wall paintings depict scenes from Nordic mythology. **Rooms 103 and 104** are dedicated to Heinrich Schliemann (see sidebar p. 94), who bequeathed his collection of Trojan antiquities to the museum. But all this pales in comparison with the ancient Egyptian treasures found in the **Ägyptisches Museum** and **Papyrussammlung,** occupying three floors in the museum's northern wing.

Neues Museum

- Map p. 83
- Bodestrasse 4
- 030 20 90 55 77
- $$$ incl. audio guide
- S-Bahn: Hackescher Markt

www.smb.museum

Priam's Gold

One of Berlin's most precious ancient treasures lies in storage at Moscow's Pushkin Museum.

The legendary gold of Troy, found by German archaeologist Heinrich Schliemann (1822–1890) in Turkey in 1873, was stolen from underground vaults by the Red Army in 1945 and kept under lock and key until it went on display in 1993. In spite of German demands that Russia return this and other museum collections stolen in World War II, the Russians appear to feel entitled to hang on to them as compensation for losses suffered in Germany's war of aggression.

Schliemann was convinced that the ancient treasure, also known as Priam's gold, belonged to the legendary king of Troy mentioned in Homer's *Iliad*. Experts later deduced that the gold was much older than that, dating from 2500 B.C. A few copies can be seen in the Neues Museum.

Upon entering, be sure to peer down at the sarcophogi in the Egyptian courtyard one floor below. You are greeted by an imposing granite statue of Pharaoh Amenenhet III (1840–1800 B.C.), surrounded by smaller busts including one of Queen Hatshepsut (1517–1484 B.C.), one of Egypt's few female pharaohs. The statues, seated and standing, accompanied in burial the person they depicted. The statues are made of granite, quartzite, limestone, bronze, and wood. Some are in exquisite condition.

The adjacent section deals with the brief period of royal eccentricity under Akhenaten (R. 1353–1336 B.C.), the pharaoh who abandoned Thebes, created a new capital (at what is now Amarna), and instituted the monotheistic worship of the sun god, Aten. The star of the collection, and one of Berlin's most famous artistic possessions, is the 1340 B.C. **bust of Nefertiti,** Akhenaten's wife. All by herself in **room 110,** this remarkably preserved painted limestone bust, found in an Egyptian sculptor's workshop, shows her as an exceptionally beautiful woman. Every few years, the Egyptian government lobbies to get her back, and the German government says *nein*.

Next up is a selective exhibit from the Berlin papyrus collection, one of the most extensive in the world. Documents on display range from fairy tales to court rulings, from a wedding contract to instructions on the execution of two wayward policemen. The documents are not only in hieroglyphics but in later derivative scripts as well.

On the upper floors, highlights in the **Museum für Vor- und Frühgeschichte** (Museum for Prehistory and Early History) include the Goldhut (Gold Hat), a shimmering conical headdress. Covered with about a pound (0.5 kg) of gold leaf, it is the best preserved of four such hats from the Bronze Age. The Grüner Kopf (Green Head) from around 500 B.C. is named after its queer greenish stone.

Altes Museum

One of the most harmonious neoclassical buildings in Berlin, the Altes Museum is often considered one of the lesser members of the Museumsinsel team. But the timeless beauty of its primary collection, the Antikensammlung (Collection of Classical Antiquities), shines like a beacon over the millennia, with extensive displays of Greek, Etruscan, Persian, and Roman artifacts.

Yet another product of architect Karl Friedrich Schinkel, the building was completed in 1830 under the orders of King Friedrich Wilhelm III.

Ionic columns facing the Lustgarten. Inside, the theme continues with more Ionic columns in the Hall of Pillars at the entrance and inside the **Rotunda,** a circular chamber inspired by the Roman Pantheon. Only the Rotunda was restored faithfully after the war, down to the 18 Roman statues copied from Greek originals.

Antikensammlung: Looping around the Rotunda are two floors of exposition space. The Antikensammlung on the ground floor starts with objects from ancient Crete, Mycenae,

Altes Museum
- Map p. 83
- Lustgarten
- 030 266 42 42 42
- Closed Mon.
- $$ incl. audio guide
- S-Bahn: Hackescher Markt

www.smb.museum

Ionic columns are a hallmark of the Altes Museum, home to classical collections.

As a frieze in the **Säulenhalle** (Hall of Pillars) proclaims, he "donated this museum for the study of every kind of antiquities and the free arts."

Badly damaged in World War II, the museum remained closed until 1966. The facade has 18 fluted

and the Cyclades, with simple statuettes and pottery dating as far back as 3000 B.C. The collection proceeds in loose chronological order; it is divided into 19 sections, each dedicated to a theme. **Sections 1** through **3** contain a battalion of bronze helmets, heroic figurines, burial votives from Olympus, and other funerary monuments.

The high point in **Section 6,** halfway through the floor, is "Der Betende Knabe" ("The Praying Boy"), an extraordinarily graceful bronze statue from 300 B.C. A detour in **Section 8** takes you through a collection of ancient gold and jewelry. Greek, Etruscan, Persian, and Roman items dominate. A golden fish that apparently decorated a warrior's shield is eye-catching. Greek theater is covered in **Section 9,** where an actor in odd woolen costume is shown playing Papposilenus, a satyr.

INSIDER TIP:

You can take photos in permanent collections run by the Berlin museum state authority, SMB, for free. In Schloss Charlottenburg and the Potsdam palaces, you need a day pass [fee].

—CAROLINE HICKEY
National Geographic travel books editor

Upstairs, the exhibition continues with displays of Etruscan and Roman art. Striking is the preoccupation with death and the afterlife, with some interesting tales attached. A detailed relief, "Medea and the Daughters of Pelias," shows preparations for the killing of King Pelias,

who was to be rejuvenated by being boiled in a cauldron with some magical herbs.

Other curious items are portraits on wood placed on Roman mummies in Egypt in the first two centuries A.D., after Egypt had been absorbed by the Roman Empire. Large, graceful pieces populate the section on Roman sculpture inspired by Greek models, such as the statue of Emperor Hadrian's lover Antinous, and another of Dionysus accompanied by a young satyr. The Garden of Delights contains ceramics with decoration depicting festivals and orgies (including a merry group of satyrs).

Hildesheimer Silberfund:
A sense of privilege pervades the room on Roman luxury, where Amor and Psyche are locked in playful embrace. Here, too, are the silver treasures of the **Hildesheimer Silberfund.** This collection of 70-odd pieces of Roman silverware had been carefully buried near Hildesheim and forgotten for centuries until an army unit stumbled across it in 1868. The remarkable collection of plates, vases, trays, goblets, and other items constitutes one of the most important such finds in the world. How this collection wound up where it was found, 174 miles (280 km) east of the Roman world's ancient frontier with Germany, remains a mystery.

Giant amphorae from Greek settlements in southern Italy, especially Taranto, fill **Section 23;** the glass example (150–80 B.C.) from the Greek colony of Olbia in **Section 25** is amazingly intact. ∎

Berliner Dom & Lustgarten

It is hard to believe that this grand, powerful cathedral, symbol of turn-of-the-20th-century imperial power at the heart of Germany, was gutted in World War II, or that East Berlin's communist regime considered pulling it down completely in the 1950s.

Built for the kaiser and his family, the Berliner Dom came close to demolition after World War II.

The Italian Renaissance–style church was erected from 1894 to 1905, replacing an earlier, 1750 cathedral that itself had been reworked by Karl Friedrich Schinkel in 1822. This was the Hohenzollern court church and main family burial place. Restoration work began in 1975 and continues today. The grand, octagonal *Predigtkirche* (main church building) is now the scene of regular choir performances.

Some of the cathedral's finest decorative elements come from its predecessor. They include the marble and onyx altar by Friedrich August Stüler, the Schinkel-designed candelabra, and the gilded lectern, probably created by Andreas Schlüter. Magnificent Schlüter-designed decorative sarcophagi for King Friedrich I and his second wife Sophie Charlotte rest in niches on the south flank of the church. The monarchs are now buried downstairs in the **Hohenzollerngruft** (Hohenzollern Crypt).

Long flights of stairs from the cathedral's south side take you past the Dom's **museum,** with 19th-century scale models of proposed cathedral designs, to an external gallery around the top of the copper **dome** (follow the signs *"Zur Kuppel"*).

In front of the church stretches the **Lustgarten,** an unadorned park today but once a splendid baroque garden. ∎

Berliner Dom
- Map p. 83
- Am Lustgarten
- 030 20 26 91 36
- $$ ($$$ incl. audio guide)
- S-Bahn: Hackescher Markt

www.berliner-dom .de

Schlossplatz & Around

This square was once the symbolic center of Berlin. On one side stood the Stadtschloss (palace) and on the other its counterweight, the Berliner Dom. The palace is now but a memory, but an elaborate reconstruction stands to restore its place in Prussian history.

Schlossplatz
🄰 Map p. 83

Humboldt-Box
🄰 Map p. 83
✉ Schlossplatz 5
☎ 018 05 03 07 07
💲 $
🚇 U-Bahn &
S-Bahn:
Alexanderplatz
**www.humboldt-box
.com**

Berlin's first princely castle, built in the 15th century, was replaced by a Renaissance palace in the 16th century. In 1699, Andreas Schlüter turned this residence into a fine baroque palace. His successor, Johann Friedrich Eosander von Göthe, doubled its size by 1716.

The palace took direct hits in air raids on February 3, 1945. Although badly damaged, it succumbed not to bombs but to ideology. Despite an international outcry, Walter Ulbricht's communist regime decided in 1950 to replace what he considered a vile symbol of German imperialism with a parade ground for "spontaneous" demonstrations.

The steel-and-concrete Palast der Republik (Palace of the Republic) built on the site was demolished in 2008. A new complex called **Das Humboldt-Forum,** which includes a facade based on the original Stadtschloss, is being raised at the location, although financing is unclear (latest estimate: €590 million/$767 million through completion in 2019). The Forum will house the Dahlem museums, the Berlin state library, and several departments of Humboldt University. An information center, the **Humboldt-Box,** holds related exhibitions.

Across the now desolate Schlossplatz stands the 1964 **Staatsratsgebäude,** another onetime GDR government building that, in this case, has become a business school. Some of the old GDR national symbols have been kept in this protected monument.

Facing it across Breite Strasse is the 1670 **Alter Marstall,** once the royal stables and Berlin's oldest baroque structure. An extension from 1901, **Neuer Marstall,** is now home to a music school. South of the Alter Marstall is the Renaissance **Ribbeckhaus,** notable for its pretty gables. ∎

Save the *Ampelmännchen!*

Berlin's first pedestrian lights were introduced in 1957, but four years later, after the city was split by the wall, new lights were installed in East Berlin: a green man with a flat hat, decisively stepping out (go), and a red fellow with his arms outstretched (wait). With reunification in 1990, it was planned to replace these with standard West Berlin lights, but fans launched a campaign to save the *Ampelmännchen* (little traffic-light man), which had become a cult figure. Most of the lights were saved, and new ones have even appeared in the western half of the city. Ampelmännchen key rings, mugs, fridge magnets, and stickers now take up as much space in souvenir stores as Berlin Wall memorabilia.

DDR Museum

By far the most popular exhibit of "Ostalgie" (nostalgia for the East) in town, this time capsule of GDR society and culture plays down the less savory aspects of the East German regime, but compensates with its entertainment value and a wealth of astonishing details.

Sixteen tightly packed, hands-on thematic sections give an excellent overview of everyday life in the DDR (Deutsche Demokratische Republik; East Germany or GDR in English). Lesser-known details of work, family, and leisure feature along-side familiar displays on the Stasi, niggling border controls, and the rubber-stamping parliament in what was supposed to be the ultimate planned society.

DDR Museum diorama of the Berlin Wall

You can slide behind the wheel of an original **Trabant,** the two-stroke, smoke-belching people's car of the East, and "drive" through a *Plattenbau* (prefab concrete) housing estate. Once you took delivery of these "plastic racers" (waiting times could be ten years or more), your troubles had just begun. Mechanics expected Trabi owners to provide their own spare parts, which were as scarce as bananas in the GDR. Made of cotton fleece and resin, the car's body proved tasty to goats.

Another big hit with visitors is a **reconstructed GDR apartment,** its 1970s interior drenched in browns and oranges. Here, you can watch sanitized Ost-TV or rummage through kitchen cupboards for typical East German foodstuffs such as *Tempobohnen* (fast-cooking white beans). In the **sports** section, a foosball table reflects the only face-off of East and West German soccer teams, during the 1974 World Cup. Sharp eyes will spot a package of Oral Turinabol tablets, used to dope the GDR's overachieving Olympic athletes. There is a quaint diorama on *Freikörperkultur* (nudism), which was promoted as a sign of class-lessness and was understandably popular given the funky synthetics of East German fashion.

You can pretend to be a Stasi officer and listen to a bugged flat, or view a prison cell. But the darker aspects of the GDR regime are dealt with more realistically at Hohenschönhausen (see pp. 162–163), although the exhibits here are better suited to young viewers. Afterward, stop by the restaurant for an order of *Falscher Hase* (Fake Hare), hamburger steak stuffed with Spree pickles. ∎

DDR Museum

🅜 Map p. 83

✉ Karl-Liebknecht-Strasse 3

☎ 030 84 71 23 73

💲 $$

🚉 S-Bahn: Hackescher Markt; U-Bahn & S-Bahn: Alexanderplatz

www.ddr-museum.de

A Walk Around Red Berlin

The working class and left-oriented intellectual circles have always had an influence on Berlin's politics, and for 40 years East Berlin was capital of the communist GDR, so it doesn't take long to uncover reminders of the city's socialist and communist past.

Begin in the Tiergarten with the **Sowjetisches Ehrenmal ①** (see p. 120), a memorial to the Soviet liberation of Berlin in 1945. A minirevolt on June 17, 1953, in East Berlin protested this "liberation"; head east to Brandenburger Tor on Strasse des 17. Juni, which takes its name from that unsuccessful uprising.

A block north of the gate, on the corner of Ebertstrasse and Scheidemannstrasse, is a makeshift **Berlin Wall memorial ②** honoring those killed attempting to cross the wall between 1961 and 1989.

A stroll east along Dorotheenstrasse into what was East Berlin leads to the **corner of Friedrichstrasse ③**, where Friedrich Engels (1820–1895), coauthor of the *Communist Manifesto*, lived for a year (1841). A plaque marks the spot, but the house was destroyed in World War II.

Walk south to Unter den Linden and turn left (east). Vladimir Ilyich Lenin (1870–1924), who led the Russian Revolution, studied at the **Staatsbibliothek ④** on your left before World War I. One building east, Karl Marx (1818–1883) studied at **Humboldt Universität ⑤**, where he forged his early ideas for communism, from 1836 to 1841.

On the east side of the university is the **Neue Wache ⑥** (see pp. 64–65), the central memorial to victims of Nazism under the East German regime. Walk south along the Spree until you come to the current **Foreign Ministry ⑦** (see p. 69) in the Nazi-era Reichsbank. In 1958, it housed the Central Committee of East Germany's Sozialistische Einheitspartei Deutschlands (SED).

Cross the Jungfernbrücke, the city's oldest bridge from about 1701, and turn left for the Schlossplatz. A monumental doorway and

NOT TO BE MISSED:

Sowjetisches Ehrenmal • Neue Wache • Staatsratsgebäude • Fernsehturm

balcony salvaged from the Stadtschloss, the palace destroyed by the East Germans (see p. 98), remains on the former **Staatsratsgebäude ⑧**, or State Council building, on the north side of the square. From this doorway, Karl Liebknecht proclaimed (in vain) the

INSIDER TIP:

To shorten waiting times at the Fernsehturm, buy tickets online or use the mobile text-message service.

—DAMIEN SIMONIS
National Geographic author

socialist republic in 1918, setting off the Spartacist Revolt (see pp. 27–28). Those events are commemorated in reliefs on the **Neuer Marstall** ❾. The East German parliament was in the now demolished Palast der Republik built over the **Stadtschloss site** ❿.

Walk east and cross the Spree again. In the square behind the Palast der Republik site stands a stiff statue to Marx and Engels in the **Marx-Engels-Forum** ⓫ (see p. 104), shunted to one side during construction of

a new U-bahn line. Continue east to reach concrete-laden Alexanderplatz, East Berlin's showcase square, topped by the city's tallest building, the **Fernsehturm** ⓬ (see p. 103). A little way north, along Spandauer Strasse, the location of the **German Communist Party (KPD)** headquarters ⓭ until 1926 is marked by a plaque at Rosenthaler Strasse 38. The party then moved to the bigger **Karl-Liebknecht-Haus** ⓮ at Kleine Alexanderstrasse, just off **Rosa-Luxemburg-Platz,** until banned by the Nazis in 1933.

◤ See also area map pp. 82–83
► Sowjetisches Ehrenmal, Strasse des 17. Juni
🕐 2 hours
↔ 3.4 miles (5.5 km)
► Rosa-Luxemburg-Platz

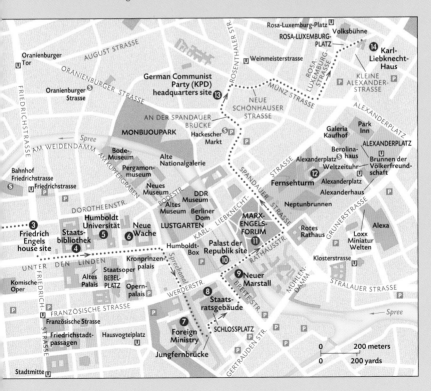

Alexanderplatz & Around

Anyone who has read (and managed to understand!) Alfred Döblin's *Berlin Alexanderplatz* cannot help being drawn to what was in the 1920s one of the busiest corners of the city. But Döblin's square ceased to exist after World War II. Heavily damaged, it was converted into a shadow of its former self by the communist authorities from the 1950s on. For all that, this onetime showplace of socialism is full of interest and worth a visit.

This onetime animal market was turned into a square and named after Russian tsar Alexander I in 1805, when he paid Berlin a state visit. In the 1848 revolt, workers clashed violently with police and erected barricades

Berlin's cylindrical AquaDom, near Alexanderplatz, may be the strangest aquarium in the city.

here. In 1882, a train station was built across the middle of the square, and a U-Bahn station was added in 1913. Döblin described the square in the 1920s, when it hosted department stores such as Wertheim and Tietz, as a playground for "delinquents, prostitutes, and the penniless."

The square got the beginnings of a facelift in 1931–32 with the construction of the Alexanderhaus and Berolinahaus by leading architect and designer Peter Behrens (1868–1940). Considered the height of modern architecture at the time, they remain standing today. In GDR times came the Interhotel Stadt Berlin (the now rather worn-looking Park Inn) and Centrum-Warenhaus (which is now part of the Kaufhof chain of department stores).

Most impressive of all was the Fernsehturm (Television Tower) southwest of the train station, the tallest structure in all Berlin at 1,207 feet (368 m). Less impressive are the rather sad **Weltzeituhr** (World Clock), a popular meeting place in East Berlin, in front of the Alexanderhaus, and the neglected **Brunnen der Völkerfreundschaft** (Friendship of the Peoples Fountain), just behind the Berolinahaus. Ambitious plans to transform the square and surrounding area

The Pope's Revenge

The highest structure in Germany, the Fernsehturm (Television Tower) is one of Berlin's most recognizable symbols. Officially, the "golfball on a stick" was supposed to improve transmissions at GDR state television, but this was a Cold War cover story. After taking over the Sputnik-era tower in 1990, telephone giant Deutsche Telekom discovered scads of spy equipment aimed directly at the capitalist West.

The 29,000-ton (26,000 tonne) concrete shaft supports a distinctive globe holding an observation deck and a revolving café at 666 feet (203 m). In East Berlin's heyday, you could enjoy propaganda films in the tower's information center on life's pleasures in the "Capital City of the GDR."

The TV Tower was given other nicknames, including "The Pope's Revenge," for the crucifix reflection that graces the sphere on sunny days. This was problematic in the GDR, officially a godless state. Walter Ulbricht, then East Germany's premier, was said to be so displeased that the tower architects weren't invited to the opening ceremony.

---

with ten 500-foot-high (150 m) buildings may fall short, although one tower may be built as part of a huge entertainment and commercial center. Shiny new shopping malls are sprouting around the perimeter. Across Grunerstrasse lie the ruddy arches of the Portuguese-designed complex Alexa, home to 180-plus stores and restaurants. Its top floor hosts **Loxx Miniaturwelten,** a vast model of Berlin with model trains and lifelike touches like a rock concert in front of the Reichstag.

The pride and joy of the GDR, the 1969 **Fernsehturm** (see sidebar above) has become a landmark. At its foot lies the only hint of Berlin's centuries of history in this part of town. The **Marienkirche** is a Gothic church rebuilt in 1380 after fire destroyed its predecessor. Inside, the main work of art is the faded 15th-century "Totentanz" ("Dance of Death"), a macabre 72-foot-long (22 m) frieze along the walls on your left as you enter by the main door. Andreas Schlüter designed the pulpit.

City Hall

Amid flowerbeds south of the Marienkirche sits the **Neptun-brunnen** (Neptune Fountain), a neobaroque effort by Reinhold Begas, commissioned in 1891 by city hall. It originally stood on Schlossplatz. The people who commissioned it worked in the **Rotes Rathaus** (Red City Hall), off the southeast corner of Alexanderplatz. Finished in 1870 and rebuilt from scratch from 1951 through 1956, the neo-Renaissance building is the political heart of Berlin. Its name comes from the red-hued brick used, but could easily refer to the city's politics. In spite of a complex electoral system that favored the ruling noble class, Berliners voted en masse for left-wing candidates in mayoral elections from the late 19th century on.

The first fully free municipal elections (in which women had the

Fernsehturm

- Map p. 83
- Panoramastrasse 1a
- 030 242 33 33
- $$$
- U-Bahn & S-Bahn: Alexanderplatz

www.tv-turm.de

Marienkirche

- Map p. 83
- Karl-Liebknecht-Strasse 8
- 030 242 44 67
- U-Bahn & S-Bahn: Alexanderplatz

www.marienkirche-berlin.de

Rotes Rathaus

- Map p. 83
- Rathausstrasse 15
- 030 902 60
- Closed Sat.–Sun.
- U-Bahn & S-Bahn: Alexanderplatz

AquaDom & Sea Life Center

🅰 Map p. 83
✉ Spandauer Strasse 3
☎ 030 99 28 00
💲 $$$
🚇 U-Bahn & S-Bahn: Alexanderplatz

www.visitsealife.com

vote for the first time) took place in 1919. The Nazis dissolved the city council in 1933 and hounded many of its members into exile or concentration camps. It is again home to united Berlin's city council, known as the Senat (Senate).

Up the grand staircase and on the right is the **Säulensaal** (Hall of Pillars), used for special events and occasional exhibitions. The **Wappensaal** (Hall of Coats of Arms), also used for special occasions, is farther in on the right.

An orderly green space south across Spandauer Strasse from Alexanderplatz has as its focal point the rather stylized (not to say poor) pair of statues of Karl Marx and Friedrich Engels. This leftover from GDR days gives the square its name, the **Marx-Engels-Forum.**

Quite indifferent to Marx and Engels are the seahorses, starfish, and sharks flitting about inside the fish tanks of the **Sea Life Center.** Thousands of other critters are on show here in some 30 tanks, but don't expect many brightly colored tropical creatures, as most come from Germany's chilly waters. The most original part of the display is the **AquaDom,** a cylindrical tank

INSIDER TIP:

No Berlin visit would be complete without trying a *Currywurst*—grilled, sliced sausage in a thick curry sauce.

—LARRY PORGES
National Geographic travel books editor

filled with fish through which an elevator slowly rises.

A surprising and lonely relic of old Berlin stands a block up Spandauer Strasse from the Sea Life Center. First built about 1300 as a hospital chapel, the **Heilig-Geist-Kapelle** (Chapel of the Holy Spirit; *Spandauer Strasse 1*) has remained standing throughout the city's troubles and is, after the Nikolaikirche (see opposite), central Berlin's oldest surviving building. In about 1520, the chapel was remodeled into its present form, although much has been restored. It is now part of Humboldt University's economics department, through whose foyer one must enter to glimpse the chapel's interior. ∎

Plattenbau Revival

For a generation of West Germans, nothing symbolized the ideological inferiority of the Communist East better than the *Plattenbau,* the unsightly apartment blocks that sprouted like shower mold behind the Iron Curtain. Over two decades after reunification, young Germans are now clamoring for Plattenbau apartments bristling with

retro furnishings and options for a loft conversion.

In the suburb of Hellersdorf, the Plattenbau Museum (*Hellersdorfer Strasse 179, tel 0151 16 11 44 40, Sun. 2–4 p.m.*) has re-created a three-room 1980 apartment complete with vintage brown-orange wallpaper, fringed lampshades, and plenty of *Plaste* (plastic).

Nikolaiviertel & Around

Just south of Rathausstrasse unwinds a compact piece of old Berlin. Narrow, cobbled streets are lined with houses from another era, some hosting cozy restaurants and cafés. At the very center rise the twin, tapered towers of the Gothic Nikolaikirche (St. Nicholas Church). It can be hard to believe that, with a few exceptions, none of this dates back farther than the 1980s.

Largely destroyed by Allied bombs and then finished off by the communist GDR regime, this area had pretty much ceased to exist. As the 750th anniversary of Berlin's foundation approached in 1987, the authorities seemed to make an act of contrition by deciding to re-create the quarter. A couple of houses in the Nikolaiviertel (St. Nicholas District), on the south side of Rathausstrasse, are the genuine, restored articles. The rest are no more than 20 years old.

The **Nikolaikirche,** built about 1230, was restored and now contains the **Nikolaikirchemuseum,** a modest museum dedicated to the story of the church. Inside, the ceiling frescoes, based on the originals, lend a surprising splash of color. Virtually across the road from the church is **Knoblauchhaus** *(Poststrasse 23, tel 030 23 45 99 91, closed Mon., $),* an 18th-century upper-bourgeois house whose museum is dedicated to the Knoblauch clan, a rich silkmaker family. Downstairs is a 19th-century restaurant, the **Historische Weinstuben** *(Poststrasse 23, tel 030 242 41 07).* This is one of the few buildings that was restored but not redone from scratch.

Ephraim-Palais *(Poststrasse 16, tel 030 24 00 21 21, closed Mon., $),*

The Gothic Nikolaikirche was damaged in World War II.

a few steps south, had a more bizarre fate. The corner mansion was built in 1766 for Veitel Heine Ephraim, court banker to King Friedrich II. The rococo-era structure was to be demolished under the Nazis in 1935 to allow road-widening work, but locals protested so much that the facade was dismantled and put into storage. In 1983, East Berliners began

Nikolaikirche-museum

- 🗺 Map p. 83
- ✉ Nikolaikirchplatz
- ☎ 030 24 72 45 29
- 💲 $$, free Wed.
- 🚇 U-Bahn & S-Bahn: Alexanderplatz; U-Bahn: Klosterstrasse

www.stadtmuseum .de

EXPERIENCE: Something's Brewing

In the early 1900s, Berlin boasted 200 breweries serving a wide variety of suds, but by the end of the century only two mass producers remained. More recently, boutique brewers have staged a comeback with specialty beers.

In Nikolaiviertel, **Georgbräu** (Spreeufer 4, tel 030 242 42 44, www.georgbraeu.de), is a brewpub adorned with gorgeous copper vats and tools of the trade. At **Brauhaus Südstern** (Hasenheide 69, Kreuzberg, tel 030 69 00 16 24, www .brauhaus-suedstern.de), you can sample the house standards—Helles or Dunkles (pale and dark ales), or Weisse (wheat

beer)—plus seasonals like Honey Brown Ale or Oktoberbier. You can also sign up for brewing courses and guided tours. **Privatbrauerei am Rollberg** supplies numerous restaurants with its organic, unfiltered suds (Am Sudhaus 3, Neukölln, tel 030 68 08 45 77, www.rollberger.de). The subterranean vaults can be visited with **Berliner Unterwelten** tours (see sidebar p. 166). More fabulous tipple is on tap at **Brauerei Eschenbräu** (Triftstrasse 67, Wedding, tel 030 462 68 37, www.eschenbraeu. de) and **Hops & Barley** (Wühlischstrasse 22/23, Friedrichshain, tel 030 29 36 75 34, www.hopsandbarley-berlin.de).

Heinrich Zille Museum

◮ Map p. 83
✉ Propststrasse 11
☎ 030 24 63 25 00
💲 $
🚇 U-Bahn & S-Bahn: Alexanderplatz; U-Bahn: Klosterstrasse

www.heinrich-zille-museum.de

Hanf Museum

◮ Map p. 83
✉ Mühlendamm 5
☎ 030 242 48 27
🕐 Closed Mon.
💲 $
🚇 U-Bahn & S-Bahn: Alexanderplatz; U-Bahn: Klosterstrasse

www.hanfmuseum.de

to reconstruct it. Its elegant rooms now host art exhibitions.

Also resurrected from the ashes in the 1980s was **Zum Nussbaum** (Am Nussbaum 3, tel 030 854 50 20, www.wirtshaus-zum-nussbaum.de), a 16th-century eatery that stood across the Spree on Fischerinsel. One of its regular guests is said to have been local artist Heinrich Zille (1858–1929), to whom the nearby **Heinrich Zille Museum** is dedicated. He was known for his satirical sketches, some on display here.

The thundering boulevard of Mühlendamm runs through what was once the Molkenmarkt, the oldest marketplace in medieval Berlin. The **Hanf Museum** is tucked away on its northern flank. It is dedicated to the serious business of hemp, its uses, and known medicinal (even dizzying) effects.

On the south side of Mühlendamm is a long, bombastic building (not open to the public).

The older half was the **Palais Schwerin** (built for a minister of Friedrich I); the newer half housed the **Berliner Münze** (mint). The entire building was occupied by the Ministry of Culture under the GDR.

The 1911 **Altes Stadthaus,** a mighty edifice with a mightier tower on Jüdenstrasse, was and remains a government administration building, now for the city of Berlin. On Klosterstrasse, which runs behind the Stadthaus, stand the ruins of the 13th-century **Franziskaner Klosterkirche,** left in a parlous state by the flames of war. Behind the Stadthaus on the corner of Parochialstrasse is the **Parochialkirche,** which in turn leads one to Waisenstrasse, an old Berlin lane that is home to the city's oldest restaurant, **Zur Letzten Instanz** (Waisenstrasse 14–16, tel 030 242 55 28, http://zurletzteninstanz.com). It is close to a modest strip of Berlin's other wall, the medieval one that encircled the then tiny town. ■

Hackescher Markt & Around

The Hackescher Markt S-Bahn is one of the most beautiful, and one of the best restored, of a series of train stations built east to west across the city in the late 19th century. The brick-and-tile station, completed in 1882, is also for many the introduction to one of the most curious corners of central Berlin, the Scheunenviertel (Barns District).

Grunge art enlivens a courtyard in the Scheunenviertel.

Back in the mid-17th century, Elector Friedrich III ordered all crops to be stored in barns outside the city center. King Friedrich Wilhelm I then ordered Jews who did not own property to move in among the barns. The area, enclosed by Karl-Liebknecht-Strasse, Torstrasse, and Rosenthaler Strasse, became Berlin's main Jewish quarter.

Much of the horror of the Nazi persecution of Jews was played out here and in the neighboring, better-off Spandauer Vorstadt district west of Rosenthaler Strasse. Here and there, especially in Rosenthaler Strasse, are scattered *Stolpersteine,* brass plaques with the names of Jewish deportees and concentration camp victims (see sidebar p. 31).

The area is known for its turn-of-the-20th-century housing blocks with interlocking internal courtyards *(Höfe).* The renovated **Hackesche Höfe,** a prime example and something of a

Hackesche Höfe

- Map p. 83
- Rosenthaler Strasse 40–41
- S-Bahn: Hackescher Markt

www.hackesche -hoefe.com

Museum Blinden-werkstatt Otto Weidt & Stille Helden

🅰 Map p. 83

✉ Rosenthaler Strasse 39

☎ 030 28 59 94 07

🚇 S-Bahn: Hackescher Markt

www.blindes -vertrauen.de

Anne Frank Zentrum

🅰 Map p. 83

✉ Rosenthaler Strasse 39

☎ 030 288 86 56 00

🕐 Closed Mon.

💲 $

🚇 S-Bahn: Hackescher Markt

www.annefrank.de

Sophienkirche

🅰 Map p. 83

✉ Grosse Hamburger Strasse 29

☎ 030 308 79 20

🚇 U-Bahn: Weinmeister-strasse

www.sophien.de

tourist attraction, are a series of buildings that house a mix of apartments, trendy boutiques, cafés, restaurants, and a cinema gathered around eight courtyards.

Down an alley off Rosenthaler Strasse is a touching piece of anti-Nazi history, the **Museum Blindenwerkstatt Otto Weidt.** Weidt ran a small factory for the deaf and blind here during the Nazi period, in which Jews and non-Jews were employed making brooms and brushes. For years, he managed to protect his employees in this "essential war industry"; in 1942, he bribed the Gestapo into returning workers arrested for deportation. This story is told in original rooms in pictures and text. The display is limited and best understood when you watch the 20-minute video (in English or German). Accessed through a separate entrance, the front rooms of the original workshop are devoted to the stories of other *Stille Helden* ("silent heroes") who worked against the Nazi regime.

Down the same alley is the **Anne Frank Zentrum,** a small exhibition on the life and sad times of Anne Frank (1929–1945), the German-Jewish girl whose years

in hiding in Amsterdam were made famous when her diary was published in 1947.

Sophienstrasse

The Sophienstrasse, which mostly survived the war, runs west off Rosenthaler Strasse. It is one of the prettiest streets in the area. Halfway along in a quiet yard is the **Sophienkirche,** which has the only original baroque bell tower in Berlin. The church was built in 1713 but did not get its 226-foot (69 m) sandstone tower until 1735.

Across the road, peer inside the courtyards of the **Handwerker-vereinshaus,** a typical series of brick houses with inner courtyards that survived war, the GDR, and, so far, renovation. Built in 1905 for a 19th-century craftsmen's guild (the sign remains carved into the facade), today it is home to the **Sophiensäle,** a leading theater and cultural center. In its post–World War I heyday, the great figures of German communism harangued the workers in its halls. Under the Nazis, the building became a print shop manned by forced labor. A few steps up

Graffiti City

If Berlin's skyline is defined by buildings like the Reichstag and Kaiser-Wilhelm-Gedächtniskirche, it is graffiti that rules the streetscape. With its abundance of vacant buildings, weedy lots, and creative nomads, the capital has become a blank canvas for urban artists far and wide, turning it into arguably the most "bombed" (slang for graffiti-covered) city in Europe. In the Mitte district, peruse the streets south of Rosa-Luxemburg-Platz U-Bahn station for work by mysterious guerrilla artist Banksy, romantic stencil master XooooX, and cut-out specialist Chin Chin. Other heavily scribbled streets include Simon-Dach-Strasse in Friedrichs-hain and Kreuzberg's Schlesische Strasse—look out for the giant "Brothers in upside and down" by Bologna street artist Blu.

Sophienstrasse is the **Sophie-Gips-Höfe,** a classic early 20th-century three-courtyard housing block with art galleries and a café.

Sophienstrasse runs into Grosse Hamburger Strasse, until World War II an elegant street where comparatively well-off Jews lived. At its Hackescher Markt end lay the **Alter Jüdischer Friedhof** (Old Jewish Cemetery), destroyed by the Gestapo in 1943. Founded in 1672 and closed in 1827, it may have held as many as 10,000 Jews. After it was turned into a temporary sports field by the Gestapo, it was used as a makeshift cemetery for almost 3,000 people killed in street fighting in the last days of World War II. A memorial to philosopher Moses Mendelssohn (1729–1786) is all that remains.

The vacant lot next door at No. 26 was the site of a Jewish seniors home. It was used by the Gestapo from 1942 on as a collecting point for the last of Berlin's Jews to be deported to the East European concentration camps.

Neue Synagoge

Just southwest, Oranienburger Strasse was long one of the main streets of Jewish Berlin, dominated since the mid-19th century by Germany's biggest synagogue. Opened in 1866, the **Neue Synagoge** (today also known as the **Centrum Judaicum**) was designed by Edouard Knoblauch (1801–1865), a student of Karl Friedrich Schinkel. The building had room for 3,000 worshippers. The beautiful facade, with its Moorish airs and gold-encrusted dome, became a Berlin land-

mark. It suffered relatively little when assaulted by the storm-troopers on *Kristallnacht* in 1938 because the local police chief chased the thugs off and so allowed the fire brigade to save the building. He was transferred the next day.

Its last religious services were held in 1940, and Allied bombing in 1943 did heavy damage. The main hall was demolished in 1958 and what remained was restored in 1995.

The restored building is as impressive as the original, and the security measures more so. Inside, you can climb up into the dome. In the first-floor exhibition room below is a cutaway model of the original building, as well as a *ner tamid* (eternal lamp) saved from destruction. The exhibition is split into two parts, one on the history of the building and the second on life in Berlin's Jewish community, then and now. ∎

EXPERIENCE:
Photoautomats

Wonder how to immortalize your moments in Berlin? Expose your happy face (and maybe those of a couple of friends) in a coin-operated Photoautomat. Dozens of these quaint photo booths, many of them revived by retro entrepreneurs, are scattered around the city's bar and club districts, like Hackescher Markt. The prints pop out in black-and-white, good enough for basic IDs and souvenirs. After dark, you'll see the booths flashing like a mad scientist's lab, and even at 3 a.m. you might need to line up. See a list and locator map at *www.photoautomat.de.*

Sophiensäle

🅜 Map p. 83
✉ Sophienstrasse 18
☎ 030 27 89 00 30
🚇 U-Bahn: Weinmeisterstrasse

www.sophiensaele.de

Sophie-Gips-Höfe

🅜 Map p. 83
✉ Sophienstrasse 21
☎ 030 28 49 91 20
🚇 U-Bahn: Weinmeisterstrasse

www.sophie-gips.de

Neue Synagoge

🅜 Map p. 83
✉ Oranienburger Strasse 28–30
☎ 030 88 02 83 00
🕓 Closed Sat.
💲 $
🚆 S-Bahn: Oranienburger Strasse

www.cjudaicum.de

Oranienburger Tor & Around

The tower that marked the old town exit from Berlin at the intersection of Oranienburger Strasse and Torstrasse is long gone. Just beyond this junction, playwright Bertolt Brecht lived and worked in his last years. Nearby are branches of the city's Humboldt University and main city hospital, the Charité, both with curious museums. A more contemporary touch comes in the Hamburger Bahnhof train station turned gallery.

Music throbs at the Kalkscheuene club in the popular nightclub area around Oranienburger Strasse.

**Dorotheen-
städtischer
Friedhof**

 Map p. 82

✉ Chausseestrasse

 U-Bahn: Oranien-
burger Tor

Wandering up Chausseestrasse, you come across the **Doro-theenstädtischer Friedhof,** a smallish cemetery with more than its fair share of Berlin lumi-naries. They range from author Heinrich Mann and philosopher Georg Hegel (1770–1831) to towering figures of 19th-century art and architecture, including Karl Friedrich Schinkel, Friedrich August Stüler, Johann Gottfried Schadow, and Christian Daniel Rauch. Also resting here are Brecht and his actress wife

Helene Weigel (1900–1971).

From 1953, the couple lived next door on Chausseestrasse in apartments overlooking the cemetery in what is now the **Brecht-Weigel-Gedenkstätte** *(Chausseestrasse 125, closed Mon., $).* You can visit some of the rooms in which they lived, three of which have been left much as they were in Brecht's lifetime—but visits are by guided tour only, and are in German. Brecht wrote to a friend: "It really is advisable...to live in former capitalist surroundings, until we finally have socialist ones." He might also have had in mind the grand-looking 19th-century mansion, the **Borsighaus** (*Chausseestrasse 13*), across the road, where industrialist August Borsig (1804–1854) established the administration offices of his nearby factories.

Around the corner on Invalidenstrasse, in aging buildings of Humboldt University, is the **Museum für Naturkunde,** an extensive and engaging natural history museum with loads of stuffed animals, fish, fossils, and a number of spiffy interactive displays. The star attraction is the giant skeleton of a brachiosaur.

West down Invalidenstrasse past the military hospital, a canal-side walkway north leads to the **Invalidenfriedhof,** a military cemetery where senior officers lie. Memorial plaques recall civilians

für Gegenwart–Berlin anymore. Converted into an enormous exposition space, it hosts contemporary art exhibitions and a permanent display. The backbone of the collection consists of works by such modern masters as Andy Warhol (1928–1987), Anselm Kiefer (born 1945), Joseph Beuys (1921–1986), and Cy Twombly (1928–2011). It also holds art from Roy Lichtenstein (1923–1997), Jeff Koons (born 1955), Damien Hirst (born 1965), and others. The range is broad, from Warhol's "Mao" portrait (1973) to the "Berlin Circle" by Richard Long (born 1945).

The complex of restored buildings comprising the central clinics and research departments of Berlin's Charité teaching hospital is home to the oddly interesting **Berliner Medizinhistorisches Museum** (Berlin Medical History

Museum für Naturkunde

- 🅜 Map p. 82
- ✉ Invalidenstrasse 43
- ☎ 030 20 93 85 91
- 🕐 Closed Mon.
- 💲 $$
- 🚇 U-Bahn: Naturkunde-museum

www.natur kundemuseum -berlin.de

Hamburger Bahnhof/Museum für Gegenwart–Berlin

- 🅜 Map p. 82
- ✉ Invalidenstrasse 50–51
- ☎ 030 39 78 34 11
- 🕐 Closed Mon.
- 💲 $$
- 🚇 U-Bahn & S-Bahn: Hauptbahnhof

www.hamburger bahnhof.de

Arts Bunker

Owned and run by ad mogul Christian Boros, this World War II air-raid shelter south of Oranienburger Tor S-Bahn station is Berlin's quirkiest contemporary art gallery. The forbidding concrete tower stored fruits and vegetables in hard-up postwar Berlin, earning it the nickname "Banana Bunker." After the Wall came down, its scarred hulk was a perfect setting for techno parties.

On display are works by contemporary maestros such as Olafur Eliasson, Anselm Reyle, and Ai Weiwei, shown in 120 concrete rooms on five windowless floors. Wartime signage, telephones, and other artifacts have been preserved. You can view the collection only on guided tours; book online at *www.sammlung-boros.de*.

and soldiers buried in mass graves here after air raids, as well as conspirators executed after the July 1944 plot to kill Hitler (see sidebar p. 132). After 1961, the Berlin Wall ran right through the cemetery.

Trains don't run to the nearby **Hamburger Bahnhof/Museum**

Museum; *Schumantrasse 20–21, tel 030 450 53 61 56, closed Mon., $$).* Shudder at the old dentist tools, be thankful if you can't read the German explanation of ancient gallstone treatments, and see what you make of the bottles floating with cancerous brains and sick lungs. ∎

Berlin's Jewish Community, Past & Present

On August 30, 1929, the *Central Verein Zeitung* (a Berlin paper "for Germanness and Jewishness") published a special edition for the 200th anniversary of the birth of Berlin Enlightenment philosopher Moses Mendelssohn. Ten years earlier, Germany's Jews had been guaranteed full equality by the Weimar Republic's constitution. These rights would hold for less than 14 years.

Berlin's Jews look forward to events such as the annual Jewish cultural festival.

Jews were present in Germany as early as the 8th century and in Berlin from the 13th century. Here, as elsewhere, they were subjected to restrictions. Residence permits could be revoked at any time, and Jews were barred from most trades. Moneylending, street peddling, medicine, and later banking were among the few options for Jewish businesses.

Although Jews were expelled from the territory of Brandenburg in 1573, they returned to the area in 1671 when Jewish families were expelled from Austria. Berlin from the 17th century was a relatively open city; its patchwork of regulations and edicts both benefited and hindered the city's Jews over the years.

The Enlightenment brought hopes of equality and, in spite of prejudice against them, many Jews identified closely enough with the "Fatherland" to march to their deaths in the carnage of World War I. Others were active in left-wing movements.

Berlin's Jewish society brought forth plenty of stars. Among Mendelssohn's descendants was the musician Felix (1809–1847). For centuries, trade had been one of the few avenues open to Jews, and some had great success. Adolf Jandorf (1870–1932) founded his KaDeWe store in western Berlin in 1907.

Then came the nightmare of the Nazis. When Hitler came to power in 1933, at least

170,000 Jews lived in Berlin, many in slum conditions in the largely Jewish Scheunenviertel north of Alexanderplatz. The Scheunenviertel area and neighboring streets were a tough district, where pimps and petty criminals gathered.

More than 100,000 Berlin Jews went into exile before World War II, and more than 50,500 perished in the Auschwitz and Theresienstadt death camps. On February 27 and 28, 1943, the last Jews in Berlin were rounded up for deportation. Around 2,000 who were married to non-Jews were herded into a former Jewish welfare office at Rosenstrasse 2–4. In an act of courage, their spouses and several thousand others, mostly women, demonstrated around the clock for their release. On March 6, they were set free. As many as 6,000 Jews in Berlin survived in hiding.

Today, Berlin's Jewish community numbers around 10,000, two-thirds of them from the former Soviet Union. It is the largest Jewish community in Germany (where the total Jewish population is about 105,000). Tensions among immigrant groups have created ill feeling; native Berliner Jews feel outmaneuvered by newcomers, and the two sides continue to argue.

1933: A Brownshirt flanks a store and a sign, "Germans! Defend yourselves! Don't buy from Jews!"

More Places to Visit in Central Berlin

Gedenkstätte Berliner Mauer

Nearly a mile (1.5 km) in length, this monument to the memory of the victims of the Berlin Wall is one of the best spots in which to confront the history of the barrier. The wall was built along the south side of the street. As it was perfected, houses were demolished to create a no-man's-land. A stretch of the main wall, death strip, and inner wall remain as a memorial on the corner of Ackerstrasse. A late 19th-century church, painstakingly restored after World War II, was left isolated in the death strip until finally demolished by the GDR regime in 1985. In 2000, a memorial chapel was built in its stead. Across the road, the documentation center offers a permanent exhibition, enlivened by a selection of documents, photos, and audio and video material. At the western end of the memorial, a separate visitors center shows a short introductory film on the history of the wall and rents out multimedia guides for a stroll through the open-air exhibits, which are continually being expanded.
www.berliner-mauer-gedenkstaette.de Map p. 83 ✉ Bernauer Strasse 111 & 119 ☎ 030 467 98 66 66 💲 Multimedia guide $$ 🚇 U-Bahn: Bernauer Strasse

Historischer Hafen

Across the southeastern tip of Museumsinsel is this floating reminder that Berlin's trade was once largely riverborne. At the turn of the 20th century, more than 400 vessels arrived in Berlin daily. The Historical Harbor is a huddle of some 20 different riverboats. One operates as a summer café and another has a small museum.
www.historischer-hafen-berlin.de Map p. 83 ✉ Märkisches Ufer ☎ 030 21 47 32 57 🕐 Museum open Sun. noon–6 p.m., May–Sept. 💲 $ 🚇 U-Bahn: Märkisches Museum

Märkisches Museum

Possibly one of the city's most eclectic museums, the Märkisches Museum presents a voyage through the history of Berlin, from the Stone Age tribes who settled in thatched huts around the Spree to the late 20th century. Highlights on the ground floor include the Gothische Kapelle (Gothic Chapel), now an exhibition space for altars, religious paintings, and sculptures, and the medieval Zunftsaal (Guild Hall), a dark paneled chamber replete with ceremonial trophies, goblets, and flags. Rooms on upper floors are jammed with items from bourgeois homes from the 18th to 20th centuries. A room on the top floor contains automatophones (barrel organs and their more mechanized successors). The museum staff cranks these up around 3 p.m. on Sundays. Labeling is in German.
www.stadtmuseum.de Map p. 83 ✉ Am Köllnischen Park 5 ☎ 030 24 00 21 62 🕐 Closed Mon. 💲 $$, free Wed. 🚇 U-Bahn: Märkisches Museum

Students behold Berlin in miniature at the Märkisches Museum.

Much more than a pretty park: the center of German political life, a concentration of art collections, and Germany's oldest zoo

Tiergarten & Around

Introduction & Map 116–117

Regierungsviertel 118–119

Tiergarten 120–121

Feature: The Shock of the New 122–123

Kulturforum 124–125

Experience: In the Air Tonight 125

Gemäldegalerie & Kupferstichkabinett 126–128

Neue Nationalgalerie 129–130

More Places to Visit in Tiergarten & Around 131–132

Hotels & Restaurants 246–247

Cooling off in leafy Tiergarten

Tiergarten & Around

This peaceful park in the center of Berlin is perfectly named. The "Animal Garden" was once the favorite hunting ground of Prussian kings living on Unter den Linden in the Berliner Schloss. Those days are long gone, but in the southwest corner of the Tiergarten the city's main zoo is full of all sorts of critters, while the park's northern edge is home to Germany's government buildings, which at times can seem like a bit of a zoo as well.

As the city spread westward in the 18th and 19th centuries, the royal hunting ground gradually became what it is today, a public park laced with walking paths and strings of pretty lakes and streams. Through its middle, the asphalt scar of Strasse des 17. Juni runs east and west, intersected at the Grosser Stern circle by a busy north–south thoroughfare. A monument to military victories past, the Siegessäule, rises from the circle. Strangely enough, these roads don't disturb the peace deeper inside the park. On summer nights, different fauna come out to play, as prostitutes and other sexual adventurers cruise the park.

Art lovers will be drawn to this part of town for the concentration of galleries and museums in the Kulturforum, which hangs onto the southeast rim of the Tiergarten. In the Gemäldegalerie awaits a cornucopia of old masters and other classics collected over the past

couple of centuries. Nearby in the Kunstgewerbemuseum (Museum of Decorative Arts) is a diverse presentation of the best in European arts and crafts down the centuries. Here you can find anything from Meissen porcelain and Renaissance silverware to art deco objects and Bauhaus furniture. A musical note is sounded in the Philharmonie and Musikinstrumenten-Museum. For a major injection of modern art, taking in anyone from Pablo Picasso to local hero George Grosz, head for the Neue Nationalgalerie's collection

NOT TO BE MISSED:

The bold architectural statements of the Regierungsviertel **118–119**

Strolling the onetime royal hunting ground of the Tiergarten **120–121**

The dome and skyscrapers at Potsdamer Platz **122–123**

Viewing the beautiful old masters of the Gemäldegalerie **126–128**

Learning about Stauffenberg's daring plot at the Bendlerblock memorial **132** (which is due to transfer to the Gemäldegalerie in upcoming years). The Neue Nationalgalerie building, a key contribution to the city from Ludwig Mies van der Rohe, will itself draw fans of modern architecture. A short walk away are the innovative buildings around Potsdamer Platz (see pp. 74–76). The imaginative new buildings of the Regierungsviertel (Government District) spread out to the north.

With a short stroll to the west of the Neue Nationalgalerie, you can learn about the efforts of Germany's resistance fighters at the Gedenkstätte Deutscher Widerstand. Those with a taste for walking will continue through the Diplomatenviertel (Diplomatic District) to admire some wonders of contemporary architecture. This promenade can be rounded off with a visit to the Bauhaus Archiv. ■

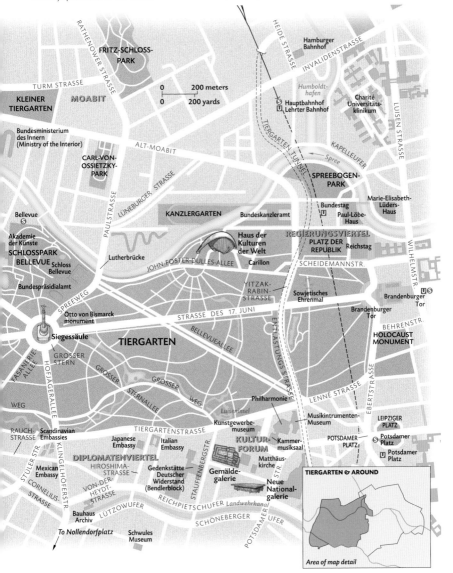

Regierungsviertel

The 1991 decision to return Berlin to its status as capital of a united Germany opened the way for an architectural revolution. A new Regierungsviertel (Government District) had to be created. There was no possibility of a return to the pre–World War II concentration of ministerial buildings on and around Wilhelmstrasse, although some buildings there are still in use.

The striking Paul-Löbe-Haus is one of several avant-garde buildings housing the government.

Sir Norman Foster's design for the modernized Reichstag building (see pp. 54–57) as the seat of parliament was only the beginning. Already considered too small when built in the late 19th century, it now required annexes. These arose north of the building on either side of what is known as the Spreebogen (Bend in the Spree).

The **Paul-Löbe-Haus** and **Marie-Elisabeth-Lüders-Haus,** named after prominent Weimar parliamentarians and Nazi opponents, house government conference rooms and offices. The buildings, which face each other over the Spree, are laden with symbolism. The Berlin Wall divided the city here at the river; the Marie-Elisabeth-Lüders-Haus stands in what was East Berlin. In the shadow of the Paul-Löbe-Haus, on the bend in the river 164 feet (50 m) north of the Reichstag building, is a silent memorial—a series of white crosses—to those who were killed while trying to cross the wall. These two buildings of the united Germany are linked across the former border by two footbridges.

Of the two buildings, both designed by Stephan Braunfels (born 1950), the seven-story Paul-Löbe-Haus is the more striking. A series of giant glass cylinders is divided by sharp-edged, implacable-looking concrete shafts. The flat roof of the Marie-Elisabeth-Lüders-Haus juts out as a precipice over a public square below. The detached giant cube with the huge circular windows contains the parliamentary library. Organized tours must be booked in advance through the Bundestag visitor bureau.

West of the Paul-Löbe-Haus stands what Berliners like to call the "washing machine": the H-shaped **Bundeskanzleramt** (Office of the Federal Chancellor; *Willy-Brandt-Strasse 1*). The nickname comes from its appearance, in which cubic forms are contrasted with large circular openings. It was designed by Berlin architects Axel Schultes (born 1943) and Charlotte Frank (born 1959) and completed in 2002. The **Kanzlergarten,** a modest garden, lies west across the river.

Just southwest of the Bundeskanzleramt along the Spree River rises the **Haus der Kulturen der Welt** (House of World Cultures). Built in 1957 by American Hugh Stubbins (1912–2006), it is used for concerts, expositions, and other cultural events. Outside, in adjacent gardens, the 68 bells of the carillon ring regularly.

About 2,000 feet (600 m) farther west along John-Foster-Dulles-Allee, you come before the gates of **Schloss Bellevue** *(Spreeweg 1),* which is as far as you will get. This late 18th-century summer residence for the Prussian royal family has been the prime reception palace for the German president (who resides in a villa in Dahlem) since 1994. Restored in 2005, it is set in private gardens that link it with the gray, elliptical **Bundespräsidialamt,** which houses presidential staff offices.

The arrival of the federal government in Berlin also changed the face of the Moabit district north across the Spree. Many public servants now live in the remarkable, snake-shaped apartment block at Paulstrasse. Some of those employees doubtless work

INSIDER TIP:

If you can, try to visit the German chancellery during the ministries' open-house day, held on the third Saturday in August.

—JEREMY GRAY
National Geographic author

about a 1,640-foot (500 m) walk to the west in the glass-fronted, riverside edifice of the **Bundesministerium des Innern** (Ministry of the Interior) at Alt-Moabit 98–101. This multistory building looks like a giant magnet with two cooling towers at the river end. ■

Haus der Kulturen der Welt

🅰 Map p. 117

✉ John-Foster-Dulles-Allee 10

☎ 030 39 78 71 75

💲 Exhibitions $–$$, Haus free

🚌 Bus: 100

www.hkw.de

Tiergarten

Bordered to the north by the Spree River, the Tiergarten is Berlin's Central Park: a great place to walk or cycle off the stress of a hard day's sightseeing. The park, established as the Prussian royal family's private hunting ground in the mid-17th century, bristles with reminders of Berlin's tumultuous past.

South of the Regierungsviertel buildings along the park's northern edge, marked by John-Foster-Dulles-Allee, the Tiergarten invites exploration. Follow Strasse des 17. Juni from the Brandenburger Tor and stroll

A statue of a Soviet soldier stands watch over the Sowjetisches Ehrenmal, raised shortly after World War II.

about 1,000 feet (300 m) west until you stumble across a historical conundrum. The **Sowjetisches Ehrenmal** is a memorial erected by the Soviets shortly after they conquered the city in the Battle of Berlin in 1945. The two T-34 tanks are said to have been the first to enter Berlin; the marble for the monument purportedly came from the ruins of Hitler's chancellery. That the locals thought of the Soviets as liberators is doubtful; the name of this avenue commemorates an uprising in East Berlin in 1953 against the Soviet-backed regime.

The broad boulevard, which used to be known as Charlottenburger Chaussee, leads across the park. Hitler staged several massive military marches along this strip, which was chosen to become the east–west axis in Hitler's grand post-victory capital, Germania.

In recent years, the avenue has been better known for gatherings of a more peaceful nature. At the western end of the park lies a traffic circle, the Grosser Stern (Great Star), with the grand **Siegessäule** (Victory Column) rising from its center. In July 2008, then presidential candidate Barack Obama addressed a throng of 200,000 listeners at the column, mindful that Reagan and Kennedy had held historic speeches at the

INSIDER TIP:

The Patio Restaurant-schiff is a cozy but chic restaurant on a pimped-out barge in a quiet bend on the Spree River. It has great views of the riverbank from the rooftop terrace.

—KEVIN COTE
Producer, Deutsche Welle TV

Brandenburg Gate. The column was originally set up in front of the Reichstag to fete Prussia's military successes. Hitler had it moved here and placed on a higher column, taking the golden statue of the goddess of victory, known to Berliners simply as *Goldene Else* (Golden Else), to a height of 220 feet (67 m). There is a viewing platform 164 feet (50 m) up the column. Berlin's homosexual community has adopted the Siegessäule as a symbol, even lending its name to a prominent gay magazine. Like the legendary Love Parade before it, the annual Christopher Street Day procession ends here in a riot of colorful costumes, floats, and concerts.

Other monuments in the park commemorate a moment of political violence that set the tone for the following years. In 1919, Communists **Karl Liebknecht** and **Rosa Luxemburg** were assassinated by right-wing paramilitary troops in the Tiergarten. The spot where Liebknecht was shot is marked along Grosser Weg by the Neuer See lake, southwest of Grosser Stern, while the easily missed memorial to Luxemburg lies south of Landwehrkanal next to the Lichtensteinallee bridge, where her body was dumped.

Behind the Luxemburg memorial are the fences that restrain animals in Germany's oldest zoo. The **Zoologischer Garten** was founded in 1844 by Alexander von Humboldt. Today it houses more than 19,000 animals in an 84-acre (34 ha) space. There is also a fascinating aquarium.

Close to the Tiergarten S-Bahn station, a leafy path threads through the open-air **Gaslatern-enmuseum** *(Grosser Weg, tel 017 98 10 67 47, http://gaslicht-kultur .de)*, featuring dozens of spindly giants from Germany and Europe. Some 44,000 gas-powered street lamps—more than half of those left on the planet—still illuminate the German capital. ∎

Siegessäule

🅰 Map p. 117
✉ Strasse des 17. Juni, Grosser Stern
💲 $
🚌 Bus: 100

Zoologischer Garten

🅰 Map p. 116
✉ Hardenbergplatz 8
☎ 030 25 40 10
💲 Zoo & aquarium $$$$
🚇 U-Bahn & S-Bahn: Zoologischer Garten

www.zoo-berlin.de

Patio Restaurantschiff

✉ Helgoländer Ufer at Kirchstrasse
☎ 030 40 30 17 00

The Iron Chancellor

When the *Junker* (landed noble) Otto von Bismarck became chancellor of Prussia in 1862, even he probably didn't imagine that in less than ten years he would succeed in uniting all Germany under Prussia's control. He thus became the first chancellor of Germany. Known as the Iron Chancellor for his toughness, he was also dubbed *Der Schmied des Reichs* (the man who forged the empire) and was thus often depicted in blacksmith's clothes, hammer in hand. Nothing could have made Berlin's working class laugh harder. Bismarck once declared in parliament: "I am a Junker and I insist on having the advantages that gives me!" He had plenty, as the towering statue of him near the Bundespräsidialamt suggests.

The Shock of the New

In the first half of 2006, workers raced to finish building a central railway station for Berlin in time for the summer football (soccer) World Cup. The former Lehrter Bahnhof, now known as Hauptbahnhof (Central Station) is touted as Europe's biggest rail junction, where local, regional, and international trains crisscross at four levels beneath an elegantly vaulted steel-and-glass roof.

Potsdamer Platz was a wasteland when the Wall came down in 1989. Some of the world's top architects have since let their imaginations run riot.

The average Berliner is used to huge new public works. Berlin has been one of the world's biggest playgrounds for an international phalanx of architects since the city came together again in 1990. The scars left by the war and Berlin Wall provided unique opportunities to create a new cityscape. The prudent city council imposed a raft of building regulations, but still left room for imagination and creative playfulness.

Potsdamer Platz (see pp. 74–76) attracted enormous attention. From a no-man's-land in 1990, it has become a thriving commercial center, graced by a variety of extraordinary and unique buildings, from the domed Sony Center and adjacent Bahntower to the kaleidoscopic mix making up the Quartier Potsdamer Platz.

Equally surprising is the Regierungsviertel complex (see pp. 118–119) around the new Reichstag building, whose glass dome by Sir

Norman Foster has become a symbol of the city.

Between Potsdamer Platz and the Reichstag building, the challenging field of ominous gray pillars that forms the Holocaust Monument (Denkmal für die ermordeten Juden Europas; see pp. 60–61) is a controversial but daring addition to the cityscape.

Eye-catching Structures

The city has been peppered with extraordinary buildings that inevitably divide opinion. The zigzag Jüdisches Museum Berlin (see pp. 180–181), which in its form seems to evoke the tortured history of German Jewry, has found a place in Kreuzberg, just as the strangely terraced and circular facade of the Ku'damm-Eck is now an accepted if odd part of the legendary Kurfürstendamm. Not far away, the Ludwig-Erhard-Haus (see p. 139), home to the stock exchange, has been nicknamed the "Armadillo" for its ranks of steel girders.

Several nations have awarded themselves new embassies. Among the eye-catchers

Mediaspree

"Paris is always Paris, but Berlin is never Berlin," quipped Jacques Lang, a onetime French culture minister. This restless dynamism is embodied by Mediaspree, a 440-acre (178 ha) real estate development along the river in Friedrichshain and Kreuzberg, a stone's throw from the futuristic O2 events arena. This humongous district marries media and services businesses with housing and leisure facilities, and stands to send adjacent rents and asset prices spiraling. Public protests ensued, and in 2008 a referendum voted overwhelmingly to tone down the upper-class elements. But the results were not binding, and the original blueprint has largely gone ahead.

are the Mexican, Scandinavian, and Austrian representations in the diplomatic district south of Tiergarten. Even the conservative CDU party got in on the act with its angular corner office building on Cornelius Strasse, near Tiergarten. Inside a glass structure floats the lentil-shaped main building.

INSIDER TIP:

A great example of Gothic expressionist architecture is Fritz Höger's 1932 Kirche am Hohenzollernplatz [Nassausische Strasse 66–67] in Wilmersdorf—less church, more a sinister, Kafkaesque factory.

–MATTHEW TEMPEST
Journalist and architecture blogger

The pace of (re)construction in Berlin has slowed since the 1990s, but various projects are still on the boil. Around Alexanderplatz (see pp. 102–104), the city has nixed ideas to build eight 500-foot (150 m) skyscrapers to compete with the Ku'damm out west. Just one tower, above the Saturn electronics store, may ever be realized, and planners have been sent back to the drawing board. Mushrooming on the periphery are shopping malls such as the three-story, art deco-inspired Alexa on Grunerstrasse and Alea 101, the faint echo of a department store from 1911.

Immediately north of the Hauptbahnhof, a forest of towers is springing up in the Europaviertel, a prestigious office and residential quarter. Though less in flux, the old West is undergoing changes of its own. The once-faded Zoo station area now sports an ultra-fancy, 32-floor Waldorf Astoria hotel, while over on Breitscheidplatz, the crumbling Bikini-Haus has been reborn as a chic shopping arcade. The more Berlin changes, the more it stays transformable.

Kulturforum

When the Nazis came to power in 1933, it spelled the end of peace and quiet for what had once been a well-to-do district on the south flank of the Tiergarten. Hitler's architect Albert Speer began tearing down houses and wiping whole streets off the map to make way for the new capital, Germania. He didn't get past demolition; Allied bombs took care of what he had not destroyed. Yet after the war, this void became one of the main cultural centers of the city.

Berlin Philharmoniker concerts regularly draw up to 2,500 fans to the Philharmonie.

Matthäuskirche
 Map p. 117
 Sigismundstrasse
☎ 030 262 12 02
🕐 Closed Mon.
 U-Bahn & S-Bahn: Potsdamer Platz

All that remains of the once peaceful community here is the **Matthäuskirche.** Built by Friedrich August Stüler in 1844 to 1846, this Evangelical church survived Speer's wrecking ball but succumbed to Allied bombs. It was patiently rebuilt in 1956 to 1960, although the interior is a bland shadow of its former self. You can climb its bell tower for the views or drop by for an organ recital from 12:30 to 12:50 p.m. *(Tues.–Sat.).*

First off the mark in the post-war construction was the **Philharmonie,** completed in 1963 (with a golden aluminum facade added in 1981) as the new home for the esteemed Berlin Philharmoniker (Berlin Philharmonic Orchestra). Designed by Hans Scharoun (1893–1972), it enjoys superb acoustics. To join the 1 p.m. tours of the Philharmonie and adjacent **Kammermusiksaal** (Chamber Music Hall), which was opened in 1987 to another Sharoun design, wait at the artists' entrance (signposted).

In the following years, the other museums that make up the Kulturforum were completed, making this an extraordinary concentration of culture, difficult to tackle in less than two days.

Music lovers will not pass up a chance to visit the **Musikinstrumenten-Museum** (Tiergartenstrasse 1, tel 030 25 48 11 78, www .sim.spk-berlin.de, closed Mon., $), next door to the Philharmonie. The collection was established in 1888 and greatly expanded. Just about every kind of classical instrument is represented. The sheer number of harpsichords, clavichords, and pianos is impressive. Among them is the piano on which Carl Maria von Weber composed Der Freischütz in 1821. Next to it is a glass harmonica invented by Benjamin Franklin.

The biggest instrument on display is a giant Wurlitzer organ, cranked up at midday on Saturdays. Wurlitzers of this ilk were made for silent film showings; this one is the largest working model of its kind in Europe.

A short walk west is the **Kunstgewerbemuseum** (Museum of Decorative Art), with an exhaustive collection (on four floors) of European decorative arts and crafts from the Middle Ages to the art deco period of the early 20th century (museum closed for refurbishing until spring 2014).

The exposition starts on the ground floor with a fashion gallery of 100-plus outfits from the 18th to 20th centuries. From here, you move to the Middle Ages section, on the floor below the ticket desk. The riches are composed primarily of church treasures, along with tapestries and furniture. The following two rooms are dedicated to the Renaissance. Exquisite

ceramics from Italy and Spain take pride of place.

The collection continues, oddly, two floors up with the baroque. Early Berlin porcelain is on show, along with French pewter and central European glassware. The next room, which extends from baroque to rococo, is home to the museum's collections of fine 18th-century porcelain from Meissen.

Thereafter comes the 19th century, with brightly polished Empire furniture, still more

porcelain, and sinuous art nouveau furniture. The top floor displays end with art deco furniture and household items.

The contemporary design section, roughly from the 1920s to the 1960s, is lodged in the basement. Look for furniture by Ludwig Mies van der Rohe. ∎

Philharmonie & Kammermusiksaal

- Map p. 117
- Herbert-von-Karajan-Strasse 1
- 030 25 48 81 56
- Guided tours 1 p.m. (Reservations required for ten or more)
- $$
- U-Bahn & S-Bahn: Potsdamer Platz

EXPERIENCE:
In the Air Tonight

Every summer near the Olympiastadion, lines snake down the street waiting to get into the Waldbühne (Glockenturmstrasse 1, tel 018 05 57 00 70, www.waldbuehne -berlin.de), **an open-air stage at the nub of a wonderfully steep amphitheater built in the 1930s. On offer is a beloved concert series by the Berlin Philharmoniker. Inside, the atmosphere is folksy as spectators consume food and drink from picnic baskets set on the balustrades. After the finale, everyone joins in the decades-old tradition of lighting candles and singing "Berliner Luft" ("Berlin Air"), the city's unofficial anthem by Paul Lincke. Tickets must be purchased in advance and include round-trip public transit fare.**

Kunstgewerbemuseum

- Map p. 117
- Matthäikirchplatz
- 030 266 42 43 36
- Closed Mon.
- $$
- U-Bahn & S-Bahn: Potsdamer Platz

Gemäldegalerie & Kupferstichkabinett

One of the greatest collections of old masters in Europe, the Gemäldegalerie warrants several hours per visit. The two strongest elements are Dutch and Flemish painting (from the Middle Ages to Rubens and Rembrandt) and the Venetian Renaissance. There is a smattering of German artists, stronger on the late medieval period, a splash of the Florentine Renaissance, and some teasers from Britain and France.

Priceless works of the old masters fill the halls of the Gemäldegalerie.

A word of warning: From 2015, some of the collection may be transferred to the Bode-Museum (see p. 90). The city plans to concentrate Berlin's collections of antiquities and art up to the 19th century in the Museumsinsel. This process will take years. Eventually, the 20th-century collection of the Neue Nationalgalerie (see pp. 129–130) will hang here.

Of the gallery's 3,000 works, about half are on display. Around the bright, elongated **central hall,** which is used for special exhibitions, spreads a number of rooms containing paintings, arranged more or less chronologically and by geographical area. The numbering is odd, switching between Roman and Arabic numerals. The following are some highlights.

The first rooms on the right contain principally German medieval religious images from the 13th century on. In **Room 2,** Nuremberg-born Albrecht Dürer (1471–1528) is represented with a couple of works. Of the two, the "Bildnis einer Jungen Venezianerin" ("Image of a Young Venetian," 1506) is more interesting. Dürer made several trips to Venice, then a cultural epicenter. The light and color in this portrait of a young Venetian woman betray the influences of the north Italian city-state.

In **Room 3,** Lucas Cranach the Elder (1472–1553) has several works. Paintings by Hans Holbein the Elder (1465–1524) and the Younger (1497–1543)—the latter represented by a series of portraits—grace **Room 1.**

Sinners & Sayings

Cranach the Elder turns up again in **Room III** with "Flügelaltar mit dem Jüngsten Gericht" ("Side Altar with the Last Judgment," 1524). A close look at this painting is enough to make the most stubborn sinners repent. Bizarre monsters torture recent arrivals in hell, bodiless heads wander around, sinners are impaled on trees and boiled in huge pots. Who is responsible for all this woe? Take a look at Adam and Eve having a bite of an apple in the left flap of the triptych. Less distressing but equally bizarre is his "Der Jungbrunnen" ("The Fountain of Youth," 1546), in which old hags arrive at the left, enter a pool, and exit to the right in the flower of youth.

Room IV is a key stop, with two grand altar tableaux by the Flemish Rogier van der Weyden (1399–1464). The fine detail in the background images of towns is striking in "Der Middelburger Altar" (ca 1445), which depicts

Christ's birth and the Three Wise Men, and "Der Marienaltar" (1435), with the Mary at its center.

Just as absorbing is "Die Niederländischen Sprichwörter" ("Dutch Sayings," 1559) by the Flemish Pieter Breughel the Elder (ca 1525–1569) in **Room 7.** In a manic medieval village scene, each character or scene is the incarnation of one of 126 old sayings. On the lower left, for instance, is a man who embraces and bites a pillar. The Dutch called religious bigots "pillar biters."

Rooms 9 and **VIII** contain a wealth of works by Peter Paul Rubens (1577–1640), the Flemish baroque master. These grand paintings display an unusual verve of brushstroke and movement, evident in "Thronende Maria mit dem Kind und Heiligen" ("Mary Enthroned with the Christ Child and Saints," ca 1627).

INSIDER TIP:

Drop the kids at the Gemäldegalerie's Kinder-Reich (Children's Realm) and its reconstructed painter's workshop.

—GABRIELLA LE BRETON
National Geographic author

After traversing a series of rooms filled mainly with landscapes, portraits, and still-life images from Dutch artists, you meet a selection by the great Rembrandt van Rijn (1606–1669). The most important are the six

Gemäldegalerie

🗺 Map p. 117
✉ Matthäikirchplatz
☎ 030 266 29 51
🕐 Closed Mon.
💲 $$
🚇 U-Bahn & S-Bahn: Potsdamer Platz

www.smb.museum

Kupferstich-kabinett

- ✉ Matthäikirchplatz
- ☎ 030 266 29 51
- 🕐 Closed Mon.
- 💲 $$, Studiensaal free
- 🚇 U-Bahn & S-Bahn: Potsdamer Platz

www.smb.museum

tableaux in **Room X,** including "Der Mennonitenprediger und seine Frau" ("The Mennonite Preacher and His Wife," 1642), next to which is a portrait of the master's housekeeper and lover, Hendrickje Stoffels (1656–1657).

Rooms 20–22 form a brief interlude between the Dutch masters and the brilliance of Renaissance Italy to come. England's Thomas Gainsborough

Book Bargains

Twice a year, culture vultures flock to the *Bücher-Sonderverkauf* **(special book sale) held by the Berlin state museum foundation in the foyer of the Kulturforum near the Gemäldegalerie. On offer are steeply discounted books, postcards, posters, and notebooks. Exhibition catalogs can be snapped up for a fraction of the cover price. Check the Berlin media in late March and late November for dates, and come early.**

(1727–1788) dominates **Room 20** with several portraits, while France's Jean-Antoine Watteau (1684–1721) is the key figure in **Room 21.** Antoine Pesne, the French court painter brought to Berlin by King Friedrich I, has a few works in **Room 22.**

Italian Masters

The next 23 rooms are a festival of Italian mastery, with particular emphasis on Venetian

Renaissance, baroque, rococo, and landscape art. You will glide by works from Giambattista Tiepolo (1696–1770; **Room 24**), Titian (Tiziano Vecellio, ca 1490–1576; **Room XVI**), Tintoretto (Jacopo Robusti, 1518–1594; **Room XVI**), and the master of Venetian scenes, Canaletto (Giovanni Antonio Canal, 1697–1768; **Room XII**).

The roll call of Florentine masters includes Giorgio Vasari (1511–1574; **Room 30**), Fra Angel-ico (ca 1395–1455; **Room 39**), Fra Filippo Lippi (ca 1406–1469; **Room 39**), and Botticelli (1445–1510; **Room XVIII**). Renaissance genius Raphael (1483–1520; **Room 29**) is represented with five works, includ-ing "Maria mit dem Kind, Johannes dem Täufer und einem Heiligen Knaben" ("The Virgin Mary with the Christ Child, John the Baptist, and a Holy Boy") a circular portrait that emanates a joyous, Mediter-ranean light. If, at this point, the luxuriant displays have not left you feeling overwhelmed, another 400 canvases by European painters from the 13th to 18th centuries are tucked away in Rooms 43–54 on the lower level.

Opposite the Gemäldegal-erie in the same building is the **Kupferstichkabinett,** a treasure of hundreds of thousands of sketches, drawings, pastels, and watercolors dating from the Middle Ages to the 19th century. Visitors may visit the **Studiensaal** (*bring identifica-tion, closes 4 p.m.*) and ask to see some of the works. Temporary exhibitions are held here and in the **Kunstbibliothek** (Art Library) downstairs. ■

Neue Nationalgalerie

The existence of Ludwig Mies van der Rohe's Neue (New) Nationalgalerie, a work of art in which to house works of art, is due to the Cold War that split Berlin and its art collections. The bulk of the city's 19th-century art remained in East Berlin in what would later be known as the Alte (Old) Nationalgalerie. Most of the 20th-century collection, especially German works from the first half of the century, was stored in the West.

The Neue Nationalgalerie is a short walk from the 19th-century Matthäuskirche.

In 1968, this wealth of 20th-century art found a new home in Mies van der Rohe's building, a low-lying, glassed-in structure with a broad roof hanging over the surrounding piazza.

Various sculptures grace the building and its **sculpture garden.** Among them are "The Archer" by Britain's Henry Moore (1898–1986), a bronze created in 1964–1965, and American Alexander Calder's (1898–1976) 1965 "Heads and Tail," the most striking of the exhibits in this outdoor gallery—a lively looking piece whose elements communicate

the idea of a confused crowd of people. Spain's Eduardo Chillida (1924–2002) contributed "Gudari," a work that, with its branchlike elements, suggests the search for place and identity.

Prior to a three-year renovation starting in 2015, the Neue Nationalgalerie is hosting rotating shows and exhibitions of works plucked from its archives.

Works from the years 1968 to 2000 are on display through the end of 2014, a swan-song retrospective before doors close for the facelift. Highlights include Joseph Beuys's "Richtkräfte" ("Directional

Neue Nationalgalerie

- Map p. 117
- Potsdamer Strasse 50
- 030 266 42 42 42
- Closed Mon.
- $$
- U-Bahn & S-Bahn: Potsdamer Platz

www.neue-national galerie.de

Forces," 1977), consisting of 100 crazily scattered chalkboards, and the immense color blocks of "Who's Afraid of Red, Yellow, and Blue IV" by Barnett Newman (1905–1970). Concept art from East German artists Werner Tübke (1929–2004), Wolfgang Mattheuer (1927–2004), and Hartwig Ebersbach (1940–) feature alongside expressionist paintings of the 1980s and photography and video creations by Jeff Wall (1946–), Stan Douglas (1960–), and Pipilotti Rist (1962–).

Early 20th Century

The heart of the permanent collection is made up of the German expressionists and their successors. Leading the way is Ernst Ludwig Kirchner. Among his better known Berlin paintings is "Potsdamer Platz" (1914), in which two ladies of the night seem to rise out of a vortex at the heart of the painting.

Other pre–World War I works on show include a mixed bag of the best. Pablo Picasso (1881–1973) and Juan Gris (1887–1927) contribute with some classics of cubism. Paul Gauguin (1848–1903) and Emil Nolde (1867–1956) add an exotic touch with their warm images from the Pacific.

The horrors of World War I had a telling effect on art and its makers. Otto Dix had served in the trenches and could hardly avoid reflecting this in his gruesome messages. As cruel as the war are paintings such as "Die Skatspieler" ("The Cardplayers," 1920), depicting three mutilated

INSIDER TIP:

To get a quick overview of what's on in Berlin's vibrant museum scene, check *www.museumsportal-berlin.de.*

—LARRY PORGES
National Geographic travel books editor

war veterans who are missing limbs and other body parts.

The Interwar Period

The feverish interwar period attracted all sorts of artists to Berlin. Among the exponents of Bauhaus were Switzerland's Paul Klee, Russia's Wassily Kandinsky, Oscar Schlemmer, and Lyonel Feininger, all represented here.

An early dada star who went on to lead the Neue Sachlichkeit (New Objectivity) group was Georg Grosz, whose "Stützen der Gesellschaft" ("Society's Props," 1926) is a fierce satire on German society: Its figures are equipped with props ranging from priestly robes and sabers to beer steins and socialist flags. Outside, the country burns.

A smattering of greatly varied international works lends the collection an eclectic flavor. Salvador Dalí (1904–1989), Joan Miró (1893–1983), Giorgio de Chirico (1888–1978), Alexander Calder, Constantin Brancusi (1876–1957), and Alberto Giacometti (1901–1966) are among those who stand out in the gallery's wide-ranging collection. ■

More Places to Visit in Tiergarten & Around

Bauhaus Archiv

Originally intended for the city of Darmstadt in the 1960s, this temple to Bauhaus design was created by the movement's father, Walter Gropius. It was finally erected in Berlin after his death. Gropius founded the original Bauhaus school, dedicated to avant-garde design, in Weimar; among his colleagues was architect Ludwig Mies van der Rohe. Local authorities forced Gropius to move, to Dessau in 1925 and then to Berlin in 1932, where the Nazis shut him down for good in 1933. This central archive building, itself late Bauhaus in design, has a permanent exhibition on the ground floor embracing household and furniture items made by Bauhaus teachers and students, including a couple by Mies van der Rohe and quite a few by Hungarian-born Marcel Breur (1902–1981). It also holds posters and art by Klee, Kandinsky, and Schlemmer, as well as models of some important Bauhaus constructions.
www.bauhaus.de 🅜 Map p. 117 ✉ Klingelhöfer-strasse 14 ☎ 030 254 00 20 💲 $$ 🚍 Bus: M29; U-Bahn: Nollendorfplatz

Diplomatenviertel

A stroll past some of the embassies in the Diplomatenviertel, the Diplomatic District, gives a visitor a tour of interesting Tiergarten architecture. This district, just south of Tiergarten and north of Landwehrkanal, was the idea of Hitler's chief architect, Albert Speer, and remnants of his era include the rather fascist-looking embassies of Hitler's World War II allies Italy and Japan, which face each other across Hiroshimastrasse (Nos. 1 and 6, respectively) on the corner of Tiergartenstrasse. More modern are the combined Scandinavian (Denmark, Finland, Iceland, Norway, and Sweden) compound to the west at Rauchstrasse 1. The curving main facade is made up of a coating of sea green ailerons that rise and fall as those inside require more or less light and privacy. Just south, the Mexican Embassy at Klingelhöfer-strasse 3 is just as intriguing. The graceful vertical columns of its facade open out like a fan when seen from the side.
🅜 Map p. 117 🚍 Bus: M29 or 200; S-Bahn or U-Bahn: Potsdamer Platz

Walter Gropius's Bauhaus Archiv has become a local landmark.

Gedenkstätte Deutscher Widerstand (Bendlerblock)

Enter the Federal Building and Town-Planning Office and you step back into the grim final year of World War II. Deep in the night of July 20, 1944, shots rang out across the courtyard as senior officer Claus von Stauffenberg and three others were executed after they failed in their attempt to assassinate the Führer (see sidebar). The building, then part of the *Wehrmacht* (army) headquarters and known as the Bendlerblock, has seen little change. The offices on the second floor where the plotters met today house this memorial to German resistance. The extensive display of photos and documents highlights sources of resistance to Nazism in Germany, ranging from military staff to minorities such as Jews and Gypsies. An English-language audio device is available; the exhibition is in German.

www.gdw-berlin.de 🄰 Map p. 117 ✉ Stauffenbergstrasse 13–14 ☎ 030 26 99 50 00 🚌 Bus: M29

Schwules Museum

Lodged in an old printing plant south of the Tiergarten, the Gay Museum hosts changing and permanent exhibitions on homosexuality in Germany since the 19th century. Most interesting are the sections on the busy gay scene in 1920s Berlin and on the subsequent repression under Hitler. The display continues with the reawakening of gay bars in 1950s Berlin, suppression in the GDR, and on to the 1980s, when AIDS reared its ugly head. Since moving into these new, spacious quarters in 2013, the museum has expanded its scope to include exhibits about sexual identity and gender diversity. Most of the labeling is in German, although some information in English is available at the counter. The museum includes a reference library, archive, café, and a venue for cultural events such as films, lectures, and literary readings.

www.schwulesmuseum.de 🄰 Map p. 117 ✉ Lützowstrasse 73 ☎ 030 69 59 92 52 🕐 Closed Tues. 💲 $$ 🚌 Bus: 106

The Plot to Kill Hitler

Claus Schenk Graf von Stauffenberg (1907–1944), a career soldier, rose through the officer class to become chief of staff of the Replacement Army in June 1944. As early as the late 1930s, discreet groups of officers and civilians had formed conspiratorial circles, especially the so-called Kreisauer Kreis (Kreisau Circle), with the aim of overthrowing Hitler. Several assassination attempts failed, and by the time Stauffenberg decided to try in July 1944, the group's hopes were limited to ending the war quickly and with some dignity. As a senior officer, Stauffenberg had access to meetings with Hitler at the Eastern Front headquarters near Rastenburg in East Prussia (today part of Poland). When he arrived on July 20, he placed a bomb in a briefcase beside Hitler and shortly

thereafter walked out of the room. As he left, someone moved the briefcase; the explosion left Hitler wounded but alive. Stauffenberg flew back to Berlin, convinced of Hitler's demise, and his co-conspirators tried to enact their coup, which envisaged the occupation of key points across the city. Reports that Hitler was alive stayed the hand of most of the wavering military, and it quickly became clear the coup had failed. Stauffenberg and three others were shot that night in the Bendlerblock (see entry above), while another committed suicide. In the coming months, more than 7,000 conspiracy suspects would be arrested and over 100 tortured, tried, and in most cases, executed in the Plötzensee prison. Hitler had the trials and executions filmed for his personal entertainment.

Royal elegance at Schloss Charlottenburg and elegant shopping along the legendary Ku'damm in this central-western district

Charlottenburg

Introduction & Map   134–135

Kaiser-Wilhelm-Gedächtniskirche   136

Käthe-Kollwitz-Museum   137

Walk: Strolling Around the
   Ku'damm   138–139

Schloss Charlottenburg   140–145

Experience: Berlin by Boat   143

Feature: Berlin's Brightest Christmas
   Lights   146–147

Experience: Festival of Lights   147

Museum Berggruen & Sammlung
   Scharf-Gerstenberg   148–149

Bröhan-Museum   150

Museum für Fotografie   151

Gedenkstätte Plötzensee   152

More Places to Visit in
   Charlottenburg   153–154

Hotels & Restaurants   247–249

Contemporary flair in Ludwig-Erhard-Haus

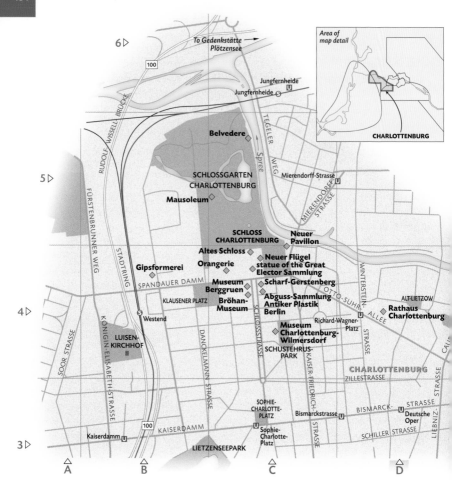

6▷ To Gedenkstätte
Plötzensee

100

Jungfernheide Ⓤ
Jungfernheide

Area of
map detail

CHARLOTTENBURG

Belvedere

5▷ SCHLOSSGARTEN
CHARLOTTENBURG

Mierendorff-Strasse Ⓤ

Mausoleum

SCHLOSS
CHARLOTTENBURG

Neuer
Pavillon

Altes Schloss

Neuer Flügel
statue of the Great
Elector Sammlung

Gipsformerei

Orangerie

SPANDAUER DAMM

Museum
Berggruen

Scharf-Gerstenberg

KLAUSENER PLATZ

Bröhan-
Museum

Abguss-Sammlung
Antiker Plastik
Berlin

ALT-LIETZOW

Rathaus
Charlottenburg

4▷

Ⓢ Westend

Richard-Wagner-
Platz Ⓤ

Museum
Charlottenburg-
Wilmersdorf

LUISEN-
KIRCHHOF
II

SCHUSTEHRUS-
PARK

CHARLOTTENBURG

ZILLESTRASSE

SOPHIE-
CHARLOTTE-
PLATZ

Bismarckstrasse Ⓤ

BISMARCK-

STRASSE

Deutsche
Oper

100 KAISERDAMM

Kaiserdamm Ⓤ

Ⓤ Sophie-
Charlotte-
Platz

SCHILLER STRASSE

3▷

LIETZENSEEPARK

A   B   C   D

Charlottenburg

A separate city until absorbed by Berlin in 1920, the onetime village of Lietzow (or Lützow) took its current name from the palace built for Queen Sophie Charlotte by King Friedrich I, renamed Charlottenburg after his wife's death. Today's municipality stretches from the quiet residential district around the palace south to the equally tranquil Wilmersdorf and southeast to the racier Kurfürstendamm.

In 1705, Friedrich I granted the title of town to a huddle of houses along the Schlossstrasse south of Schloss Charlottenburg. In the mid-19th century, industry set up along the Spree River, housing was spreading, and by 1900, Charlottenburg had become the richest city in Prussia.

The laying of the Kurfürstendamm boulevard in the late 19th century created a new attraction to rival Unter den Linden in the city center. Today the Ku'damm is largely a label-slaves' shopping strip—but not exclusively. Among the fashion houses and mansions glitter several jewels of interest. At its eastern end rises one of Berlin's best known monuments, the Kaiser-Wilhelm-Gedächtniskirche. Shoppers, especially those with a weakness for gourmet products, will want to head east to one of Europe's greatest department stores, KaDeWe. Bahnhof Zoologischer Garten (Bahnhof Zoo for short) has long had an edgy flavor; the sex shops around it remain in action despite a cleanup. Indulge a little erotic fantasy at the Erotikmuseum or admire provocative fashion photography at Helmut Newton's nearby Museum für Fotografie. Rather less playful is the art on show at the Käthe-Kollwitz-Museum, just south off the Ku'damm.

Another world altogether lies west around Schloss Charlottenburg. The long, low palace and its gardens are a magnet for tourists and locals alike. Three fine museums stand across the road from the palace. One, Museum Berggruen, is dedicated to Pablo Picasso and three other modern artists, while its sister collection, Scharf-Gerstenberg, explores the work of surrealists and their precursors. The Bröhan-Museum is a gold mine of the applied arts, especially from the art nouveau period. ■

NOT TO BE MISSED:

Reminders of war's folly at Kaiser-Wilhelm-Gedächtniskirche   136

Eyeing the boutiques and swanky villas of the Ku'damm   138–139

Taking in the trappings of royalty at Schloss Charlottenburg   140–145

Art deco riches at the Bröhan-Museum   150

Newton's giant nudes at Museum für Fotografie   151

Honoring resistance heroes at Gedenkstätte Plötzensee   152

Kaiser-Wilhelm-Gedächtniskirche

A stranger destiny could not have befallen such a public building. Erected by a warlike emperor to the memory of his grandfather, the Kaiser-Wilhelm-Gedächtniskirche almost fell victim to the ravages of another war unleashed by the successors to the emperor's fallen empire. After coming within an ace of demolition, the shattered church, lit up at night, is an especially powerful sight and a symbol of modern Berlin.

Kaiser-Wilhelm-Gedächtniskirche

- 135 F2 & 139
- Breitscheidplatz
- 030 218 50 23
- Entrance hall closed Sun.
- U-Bahn & S-Bahn: Zoologischer Garten

The eerily lit ruins of the Kaiser-Wilhelm-Gedächtniskirche

Kaiser Wilhelm II ordered the neo-Romanesque church to be built in honor of his grandfather, Kaiser Wilhelm I. The central portion was rich in mosaics and stained glass; the memorial hall was decorated with reliefs depicting the history of the Hohenzollern dynasty. For all that, the church was not considered a monument of great importance in the pre–World War II cityscape of Berlin.

Allied bombs destroyed the church in 1943, leaving little more than the truncated bell tower. In the 1950s, plans to pull down these remnants, by then affectionately dubbed the "Rotten Tooth" by Berliners, called forth such an outcry that it was decided instead to create a memorial.

The exterior remains partly blackened and pockmarked, while parts of the interior mosaics in the entrance hall have been restored. They include a series showing the German emperors, including Wilhelm I and Wilhelm II (*guided tours in English 1:15, 2, & 3 p.m., $, www.gedaechtniskirche-berlin.de*).

In front of the entrance is a modern chapel. Just to the right as you enter is a charcoal drawing known as the Stalingrad Madonna. Dr. Kurt Reuber, chief field doctor with the German army trapped in Stalingrad in 1942–1943, drew it on the back of a Russian map and wrote: "Christmas 1942 in the Stalingrad Pocket. Light, Life, Love." Reuber died in a Siberian POW camp. ■

Käthe-Kollwitz-Museum

Housed in a late 19th-century home off the Ku'damm, this museum is the most complete collection of the works of one of Germany's finest expressionist artists. Käthe Kollwitz's art—mostly drawings, etchings, and woodcuts—always had an intensely socially conscious message.

Kollwitz depicted human suffering, such as that of the Silesian weavers in her 1897 lithographs.

Married to a doctor, Kollwitz lived most of her life in Prenzlauer Berg (on what is today Kollwitzstrasse). She first captured the public's attention with her series "Ein Weberaufstand" ("A Weavers' Revolt") in 1897.

The exhibition begins on the first floor. One room is dedicated to post–World War I antiwar posters and others appealing for aid for children and POWs. Kollwitz had been hit hard by the death of one of her sons, Peter, on the Western Front in 1914. This is reflected in a series of sketches depicting a woman pursued by Death.

The complete series of "Ein Weberaufstand" is on the second floor; the six pieces portray the abject misery in which cottage-industry weavers lived in late 19th-century Germany. Another series, "Bauernkrieg" ("Peasant War"), includes such chilling scenes as "Vergewaltigt" ("Raped"), showing a woman lying unconscious in a field. One room is dedicated to self-portraits from 1888 to 1938.

Death dominates the fourth floor, especially in its relationship with mothers. For instance, Death stretches out his hand to a mother with cowering children in "Frau Vertraut Sich dem Tod an" ("Woman Entrusts Herself to Death").

In 1936, the Nazis banned Kollwitz's art. She died on April 22, 1945, about two weeks before World War II ended. ∎

Käthe-Kollwitz-Museum

🅐 135 E2 & 139
✉ Fasanenstrasse 24
☎ 030 882 52 10
💲 $$
🚇 U-Bahn: Uhlandstrasse

www.kaethe-kollwitz.de

Strolling Around the Ku'damm

Long before Berlin was divided in two, the broad Kurfürstendamm exerted a magnetic charm with its boutiques and cafés. During the Cold War, the Ku'damm, as it is better known, became West Berlin's central artery. It suffered after reunification, as everyone's interest in the city shifted to the scarred but reunited center. Since the dawn of the new century, the Ku'damm has again taken its place in Berlin's sun.

Shoppers in Europe's biggest department store, KaDeWe, enjoy one of its gourmet bars.

NOT TO BE MISSED:

Käthe-Kollwitz-Museum
• The Story of Berlin • Museum
für Fotografie

When West Berlin was a separate city, all mainline trains terminated at **Bahnhof Zoologischer Garten ❶**. In the 1970s and 1980s, the station and its surroundings developed a grim reputation as a junkies' gathering point and prostitution strip. The station has been cleaned up since then, but its glory days are past, as most mainline trains pour into the new Hauptbahnhof to the northeast.

A phalanx of cheap porno-film joints still ekes out a living around the station, and it is hard to imagine a more appropriate spot for the **Beate Uhse Erotikmuseum ❷**, a few steps down Joachimstaler Strasse *(Joachimstaler Strasse 4, tel 030 886 06 66, $$)*. Created by Germany's late sex-shop queen, the collection of 5,000 sex-related objects and art spreads over two floors.

A brisk walk east along Kantstrasse takes you to the dramatic **Kaiser-Wilhelm-Gedächtniskirche ❸** (see p. 136). Past it stretches the busy Breitscheidplatz, dominated by the Europa-Center, a shopping and office center. About 1,150 feet (350 m) down Tauentzienstrasse on Wittenbergplatz is the **Kaufhaus des Westens ❹** (Department Store of the West), better known as KaDeWe and one of the world's great stores. It claims to be continental Europe's biggest such store, serving 40,000 to 50,000 customers a day. The fine foods department is also Europe's biggest.

Walk back to Breitscheidplatz, where Ku'damm begins, stretching west. Lined on either side by elegant (mostly restored) late 19th- and early 20th-century buildings, it is rich in international name stores.

A short way west of Breitscheidplatz, take a detour left down Fasanenstrasse to visit the **Käthe-Kollwitz-Museum ❺** (see p. 137).

Taking a left back on Ku'damm, you reach **The Story of Berlin ❻** *(Kurfürstendamm*

207–208, relocating in fall 2014, tel 030 88 72 01 00, www.story-of-berlin.de, $$$). This multimedia tour of eight centuries of Berlin history is not a bad introduction to the city, although a trifle cheesy. You can also tour the 1970s nuclear fallout shelter below ground: It can hold 3,600 people in cramped conditions for two weeks in case of nuclear assault. What they are supposed to do after that is anyone's guess.

Back on the surface, return to Kantstrasse via Knesebeckstrasse and elegant, restaurant-lined Savignyplatz. From Kantstrasse, a quick nip south down Fasanenstrasse is the **Jüdisches Gemeindehaus ❼** (Fasanenstrasse 79–80), the Jewish community center. It stands on the site of a synagogue damaged in the 1938 *Kristallnacht*, then again by Allied bombing, and finally demolished in 1958. A few remainders of the old facade have been erected in front of the modern building.

Back north on the corner of Kantstrasse is one of Berlin's peculiar new buildings,

Kantdreieck ❽. Holding offices of the city's gas company, Vattenfall, it is topped by what looks like a cross between a sail and an aircraft wing. Immediately opposite stands the wedding-cake facade of **Theater des Westens ❾** (Kantstrasse 12, tel 030 31 90 30), where tenor Enrico Caruso made his Berlin debut in 1905. It now hosts lavish musical productions. North up Fasanenstrasse, **Ludwig-Erhard-Haus ❿** (Fasanenstrasse 85) houses Berlin's stock exchange. Its mix of arches and straight glass lines won it the nickname "armadillo." On your way back to the train station, the **Museum für Fotografie ⓫** (see p. 151), on Jebensstrasse, is a worthwhile detour.

⓰	See also area map p. 135
▶	Bahnhof Zoo
⏱	3 miles (4.8 km)
⬌	2.5 hours
▶	Museum für Fotografie

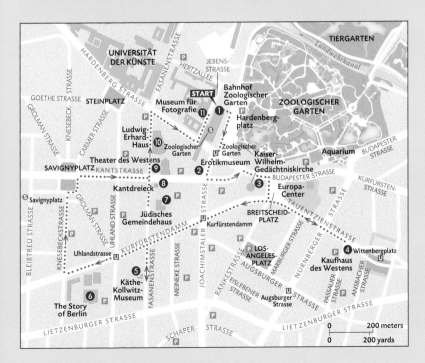

Schloss Charlottenburg

One of the most popular sights in Berlin, the Charlottenburg palace and its gardens could easily occupy a day of your time. If you want to see everything, get here in the morning, and try to avoid weekends and summer holidays as the crowds are enough to make you claustrophobic.

Schloss Charlottenburg was restored after World War II.

The original, sober baroque summer palace was built for Sophie Charlotte, second wife of Friedrich III, who would become Prussian king in 1701. It went up in 1695–99 under the direction of architect Johann Arnold Nering. Relatively close to the central Hohenzollern winter palace—the Berliner Schloss, now being reconstructed in Mitte—it was surrounded by thick woodland. The location on the Spree appealed to the Hohenzollerns, who liked nothing better than parading from residence to residence by river.

Sophie Charlotte turned the palace, which she dubbed Lietzenburg after the nearby hamlet of Lietzow, into an intellectual salon, surrounding herself with musicians, poets, and philosophers. Having crowned himself Prussia's King Friedrich I, the monarch wanted grander residences to match those of other European monarchs. The new court architect, Johann Friedrich Eosander von Göthe, set to work in 1702, lengthening the palace on either side and adding two south wings to create a grand courtyard. Then came the majestic dome atop the core of the palace and the western Orangerie, a low-slung addition that was supposed to be mirrored on the east side. Queen Sophie Charlotte did not live to see the work finished. After her death in

1705, the palace and the surrounding district became known as Charlottenburg.

Friedrich Wilhelm I's arrival on the throne in 1713 put an end to work on what he considered frivolous projects. Only when Friedrich II (Frederick the Great) replaced him in 1740 was the Neuer Flügel (New Wing) added in place of the eastern Orangerie that had been canceled by his father. Later would come the theater, the Neuer Pavillon (New Pavilion, a separate house at the east end), and the buildings erected in the gardens.

A good deal of the palace was destroyed in British Royal Air Force night-bombing raids in 1943. The decision to restore the palace was partly political. After the Berliner Schloss was demolished in East Berlin in 1950, the West Berlin administration decided to demonstrate its greater sensibility to German heritage by giving the nod to restoration (after having seriously considered demolition). Ironically, the palace was in the British occupation sector. The people who had bombed it to smithereens now encouraged its reconstruction.

Altes Schloss

Start a visit in the Altes Schloss (Old Palace), the original Nering-designed core, most of which can be seen only by a guided tour. You approach the domed palace building through the main courtyard, presided over by Andreas Schlüter's equestrian **statue of the Great Elector Friedrich Wilhelm** (completed in 1708). This originally stood

in the center of Berlin and was placed here after World War II.

Guided tours are given throughout the day, or you can take the self-guided audio tour (the English version is rather confusing, as the room numbers do not correspond to your LCD display). You pass a series of 19th-century royal apartments to reach the garden side of the palace and enter the queen's **Audience Chamber,** featuring a large portrait of Sophie Charlotte by Friedrich Wilhelm Weidemann.

A Statue's Odyssey

Located in the forecourt of Schloss Charlottenburg, the statue of Elector Friedrich Wilhelm I has an interesting backstory. During World War II, the imposing bronze figure was moved outside Berlin for safekeeping. In 1947, the barge holding it sank, and his royal highness spent two inglorious years on the bottom of the Tegeler See. The likeness was eventually recovered and returned in 1951.

On the right side of the room, you can peer into the **Old Gallery,** finished in carved oakwood and lined with portraits of the Prussian royal family—note how unflatteringly realistic many of them are. Now turn west to cross some of Sophie Charlotte's apartments (various items of furniture were saved from the Berliner Schloss) before entering the **Ovaler Saal**

Altes Schloss

- 🅰 134 C4
- ✉ Spandauer Damm 20–24
- ☎ 030 32 09 11
- 🕐 Closed Mon.
- 💲 $$$, incl. guided tour or audio guide
- 🚇 U-Bahn: Richard-Wagner-Platz; Bus: 109, M45, or 309

www.spsg.de

Neuer Flügel

- 🅰 134 C4
- ✉ Spandauer
  Damm 20–24
- ☎ 030 32 09 11
- 🕐 Closed Mon.
- 💲 $$, incl.
  audio guide
- 🚇 U-Bahn: Richard-
  Wagner-Platz;
  Bus: 109, M45,
  or 309

www.spsg.de

(Oval Hall), at the center of the palace beneath the dome, looking onto the garden.

The series of royal apartments continues. In the **Rote Tresenkammer** (Red Damask Room), the precious wall covering is braided with gold, while two emblems of the royal couple, the Prussian eagle and galloping Horse of the Guelphs, grace the wainscoting below. In the **study of Friedrich I,** depictions of the four seasons rim the ceiling fresco presided over, in the center, by Apollo and the constellations. Friedrich's adjacent **bedroom** features a "wind clock" that was originally linked to a weather vane on the roof.

INSIDER TIP:

Across the street from Schloss Charlottenburg, try quaint brew-pub Brauhaus Lemke [Luisenplatz 1] for a post-palace quaff.

—JUSTIN KAVANAGH
National Geographic international editions editor

In many restored rooms, only the stucco has been renewed in the ceilings and no frescoes painted. Frequently this is because none had ever been painted; in others, no hint remained as to what they had looked like.

You wind up in the gaudy **Porzellankabinett,** which contains a wall-to-wall display of some 2,700 pieces of porcelain of limited artistic, but great show-off, value. The purpose of the chamber was to provide an impressive talking point for visiting dignitaries. It is followed by the palace **chapel,** now used for concerts. The fittings include a raised oakwood pulpit, a quaint, fat-piped organ from 1706, and an immense gilded crown seeming to hover in midair, just opposite the royal box.

You may freely wander the second floor, formerly the apartments of King Friedrich Wilhelm IV and his family. Harder hit by the bombs, the floor has been rebuilt as exhibition space. The main attractions here are the **Kronprinzensilber** (Crown Prince's Silver) and the **Kronschatz.** The first is a dazzling collection of early 20th-century Prussian silverware presented to Crown Prince Wilhelm, son of Kaiser Wilhelm II, on his wedding day in 1904. The latter is a modest but intriguing collection of Hohenzollern crowns and Friedrich II's diamond-studded snuffboxes. In between lie several rooms of ornate porcelain made by the Königliche Porzellan-Manufaktur (KPM, Royal Porcelain Factory) and Saxony's Meissen.

Neuer Flügel

If you like, take some refreshment in the café-restaurant in the Kleine Orangerie nearby. Then it is time to tackle the Neuer Flügel *(closed until spring 2014).* Pick up the informative audio tour for this self-guided stroll. Climb the stairs and turn left into the **Weisser Saal** (White Room), a magnificent dining hall that Friedrich II rarely

EXPERIENCE: Berlin by Boat

Long before techno rang out from makeshift party rafts, Berlin had a special affinity for its waterways. In the 13th century, its wily margraves taxed shipments of merchants attempting to transit Mühlendamm in today's medieval quarter. The Hohenzollerns boated from palace to palace, and Frederick the Great—ever mindful of its commercial and military potential— expanded the canal network with great zest. The result is 100 miles (160 km) of navigable waterways and, as riverboat captains will happily tell you, more bridges than Venice.

During the Cold War, long stretches of Berlin's rivers, lakes, and canals were cut off in border zones and abandoned industrial estates along the Wall. In the years since reunification, these arteries have become pass-able again and beckon to be explored. Some of them usher you into surrounding networks of lakes and (eventually) the Baltic Sea and the Oder and Rhine Rivers.

A Spree River boat motors past Museum Island.

Captain of Your Destiny

If you prefer to skipper yourself, consider the first choice of smooching couples and Ray-Banned revelers at **Rent-a-Boat** (tel 0177 299 32 62, www.rent-a-boat .com), based near the Insel der Jugend (Isle of Youth) in Treptower Park. Unusually for Germany, without as much as a learner's license you can cruise past riverside forests to the Bay of Rum-melsburg in Friedrichshain, paddle among the swans and weeping willows on the Landwehrkanal, and dock for an impromptu refreshment at Club der Visionäre (see Travelwise p. 264). You can also venture farther out to the Müggelsee, the former playground of GDR elite at Köpenick (see pp. 170–171),

and admire the rowing clubs tearing up the Dahme River.

The west offers its own delights, as canoes, kayaks, and barges can laze along the Spree as it flows into the Havel River outside Charlot-tenburg. Here, a good rental option is **Der Bootsladen** (Brandsteinweg 37, tel 030 362 56 85, www.der-boots laden.de) in Spandau (see pp. 192–193), which provides maps and gear for excursions into the canals of Berlin's "Little Venice" and the watery wilds beyond.

Organized Tours

These XXL riverboats get to parts that little private craft don't reach, so it's

worth braving the crowds to get a unique view of the city's bridge-filled canals, architectural treasures, and monuments around Museum Island. Companies like **Ree-derei Riedel** (Planufer 78, tel 030 67 96 14 70, www.reeder eiriedel.de), **Reederei Bruno Winkler** (tel 030 349 95 95, www.reedereiwinkler.de), and **Exclusiv Yachtcharter & Schifffahrt** (Holsteiner Ufer 32, 030 43 66 68 36, www .exclusiv-yachtcharter.de) operate tours down the Spree and into its side canals, looping through Berlin's historic center. Most Berlin-ers do it once for themselves and reload on occasion for visiting relatives.

Neuer Pavillon

- 134 C4
- ✉ Spandauer Damm 20–24
- ☎ 030 32 09 11
- 🕐 Closed Mon.
- $ $
- 🚉 U-Bahn: Richard-Wagner-Platz; Bus: 109, M45, or 309

www.spsg.de

used. The still more impressive **Goldene Galerie** (Golden Gallery), a 138-foot-long (42 m) ballroom, follows. Its aquamarine walls and ceiling are liberally festooned with gold-painted floral stucco motifs. The king used the four modest rooms that follow as his private chambers. Among the paintings is "Einschiffung nach Cythera" ("Boarding for Cythera," 1718–1719) by Antoine Watteau (1684–1721).

You then return to the stairway and walk through the rooms that stretch to the west. The first six, among Friedrich II's private rooms on the south side, were renovated as winter quarters by King Friedrich Wilhelm II in late 18th-century neoclassicist style. He died before seeing them finished, and his daughter-in-law, Queen Luise (1776–1810), wife of King Friedrich Wilhelm III, moved in. In the sixth room is the bed she slept in. Destroyed in 1943, the rooms were restored in 1983–1995.

More of Friedrich's private rooms lie along the garden side. The most interesting is the **Bibliothek** (Library). Six original cedar cabinets contain a collection of the king's favorite reading (these books came mostly from Potsdam). The king liked to read in French rather than German and kept copies of the same books in all his residences so that he could consult them wherever he was.

Downstairs, you enter a vestibule with a model and photos of the Berliner Schloss, the former principal royal palace in central Berlin. The bulk of the remaining rooms constituted the apartments of King Friedrich Wilhelm III. Worth seeing in **Room 317,** an antechamber, is Jacques-Louis David's (1748–1825) stirring portrait of Napoleon as first consul leading the French army across the St. Bernard Pass from Switzerland into Italy in 1798. It was brought to Berlin from Paris as war booty after Napoleon's defeat at Waterloo in 1815.

Neuer Pavillon

Just beyond the Neuer Flügel stands the Italian-style Neuer Pavillon, built as a separate summer house by Karl Friedrich Schinkel in 1824–1825 for King Friedrich Wilhelm III and his morganatic wife, Auguste, Princess of Liegnitz and Countess of Hohenzollern. It was rebuilt in 1970 as it appeared originally.

The building has been filled with period furniture and a modest collection of art, porcelain, and other objects. A strikingly long settee in the **Garden Saloon** afforded a splendid view of the Schloss. In the

In winter, the Schloss Charlottenburg pond becomes a perfect location for ice-skating.

upstairs study and various other rooms, you can see images of Berlin and landscapes, in particular by Eduard Gärtner. His 1839 panorama of the Kremlin in Moscow is a highlight. A large part of this floor is given over to works by Schinkel and 19th-century contemporaries such as Carl Blechen, whose romantic-realistic style recalls that of Caspar David Friedrich.

Back outside, a walk west past the Neuer Flügel and Altes Schloss leads to the slender west wing of the palace. This is the **Orangerie,** now used for classical concerts played by musicians in 18th-century dress. It is capped by the theater added to the building by Carl Gotthard Langhans (1732–1808), designer of the Brandenburger Tor, in 1788–1791. Used for storage from 1902, most of its original decoration, art, and furnishings were lost.

Schlossgarten

The Schlossgarten Charlottenburg is a mixed garden reflecting different periods of the palace's history. An imitation of the French royal Palace of Versailles, the garden was originally a rigidly geometrical affair. In the 19th century, it was completely reworked in the English style, which sought to replicate the randomness of nature. Peter Joseph Lenné (1789–1866), Berlin's top landscape architect, was behind this change. Having been used as a potato field in the immediate postwar years, it is today a compromise: The part behind the Altes Schloss follows the French model, while most of

the rest is primarily in the English manner. A couple of buildings lurk amid its greenery. Not far from the Karpfenteich (Carp Pond), the neoclassical **Mausoleum** *(closed Nov.–March & Mon. April–Oct.)* was built in 1810 to house the tomb of Queen Luise. It was later expanded for her husband, King Friedrich Wilhelm III, and, much later, Kaiser Wilhelm I and his second

INSIDER TIP:

Reach the baroque gardens of Schloss Charlottenburg by riding a rented bike from the Reichstag along Spree River pathways.

—KEVIN COTE
Producer, Deutsche Welle TV

wife, Augusta. Sitting alone in the garden's northern reaches is the **Belvedere** *(closed Mon., $)*, a dainty three-story tower conceived as a teahouse in 1788 by Langhans. Rebuilt after World War II, it houses a collection of Berlin porcelain.

Porcelain manufacture—mainly by two producers, the Wegely and Gotzkowsky houses—began in Berlin in 1751. From 1763, all production was brought together under KPM. The ground floor is mainly given over to decorative porcelain (wall fittings, vases, and statuettes), the second floor to dinner service sets, and the third floor to delicate tea sets. ∎

Berlin's Brightest Christmas Lights

For some, the onset of the northern winter is like a long icy ride down a dark tunnel until the following spring. In Berlin, there's no need for that sort of gloom. The German tradition of the *Weihnachtsmarkt* (Christmas market) fills the city with concentrated cheer. Across Berlin, better and lesser known markets set up in the squares, some with amusement park attractions, others with stands selling plenty of Christmas gifts.

Berlin prides itself on its Christmas street decorations, such as these lights along Tauentzienstrasse.

All the fairs are laden with traditional food and drink offerings. Standard traditional elements include sausages, *Glühwein* (mulled wine), *Zuckerwatte* (cotton candy), and *kandierte Äpfel* (candied apples).

The action usually starts around November 23; most markets finish a few days before Christmas Day. Although most Christmas markets open up around 11 a.m. and continue until about 9 or 10 p.m., they are at their most atmospheric when lit up at night (which means beginning around 4:30 p.m., when it is already pitch dark).

As many as 60 markets set up across Berlin. Some of the tried-and -true remain the best. Easily the best known and biggest Weihnachtsmarkt in Berlin is held in the old town of Spandau in the northwest suburbs. It is worth the trip. The village setting lends it more of a cozy feel than some of the big city center markets. More than 250 stands open, and gourmands can cruise the international food and drink specialty stands. Brass bands perform on most nights; on Fridays, there are Christmas concerts. In addition to Glühwein, you'll definitely find *Feuerzangenbowle*, a red-wine-and-rum punch with kick.

Those with kids may head for Alexanderplatz in Mitte, where a giant Ferris wheel and other amusement park rides are set to get you screaming for dear life. After some of these, a Glühwein is definitely in order. Central and popular with families, Alexanderplatz tends to get crowded at night.

Another of the big markets takes place over on the west side of town at Breitscheidplatz by the Ku'damm. Rides are usually limited to a few merry-go-rounds for young children. The place is jammed with stands selling all sorts of (mostly useless) trinkets. Even so,

EXPERIENCE:
Festival of Lights

Since its debut in 2004, Berlin's Festival of Lights *(Oct., 7 p.m.–midnight, http:// festival-of-lights.de for dates)* has rivaled the popularity of the city's Christmas markets, drawing more than 600,000 Berliners and visitors every October. During two weeks of (hopefully) crisp autumn evenings, around 70 landmarks such as the Fernsehturm, Gendarmenmarkt, and Siegessäule are transformed into parchments for elaborately staged illuminations, fireworks, and videos. They get more sophisticated every year: In 2012, the Brandenburger Tor hosted projections of a weirdly convincing *Plattenbau* (GDR-era concrete prefab), while the U.S. Embassy melted into waterfalls and the Golden Gate Bridge. Visitors can take "lightseeing" buses from site to site.

INSIDER TIP:

The Yuletide window displays at the KaDeWe department store [see p. 138] on Wittenbergplatz are as elaborate as those of Macy's in New York or London's Harrods.

—CAROLINE HICKEY
National Geographic travel books editor

the atmosphere is fun, although again it can become very crowded.

Perhaps the classiest of the city's Christmas markets is the one held at Gendarmenmarkt. The setting is the prettiest in central Berlin. There are no rides, but lots of attractive stands sell all manner of goods, from crafts to gourmet food. The entry fee *($)* and relatively high prices for your Glühwein help to keep crowds down to manageable levels.

Similarly genteel is the market that fills the passages behind the Opernpalais off Unter den Linden. One of the most intimate venues is the Kulturbrauerei, devoted to Scandinavian arts and crafts in the courtyards of a 19th-century brewery in Prenzlauer Berg. After browsing, you can huddle around the bonfire sipping grog or warm yourself by slipping into a heated reindeer-skin coat.

Less atmospheric than the Kulturbrauerei is the Potsdamer Platz market, but it does set up an artificial snow slope so that you can try out your sledding technique with a toboggan or inflated inner tube. The market also has a free ice-skating rink.

For more information on the present year's markets in Berlin and elsewhere, take a look at *www.weihnachteninberlin.de.*

Berlin's cheer is not limited to its markets; the streets light up for Christmas, too. The best are along and around the Ku'damm. Close behind come those on Friedrichstrasse and Unter den Linden.

Museum Berggruen &
Sammlung Scharf-Gerstenberg

Beneath a circular core culminating in a dome, the Berggruen collection (named after collector Heinz Berggruen, 1914–2007) is devoted to four giants of 20th-century art: Pablo Picasso, Henri Matisse (1869–1954), Paul Klee, and Alberto Giacometti. The biggest part of the collection is dedicated to Picasso, with more than 80 of his works. Paired with the museum is the Sammlung (Collection) Scharf-Gerstenberg across the street, focusing on surrealists.

Alberto Giacometti's lithe figures adorn several rooms of the Museum Berggruen.

Museum Berggruen

 134 C4

 Schlossstrasse 1

 030 326 95 80

 Closed Mon.

💲 $$

🚇 U-Bahn: Sophie-Charlotte-Platz or Richard-Wagner-Platz
Bus: M45, 109, or 309

www.smb.museum

Center stage beneath the Berggruen's dome is occupied by a typically spindly Giacometti bronze, "Stehende Frau" ("Standing Woman"). The first two rooms are filled with an eclectic collection of works by Matisse, from an early portrait of Lorette, done in 1917, to some of his later, more abstract pieces, including "Die Seil-springerin" ("Woman Skipping Rope"), a 1952 blue-on-white work in strips of gouache.

Matisse gives way to early Picasso in the third room. Works include a page from a sketchpad in which he practiced quick drawings, such as a pensive one of his art-teacher father. In the same rooms are portraits from his so-called blue and pink periods of the early 1900s. The second floor is devoted mostly to Picasso's works from the cubist period through to his sketches of female nudes in the 1960s and 1970s. There are a couple of works by his cubist contemporary, Georges Braque (1882–1963).

On the top floor, Klee's art, interspersed with some of

Giacometti's bronzes, takes a different tack. Klee's work ranges from elegant, geometrical pieces to satirical sketches, such as "Der Grosse Kaiser Reitet in den Krieg" ("The Great Kaiser Rides Off to War," 1920). In 2013, an extension opened in an old Prussian officers' club next door, providing space for another 50 works.

Sammlung Scharf-Gerstenberg

Museum Berggruen is entwined with another collection across the street: The quirky Sammlung Scharf-Gerstenberg, dedicated to surrealists and their forerunners. Surrealism was as "beautiful as the chance meeting on a dissecting table of a sewing machine and an umbrella," quipped Andre Bréton, who founded the surrealist movement in Paris in 1924.

The idea obviously appealed to Otto Gerstenberg (1848–1935), one of Berlin's greatest art collectors. The insurance magnate kept a villa in Grunewald where he stored the works he picked up from Paris dealers. His grandson, Dieter Scharf, is now the curator. Before the collection opened in 2008, few pieces were ever displayed in public.

The permanent exhibition, "Surreal Worlds," absorbs three floors of the neoclassical **Stülerbau,** its intimate rooms radiating from a central staircase with soaring cupola. Prime time is given to surrealist René Magritte (1898–1967), dada pioneer Max Ernst (1891–1976), and the multi-talented Klee.

The strength of this exhibition lies not in its star power, but in the bizarre nature of its material. Highlights include dungeon architecture by Italian artist Giovanni Battista Piranesi (1720–1778), ghoulish etchings by Spain's Francisco Goya (1746–1828), and ethereal canvases by French symbolist Odilon Redon (1840–1916). The annex, a former stable, comes as a surprise behind the modern extension. You pass through the Gate of Kalabsha, covered with

INSIDER TIP:

A *Bereichskarte* (area ticket) bought at Museum Berggruen, Sammlung Scharf-Gerstenberg, or Museum für Fotografie entitles you to same-day entry to all three museums.

—JEREMY GRAY
National Geographic author

hieroglyphs from 30 B.C., to a separate hall of paintings and sculptures. Here, oddities abound such as Magritte's "Gaspard de la Nuit" ("Gaspard the Somnabulist," 1965) showing a hawk contemplating a burning ruin.

The onetime Sahurê Temple annex has been converted into a movie theater, showing surrealist classics throughout the day, such as *Un Chien Andalou (An Andalusian Dog)* by Salvador Dalí and Luis Buñuel (1900–1983). ∎

Sammlung Scharf-Gerstenberg

🅰 134 C4
✉ Schlossstrasse 70
☎ 030 266 42 42 42
💲 $$
🚇 U-Bahn: Sophie-Charlotte-Platz or Richard-Wagner-Platz Bus: M45, 109, or 309

www.smb.museum

Bröhan-Museum

After decades of neglect, the whimsical style of decorative arts known as art nouveau is again attracting attention in Europe. Known in Germany as *Jugendstil* (youth style), it swept Europe in art, architecture, and design in a wave of youthful creativity in the first decades of the 20th century. This period, along with the later movements of art deco and functionalism, is the subject of this original museum.

Bröhan-Museum
- 134 C4
- Schlossstrasse 1a
- 030 32 69 06 00
- Closed Mon.
- $$
- U-Bahn: Richard-Wagner-Platz; Bus: 109, M45, or 309

www.broehan -museum.de

The first floor holds a collection of glassware and vases produced in the French city of Nancy, a leader in the art nouveau movement. A room is dedicated to porcelain and cutlery by Hamburg-born Peter Behrens (1868–1940), who was better known for his architecture. His was a sober, geometrical approach to design, with clean lines, gentle curves, and restrained decorative motifs.

Equally striking is the **dining room** furnished by Eugène Gaillard (1862–1933). The designs were originally done around 1900 for the Galeries de l'Art Nouveau in Paris, run by art dealer Siegfried Bing (1838–1905). Some consider Bing to be the father of art nouveau, his term for a fresh new style influenced heavily by Japanese art and natural forms. Their expression could not be clearer than in the furniture of Hector Guimard (1867–1942). His buffet cabinet is a unique piece. Above the main cabinet, a smaller cabinet is raised as if on exposed tree roots.

Most of the museum's art collection is displayed on the third floor. The paintings, drawings, and pastels gathered here include works by Berlin turn-of-the-20th-century Secession artists like Karl Hagemeister (1848–1933) and Hans Baluschek (1870–1935).

On the top floor, one room is devoted to the Belgian exponent of art nouveau Henry van de Velde (1863–1957). In 1895, van de Velde designed a house, the Bloemenwerf, outside Brussels for himself and his wife. A striking example of his artistic style is a lamp whose arms dangle like tropical branches. ■

Art nouveau treasures of the Bröhan-Museum range from designer furniture of the period to lovingly crafted vases.

Museum für Fotografie

A man obsessed with photography and women, fashion photographer Helmut Newton (1920–2004) was born in Berlin and picked up his first camera at the age of 12. Forced into exile as a Jew in 1938, he lived abroad most of his life. In 2003, he gave this gallery of his work to the city that turned its back on him. It shares its premises with the extensive photography collection of the Kunstbibliothek (Art Library).

The female form in various states of undress dominates Helmut Newton's photography.

The Newton collections span two floors. "Private Property," the exposition on the first floor, is the most personal, with pictures from Newton's young Berlin years and his later years in Australia.

His wife, June Newton, is also an accomplished photographer who uses the name Alice Springs. You can view a series of her shots of him as well as some fascinating video footage of Newton on shoots with the likes of Pierre Cardin and Vanessa Redgrave.

Photos from his books and magazine articles appear, along with an extensive series of posters for his many exhibitions.

A separate theme, entitled "A Gun for Hire," leads you through a selection of his most stunning fashion photography, produced for names like Chanel, Yves Saint Laurent, and Versace. Some of his more erotic photography is also on display, along with landscapes.

On the top floor, temporary exhibitions are held in the newly restored Kaisersaal. Historical images from the Kunstbibliothek archives, some going back to the early days of photography, can be viewed in the art library on request. ■

Museum für Fotografie

🅰 135 E3 & 139

✉ Jebensstrasse 2

☎ 030 266 42 42 42

🕐 Closed Mon.

💲 $$

🚇 U-Bahn & S-Bahn: Zoologischer Garten

www.smb.museum

Gedenkstätte Plötzensee

On August 8, 1944, a group of 89 people who were condemned to death in connection with the July plot to assassinate the Führer (see sidebar p. 132) were killed in Plötzensee: Eight were hanged on butcher's hooks in Hitler's perverted justice system. Hitler had their final agony filmed in this prison, north of central Berlin.

Policemen lead Peter Graf Yorck von Wartenburg, one of the 1944 conspirators, to court. He died at Plötzensee.

Gedenkstätte Plötzensee

🗺 134 C6
✉ Hüttigpfad
🚌 Bus: TXL

www.gedenkstaette-ploetzensee.de

Today, the Nazi-era victims held in the prison are remembered in the former execution chamber, now the Plötzensee Memorial Center.

Prisoners on death row were held in Haus III, most of which was destroyed in World War II. Part of the shed survived, however, and has been turned into a **memorial** to the sufferers of Nazi rough justice. Around it, a modern prison still operates today, but the ruins of Haus III were torn down.

The prison, which Berliners soon dubbed "the Plötz," opened its doors to inmates in 1879. It was built under Kaiser Wilhelm I with a view to holding large numbers of rebels (its capacity was around 1,200) should Berliners ever rise against the government and kaiser. In the end, it was used mainly for common criminals.

From 1890 to 1932, almost 40 inmates were executed by beheading. In the 12 years of Nazi dictatorship, 2,891 people met their end in Plötzensee. Most were political prisoners who in some cases had spent months here being interrogated under torture before they were convicted in rigged trials. At first, prisoners were beheaded by the executioner's axe, but Hitler ordered a switch to the guillotine in 1936.

Prisoners condemned to death in cells in Haus III would spend their last hours in special cells on the first floor, known to inmates as the *Totenhaus* (house of the dead). What you see today is a simple **execution room,** with five butcher's hooks hanging from a steel beam. Instead of being beheaded, many prisoners convicted of treason, including the July 1944 conspirators, were hanged from these hooks. Today you will probably find fresh wreaths there dedicated to the memory of the dead.

Next door, the story of the prison is told in a series of panels. Finally, you can check the names of the executed on a computer. ∎

More Places to Visit in Charlottenburg

Abguss-Sammlung Antiker Plastik Berlin

This curious collection of plaster casts of ancient statuary is aimed at students and professors, but grabs quite a few passing visitors, too. Copies of statues and reliefs dating back as far as the third millennium B.C. and reaching about A.D. 500 form the bulk of the display. The focus is on Greek, Roman, and, to a lesser extent, Byzantine work. The place looks like a frenetic sculptor's workshop. Shelves are lined with plaster heads, cabinets are stuffed with figurines, and phalanxes of classical statues in all manner of poses seem to have a problem with breaking ranks. In this one higgledy-piggledy spot, you can dive into (copies of) treasures of antiquity held in museums around the world, including Athens, Rome, London, Paris, and Vienna. In all, about 2,000 items are on show. Among them are a gold-painted statue of a discus thrower by Myron (ca 450 B.C.), one of the greatest sculptors of classical Greece. The "Apoll vom Belvedere" ("Belvedere Apollo") is a particularly gracious statue of the god. The original was unearthed in the 15th century and was itself a Roman copy of a Greek bronze originally in Athens's Temple of Apollo. Oversize pieces dominate in the rear display room, notably the massive Farnese Bull of Hellenic myth. The 13-foot (4 m) statue shows Dirce, the first wife of Theban king Lykos, being tied to a steer as punishment for her cruelty to her niece Antiope, who gave birth to twins fathered by Zeus. The original in Rome is the largest sculpture ever recovered from antiquity. The pieces are cast not here but at the nearby Gipsformerei (Museum Replica Workshop; *Sophie-Charlotten-Strasse 17–18, tel 030 321 70 11, $*), whose shop bristles with busts and jewelry. German-language tours of the workshop and archives are given on the first and third Wednesday of the month. *www.abguss-sammlung-berlin.de* 🅼 Map p. 134 C4 ✉ Schlossstrasse 69b ☎ 030 342 40 54 🕐 Closed Mon.–Wed. 🚇 U-Bahn: Richard-Wagner-Platz; Bus: 309 or M45

Ahmadiyya-Moschee

A wholly unexpected sight in leafy, suburban southwest Berlin is this grand mosque, built in 1924–1928 in Indian Mogul style by German architect K.A. Hermann for the Ahmadiyya Anjuman religious association, founded in the 19th century to propagate the Muslim faith. The bright white mosque is surmounted by a series of slender towers, parapets, and a bulbous metallic dome topped by the crescent of Islam. It is the oldest mosque in Germany and, like so much of the city, nearly met its end in the dying days of World War II. Used by German soldiers as a machine-gun post to snipe at advancing Russian soldiers, much of the building was destroyed. It was partly restored by the British and Indian military after the war and since 1993 has been cataloged as a monument. Both minarets have been rebuilt and the mosque serves as a local information center. It is generally open from around 1 p.m. for Friday prayers. *http://berlin.ahmadiyya.org* 🅼 Map p. 135 E1 ✉ Brienner Strasse 7–8 ☎ 030 873 57 03 🚇 U-Bahn: Fehrbelliner Platz

The Currywurst Story

On the afternoon of September 4, 1949, 36-year-old Herta Heuwer grew bored waiting for customers at her Charlottenburg sausage stand and began to mess around with toppings. She mixed tomato sauce, chili, curry powder, Worcester sauce, and other ingredients, poured the concoction over a sliced, skinless sausage, and voilà—the Currywurst was born. Heuwer's secret "Chillup" sauce was patented in 1959. Look for the memorial plaque at Kantstrasse 101.

Ahmadiyya-Moschee, the oldest mosque in Germany

Camera Work

A magazine started by photographer Alfred Stieglitz (1864–1946) inspired this Bauhaus-flavored gallery that resembles a fire station. Past exhibitions read like a who's who of photography, including Man Ray (1890–1976), Irving Penn (1917–2009), Diane Arbus (1923–1971), and Berlin native Helmut Newton. Photographers sign books and chat with visitors on opening nights. The gallery, which is half-hidden in a quiet rear courtyard, also serves as a launch pad for artists on their way up: Martin Schoeller (1968–), Jean-Baptiste Huynh (1966–), and Robert Polidori (1951–) all made their German debuts at Camera Work.

www.camerawork.de 🅰 Map p. 135 E2 ✉ Kantstrasse 149 🕐 Closed Sun.–Mon. 🚆 S-Bahn: Savignyplatz

Museum Charlottenburg-Wilmersdorf

Something of a hidden gem, this local history and art museum is lodged in a comely neo-Renaissance villa that once belonged to the Mendelssohns and the Oppenheims, leading Jewish families in Charlottenburg society. On the ground floor is a modest permanent exhibition of historical objects, letters, and photos, while the adjacent room has changing displays on prominent residents like Josef Block, a painter of the Berlin Secession movement. The real draw is upstairs—around 50 paintings, sketches, and sculptures from Charlottenburg's vast art archives, displayed in spacious modern quarters. The emphasis is on the 19th century and Berlin Secessionists. Many works have a local flavor, including "Badende Jungen" ("Boys Bathing") in the Havel River, by Impressionist Philipp Franck (1860–1944) and "Zur Grube" ("To the Mine") by Hans Baluschek (1870–1935), showing lamp-bearing laborers.

www.villa-oppenheim-berlin.de 🅰 Map p. 134 C4 ✉ Schlossstrasse 55 ☎ 030 902 91 32 01 🕐 Closed Mon. 🚆 U-Bahn: Richard-Wagner-Platz; Bus: 309 or 109

Rathaus Charlottenburg

With its 287-foot (87.5 m) tower and mix of Gothic and art nouveau ornament, this imperious building seems oversize for a seat of local government. When it was opened in 1905, Charlottenburg was still a separate and proud city. Designed by local architects Heinrich Reinhardt (1868–1947) and Georg Süssenguth (1862–1947) and expanded in 1911–1916, the building was mostly destroyed in World War II. It was then patiently rebuilt by 1958. The colossal statuary on the facade represents trade guilds and various allegories. Through the wrought-iron main doors is a majestic stairway that leads you into the labyrinth inside.

🅰 Map p. 134 D4 ✉ Otto-Suhr-Allee 96–102 🕐 Closed Sat.–Sun. 🚆 U-Bahn: Richard-Wagner-Platz

The districts of what was East Berlin, from café-crammed Prenzlauer Berg to Köpenick's country palace

Prenzlauer Berg, Friedrichshain, & the East

Introduction & Map   156–157

Walk: A Prenzlauer Promenade   158–159

Volkspark Friedrichshain   160

Experience: A Moveable Fete   160

Lichtenberg   161–163

Feature: Berlin Design   164

Pankow & Weissensee   165

Experience: Berlin's Fascinating
   Underworld   166

East Side Gallery   167

Treptower Park   168

Karlshorst   169

Köpenick   170–171

Grosser Müggelsee & Grünau   172

More Places to Visit in Prenzlauer Berg,
   Friedrichshain, & the East   173–174

Hotels & Restaurants   249–252

Painter Thierry Noir stands in front of his artwork at the Berlin Wall.

Prenzlauer Berg, Friedrichs-hain, & the East

Berlin's East has become a fascinating mix since the days of the German Democratic Republic. Prenzlauer Berg, once a relatively poor district, has become gentrified and hip. Friedrichshain to the south is winning a name for itself with a busy nightlife scene. Farther out, quiet, working-class suburbs hide keys to the city's rough-and-tumble 20th century.

Little more than countryside until the mid-19th century, Prenzlauer Berg became a densely populated working-class district by the 20th century. Neglected and crumbling in GDR days, it has been renovated, prices have soared, and a young population of go-ahead folk has moved in. Catering to their needs, especially around Kastanienallee and

Kollwitzplatz, is a spectrum of restaurants, bars, and shops. One of Berlin's biggest synagogues managed to survive here, a couple of 19th-century breweries have been imaginatively recycled, and the area is one of the best preserved in the city.

Nearby Friedrichshain is bisected by a curious experiment in 1950s Soviet-style town planning and architecture, the somehow captivating Karl-Marx-Allee. Nearby Boxhagener Platz has become a focal point of nightlife for the many students and other restless young people who bailed out of Prenzlauer Berg.

Each of the outermost districts has one or two rough-edged gems: a neglected palace in Pankow, a GDR prison in the high-rise housing districts of Hohenschönhausen and Lichtenberg, or a curious war museum among the pleasant villas of Karlshorst. Close by, the sprawling Tierpark Berlin happens to be Europe's largest zoo. To the southeast, the giant Sowjetisches Ehrenmal in Treptower Park is a study in Stalinist pomp, while peaceful Köpenick beckons with a restored Hohenzollern palace and a bucolic string of lakes. ∎

NOT TO BE MISSED:

Exploring the hipster hub of Prenzlauer Berg   158–159

Pretty ponds and political relics in Volkspark Friedrichshain   160

Looking behind the scenes at the Stasi's onetime command center   161–162

Visiting Europe's largest Jewish cemetery at Weissensee   165

The enormous Sowjetisches Ehrenmal in Treptower Park   168

The fascinating German-Russian Museum in Karlshorst   169

Köpenick's majestic town hall and its clever "captain"   170–171

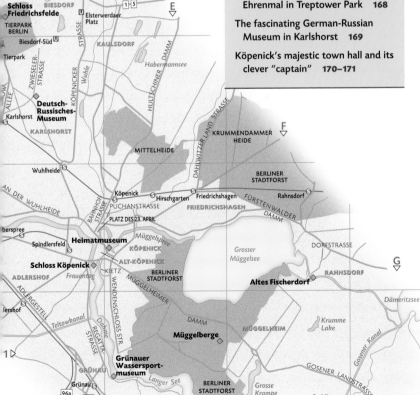

A Prenzlauer Promenade

More than many other of Berlin's inner suburbs, Prenzlauer Berg oozes atmosphere and invites a gentle stroll. There are few major sights, but you can visit several lesser sources of curiosity and find plenty of opportunities for refreshment along the way.

Visitors find plenty of charming stores and cafés in Prenzlauer Berg.

Start at the Rosenthaler Platz U-Bahn station, through which the city's defensive wall once ran. A slightly uphill stroll along Weinbergs-weg (Vineyard Way) takes you past the Volkspark am Weinbergsweg, which was a vineyard in the 18th century. Turn left on Fehrbelliner Strasse and then right to tower-ing **Zionskirche** ❶ on the square of the same name.

The grand brick church was built under Kaiser Wilhelm I and opened in 1873. Designed by August Orth (1828–1901) in a mix of neo-Romanesque and neo-Gothic styles, it stands with a 220-foot (67 m) tower on central Berlin's highest natural point. Evangelical theologian Dietrich Bonhoeffer (1906–1945) was once Zionskirche's parish priest. This opponent of the Nazis, who was active in the underground from 1940 on, was arrested in 1943 and died in Flos-senbürg concentration camp in April 1945.

NOT TO BE MISSED:

Zionskirche • Kulturbrauerei
• Synagoge Rykestrasse
• Museum Pankow

Zionskirchstrasse leads east past pleasant Teutoburger Platz to Christinenstrasse and the back of the onetime **Pfefferberg brewery** ❷, whose tenants include art galleries, a youth hostel, and a cowboy-style nightclub. A walk around its north flank leads to Schönhauser Allee, north of which lies the historic, leafy **Jüdischer Friedhof** ❸. Established in 1827, this Jewish cemetery was in use until 1976 and holds the remains of composer Giacomo Meyerbeer and painter Max Liebermann. Across Schön-hauser Allee stands the redbrick neo-Gothic

Segenskirche ④, a 1908 church with a northern Italian flavor. A short walk farther north on Schönhauser Allee brings you to the massive **Kulturbrauerei ⑤**. Built in 1889, this dazzling complex of 20 red-and-yellow brick buildings, once a brewery, is an entertainment center, with clubs, bars, a cinema, a theater, and stores. One of the city's great beer gardens, the **Prater ⑥**, is around the corner on Kastanienallee.

Walk east along Danziger Strasse and then south (right) down Husemannstrasse, lined with shops, restaurants, and bars. Husemannstrasse leads into charming **Kollwitzplatz ⑦**, named after artist Käthe Kollwitz (who lived nearby on what is now the elegant, cobbled Kollwitzstrasse), the scene of a bustling Saturday market.

A block east on Knaackstrasse stands the

Synagoge Rykestrasse ⑧, one of only two to survive Nazi savagery and war damage. Straight ahead in the small green park on the right rises what locals refer to as Dicker Hermann (Fat Hermann), a former **Wasserturm ⑨**, or water tower, that Hitler's SA turned into a prison for Jews. It is now a highly original apartment block.

Around the corner, on Prenzlauer Allee, you can learn a little more about local history in the **Museum Pankow ⑩** *(Prenzlauer Allee 227–228, tel 030 902 95 39 17, closed Sat.–Sun.).*

Ⓜ See also area map p. 156
▶ Rosenthaler Platz
🕐 1.5 hours
↔ 2.4 miles (3.8 km)
▶ Museum Pankow

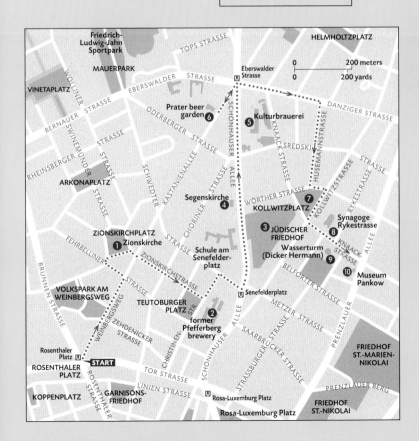

Volkspark Friedrichshain

Central Berlin's prettiest park after the Tiergarten, and one of the city's more interesting green spaces, the Friedrichshain People's Park straddles the municipal frontier between hip Prenzlauer Berg and frumpier, working-class Friedrichshain. It is filled with historic symbolism, although for locals it is simply a lovely spot for a Sunday stroll or jog.

Volkspark Friedrichshain

🗺 156 B4

🚉 S-Bahn: Landsberger Allee

Located less than a mile from Alexanderplatz, the park owes its form to World War II. It was Berlin's first communal park, laid out in the late 19th century to give a little relief to the local working-class masses. During World War II, air-raid shelters were built here. After 1945, creative builders used the masses of rubble left over from air raids to create two hills over the shelters. The result was the 256-foot-high (78 m) **Grosser Bunkerberg** (Big Bunker Hill) in the heart of the park and the smaller 157-foot (48 m) **Kleiner Bunkerberg** (Little Bunker Hill) to the east. Between them lies a pleasant lake. One thing that remained unchanged after 1945 was the 1913 **Märchenbrunnen** (Fairytale Fountain), fronted by a gracious colonnade, in the park's northwestern corner.

Memorials to violent events abound. The **Friedhof der Märzgefallenen,** the original burial place of 183 Berliners killed by royal troops in the March 1848 uprisings, lies at the southern end of the park (*off Landsberger Allee*). Few gravestones remain; the cemetery is now also a memorial to rebels killed in a mutiny that accelerated Germany's capitulation in 1918.

Only 18 years later, civil war broke out in Spain and some Germans volunteered to join the International Brigades that aided the left-wing government forces. A monument to them stands on the western Friedenstrasse side of the park.

At the east end of the park is another memorial—this time to Polish soldiers and resistance fighters of World War II as well as to members of the German resistance. The monument was raised in 1972 in an act of socialist brotherhood between the Warsaw Pact allies. ∎

EXPERIENCE:
A Moveable Fete

All dressed up and no place to go? Catch the **M10,** Berlin's party tram connecting the Eberswalder Strasse U-Bahn station with the ground zero of the city's nonstop revelers, Warschauer Strasse in Friedrichshain. Notice how virtually every passenger is holding an open bottle of beer? No one bats an eyelid, not even the police—public quaffing is legal provided you behave yourself. Along the 5-mile (8 km) route are dozens of clubs beckoning to be torn apart, and if you're worrying about missing the last metro back, relax. From Friday to Sunday, Berlin's U- and S-Bahns run all night at 15- to 20-minute intervals. Plan your journey on Berlin's public transit network online at *www.bvg.de.*

Lichtenberg

A visit to and around the eastern suburbs of Lichtenberg is a voyage into the dark side of Berlin's more recent past. Here stand the former Ministerium für Staatssicherheit (Ministry for State Security, or Stasi for short) and the former Stasi prison of Hohenschönhausen. Many of the German Left's greatest historical figures (along with a swath of less reputable GDR chiefs) lie buried in the nearby Friedrichsfelde cemetery. For a little relief, make for Berlin's second zoo.

View the workings of East Germany's security apparatus at the Gedenkstätte Normannenstrasse.

Housed in the anonymous, sprawling complex that was the Stasi ministry is the **Gedenkstätte Normannenstrasse,** also known as the Stasi Museum. Many of the buildings here today have other tenants, above all the Deutsche Bahn (German Railways). The onetime nerve center of the ministry now hosts a documentation center and permanent exhibition on the ministry's misdeeds.

Head for **Haus 1.** In the foyer stands a model of the typical vehicle used to transport Stasi prisoners. It is a harmless-looking thing with five tiny, windowless and airless cells. The first floor of the building is given over to displays on bugging devices and other elements of the surveillance trade. The bugs are curious, but more so are the assorted hidden cameras. Everything from tree trunks to cigarette cases and from watering cans to handbags could be used.

On the next floor are the central offices of Erich Mielke, state security minister from 1957 to 1989 (see sidebar p. 163), and his staff. The austere offices have been left as they were. Labeling is

Gedenkstätte Normannenstrasse

🅰 156 C4
✉ Ruschestrasse 103
☎ 030 553 68 54
💲 $$
Ⓜ U-Bahn: Magdalenenstrasse

www.stasi-museum.de

Zentralfriedhof Friedrichsfelde

🅐 156 C4
✉ Gudrunstrasse
🚈 S-Bahn: Friedrichsfelde-Ost

Gedenkstätte Berlin Hohen-schönhausen

🅐 156 C5
✉ Genslerstrasse 66
☎ 030 98 60 82 30
🕐 Guided tours in English 2:30 p.m.
💲 $$, free Wed.

in German and (mostly) English. Some of the boss's personal effects are on display, including birthday cards from common folk, a hunting rifle, and exact instructions on how underlings should prepare the spook's breakfast.

About 1 mile (1.5 km) east of Stasi headquarters is the **Zentralfriedhof Friedrichsfelde.** It was primarily a poor people's cemetery in the 19th century, but gradually became the burial place for important socialists and communists. One of the earliest great socialists in Germany, Paul Singer (1844–1911), was given a hero's burial here. Singer lies with other

Hohenschönhausen Memorial

From the cemetery, the easiest route to Berlin's former central Stasi prison, the **Gedenkstätte Berlin Hohenschönhausen** (Berlin Hohenschönhausen Memorial), is by tram. Take any northbound tram along Rhinstrasse from outside the Friedrichsfelde-Ost S-Bahn station and change for westbound trams 6 or 7 at Landesberger Allee. Get off at Genslerstrasse. Only guided tours are possible; these take up to two hours and are given once daily in English.

For those who understand

A tiger presides over the Tierpark, Berlin's second zoo, in Friedrichshain.

socialists of the era, like Wilhelm Liebknecht (1826–1900) and Friedrich Ebert. In the inner circle, gathered around a monument to socialism, are Rosa Luxemburg and Karl Liebknecht, alongside GDR leaders such as the detested Walter Ulbricht.

German, this tour is a chilling and moving experience, as many of the volunteer guides are former inmates. The prison (with more than 200 cells and interrogation rooms) was set up in 1951 in what had been a Soviet prison camp since 1945. The tour starts with

The Rise & Fall of Erich Mielke

After three decades at the top, Erich Mielke (1907–2000) must have seen the collapse of the GDR and its aftermath as a nightmare. Born into a working-class family in Berlin's northern suburb of Wedding, Mielke was a militant in the German Communist Party by the late 1920s. In street fighting in 1931, he shot two policemen dead (a crime for which he received a prison sentence in 1993) and fled to Moscow. After fighting in the Spanish Civil War (1936–1939) and hiding in France during World War II, he returned to Berlin in 1945.

A protégé of East German president Walter Ulbricht, Mielke was named minister for state security in 1957 (see pp. 161–162). His spy network had files on virtually the entire East German population. Feared rather than liked, this "hero of the working class" was quickly dropped by the ruling SED party after the Berlin Wall came down in November 1989. In mid-1990, he went on trial several times on murder and fraud charges. After a few years in jail, he was freed in 1995 and all further cases against him were dropped in 1998 on health grounds.

a half-hour film on the prison's history. Visitors are then taken to the cellar prison (known as the U-Boot, or "Submarine"), a series of unspeakable, dank, lightless cells, including some with standing water, where Soviet intelligence interrogators and then their Stasi successors tortured political prisoners. In the newer 1960s prison buildings, cells are not quite as awful, but treatment was brutal and arbitrary for the flimsiest of political "crimes." The cells were in use until 1989.

Tierpark Berlin

Berlin's post–World War II past has also resulted in a pleasant alternative to all this weighty history. The city's division left East Berlin without a zoo, and so the Tierpark Berlin was created from scratch and opened in 1955.

The biggest animal park in Europe, it has some 7,600 occupants. The generous layout is the zoo's strong point, leaving plenty of open space for herds of camels, deer, and many others, caged only by moats. The pink flamingo island is a high point. Others include the bear enclosures, the Dickhäuter-haus (the "thick-skinned" domain of elephants and rhinos), and the snake farm.

Schloss Friedrichsfelde

At the northwest end of the park stands Schloss Friedrichsfelde, a palace that lay far from Berlin in the countryside when it was first built in 1695. It was given its present appearance in 1719 by Martin Böhme, Berlin's official palace architect at the time. After World War II, it slowly decayed until being restored in 1981.

The palace can be visited only by guided tours, which take place four times a day. On show is a cornucopia of 18th-century arts and crafts, from Berlin porcelain and silverware to paintings by such artists as Eduard Gärtner. On either side of the palace stretch elegant manicured gardens. ∎

Tierpark Berlin
- 157 D4
- Am Tierpark 125
- 030 51 53 10
- $$$
- U-Bahn: Tierpark

www.tierpark-berlin.de

Schloss Friedrichsfelde
- 157 D4
- Am Tierpark 125
- 030 51 53 14 07
- Tues., Thurs.–Sat. 11 a.m.–5 p.m.
- Included in Tierpark entry
- U-Bahn: Tierpark or Friedrichsfelde

www.schloss-friedrichsfelde.de

Berlin Design

Paris, Milan, London...Berlin? Germany's capital is home to no fewer than seven fashion schools. Ever since the first Bread & Butter fashion show was held in Spandau in 2000, the city has elbowed its way into the European fashion fair business.

The Walk of Fashion is one of several shows that have put Berlin on the fashion map.

Bread & Butter includes hundreds of established and emerging local designers of urban streetwear. Its philosophy of steering clear of government aid and pooling with more high-end fashion shows has given it an identity that reflects the unfettered, quirky Berlin milieu in which it blossomed. After moving to Barcelona for a couple of years, the show is now held in the gritty hangars of Berlin's old Tempelhof airport.

Fashion Shows

Berlin's rise and rise as a threads capital has spawned more fashion shows. Some are popular enough to be held twice a year, in January and July. A high-profile event is Berlin Fashion Week, set up in 2007 as a counterpart to those in New York, London, Paris, and Milan. The summer show is held on a raised catwalk in front of the Brandenburg Gate. Leaning toward haute couture,

Premium is held in a defunct railway depot in Kreuzberg. Others to watch include Show & Order, presenting high-end labels in an old power station; Gallery Berlin, focusing on edgy, avant-garde design; and Berlin's take on the New York–flavored Capsule.

Shopping

How did it all happen? West Berlin had long been the stage for Germany's most pulsating counterculture scene, and the fall of the Wall in 1989 opened up new opportunities for young creators in need of low rents. They poured into the then-burgeoning artists' quarter of Prenzlauer Berg (initially on Kastanienallee) and have since spread farther afield. Among the designers who gave Kastanienallee its fame for fashion flair are Eisdieler (Kastanienallee 12, www.eisdieler.de) and Thatchers (Kastanienallee 21, www.thatchers.de). Thatchers designs mainly women's fashion using fine materials and unusual lines.

Several more cheeky Berlin labels can be found on Kastanienallee and around the corner on Oderberger Strasse. Flagshipstore (Oderberger Strasse 53, www.flagshipstore-berlin.de) carries 30-plus labels of emerging Berlin talent. These trippy garments are produced in small batches or as one-offs.

Put off by rising rents in rapidly gentrifying Prenzlauer Berg, some designers have shifted to new "in" areas, namely, Friedrichshain and parts of Kreuzberg, Tiergarten, and Wedding. F95 (Luckenwalder Strasse 4–6, www.f95store.com) features apparel from the Premium trade show. The airy warehouse space of Andreas Murkudis (Potsdamer Strasse 77–87, www.andreasmurkudis.com) sells not only clothing but anything from designer furnishings to porcelain objets d'art.

Pankow & Weissensee

Pankow is a quiet northern suburb. Long a working-class district and relatively undamaged at the end of World War II, it became home for most of the GDR's party *Bonzen* (bigwigs) until the East German state's demise in 1990. Along with Weissensee to the southeast, it remains essentially residential, with plenty of generous green spaces and a couple of attractions.

Schloss Schönhausen and its 40-acre (16 ha) garden lie at the heart of Pankow. A mansion and some kind of green space have been here since the 17th century, but what you see today is largely the result of gardens laid out in 1829–1831 by Peter Joseph Lenné. Broad, leafy alleys crisscross the park, a favorite with summer picnickers. The newly restored palace was given its present form for

INSIDER TIP:

The spirit of old Pankow can be felt in Breitestrasse, with a 15th-century parish church and a town hall bristling with turrets.

—KAREN CARMICHAEL
National Geographic writer

Queen Elisabeth Christine, wife of Friedrich II, in 1764. The elegant **Festsaal** is Berlin's sole remaining example of a rococo ceremonial hall.

A few miles southeast of Pankow is Weissensee, another suburban area mostly made up of GDR-era housing blocks. In the middle of it all is Europe's largest Jewish cemetery, the **Jüdischer**

Friedhof Weissensee (*Herbert-Baum-Strasse 45, tel 030 925 33 30, www.jewish-cemetery-weissensee.org, closed Sat., M4 tram: Albertinenstrasse*). Laid out in 1880, the cemetery suffered some wartime damage but, remarkably, was left largely untouched by the Nazis. A memorial near the entrance honors the six million Jews who perished in the Holocaust.

To visit the cemetery, you need some kind of headwear. The flower shop at the entrance can lend you a head covering. Toward the southern end of the cemetery behind the UI and UII plots is a burial ground for German Jewish soldiers who fell in World War I. ∎

Schloss Schönhausen

🅰 156 A6
✉ Tschaikowskistrasse 1
☎ 0331 969 42 00
🕐 Closed Mon.
💲 $$
🚇 U-Bahn & S-Bahn: Pankow & M1 tram to Tschaikowskistrasse

www.spsg.de

Jews buried at Weissensee cemetery include World War I soldiers.

EXPERIENCE: Berlin's Fascinating Underworld

Things change fast in Germany's once deprived capital (popular slogan: "Poor but Sexy"). The old East German parliament building has been torn down and a replica of a Prussian palace is being built in its place. But underground it's a different story. The people from Berliner Unterwelten will show you bunkers past and present, ghost U-Bahn stations of the divided Berlin, and escape routes from East to West.

Around 100 wartime bunkers have survived in, around, and under Berlin, fairly intact but nearly invisible unless you know where to look. Toward the end of World War II, there were more than 1,000, and as Allied bombing intensified, the Germans moved the war effort underground. A railway tunnel at Tempelhof airport was used to make fighter aircraft. With the Russians closing in on Berlin, the Nazis flooded the passages to thwart invaders, and untold numbers drowned.

In 1997, local enthusiasts founded the society Berliner Unterwelten to document the city's "subterranean architecture" and make it accessible to the public. In the northern district of Wedding, they reconstructed an air-raid shelter deep under Gesundbrunnen U-Bahn station, creating a backdrop for museum exhibits. Seminars, theater performances, and concerts are now held in the depths. The society also conducts guided tours in eight languages at a handful of sites, revealing a world that few Berliners realize still lies beneath their feet.

Dark Worlds

The tours are cold, dusty, claustrophobic, and more than a bit creepy. Under Gesundbrunnen station, the **"Dark Worlds" tour** (*Brunnenstrasse 105, tel 030 49 91 05 18, www.berliner -unterwelten.de, $$$; daily 11 a.m. April–Oct. & Thurs.– Mon. Nov.–March*) departs from a steel door that hundreds of commuters normally pass unnoticed. Squeezing through the narrow passages, past signs in luminous paints, you get an idea of how grim life was: the triple-bunk beds, rows of toilets with no privacy, the hand-powered ventilators to keep deadly CO_2 at bay.

Cases display uniforms, weapons, and documents. Among the prized objects are an IBM machine that cataloged Jewish detainees and an Enigma coding device. Remarkable, too, is a mural painted by Hitler's drivers in the *Führerbunker*, depicting SS soldiers raising shields above the *Volk* (people).

Waiting Out the Bomb

Another spooky circuit, **"U-Bahns, Bunkers, and the Cold War,"** reveals deradiation shower facilities and details of GDR morale control, such as the absence of exposed pipes from which residents might hang themselves. These chambers could sustain life for only a few weeks. Those who sought refuge were told precious little about the fleeting, irradiated lives they would lead after a nuclear strike.

Underground tours reveal Berlin's grim wartime shelters.

East Side Gallery

The longest surviving stretch of the Berlin Wall, at just under a mile (1.5 km), was transformed into a popular open-air art gallery after German reunification. The forbidding barrier became a parchment to express biting farewells to the East German regime.

Now covered by a kaleidoscope of murals, it is known as the East Side Gallery and ranks with the Brandenburg Gate and Holocaust Monument as one of the city's most visited sights. Some 118 artists from 24 countries are represented. Many artworks faded away in the early years but underwent a thorough restoration in 2009. In true Berlin fashion, graffiti immediately appeared on the refreshed surfaces (and indeed, some observers contend graffiti is an integral part of the work). In early 2013, some 10,000 people gathered to hear David Hasselhoff, the onetime *Baywatch* star, sing "Looking for Freedom!" to protest the demolition of part of the gallery to make way for luxury high-rises.

Information plaques mark the best known works. These include a Trabant car busting through the masonry, a series of cartoon portraits, and a take on Eastern Bloc leaders Leonid Brezhnev and Erich Honecker kissing.

To view the gallery, walk from Schlesisches Tor or ride the No. 265 bus east of Ostbahnhof along Schlesische Strasse. Where the street changes name to Puschkinallee, you cross the boundary of what was East Berlin. A solitary leftover **Wachturm**

"Molecule Man," by Jonathan Borofsky, rises from the Spree River near the Oberbaumbrücke.

(watchtower) stands guard in the park, Am Schlesischen Busch, which was created from the death strip around the wall.

Oberbaumbrücke

Hard though it may be to believe, Berlin has more bridges than Venice. Of the 1,700 scattered throughout the greater Berlin area, easily the loveliest is the 19th-century Oberbaumbrücke, visible from the parkland lining the Spree side of the East Side Gallery. The multitowered, faux-Gothic structure was once one of eight crossover points between West and East Berlin and is now illuminated at night. ∎

East Side Gallery
- 156 B4
- Mühlenstrasse
- U-Bahn: Schlesisches Tor to walk; S-Bahn & U-Bahn: Warschauer Strasse to go directly to gallery

www.eastsidegallery .com

Treptower Park

Just east of the S-Bahn station, next to a mooring dock of Spree pleasure boats since GDR times, a brisk march along Puschkinallee takes you into Treptower Park, site of the Great Industrial Exhibition of 1896 and, for a short while, the world's longest telescope. At its heart looms the immense Sowjetisches Ehrenmal (Soviet Memorial).

Treptower Park
 156 B3
 Am Treptower Park
 S-Bahn: Treptower Park

This mausoleum cum monument celebrates the Soviet victory over "fascist Germany" in the Great Patriotic War of 1941–45 (for the Soviets, World War II didn't get started until the U.S.S.R. was invaded). Of the more than 20,000 Soviet casualties resulting from the 1945 Battle of Berlin, 7,000 are buried here.

Graveyard of Fun

In the depths of the Plänterwald, a forest southeast of Treptower Park, you may stumble across a silent, time-warped tract with Ferris wheel, swan-shaped boats, and life-size replicas of dinosaurs, some toppled in mid-snarl. This is the Spreepark, until 1989 one of East Germany's most beloved amusement parks. After reunification, it was privatized, only to go bankrupt in 2002. The park's owner, Norbert Witte, fled his creditors to Peru and was caught trying to smuggle 400 pounds (181 kg) of cocaine in his 1001 Nights Magic Carpet Ride. Most of the amusements are defunct, but on weekends you can take a spin around the grounds on the narrow-gauge train (*$, check the schedule at www .berliner-spreepark.de*).

A stone triumphal arch on the right as you head southeast along Puschkinallee signals arrival. You reach a statue of weeping Mother Russia and then, to your left, behold the monument. Two triangular structures adorned with the hammer and sickle of the U.S.S.R. and encased in rose marble—purportedly recycled from the ruins of Hitler's chancellery—serve as a symbolic entrance. What look like 16 giant sarcophagi, actually representing the ex-Soviet republics, are laid out before you. They are decorated with reliefs depicting wartime heroism.

The monument culminates in a hilltop hero's grave, capped by a 38-foot-high (11.5 m) bronze of a Soviet solder crushing a swastika underfoot, sword in one hand and a German child he has saved in the other. (This touch was inspired by a real incident during fighting around here.)

Archenhold Observatory

About 1,150 feet (350 m) east of the war memorial, halfway between a large carp pond and the Zenner beer garden, lies the Archenhold Observatory. The building boasts an enormous refractor telescope, a 69-foot (21 m) beast known as the Himmelskanone (Heavenly Cannon). In the neo-Renaissance building below, on June 2, 1915, Albert Einstein gave his first public speech on his Theory of Relativity. ∎

Karlshorst

In the four years before the final Soviet pullout from Berlin in September 1994, this area was one of the strangest parts of town. The recently reunited city may not have had a wall anymore, but its citizens still lived in parallel worlds. In another dimension altogether, however, were the Soviet officers and soldiers who had made Karlshorst their headquarters in Berlin since the end of World War II.

**Deutsch-
Russisches-
Museum**

🗺 157 D3

✉ Zwieselerstrasse
4

☎ 030 50 15 08 10

🕐 Closed Mon.

🚆 S-Bahn:
Karlshorst &
396 bus

**www.museum-
karlshorst.de**

The final act of German surrender was signed in 1945 in what would become the Soviet headquarters in East Germany.

All that remains of the Soviet presence is the **Deutsch-Russisches-Museum** (German-Russian Museum). In this building, a German officers' school and club built in 1936, Germany signed its final, unconditional surrender to Allied forces on May 8, 1945. From that spring on, it was the headquarters of the Soviet Fifth Army. The building was converted in 1967 into the elaborately titled "Museum of Fascist Germany's Unconditional Surrender in the Great Patriotic War of 1941–45."

In 1995, the current museum opened as a joint Russo-German effort commemorating the events of the war on the Eastern Front. It is a difficult balancing act. Prewar relations, war planning on both sides, and the course of hostilities on the Eastern Front are presented with a mixture of German and Soviet texts, photos, audio and video streams, and some military gear (such as uniforms, medals, and weaponry) from both sides.

Most interesting of all is the hall in which the capitulation was signed, the so-called Surrender Room. The Germans sat at a separate, low table to the right of the main table, which seated representatives of the victorious Allied forces. After the formalities, the Germans were ushered out and the victory banquet started. The scene has been set up as it was back in 1945. A silent video shows the events of that day. ■

Köpenick

Southeast of central Berlin, Köpenick was once a separate fishing village huddled on an island at the junction of the Spree and Dahme Rivers. Bronze Age families, Slavic tribes, and, from the 12th century, German colonists all built forts here. Surrounded by riverways and villas, the compact old town oozes charm. At its center stands the baroque Schloss Köpenick, which alone merits the trip from downtown Berlin.

Schloss Köpenick sits tranquilly on an island, a short stroll from the old center of Alt-Köpenick.

Schloss Köpenick

- 🗺 157 D2
- ✉ Schlossinsel
- ☎ 30 266 42 42 42
- 🕐 Closed Mon.
- 💲 $
- 🚇 S-Bahn: Köpenick & 68 tram

www.smb.museum

From the S-Bahn station, you can walk about 20 minutes south along Bahnhofstrasse or catch the 68 tram to Alt-Köpenick, the old center. On the way, you may notice a statue in the middle of a park called **Platz des 23. April**. The square's name commemorates the arrival of the Soviet army in Köpenick in 1945; the statue honors the 91 people shot here by the Nazis in a roundup of opponents in June 1933. A display in the nearby old **court cells** (*Puchanstrasse 12, open Thurs.*) describes this incident.

At the park, turn left and follow the tramlines over a bridge into the old town center. On the corner of Alt-Köpenick rises the bombastic, neo-Gothic *Rathaus* (city hall). The onetime mayor thought it a grand idea to tear down the building's medieval predecessor in 1904 and replace it with this edifice. The site became famous two years later when it

The Captain of Köpenick

Köpenick owes its fame to the startling escapade of a 60-year-old cobbler and part-time con man in October 1906. Out of work and in need of cash, Friedrich Wilhelm Voigt had an idea. Betting on the famed obedience of Prussian soldiers, Voigt bought a secondhand captain's uniform, commandeered a ten-man squad of troops he found passing by, and ordered the occupation of Köpenick City Hall. While local police maintained order outside, he arrested the mayor and had him sent to central Berlin. Then he

impounded the cash box, taking 4,000 Marks. Voigt was later arrested and sentenced to four years in prison (he served two). They say Kaiser Wilhelm was rather pleased by the incident, as it confirmed the perfect subordination of his troops to officers!

The story of *Der Hauptmann von Köpenick (The Captain of Köpenick)* was turned into a play by Carl Zuckmayer (1896–1977) in 1931. In 1956, director Helmut Käutner (1908–1980) brought the story to the silver screen.

was stormed by the "captain of Köpenick" (see sidebar). A statue of this enterprising man stands at the foot of the entrance stairs, while inside, a small museum in the old treasurer's office retells the tale by means of photos, documents, and officers' uniforms.

A few minutes' walk south leads to **Schloss Köpenick,** the 17th-century royal palace that today holds part of the collection of the **Kunstgewerbemuseum** (Museum of Decorative Arts)—in spring 2014, the main collection reopens in the Kulturforum (see p. 125). Rutger van Langerfeld (1635–1695) built the palace over its Renaissance predecessor in 1685 for Prince Friedrich.

Over four floors, a collection of fine furniture, marquetry, Berlin porcelain, pewter, and other 16th- to 19th-century objects graces the beautifully stuccoed palace rooms. The highlight is the second-floor collection of decorative gold-plated silverware; it has been set out as it was in the Rittersaal (Knights' Hall) of

INSIDER TIP:

Attend a soccer game of the legendary FC Union at the Alte Försterei stadium in Köpenick. The atmosphere is great!

—HEINER SCHUSTER
National Geographic contributor

the Berliner Schloss (see p. 98) in central Berlin. At the other end of the same floor is the **Wappensaal** (Coats of Arms Hall), holding a banquet table set with delicate porcelain and crystal.

The palace looks onto a calm body of water, the Frauentog. Fishermen used to spread their nets from the **Kietz** on the east bank. This pleasant, cobbled street is lined by charming cottages where fishing families once lived. To the northeast stands a 17th-century house that today is home to the **Heimatmuseum.** Its display of documents and artifacts recounts the long history of Köpenick. ∎

Heimatmuseum

- 157 E2
- Alter Markt 1
- 030 902 97 33 51
- Closed Mon. & Fri.–Sat.
- S-Bahn: Köpenick & 68 tram

www.heimatmuseum
-treptow.de

Grosser Müggelsee & Grünau

Berlin's biggest lake, the Grosser Müggelsee, opens up about 1.2 miles (2 km) east of central Köpenick. Stressed Berlin urbanites take the 3-square-mile (7.7 sq km) lake by storm on summer weekends for boat tours, swims, and lakeside walks. Several boat companies crisscross the lake, and swimmers can find a handful of limited beaches (some of them for nude bathing). In colder winters, the lake freezes over and becomes a popular natural ice-skating rink.

Boat tours cruise the Müggelsee in the warmer months.

Grünau

 157 D1

S-Bahn: Grünau; Tram: 68 from Köpenick

Grünauer Wassersportmuseum

157 E1

Regattastrasse 191

030 674 40 02

Open Sat. 2–4:30 p.m. April–Sept.

S-Bahn: Grünau

www.wassersportmuseum-gruenau .de

A walk along the wooded south bank is a pleasant way to pass an hour. The 377-foot (115 m) mound just to the south of the lake is the **Müggelberge,** one of the city's highest points. Of the villages that face the lake, eastern **Rahnsdorf** *(S-Bahn: Rahnsdorf)* is the most pleasant. Villas and gardens surround the original core, once a fishing settlement. To soak up the atmosphere, walk along cobbled Dorfstrasse and follow the signs to the Altes Fischerdorf (Old Fishermen's Village).

Just over a mile (2 km) southwest of Köpenick lies the quiet settlement of Grünau, founded in 1749. It's a pleasant spot for a stroll on the Dahme River, which widens into the Langer See (Long Lake). As watersports gained in popularity in the late 19th century, some Berliners built themselves lakeside residences. The spot was also chosen for the 1936 Olympics' rowing events. To learn more, see the **Grünauer Wassersportmuseum** on the edge of Langer See. What started as a private collection in 1980 has developed into a specialized museum dedicated to local watersports, with emphasis on the 1936 Olympic Games. Boats, photos, medals, and other such paraphernalia make up the bulk of the collection. ■

More Places to Visit in Prenzlauer Berg, Friedrichshain, & the East

Ernst-Thälmann-Park

This modest suburban park in Prenzlauer Berg bears one of the names dearest to German communists. The park was created in the 1980s as part of a high-density GDR housing project. Its high-rise apartments, designed to accommodate 4,000 people, tower above the park, which was intended to provide them with a little green space. Facing Greifswalder Strasse is an enormous, 43-foot-high (13 m) bronze bust to the memory of Ernst Thälmann (1886–1944), his fist clenched in communist salute. Behind him flutters a revolutionary flag. Thälmann was born in Hamburg and by the age of 20 was active in the city's trade union movement. As a dockworker, warehouse employee, and member of the German Socialist Party, he was politically active until sent to the Western Front in World War I.

INSIDER TIP:

Join in a Sunday afternoon session of karaoke in the "Bearpit'"amphitheater of Prenzlauer Berg's Mauerpark. Up to 2,000 spectators turn up.

—JEREMY GRAY
National Geographic author

In the 1920s, Thälmann rose in the ranks of the German Communist Party (KPD) and led the Roter Frontkämpferbund (Red Front Fighters' Association), which spearheaded street battles with the Nazis' Sturmabteilung (SA) para-military units in the mid-1920s. The KPD was tightly linked to the Soviet Union; Thälmann became party president with Josef Stalin's explicit backing and stood for president of the Weimar Republic in 1932. Shortly after Adolf Hitler's arrival in power in 1933, Thälmann was arrested and accused of high treason. He was shunted from prison to prison and eventually wound up in Buchenwald concentration camp in August 1944, where he was shot dead on Hitler's orders.

On the northwest side of the housing project is the Zeiss Grossplanetarium *(Prenzlauer Allee 80, tel 030 421 84 50, www.astw.de),* a planetarium added in 1987 and popular with local children.

🅰 Map p. 156 B5 ✉ Greifswalder Strasse
🚇 S-Bahn: Greifswalder Strasse

Gethsemanekirche

Prenzlauer Berg's brick Gethsemanekirche was one of an extraordinary 53 churches built on the orders of Kaiser Wilhelm II between 1890 and 1905. The kaiser hoped thus to draw the working classes away from the dangers of socialism. The building was designed by August Orth in a mixed style combining Romanesque and neo-Gothic elements and finished in 1893. The church community, far from becoming an instrument of established power, developed a reputation for dissent, especially under the Nazis and then during the 40 years of the GDR. In October 1989, shortly before the GDR edifice began to collapse, a peaceful protest in front of the church was violently broken up by Stasi agents.

🅰 Map p. 156 A5 ✉ Stargarder Strasse 77
🚇 S-Bahn: Schönhauser Allee

Karl-Marx-Allee

Of the myriad problems assailing postwar Berlin, the housing shortage was the most pressing. In 1952, East Germany launched a *Nationales Aufbauprogramm* (national

Communist hero Ernst Thälmann is commemorated in the East Berlin park bearing his name.

rebuilding program). The jewels in the crown were to be the grand blocks of residential, office, and shopping space along Karl-Marx-Allee (at the time called Stalinallee), between Strausberger Platz and Frankfurter Tor, in East Berlin. Built in the Soviet-inspired *Zuckerbäckerstil* (wedding cake style), these buildings exude a certain grandeur, much derided in the West but now making this strip worthy of national heritage protection. The buildings are multitiered, some with fluted columns and/or clad in Meissen tiles. At No. 84 on the south side, on the site of what was from 1906 to 1945 the Rose Theater, the building has reliefs depicting working-class heroes. Drop in to **Café Sibylle** *(Karl-Marx-Allee 72, tel 030 29 35 22 03)* to see a small display on the boulevard's development—or just to eat some cake. Upstairs from the café, you can visit the observation deck *($)* for views of the Zuckerbäcker buildings.

Strausberger Platz and Frankfurter Tor have a monumental appearance. East of Frankfurter Tor, the Zuckerbäcker style continues in rather more dilapidated-looking buildings a short way along Frankfurter Allee (as far as Niederbarnimstrasse). Whatever you make of the style, the apartments themselves represented unprecedented luxury for Berliners in the tough postwar period.

Map p. 156 A4–B4   Karl-Marx-Allee U-Bahn *&* S-Bahn: Alexanderplatz

Mauerpark

A spacious tract of greenery in Prenzlauer Berg's urban jumble, the Mauerpark (Wall Park) casts a folksy charm over a mile (1.5 km) of erstwhile death strip between East and West Berlin. On warm summer days, hordes of Berlin residents come to picnic, read, and sunbathe, while Frisbee artists, jugglers, and buskers strut their stuff. It's a scene and a half. On the western boundary sprawls the ever-expanding **Flohmarkt Mauerpark,** the city's largest flea market. Every Sunday, thousands of bargain hunters pick over antique furniture, GDR memorabilia (both real and fake), vintage clothing, and boxes filled with used LPs. In the shadow of Friedrich-Ludwig-Jahn sports stadium, a grassy slope rises to an old section of wall that's popular with graffiti artists. A deep recess nearby reveals a stone amphitheater known as the Bearpit, home to lively public karaoke sessions. The intrepid host, Joe Hatchiban (in real life, Gareth Lennon from Dublin), turns up on a strange-looking bicycle fitted with loudspeaker, microphone, and Macbook. Sunday afternoon at 3 p.m., weather permitting, up to 2,000 spectators fill the galleries to rate hopefuls belting out evergreens like AC/DC's "Highway to Hell." *www.mauerparkmarkt.de* Map p. 156 A5 Bernauer Strasse 63–64 U-Bahn: Bernauer Strasse or Eberswalder Strasse

Must-see museums and a string of minor pearls of historical interest in a broad swath of southern Berlin

Schöneberg to Kreuzberg

Introduction & Map   176–177

Berlinische Galerie   178–179

Experience: Art Gallery Hopping   179

Jüdisches Museum Berlin   180–181

Feature: Marvelous Marlene   182

Kreuzberg & Viktoriapark   183

Deutsches Technikmuseum Berlin   184

Tempelhof Park   185

More Places to Visit in Schöneberg & Kreuzberg   186

Hotels & Restaurants   252–254

The Oberbaumbrücke links Friedrichshain and Kreuzberg.

Schöneberg to Kreuzberg

The eastward sweep from sleepy residential Wilmersdorf across trendy Schöneberg and into the predominantly Turkish quarters of eastern Kreuzberg presents a cross-section of modern Berlin. Concentrated in western Kreuzberg are three major museums with completely different themes: The Berlinische Galerie presents a cornucopia of contemporary art, the Jüdisches Museum Berlin a provocative panorama of German-Jewish history, and the Deutsches Technikmuseum a panoply of human ingenuity.

One of the sultriest actresses ever to grace the silver screen, Marlene Dietrich was born and buried in Schöneberg. Not far from where she rests in peace, a rather different star put in a memorable appearance in 1963. President John F. Kennedy made his unforgettable *"Ich bin ein Berliner"* speech at the Rathaus Schöneberg in West Berlin.

Nearby Tempelhof airport, once the biggest in Europe, was made famous by the Berlin Airlift in 1948–1949. A memorial commemorates the airlift; the buildings themselves are a fascinating example of Nazi-era architecture.

The old airfield, meanwhile, has been turned into a public park.

Scratch the surface and other traces of Berlin's troubled 20th-century history emerge. On Kleistpark stands the building where the Nazis held show trials in the so-called People's Court, while a bunker disguised as an apartment block helps to recall a demolished sports arena, the Sportspalast, where the Third Reich spewed propaganda to the masses.

South of the Napoleon-era monument in Viktoriapark, an isolated corner of Kreuzburg hosts a ridiculously heavy concrete tower,

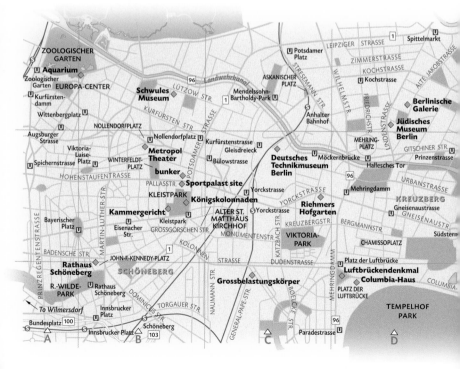

the Grossbelastungskörper, designed to test the foundations of Hitler's megalomanic architecture project, Germania.

Key points across Schöneberg and Kreuzberg lend themselves to meandering strolls by day and night. In Kreuzberg, head for Little Istanbul around Kottbusser Tor. A few minutes' walk south, a huge Turkish market takes place on Tuesdays and Fridays on the Maybach Ufer of the Landwehrkanal. They still call this area SO36, the old postal code for what was once an alternative urban scene in Berlin. It has calmed down since the fall of the Wall, but the area retains an edgy feel and pulsates with life once the sun goes down. Görlitzer Park, Wiener Strasse, Oranienstrasse, and Maybach Ufer are lined with bars and eateries. Some of Kreuzberg's magic has rubbed off on parts of Neukölln, its crunchier neighbor to the south.

The heart of the action in Schöneberg was and remains Nollendorfplatz. Famous in the 1920s as the busiest gay quarter in Europe, it was a cauldron of intellectual life as well. The revolutionary stage director Erwin Piscator opened up the Metropol Theater on Nollendorfplatz in 1927. Nearby, one of the city's most attractive produce markets takes place on Saturdays in Winterfeldplatz. Although not nearly as outrageous as in the 1920s, the area retains plenty of nightlife, gay and otherwise. ■

NOT TO BE MISSED:

Taking in the contemporary artworks of the Berlinische Galerie   178–179

Remembering lives "Between the Lines" at the Jüdisches Museum Berlin   180–181

Scaling the "mountain" of Kreuzberg in Viktoriapark   183

The trains, boats, and planes of the Deutsches Technikmuseum   184

Walking or cycling through the lush expanses of Tempelhof Park   185

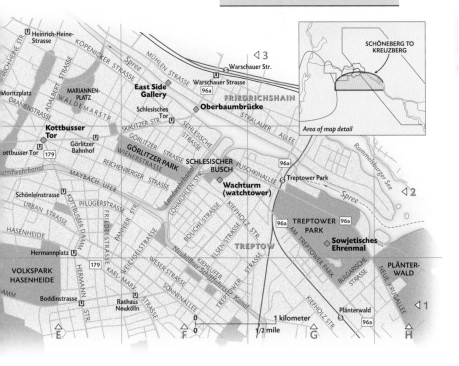

Berlinische Galerie

Berlin's feverish cultural activity seems to know no bounds. In 2004, this airy museum (formally a state museum for modern art, photography, and architecture) opened up in northern Kreuzberg. Its substantial permanent collections include modern paintings, photography, and architectural models and designs. How many of these attractions you get to see depends on the extent of the museum's temporary exhibitions.

You never know what you might see in the Berlinische Galerie, a highlight on the city's art circuit.

Berlinische Galerie

- 176 D3
- ✉ Alte Jakobstrasse 124–128
- ☎ 030 78 90 26 00
- ⏱ Closed Tues.
- 💲 $$
- 🚇 U-Bahn: Hallesches Tor

www.berlinische galerie.de

Otto Dix is a prime representative of the Realists of the 1920s. A striking work is his 1926 portrait of poet Iwar von Lücken, a gaunt man in an ill-fitting suit in a Berlin apartment.

Austrian Oskar Kokoschka (1886–1980) makes an appearance with paintings such as "Bildnis von Nell Walden" ("Portrait of Nell Walden," 1916), in which the essence of the woman in question seems to leap from the canvas.

The onetime star of Dada in Berlin, George Grosz, who became a leading figure of the Neue Sachlichkeit (New Objectivity) movement, also has works here. Among them is the satirical "Daum Marries Her Pedantic Automaton George in May 1920" (1920).

Hannah Höch (1889–1978) was another engaging painter of the Neue Sachlichkeit period. Her paintings have a provocative zest about them. "Roma" (1925) turns sunny Roman scenes on their head and focuses them on the image of a woman in a bathing suit, but with the face of Italian Fascist dictator Benito Mussolini. "Die Journalisten" ("The Journalists," 1925) is a study in alienation with six grotesque heads either floating or plopped on the bodies of scribes she reviled.

An important slot is occupied by the somber realism of Karl Hofer. Most of his earlier works were destroyed in a fire toward the end of World War II, but a disturbing exception made it into this collection. "Die Gefangenen" ("The Prisoners," 1933), created as Hitler came to power, is a disturbingly prophetic look into the future. Hopeless, starving, hairless prisoners look out from a bleak background at the observer. "Schwarzmondlicht" ("Night of the Black Moon," 1944) depicts refugees under a lunar eclipse.

A noted neoexpressionist, Georg Baselitz (1938–) is represented with two versions of "Ein moderner Maler" ("A Modern Painter") from 1966 and 2007. Both show a paint-flecked artist contemplating the landscape of a destroyed Germany.

Aside from painting, the collections include drawings, photomontages, watercolors, and more by these and other artists of the same periods. Christian Schad (1894–1982), Max Beckmann, and Dix are among them. Another Berlin accent is applied with works from the Novembergruppe (November Group), which included the likes of Ludwig Mies van der Rohe (better known as an architect).

The **architecture collection** is enormous; only a tiny portion is likely ever to be on display. It includes 300,000 plans and drawings and about 2,500 models reflecting 20th-century city planning in and around Berlin. Models include that of the Bundespräsidialamt (see p. 119) and the fascinating Sternkirche, a sci-fi-looking church design by Otto Bartning (1883–1959) that never got past the drawing board.

The **photographic collections** could constitute several separate exhibitions. Archives range from late 19th-century images taken in and around Berlin to intriguing shots from the

EXPERIENCE:
Art Gallery Hopping

In the warmer months, Berlin's art lovers hit the streets for open gallery nights. The nexus of the action is Mitte, a district peppered with exhibition spaces ranging from gritty pop-up studios to chic designer showrooms. It's quite a scene, with visitors spilling onto the sidewalks to chat and sip wine. To get a taste, start at Oranienburger Strasse S-Bahn station and work your way east down Linienstrasse. Then jump a block south and walk back on Auguststrasse. The most popular events are organized by **Open Gallery Weekend** (*www.gallery-weekend-berlin.de*) in spring and **Galerien Berlin Mitte** (*www.galerien-berlin-mitte.de*) in late summer.

former East Germany. Fascinating early photos from Heinrich Zille (1859–1928) include "Handstand machende Jungen an einem Sandhang" ("Youths Doing Handstands on a Sandbank," 1898). A postwar Berlin drained of vigor is reflected in Michael Schmidt's (born 1945) series from the 1970s, "Berlin-Wedding," photos of empty cityscapes during the Wall era. ∎

Jüdisches Museum Berlin

Its creator called the design "Between the Lines." Architect Daniel Libeskind (born 1946), faced with the delicate task of creating a modern museum on the often tragic history of Jews in Germany, came up with a powerful statement. Inside, an absorbing exhibition on German-Jewish culture awaits.

The "Shalechet" ("Fallen Leaves") art installation contains 10,000 iron faces.

Libeskind created a gleaming, low-slung, zinc-clad edifice to house the museum. Like an exploding Star of David, its angular and seemingly erratic ground plan reflects the complex twists and turns that life took for Germany's Jews through the centuries.

The remarkable building is attached like a metallic scribble to a stately baroque building (formerly a Prussian court and then city museum) that serves as the entrance. An intentionally disorienting subterranean corridor connects the two. This **Axis of Continuity** is intersected by two others, the **Axis of Exile,** with names of the cities to which Jews fled from Nazi Germany, and the **Axis of the Holocaust,** with the names of concentration camps. The latter ends outside in the dim, unheated silo of the **Holocaust Tower,** where a single shaft of light evokes terrifying scenes of deportation in cattle cars. Nearby, the **Garden of Exile** is a bundle of sloping pillars that symbolize the isolation and confusion of émigrés who faced a life away from the world they knew.

In the new building, the permanent exhibition starts on the top floor with the arrival of Jews in medieval Germany. It continues with images, audiovisual displays, household objects, and engaging texts in 13 sections spread over two floors. Treated as second-class citizens, German Jews were at the forefront of German Enlightenment thinking and, later, 19th-century literature. Their contributions are illustrated by displays on the life of philosopher Moses Mendelssohn. Other displays take you inside German-Jewish homes at the turn of the 20th century.

The final rooms deal with the emigration, deportations, and massacre of German Jews in the Nazi period with honesty but restraint. They finish by describing the slow re-creation of a small Jewish community in Germany since the war.

In a computer center on the ground floor, visitors can click their way through stories about famous personalities and cultural aspects of Jewish life. One of the more chilling exhibits is "Shalechet" ("Fallen Leaves"), where you can walk across thousands of little iron faces, producing a grating sound not unlike bones being ground together. This space itself is called the **Memory Void.**

Behind the baroque building lies a U-shaped **courtyard** for special events called the Sukkah, or thatched hut. The glass roof rests on treelike pillars that spread into a canopy of branches. In contrast to the somber mood of the new building, the courtyard is designed to encourage socializing. This area is the scene of regular concerts, readings, and markets for arts and crafts.

The Jewish Academy

Across the street is the Jewish Academy, a new Libeskind extension that houses a center for educational events, the museum's ever expanding library, and its archive, which has doubled in size over the past decade. The front section consists of a tilted cube that penetrates the wall of the main building, mimicking elements

INSIDER TIP:

All that remains of Albert Speer's proposed Germania, Hitler's megalomaniacal metropolis, are the foundations of a gigantic Triumphant Arch on General-Pape-Strasse about 2 miles [3.2 km] southwest of the Jewish Museum.

—RORY MACLEAN
Author of Berlin: Imagine a City
[a historical portrait]

of the glass courtyard and the Garden of Exile. One of the first things you see is a quote from Jewish philosopher Moses Maimonides—"Hear the truth, whoever speaks it"—splashed across the facade in five languages. Two large skylights, shaped like the Hebrew letters *aleph* and *beth* (*A* and *B*) light the cube's interior, serving as a reminder of the importance of learning and knowledge. ∎

Jüdisches Museum Berlin

🅰 176 D3
✉ Lindenstrasse 9–14
☎ 030 25 99 33 00
💲 $$
Ⓜ U-Bahn: Hallesches Tor

www.jmberlin.de

Marvelous Marlene

An ice-cool siren of stage and screen, Marlene Dietrich was the icon of a generation. Born into an upright, bourgeois family in suburban Berlin, she plunged into the twilight whirlwind of the city in the liberal 1920s, becoming the queen of Hollywood and sweetheart of GIs across Europe.

Berlin-born Marlene Dietrich was one of the great seductresses of the silver screen.

Born Marie Magdalene Dietrich von Losch in Berlin's Schöneberg district on December 27, 1901, she grew up the daughter of a Prussian police officer. In 1922, she made her first stage appearance, studying under director Max Reinhardt. Fame came in 1930, when she starred in Josef von Sternberg's *Der Blaue Engel* (*The Blue Angel*).

Five years earlier, she had married Rudolf Sieber, a production assistant with whom she had her only child, Maria, but their open marriage soon flagged (although they never divorced and Dietrich always traveled as Mrs. Sieber). Von Sternberg became her lover and convinced her to move to Hollywood, where they churned out movies to great acclaim, including *Morocco* (1930) and *Shanghai* (1932). They split in 1935, and her film career began to falter, although she remained for a while the highest-paid actress in Hollywood.

Dietrich's tumultuous life gave the lie to her apparent on-screen control. Her string of Hollywood lovers included Douglas Fairbanks, Jr. (who wrote to her from London: "The bed is lonely, my heart is lonely and I love you so much"), John Wayne ("The most intriguing woman I have ever known"), Gary Cooper, and James Stewart. The number of women lovers, including British Marion "Joe" Carstairs, was just as long.

In 1937, Nazi Germany's propaganda minister, Joseph Goebbels, tried to lure Dietrich back to the Reich. She became a U.S. citizen instead. She once told reporters: "I don't hate the Germans, I hate the Nazis." During the war, she threw herself into the Allied cause, performing for GIs from the Pacific to France.

Postwar Years

Her postwar film career was unspectacular. One of the better efforts was a starring role in Billy Wilder's *A Foreign Affair*, set in postwar Berlin. From then on, she dedicated herself to singing and cabaret until the 1960s. Dietrich returned briefly to Berlin in November 1945, but would not set foot in her hometown again for another 15 years, when she appeared during a European tour. Considering her a traitor, some of the locals picketed her show with posters demanding "Marlene Go Home." The Americans, however, awarded her the Medal of Freedom in 1947, while the French made her a *chevalier* (knight) of the Légion d'Honneur in 1950.

By the early 1970s, Dietrich had largely withdrawn from the world to her Paris apartment. In 1992, she passed away quietly in Paris and was buried beside her mother in Berlin's 19th-century Friedhof Stubenrauchstrasse, in Schöneberg.

Kreuzberg & Viktoriapark

The suburb of Kreuzberg takes its name from the neoclassical cast-iron monument, topped by a cross, that was erected here by Karl Friedrich Schinkel in 1817–1821. The memorial commemorates Napoleon's demise in 1815.

When the area was largely rural, the monument, mounted on a hill (hence Kreuzberg, or Cross Hill), could be seen for miles around. As suburban and industrial sprawl invaded the area in the second half of the 19th century, the monument was raised higher and placed above an octagonal stone structure with a neo-Gothic, fortress-like appearance. In 1888, the Viktoriapark was established around it.

The monument was erected both to the memory of the fallen and in thanks to the survivors of the early 19th-century Napoleonic Wars. Around the base are inscribed the names of various conflicts. The Iron Cross atop the monument would, in miniature, become the most coveted of military decorations. It was the first in Prussia that could be awarded to anyone for courage, regardless of rank or class. Previously, most awards and medals had been the preserve of officers.

The other attraction in the park is an artificial waterfall, along with what is claimed to be the northernmost vineyard in Germany.

A short walk north of the park is **Riehmers Hofgarten,** an elegant residential estate raised by master builder Wilhelm Riehmer (1830–1901) between 1881 and 1899. Designed in neobaroque and late classical style, the property consists of 18 five-story apartment buildings around a leafy courtyard. Particularly striking are the magnificent facades on Grossbeerenstrasse and Yorckstrasse, where two muscular titans frame the entrance. Note the Roman greeting, *salve* (hail), written in the floor mosaic. The ensemble was restored in the 1970s and today hosts a hotel and restaurant. ∎

Viktoriapark

🏛 176 C2

🚇 U-Bahn: Platz der Luftbrücke

Riehmers Hofgarten

🏛 176 D2

✉ Yorckstrasse 83–86

🚇 U-Bahn: Mehringdamm

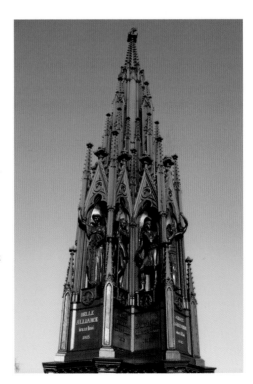

The cast-iron memorial dominating Viktoriapark gave the area its name.

Deutsches Technikmuseum Berlin

Until 1945, Anhalter Bahnhof was Berlin's biggest train station, the gateway to southern Germany and Europe. All that remains after World War II and demolition is the ruined facade on Askanischer Platz and, a long block south, the locomotive sheds now at the heart of this German Museum of Technology.

One of Europe's biggest rail-shunting yards is now a museum of the wonders of human invention.

Deutsches Technikmuseum Berlin

🅐 176 C2

✉ Trebbiner Strasse 9

☎ 030 90 25 40

🕐 Closed Mon.

💲 $$

🚇 U-Bahn: Gleisdreieck

www.sdtb.de

The new building at the front of the complex can't be missed, as outside dangles an American Douglas C-47 transport plane of the kind used during the Berlin Airlift (see sidebar p. 185).

You could spend hours in here. Upstairs from the ticket desk are displays on textile production and telecommunications; the latter includes Siemens's first telephone (1878). Displays on paper production (with demonstrations), printing, and typesetting are on the third floor.

In the new building are four floors on shipping and air travel. The sea travel section contains a massive engine room and a 1901 steam tugboat.. The flight section holds World War II wrecks, including a Junkers Ju-87 Stuka dive-bomber and part of a British RAF Lancaster bomber. Trainspotters will love the train-shunting yards, jammed with locomotives from mid-19th-century steam jobs on. Also remembered is the railways' role in the deportation of Jews.

You can visit a brewery, mills, and a depot full of classic cars outside the main buildings. A hands-on children's exhibit and workshop, Science Center Spectrum, resides at the front of the old freight station. ∎

Tempelhof Park

In 1935, Hitler decided to rebuild the venerable Tempelhof Aerodrome in monumental style. Architect Ernst Sagebiel (1892–1970) created an airport with 30 times the required capacity. Thirteen years later, the airport became a symbol of West Berlin's struggle to remain free during the Berlin Airlift.

Berliners shed a tear of nostalgia when Tempelhof, once Europe's biggest airport, was closed in 2008. After much debate, the old airfield was turned into a vast public park officially called Tempelhofer Freiheit (Tempelhof Freedom), and the grounds continue to evolve. The former runways are marked with separate paths for joggers, cyclists, and skaters, while picnic areas, vegetable patches, and a beer garden dot the green pastures.

Approaching from the west, you reach Platz der Luftbrücke (Airlift Square), at whose center rises the **Luftbrückendenkmal,** a monument to the Berlin Airlift (see sidebar). It bears the names of servicemen who died during the operation. The atmospheric baggage hall, hangars, and administrative buildings can be visited on guided tours. At **Columbia-Haus,** on the north side of Platz der Luftbrücke, the Gestapo ran a prison from 1933 on. More than 8,000 people passed through its gates, including Erich Honecker, later East Germany's president. ■

INSIDER TIP:

A guided tour through the secret underground passages and monumental halls of Hitler's onetime "World Airport Tempelhof" [see. p. 166] is an unforgettable experience.

—MAIK KOPLECK
PastFinder Berlin *author & publisher*

Tempelhof Park

- 🅰 176–177 D1–E1
- ✉ Columbiadamm
- ☎ 030 901 66 15 00
- 💲 Park entry free; $$ guided tours
- Ⓤ U-Bahn: Platz der Luftbrücke

Look Upon This City!

When the Soviet Union cut off road access to West Berlin in the summer of 1948, the western Allies decided to bust the blockade by air. From June 26, 1948, to May 12, 1949, U.S. and British aircraft flew 200,000 sorties, mostly into Tempelhof (see above). At the height of the effort, an aircraft was landing every 90 seconds. They flew in 1.5 million tons (1.36 million tonnes) of material; 71 Allied servicemen and 8 Germans died in accidents.

On September 9, 1948, West Berlin's soon-to-be mayor, Ernst Reuter, gave a rousing speech before the Reichstag ruins: "We will live to see the day of freedom!... Peoples of the world, look upon this city, look upon Berlin!" In the end, the threat of a U.S. nuclear strike on Moscow forced the Soviets to back down.

More Places to Visit in Schöneberg & Kreuzberg

Kleistpark

Berlin's botanical garden until 1903, this tidy little park is drenched in history. The neobaroque Kammergericht building, which houses the Berlin branch of the national constitutional court, was the scene of show trials in Hitler's Volksgerichtshof (People's Court). After the July 1944 attempt on the Führer's life (see sidebar p. 132), the court of much-feared judge Roland Freisler (1893–1945) moved into top gear, executing about 140 people in the ensuing months. Freisler was killed by a bomb here on February 3, 1945.

At the Potsdamer Strasse entrance to the park stretch the baroque **Königskolonnaden** (King's Colonnades), built by Carl von Gontard (1731–1791) in 1780. They were moved here from a spot near Alexanderplatz in 1910. A brief walk north and a left turn onto Pallasstrasse brings you to a postwar apartment complex that bridges the road, disguising an enormous concrete antiaircraft tower and bunker that resisted demolition attempts. Opposite it stood the Nazi-era Sportpalast (now vanished), a popular location for rousing harangues. On February 18, 1943, Propaganda Minister Joseph Goebbels gave the speech of his life: "I ask you: Do you believe, with the Führer and us, in the final and total victory of the German people?...I ask you: Do you want total war?" His broadcast voice was drowned out by applause. (He was later heard to mutter: "What idiocy! If I'd asked them to jump from the third floor of the Columbia-Haus [a Gestapo prison at Tempelhof airport], they'd have done it.") About a ten-minute wander east of Kleistpark lies the **Alter St. Matthäus Kirchhof**, a cemetery founded in 1856. The brothers Grimm, known for their collections of fairy tales, are buried here.

🅰 Map p. 176 B2 ✉ Potsdamer Strasse
🚇 U-Bahn: Kleistpark

Rathaus Schöneberg

The huge, rather pompous-looking Schöneberg city hall, finished shortly before World War I, was part of the citywide tendency to equip each district with centers of local government. From the 1940s until reunification, it served as West Berlin's city hall. Crowds gathered here on June 26, 1963, to hear U.S. President John F. Kennedy's

INSIDER TIP:

Travel back to the '50s at Babylon Kreuzberg, a cinema hidden behind Kottbusser Tor at Dresdener Strasse 126, with a great program of films in their original languages.

—PASCAL EDELMANN
Press Officer, European Film Academy & European Film Awards

famous Cold War speech: "All free men, wherever they may live, are citizens of Berlin and...I take pride in the words *Ich bin ein Berliner.*" (According to some sources, a slight grammatical hitch meant that these words sounded like he was claiming to be a jelly doughnut, but more recently Germans have come to his defense and said that he had it right.) The crowds returned to the hall on November 22 on hearing of Kennedy's assassination. A plaque commemorates his speech and death. Inside is an exhibition about German chancellor and Berlin mayor Willy Brandt.

🅰 Map p. 176 B1 ✉ John-F.-Kennedy-Platz
☎ 030 756 00 🚇 U-Bahn: Rathaus Schöneberg

In Berlin's quiet western suburbs, surprises ranging from a Renaissance citadel to an extraordinary ethnological museum

Spandau, Dahlem, & the West

Introduction & Map   188–189

Olympiastadion   190–191

Spandau Altstadt & the Zitadelle   192–193

Feature: The Strange Story of Rudolf Hess   194–195

Museen Dahlem—Kunst und Kulturen der Welt   196–199

Experience: Domäne Dahlem   197

Grunewald   200–202

Experience: Never Too Cold to Party   202

Wannsee   203–204

More Places to Visit in Spandau, Dahlem, & the West   205–206

Hotels & Restaurants   254

The Final Solution was born at the Wannsee Conference in this villa.

Spandau, Dahlem, & the West

Spandau, Dahlem, and Wannsee, in Berlin's western extremity, still seem more like country towns than parts of a European metropolis. But among the spacious houses and gardens is scattered an array of sights so varied that few visitors will resist the temptation and a longer-than-usual U-Bahn or S-Bahn trip to seek them out.

As is commonly the case in Berlin, paradoxes are not lacking. The Nazi Olympic stadium, stage of one of Adolf Hitler's early propaganda triumphs, survived the war to play a double role today as a protected monument—a symbol of the Nazi misuse of sports—and as Berlin's modern-day football (soccer) temple.

To Berlin's west, Spandau's compact town center makes for a pleasant stroll, but the main sight is the Zitadelle, an enormous Renaissance fortress that saw action during the Napoleonic Wars. Miraculously, it was left mostly untouched in the final days of World War II.

South of the Olympic stadium stretches the forest paradise of Grunewald (Green Forest). At its northern end is the Teufelsberg, a 377-foot (115 m) "mountain" made entirely of rubble left behind by the bombing of Berlin and the final months' fighting. Nature lovers can follow a path from near the stadium south along the east bank of the broad Havel River to Wannsee and even on to Potsdam.

On the eastern flank of the forest, in another onetime village, Dahlem, is a center of culture. The Museen Dahlem constitute some of the world's most extensive and impressive ethnological collections. Dahlem also holds the art gem of the Brücke Museum and the nearby Alliierten-Museum, dedicated to the history of the three western Allied powers in occupied West Berlin.

The Havel swings slowly southwest to Potsdam, passing Wannsee, Berlin's extreme southwest corner, along the way. From the summertime beach activity at Strandbad Wannsee to the princely Schloss Glienicke, the walker will come across traditional eateries, the pleasant Pfaueninsel, and, unhappily, another reminder of Nazi evil: the villa where the Wannsee Conference on the Final Solution was held. ∎

NOT TO BE MISSED:

The grand Olympiastadion, site of the 1936 games 190–191

Touring Spandau's glorious Renaissance citadel 192–193

Dahlem's splendid Ethnology Museum 197–199

Walking through the lordly hunting lodge and leafy paths of Grunewald 200–202

The sculpted gardens and follies of Peacock Island 204

Luftwaffen-museum

KLADOW

Meierei

Pfaueninsel (Peacock Island)

Schlösschen

PFAUENINSEL-CHAUSSEE

VOLKSPARK KLEIN-GLIENICKE

Schloss Glienicke

DÜPPEL FOREST

WANNSEE

KÖNIGSTRASSE 1

To Potsdam

Pohlesee

Griebnitzsee

Stölpchensee

A

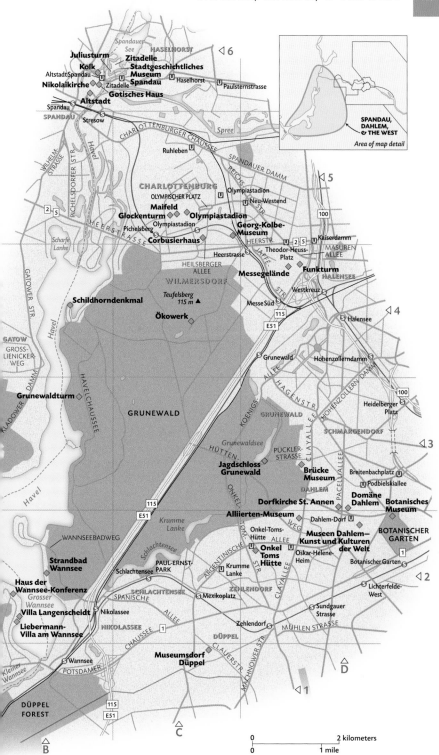

SPANDAU,
DAHLEM,
& THE WEST
Area of map detail

6
HASELHORST
Juliusturm
Zitadelle
Kolk   Stadtgeschichtliches
Altstadt Spandau   Museum
Nikolaikirche   Spandau   Haselhorst   Paulsternstrasse
Gotisches Haus
Altstadt
Spandau
SPANDAU   Stresow
CHARLOTTENBURGER CHAUSSEE   Spree
Ruhleben   SPANDAUER DAMM
5
CHARLOTTENBURG
OLYMPISCHER PLATZ   Olympiastadion
Neu-Westend
Maifeld   REICHS   STR
Glockenturm   Olympiastadion   100
Pichelsberg   Olympiastadion
Corbusierhaus   Georg-Kolbe-
Museum
HEERSTR.
JAFFÉ   2   5   Kaiserdamm
Heerstrasse   Theodor-Heuss-   MASUREN
HEILSBERGER   Platz   ALLEE
ALLEE
WILMERSDORF   Messegelände   Funkturm
HALENSEE
Teufelsberg
Schildhorndenkmal   115 m ▲   Westkreuz
Ökowerk   Messe Süd   4
E51   Halensee
Grunewald
GATOWER   Hohenzollerndamm
STR   ALLEE
HAGENSTR
Grunewaldturm   HOHENZOLLERN DAMM   100
HAVELCHAUSSEE   Heidelberger
GRUNEWALD   GRUNEWALD   Platz
KOENIGS   CLAYALLEE   SCHMARGENDORF   3
Grunewaldsee   PACELLIALLEE
HÜTTEN   PÜCKLER-   Breitenbachplatz
Jagdschloss   STRASSE   Podbielskiallee
Grunewald   Brücke
Museum   DAHLEM   Domäne
ONKEL   Dorfkirche St. Annen   Dahlem   Botanisches
Museum
Alliierten-Museum   WEG   Dahlem-Dorf   BOTANISCHER
TOMS   Onkel-Toms-   GARTEN
Krumme   Hütte   ALLEE   Museen Dahlem—
Lanke   Onkel   Kunst und Kulturen
E51   Toms   der Welt   1
Hütte   Oskar-Helene-
115   STR   Heim   Botanischer Garten
WANNSEEBADWEG   ARGENTINISCHE   CLAYALLEE
Strandbad   PAUL-ERNST-   2
Wannsee   PARK   Lichterfelde-
Schlachtensee   West
Haus der   SPANISCHE   SCHLACHTENSEE   Sundgauer
Wannsee-Konferenz   Mexikoplatz   Strasse
Grosser   ZEHLENDORF
Wannsee   Villa Langenscheidt   Nikolassee   MÜHLEN STRASSE
Liebermann-   ALLEE   Zehlendorf
Villa am Wannsee   NIKOLASSEE   1   DÜPPEL
Wannsee   CHAUSSEE   CLAUERTSTR   MACHNOWER STR
POTSDAMER   Museumsdorf   D
Düppel
1
115   C
E51   DÜPPEL
FOREST   0   2 kilometers
B   0   1 mile

Olympiastadion

Hitler's 1936 Olympic stadium had to wait 70 years for international redemption. Recently modernized, the stadium was selected for the finals (including the final match) of the 2006 FIFA World Cup football (soccer) fest. Amid the football fever, one wonders how many onlookers had flashbacks to 1936.

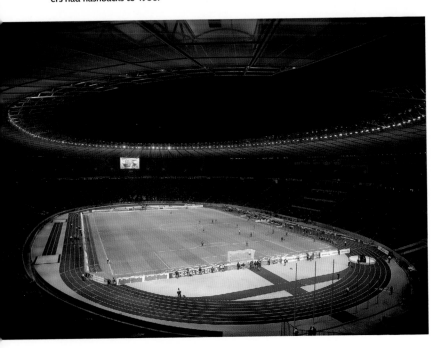

The 2004 renovation of the Olympiastadion cost nearly 30 times as much as the original structure.

Olympiastadion

- 189 C5
- Olympischer Platz 3
- 030 25 00 23 22
- Tours mid-March–Oct. 11 a.m., 1 & 3 p.m.; Nov.–mid-March 11 a.m.
- $$; guided tour $$$
- U-Bahn: Olympiastadion

www.olympia stadion-berlin.de

Built in 1934–1936 by Werner March (1894–1976) in monumental Nazi style, the stadium's solid lines and powerful stonework remain those of Hitler's day; the stadium is cataloged as a national monument. The old stonework is combined with the latest in stadium technology, most evident in the partial roof that protects nearly all the seats from inclement weather. The stadium is thus at once a homage to modern sports and a quiet reminder of the past.

The original was quite an achievement for its day, holding up to 100,000 people (today reduced to 74,400, largely because of fire safety requirements). Every element had a message. The reinforced concrete structure was partially coated in hand-cut Bavarian limestone, in a typically Nazi tribute to traditional values. The two towers of the **East Gate** represent Prussia and Bavaria linked by the five Olympic rings. (The two regions historically loathe one another, but not according to Hitler.) The opposite end of the stadium was dubbed the **Marathon Gate.** Here the Olympic flame burned; in fact, the Germans came up with the idea of the relay that brings the Olympic flame from Greece to the current stadium.

The names of the 1936 gold-medal winners are engraved on the walls here, led by African-American athlete Jesse Owens, who took four. Protocol dictated that the head of state give all champion athletes a handshake. "Do you really think I will allow myself to be photographed shaking hands with a Negro?" the Führer frothed when Owens's turn came. And so he ducked out on an affair of state.

Beyond the stadium to the west is the **Maifeld** (May Field), designed for massive Nazi May Day parades. The rather ominous **Glockenturm** (Bell Tower), rebuilt in the 1960s, was another Nazi Olympic touch. A giant bell inside it tolled to open the games. The bell has been placed on the south flank of the stadium.

Beneath the grandstand of the Maifeld is the **Langemarck-Halle,** a Gothic-style memorial hall commemorating soldiers who died in Belgium during World War I. On the ground floor, a permanent exhibition tells the fascinating history of the Olympiastadion. In the small cinema opposite, a short documentary examines the link the Nazis sought to forge between sports and self-sacrifice in battle.

INSIDER TIP:

Just west of Olympiastadion, paddle among reedbeds in Klein Venedig (Little Venice), nestled in the erstwhile fishing village of Tiefwerder.

—AXEL SAUER
Owner, Der Bootsladen boat rentals

Nowadays, the stadium is home field to Berlin's top first-division football team, Hertha BSC. You are free to visit the stadium alone, but joining an hour-long tour *(1–3 times a day, but not held during events)* has the advantage of taking you into spots otherwise off-limits. ∎

The Nazi Olympics

After World War I prevented Germany from hosting the 1916 Olympic Games, the country managed to secure the 1936 games for Berlin. By the time they were held, Hitler had been in power for three years. He used the athletic contests masterfully as a propaganda vehicle. These were the first televised Olympics and the first in which telex was used to transmit results. Some 4,000 athletes from 49 countries attended the games. To divert international media attention from the unpleasant realities of Nazi rule, all posters and other signs of anti-Semitic policy were removed for the duration.

The '36 games were an unqualified success for Nazi Germany, which took 89 medals, leaving the United States in second place with 56.

Spandau Altstadt & the Zitadelle

The history of the medieval village of Spandau, about 9 miles (15 km) west of central Berlin, reaches back to the eighth century. Declared a city in 1232, the market and fortress town at the confluence of the Havel and Spree Rivers was swallowed up by Greater Berlin in 1920. For centuries, Spandau was one of Berlin's main defensive bastions; its 16th-century fortress, or *Zitadelle,* is a gem of Renaissance military architecture.

The weapons of another age are lined up in the Renaissance-era *Zitadelle* in Spandau.

Zitadelle

- 189 C6
- Am Juliusturm
- 030 354 94 42 00
- $
- U-Bahn: Zitadelle

www.zitadelle-berlin .de

Spandau was also a major arms-production center by the late 19th century. The 1919 Versailles peace treaty was a disaster for the town, as it forbade weapons manufacture and cost Spandau 44,000 jobs. After World War II (during which it was again an important arms center), the area was assigned to the British sector of divided Berlin. In 1947, a 19th-century military prison a few miles from the town center *(on Wilhelmstrasse)* was turned into a high-security compound for just seven top Nazis condemned for war crimes. The prison was

demolished after its last inmate, Hitler's unrepentant right-hand man Rudolf Hess, committed suicide in 1987 (see pp. 194–195).

Spandau's fortress, the Zitadelle, was overrun during the Thirty Years' War in the 17th century and taken by the French without a shot being fired in 1806. The fort miraculously survived the Allied bombings that heavily damaged the nearby Altstadt (Old Town) in World War II. Nor was it harmed by the last days of street fighting between German and Soviet troops.

The fortress was built from 1560 to 1594 in the style of

complex Renaissance Italian forts, its walls designed to deflect artillery shot. The square-based citadel replaced an earlier medieval castle, of which the 13th-century crenellated **Juliusturm** is about the only reminder. You can climb this tower for views over all Spandau. The local history museum, the **Stadtgeschichtliches Museum Spandau**, is housed in the armory (*Zeughaus*), but for the history of the fortress itself you need to wander over to the **Kommandantenhaus** building, where a modest display explains all. Other rooms are given over to exhibition space, galleries, and a luxurious, medieval-style restaurant. The citadel's tunnels and other darker corners also attract up to 10,000 wintering bats every year (see sidebar).

Today, the tiny Altstadt has recovered some of its medieval appeal, with cobbled lanes leading into the main square, the Reformationsplatz. At its center rises the 14th-century **Nikolaikirche** (Church of St. Nicholas), a late Gothic brick church inside which you can see a medieval baptismal font and a 16th-century Renaissance altar. It is possible to climb the doughty fortified west tower. The name of the square is no coincidence. The first Protestant service was held here in 1539 after Elector Joachim II (1505–1571) adopted the new faith.

Nearby, Spandau's tourist office has taken refuge in what is thought to be Berlin's oldest house, the mid-15th-century brick **Gotisches Haus** (Gothic House; *Breite Strasse 32, tel 030 333 93 88, closed Sun.*), which frequently

holds temporary art and history exhibitions beneath its roof.

The oldest part of the Altstadt, known as the **Kolk**, lies north of Am Juliusturm street. Its endearing, wood-framed houses are called *Fachwerkhäuser* (timbered houses).

Luftwaffenmuseum

About 6 miles (10 km) south of the old center of Spandau is an air force buff's dream destination, the **Luftwaffenmuseum**, once the Gatow Aerodrome. Built for the Luftwaffe (air force) in 1935, it was home to one of four air force officer schools under the Third Reich. From 1945 until 1994, it was a British Royal Air Force base and, along with Tempelhof airport, was used to fly supplies into West Berlin during the 1948 Soviet blockade. The German Luftwaffe moved in again in 1995 and turned the place into a grand museum.

More than a hundred military aircraft are displayed in hangars and around the base, including many World War II classics, such as the Messerschmitt Bf 109 and the Heinkel He 111. ∎

Nikolaikirche

🗺 189 B6
✉ Reformationsplatz
☎ 030 333 56 39
🕐 Museum closed Mon., Tues., & Thurs.; tower open for tours Sat. 12:30 p.m., Sun. 2:30 p.m. April–Oct.
💲 Tower: $
🚇 U-Bahn: Altstadt Spandau

www.nikolai-spandau.de

Luftwaffen-museum

🗺 188 A3
✉ Berlin-Gatow Aerodrome, Ritterfelddamm / Am Flugplatz, Gatow
☎ 030 811 07 69
🕐 Closed Mon.
🚇 U-Bahn: Rathaus Spandau & bus 135 to Kurpromenade; follow Am Flugplatz Gatow east to museum

www.luftwaffen museum.de

Going Batty

The world's sole flying mammal is notoriously reclusive. But the dark vaults of Spandau Citadel happen to shelter a massive indigenous bat colony. In the Fledermauskeller (Bat Cellar), you can view short-tailed bats and larger Egyptian fruit bats swarming in their dimly lit cave, protected by a sheet of plexiglass. During the summer, you can take a guided tour of the casemates, home to around 10,000 bats (*tel 030 36 75 00 61, www.bat-ev.de*).

The Strange Story of Rudolf Hess

At the 1946 Nuremberg war crimes trials after World War II, Adolf Hitler's onetime right-hand man, Rudolf Hess (1894–1987), was asked if he was guilty. His reply was a simple *Nein*.

Rudolf Hess (left, behind Hitler)

Earlier in the trial, Hess had asserted that, given the choice, he would have done it all again, "even in the knowledge that I would end up burning at the stake!" In spite of doubts about his sanity, Hess was found guilty of planning a war of aggression and of being part of a conspiracy against world peace. He was not found guilty of war crimes or crimes against humanity. He was one of seven top-ranking Nazis to receive long jail sentences.

Hess, the son of a salesman, fought in the infantry and air force in World War I. An economics and history student in Munich, he joined Hitler's Nazi Party as member No. 16 in 1920. The two spent much of 1924 in prison after Hitler's failed Munich coup attempt in 1923. To while away the hours, Hitler dictated *Mein Kampf* to Hess. After their release, Hess became Hitler's personal secretary. Although

from 1933 he was made the "Führer's Deputy," he gradually lost influence. Hess remained blindly loyal to Hitler to the end, but the Führer had less and less time for a hypochondriac who believed in astrology and the occult (as well as Nazism).

Perhaps that loss of influence prompted Hess, on May 10, 1941, to make a secret flight to Britain. Hess piloted the Messerschmitt 110 himself on the same night that hundreds of Luftwaffe bombers launched one of the heaviest air raids of the war on London. He parachuted into Scotland and was sent as a POW to London, where he claimed to be bringing a peace offer. Perhaps his thinking was: If I can convince the British to exit the war, Hitler will be free to concentrate on the coming invasion of Russia and I shall be back among the big boys in the Nazi hierarchy.

The British thought he might be unbalanced and subjected him to psychiatric examination. As if to confirm their suspicions, on May 11 Hitler disavowed his former pal and declared him a psychopath. The whole affair is so odd that historians still speculate on Hess's motives.

Four Power Agreement

During the Cold War, two Berlin-based institutions were subject to the Four Power Agreement, a pact defining the responsibilities of the western Allies and the Soviet Union in occupied Germany. Spandau Prison was one. Based in Kleistpark (see p. 186), the other was the Berlin Air Safety Center (BASC), which regulated flights through "corridors" in GDR airspace.

After sharing jail time with Hitler, Rudolf Hess became the Führer's right-hand man.

Was it as Hess told it? Alternative theories abound. One suggests Hess fell into a trap set by the British secret service, while another claims the man was a double (but why, and what happened to the real Hess?). British documents on the case will not enter the public domain until 2018.

Hess and his companions were incarcerated not in Spandau's citadel, but in a prison built for the purpose west of Spandau's old town center and jointly run by the four Allied powers. All prisoners but Hess were set free by 1966. Repeated appeals for his release were stubbornly vetoed by the Soviet Union, and he finally committed suicide in 1987. The building was demolished shortly thereafter.

Museen Dahlem—Kunst und Kulturen der Welt

This museum complex set in peaceful Dahlem in southwest Berlin is a treasure chest of artifacts. They come primarily from non-European cultures, ranging from the Arctic to the South Seas and from Japan to Africa. You would need a full day to give the collections—divided into four museums spread over three floors—even a fraction of the attention they deserve. The itinerary suggested below is just one option. Pick and choose the elements that most attract you.

Priceless statuary stands in the Museum für Indische Kunst.

Museen Dahlem— Kunst und Kulturen der Welt

🅰 189 D2
✉ Lansstrasse 8
☎ 030 830 14 38
🕐 Closed Mon.
💲 $$
🚇 U-Bahn: Dahlem-Dorf

www.smb.museum

Ticket in hand, head toward the café and turn left into the **Museum für Indische Kunst** (Museum of Indian Art), a multi-faceted excursion into the world of Indian art, with some detours into neighboring countries.

The collection starts with a tiny terra-cotta statuette of a female figure from about 3300 B.C., but rapidly moves to more recent times. A curious early piece is a standing Bodhisattva with tight curly hair and a friendly smile. This statue was found in Afghanistan and dates to at least the third century B.C. Take time to examine the series of small, intricate reliefs set in the middle of the first room. Carved mostly from schist, they recount various Buddhist scenes. The green soapstone bust of the four-headed god Harihara, made in the ninth century in Kashmir, is a beautiful piece. Brief sections on Islam and the Jain faith in India follow. The former includes beautifully carved wooden doors and colorful, glazed ceramics with geometrical patterns. Nearby is a huge temple wall hanging of the Krishna cult from Rajastan.

Objects from Southeast Asia, especially Thailand and Cambodia, occupy the mezzanine level. Among them are pottery, jewelry, and bronze statues. A beautiful illustrated manuscript from Thonburi, Thailand, dates to 1776. The display rounds off with Nepalese painted-cloth images of Vishnu.

Ethnology Museum

Walk back past the café to the beginning of the Ethnologisches Museum (Ethnology Museum), the backbone of the Dahlem collections. It starts with a long hall crammed with an extraordinary array of statuary, ceramics, figurines, and jewelry from across pre-Columbian South America. Giant steles lead the way. Found in a Maya temple complex near Santa Lucía Cozumalhuapa in Guatemala in the 1860s, they date from the Preclassical period, roughly 1500 B.C. to A.D. 200. There follows a collection of artifacts from Preclassical Maya culture, mostly in ancient Mexico. Curious human figurines in jade, basalt, and other hard stones are among the more intriguing objects.

South Seas Collections: The door at the end of this hall leads into what is for most visitors a still more fascinating world, the

---

EXPERIENCE:
Domäne Dahlem

Sleepy as pigs after feeding time, the former village of Dahlem has transformed a centuries-old Prussian manor and farm into an open-air museum *(Königin-Luise-Strasse 49, tel 030 666 30 00, www.domaene-dahlem.de, closed Tues., $).* The master's residence has meaningful displays on subsistence living, but more popular draws are in the outbuildings, where families from all over Berlin converge for pottery workshops, classical music recitals, and readings of Grimm's fairy tales. Chattering visitors make a leisurely loop through the 30-acre (12 ha) tract, pausing to read the crop signs and pet farm animals. At Christmastime, vendors sell regional produce and handicrafts from market stalls, while the shop and beer garden are open all year, seemingly a world away from the big city.

South Seas collections. Objects from across the South Pacific present an utterly unexpected diversity. Among the first items you see on entering are enormous, decorated wooden carvings of fish, examples of Malanggan ceremonial burial art in New Ireland. Near them are some fairly scary masks used in ceremonies in New Britain and a pair of towering New Guinean ancestral poles, which depict men sitting or standing on each other's shoulders.

It is difficult to resist the temptation to skip all of this and head straight for the **island boat collection.** Brought to Berlin more than a century ago, these wooden vessels used in the Pacific fire the imagination. Most impressive is the one at extreme left, a deep-hulled Micronesian affair powered by sail and paddles and used for war and trade. It could carry up to 50 people.

Facing the boat collection are more masks, representing the recently dead who, in this form, were said to visit the living. Made of wood, leaves, woven textiles, and other materials, they are all quite different from one another and uniformly unnerving. In the center of the hall stands a reconstructed thatched-roof men's clubhouse from the Pacific island of Palau.

The South Seas collections continue upstairs, with furniture, jewelry, and dresses from Palau and the Marianas island group. Interesting items include Maori wood carvings—particularly the complex boat prows and sterns— Easter Island wooden statuary, and bark cloth from Tahiti.

North American Indian Collection: From here, return downstairs to the South American collection and follow the signs to the North American Indian collection. You start with the Eskimos. Among the predictable items of clothing (caribou-skin coats, snowshoes, fur boots) is an interesting piece: a canoeist's raincoat made of a seal's intestinal lining. The collection soon takes you to the United States, with displays on the proud past and difficult present of various Indian tribes.

From the spot where the North American Indian collection begins, follow a side hall up a few stairs into the **Goldkammer** (Gold Chamber), a collection of gold jewelry, figurines, bottles, and the like from pre-Columbian Colombia, Mexico, and Peru.

The succeeding rooms are

European displays at the Museen Dahlem include nativity scenes from Krakow.

Market of Continents

On the lookout for hand-woven African fabrics, jewelry from India, or felt boots from Kazakhstan? On four weekends before Christmas, 50-plus vendors gather in the Dahlem museum complex to offer exotic arts and crafts from around the globe. The emphasis of this Market of Continents *(www.marktderkontinente.de)* is on goods produced in a variety of international locations, with the proceeds from the market going to social and structural projects in those areas.

Each weekend is devoted to a different continent, and concerts, workshops, and special exhibitions are held throughout the day.

dedicated to **South American archaeology** and are dominated by ceramics, busts, and textiles from the Inca Empire. They were found in an area around the Andes mountains stretching from Ecuador in the north via Peru to Chile in the south.

Besides the South Seas collections, the next floor hosts a display of **African art,** notably wooden statuary, weapons, and the like from the Congo region, Cameroon, and Benin. The collection, one of the most important of its kind in the world, covers five centuries of African history.

The other star attraction on this floor is the **Museum für Ostasiatische Kunst** (Museum of East Asian Art). Pick up the handy room plan as you enter. The collections are divided between Chinese items—bronzes, porcelain, religious objects, paintings, and graphic arts—and a similar array of Japanese material. In one of the central rooms is a 17th-century Qing dynasty rosewood imperial throne with mother-of-pearl lacquer and a huge Qing dynasty vase. Among the Japanese crafts is a series of masks used in traditional Noh theater.

The displays rather peter out on the top floor, which houses a small collection of **musical instruments** from Southeast Asia (including a gamelan ensemble from Indonesia), the Middle East, and Africa. Also here is a section on daily life in East Asia, featuring a mixed bag of art and religious and household items from Japan and China.

Museum of European Cultures

In a separate building behind the main complex, the Museum Europäischer Kulturen (Museum of European Cultures) ponders social change and cultural diversity as embodied by such objects as a 36-foot Venetian gondola from 1910 and an ornate royal coach. Tucked away in the basement, a highlight is the mechanical *Weihnachtsberg,* a huge nativity scene from the Ore Mountains, famed for its Christmas decorations.

The room next door contains the **Juniormuseum,** an interactive journey from Berlin to the four corners of the world aimed at young children (at least, those who read German). ■

Grunewald

If you walk or cycle through the Grunewald woods now, you'll find it hard to believe that two-thirds of this forest was destroyed by the end of World War II. Since 1949, the woods have been reforested with more than 20 million conifers and broad-leaved trees. Always popular with Berliners in need of fresh air, the area took on special significance for West Berliners after the Wall went up in 1961. This was the only bit of countryside they could enjoy.

The peaceful Schlachtensee is just one of several lakes around the woods of Grunewald.

Alliierten-Museum

🅰 189 D2

✉ Clayallee 135

☎ 030 818 19 90

🕐 Closed Wed.

🚇 U-Bahn: Oskar-Helene-Heim

www.alliierten museum.de

Even in this bucolic corner of town, one is reminded of those Cold War days at the **Alliierten-Museum** (Allied Museum). The museum, which may soon move to a more central location, tells the story of the western Allied occupying forces—the United States, Britain, and France—in Berlin in the Cold War years.

A British Hastings transport plane of the kind used in the Berlin Airlift stands in the yard between the museum's two buildings. Behind it is a French military train wagon and the last of the U.S. Checkpoint Charlie buildings (in use from 1986–1990), moved here from central Berlin after reunification. The permanent exhibition contains Allied uniforms, medals, and equipment, complemented by a wealth of documents, letters, newspaper clippings, and a huge store of photos, only a fraction of which is ever shown. The display is split between the **Outpost Theater,** which covers the period from 1945 to 1950 (with particular coverage of the airlift), and the **Nicholson Memorial Library,** which runs from 1951 to 1994, the year all foreign troops withdrew from Berlin. Among the items are the front of the first Checkpoint Charlie, erected in 1961, a re-creation of a spy tunnel built by the Allies under East Berlin to tap Soviet communications, and an array of Cold War–era signs and newspaper front pages.

Brücke Museum

The Brücke Museum is just a quick bus ride north of the Alliierten-Museum on the edge of the Grunewald woods. It holds an impressive collection of paintings, sketches, watercolors, and other works by a singular group of pre–World War I artists. Works on display include material by the group's main protagonists, Ernst Ludwig Kirchner, Erich Heckel (1883–1970), Otto Müller (1874–1930), and Karl Schmidt-Rottluff (1884–1976). They were joined briefly by Emil Nolde (1867–1956) and Max Pechstein (1881–1955).

Young and rebellious, the art-ists founded the Brücke ("bridge") association in Dresden in 1905 and swore never to abandon one another. They drifted to Berlin in 1911, where big-city distractions, rivalry, and the increasing desire of each to win recognition led to the dissolution of the group in 1913.

In that brief period, these young artists turned out a prolific collective oeuvre, which represents the dawn of German expression-ism. The museum, whose creation was largely promoted by Schmidt-Rottluff, contains the single most extensive collection of the artists' graphic works (lithographs, woodcuts, and crayon and pencil drawings). Given his key role in the creation of the museum, it is not surprising that many of Schmidt-Rottluff's primary-colored later works are also held in the museum's archives.

The best known of the Brücke artists was, however, Kirchner. To him we owe a rich collection of Berlin street scenes and not a few nudes. His human figures are often long and angular, with a resemblance to African art, and the colors strong but dark.

Brücke Museum

- ⬛ 189 D3
- ✉ Bussardsteig 9
- ☎ 030 831 20 29
- 🕐 Closed Tues.
- 💲 $$
- 🚇 U-Bahn: Oskar-Helene-Heim & bus 115 to Pücklerstrasse

**www.bruecke
-museum.de**

Berlin, Capital of Wild Boar

Fierce-looking, nimble, and usually hungry, wild boar occasionally venture into urban Berlin from forests such as the Grunewald, wreaking havoc on soccer fields, public parks, and the nerves of residents. Their local numbers estimated at over 3,000, these animals can weigh more than 300 pounds (136 kg) and have been sighted in the middle of the city. In 2002, a marks-man was called to bag an ornery specimen on Alexanderplatz.

So what's the attraction? In the green spaces of the capital, most of the trees are oaks, and acorns happen to be a boar's favorite food. But in a pinch, fresh fruit and vegetables, or even wormy compost, will do—all abundantly on offer in Berlin's many *Kleingärten* (garden allotments).

He and his pals spent a fair amount of time in Berlin's bordel-los and cabarets and with their models. Kirchner's "Erich Heckel und Otto Müller beim Schach" ("Erich Heckel and Otto Müller Play Chess," 1913) shows his two colleagues playing chess, taking no notice of a nude woman draped on a sofa like a coat. Heckel was

Jagdschloss Grunewald

🗺 189 D3

✉ Hüttenweg 10

☎ 030 813 35 97

🕐 Closed Aug. & Sept., Mon. April–July & Oct.; guided tours Sat. & Sun. Nov.– March

💲 $$

🚇 U-Bahn: Oskar-Helene-Heim & bus 115 to Pücklerstrasse

www.spsg.de

Onkel Toms Hütte

🗺 189 D2

✉ Onkel-Tom-Strasse 100

🚇 U-Bahn: Onkel-Toms-Hütte

prolific; many of his paintings and sketches are on display, such as his nude "Junger Mann und Mädchen" ("Young Man and Girl," 1909). Pechstein is also known for his nudes, including "Tanz" ("Dance," 1909), a wildly cavorting couple.

Jagdschloss Grunewald

Stroll for about 15 minutes west from the Brücke Museum down Pücklerstrasse and follow a forest path through quiet woods to the enchanting Jagdschloss Grunewald, a lordly hunting lodge on the edge of a pretty lake, the Grunewaldsee. Elector Joachim II of Brandenburg had this three-story Renaissance-era mansion built in the Green Forest in 1542. Baroque alterations and lower outbuildings that form a courtyard around the mansion were added in the 18th century. The hunt was a popular

EXPERIENCE:
Never Too Cold to Party

If Jack Frost stops by long enough, the Spree River freezes over and Berlin's insatiable community of merrymakers comes out to throw an ice rave. Don't miss this for the world! Vendors arrive on makeshift carts to sell bratwurst and mulled wine, while DJs spin tunes on portable stereos. Red-cheeked dancers wobble on the frozen expanse. After nightfall, lanterns are hung on riverside trees and the mood shifts up a gear. Try the shallower inlets of the Wannsee, Müggelsee, or Rummelsburger See, and don't forget your spikes or skates (Kaufhof department store is an easy option, see Travelwise p. 257).

INSIDER TIP:

Onkel Toms Hütte, on the southeastern edge of the Grunewald, is a UNESCO-protected Modernism development worth a visit.

—BEN BUSCHFELD
National Geographic contributor

activity with the rulers of Brandenburg and Prussia, and the *Jagdschloss* was in use until World War I. The long, low building that faces the mansion stored hunting material and is lined with the antlers of felled beasts. Inside there is a museum on the business of the hunt, with weapons and other equipment. The most impressive part of the *Schloss* itself is the main hall on the first floor. The building now has a mixed collection of 15th- to 18th-century art, including works by Lucas Cranach the Elder (1472–1553) and the Younger (1515–1586).

Ökowerk

Lodged in and around a handsome 19th-century waterworks south of the Teufelsberg (see p. 206), the nature center Ökowerk *(Teufelsseechaussee 22, closed Mon., S-Bahn: Heerstrasse & walk 25 min.)* boasts a large organic garden, ponds filled with frogs, and a charming lunch café. An aquatic information display is set up in the old filter works. Family-friendly workshops, field trips, and guided tours are offered throughout the year. ∎

Wannsee

Tucked away in the extreme southwest of Berlin, Wannsee is a peaceful, wooded outpost of villas and boat clubs on the south shore of the Havel River. One of the grandest villas was the location for the 1942 Nazi conference that decided on the extermination of European Jews. A few villas away is Berlin artist Max Liebermann's former summer house, now a museum. Long-ish walks in the woods lead to Pfaueninsel, the island site of a onetime royal country palace.

In summer, swans and Berliners alike flock to lake beaches.

Coming from central Berlin, your first stop can be the lakeside beaches of **Strandbad Wannsee,** although it might be more logical to finish a day of sightseeing by flopping on the beach last of all. The southern end is about a ten-minute walk from the Nikolassee S-Bahn stop. The sandy beach, with snack stands, beach basketball, and a playground, is a popular draw. The beach's supporting buildings are a century old.

Southwest of the beach across the Grosser Wannsee lake stands the **Liebermann-Villa am Wannsee,** which Liebermann built in 1910 as a summer retreat. In early 2006, it reopened as a museum dedicated to the Berlin impressionist's life and works. The original layout of the picturesque hedge garden will be restored and unveiled in 2014. Liebermann, born into a wealthy Jewish family, became head of the Prussian Art Academy after World War I. He

Strandbad Wannsee

🅐 189 B2

✉ Wannseebadweg

🕐 Closed Oct.–March

💲 $

🚇 S-Bahn: Nikolassee

Liebermann-Villa am Wannsee

- Ⓜ 189 B2
- ✉ Colomierstrasse 3, Am Grossen Wannsee
- ☎ 030 80 58 59 00
- 🕐 Closed Tues.
- 💲 $$
- 🚆 S-Bahn: Wannsee & bus 114 to Liebermann-Villa

www.liebermann -villa.de

Haus der Wannsee-Konferenz

- Ⓜ 189 B2
- ✉ Am Grossen Wannsee 56–58
- ☎ 030 805 00 10
- 🚆 S-Bahn: Wannsee & bus 114 to Haus der Wannsee-Konferenz

www.ghwk.de

Pfaueninsel

- Ⓜ 188 A2
- ☎ 030 80 58 68 31 (Schlösschen)
- 🚆 S-Bahn: Wannsee & bus 218 & ferry

www.spsg.de

Schloss Glienicke

- Ⓜ 188 A1
- ✉ Königstrasse 36
- ☎ 030 805 30 41
- 🕐 Closed Mon.
- 💲 $
- 🚆 S-Bahn: Wannsee & bus 316

www.spsg.de

The Final Solution

The "solution of the Jewish question" was discussed at Wannsee like any other bureaucratic matter. That the topic was how to destroy 11 million European Jews (from neutral Portugal and unconquered Great Britain to the Soviet Union) seems to have fazed no one. From a policy of forced emigration, halted in 1941, the Nazis had moved to deportation of Jews (mostly to Polish work and death camps). The ultimate aim was genocide. The matter-of-factness of the 15 pages of minutes from the 1942 meeting, which can be downloaded from the museum website, is hard to believe.

later resigned in disgust at the Nazis' anti-Semitic policies. On the first floor of the two-story villa is a collection of memorabilia, while the top floor, which has his restored studio, displays some of his paintings.

Across the street is the striking wood-framed caprice known as the **Villa Langenscheidt,** which still belongs to the German dictionary dynasty that had it built. A short walk farther north is the **Haus der Wannsee-Konferenz.** The sprawling gardens and magnate's villa were acquired by the SS paramilitary security organization in 1941. On January 20, 1942, a group of 15 high-ranking

Nazi Party officials gathered here to discuss the *Endlösung* (Final Solution)—the extermination of European Jewry. Displays cover the history of Jewish persecution in Nazi Germany and occupied Europe from 1933 to 1945.

After this sobering visit, you may need a long walk. Follow the riverbank walkway west for just over a mile (1.6 km) and you reach a ferry *(fee)* to **Pfaueninsel** (Peacock Island), named for its resident birds. A stroll around the 185-acre (75 ha) island is a delight. Apart from the sculpted gardens, you can visit the late 18th-century white **Schlösschen** (Little Castle) near the ferry landing, from late

INSIDER TIP:

Buy your train tickets from DB machines rather than the ticket counter, which adds a surcharge.

—KAREN CARMICHAEL
National Geographic writer

April to October *(closed Mon., $),* and the **Meierei** *(weekends only, Nov.–March, $),* a farm also created by Prussia's royals in the 18th century, at the island's northeast end. Check times for the last ferry.

Hardy walkers can go another 2 miles (3 km) west along the Havel's banks to reach the rear entrance to **Schloss Glienicke.** This neoclassic palace built by Karl Friedrich Schinkel in 1824 is the scene of regular concerts. ∎

More Places to Visit in Spandau, Dahlem, & the West

Botanischer Garten

A great way to get warm on a winter's day in Berlin is to visit the *Gewächshäuser* (hothouses) of this extensive suburban botanical garden. The central house is by far the biggest, a sweaty haven with soaring palms and bamboo trees. Giant rulers next to some of the latter mark the amazing rapidity of their growth. Another house is filled with the perfume of rhododendrons and camellias. Other structures are dedicated to Australian, South African, or Mediterranean plants; everything from cacti to orchids is on display. All manner of trees and plants spread out in the surrounding gardens—it is definitely better to visit in summer to enjoy this part of the site. Those wanting to understand the flora in the garden a little better can pop into the **Botanisches Museum,** where models and other displays reveal the inner workings of plant life. There are sections ranging from poisonous mushrooms to the many uses of plants.
www.bgbm.de Map p. 189 D2 ✉ Königin-Luise-Strasse 6–8 ☎ 030 83 85 01 00 💲 $$ 🚇 S-Bahn: Botanischer Garten

Dorfkirche St. Annen

Just across Pacelliallee from the Domäne Dahlem is the village church of St. Anne, a charming little stone, brick, and *Fachwerk* (timbered) place of worship set amid a crowded cemetery. A church has stood here since the 13th century, but what you see was built in the 17th century. The late Renaissance-style wooden pulpit was inserted in 1679. The carved altar dates to around 1500, while the crucifix on the altar, from 1490, was in the Klosterkirche in central Berlin, a church destroyed in World War II.
www.kirchengemeindedahlem.de 🗺 Map p. 189 D3 ✉ Königin-Luise-Strasse 55 ☎ 030 841 70 50 🕐 Open Sat.–Sun. 11 a.m.–1 p.m. 🚇 U-Bahn: Dahlem-Dorf

Funkturm

One of the symbols of the city, this radio-transmitter tower set amid the Messegelände (Trade Fair Grounds) was built in 1924–1926. Nicknamed *der lange Lulatsch* (lanky lad) by quick-witted Berliners, it looks a little like a simplified version of Paris's Eiffel Tower. In 1935, the world's first regular TV

The Corbusierhaus apartment building rises like a monolith in suburban Berlin.

transmission began from this tower, but since 1962 it has been used only as a relay station for amateur and police radio. Nowadays tourists and trade fair visitors stop by to take an elevator to the top for views around Berlin. Some stop off a third of the way up for a meal and view in the **Funkturm Restaurant.** Marlene Dietrich ate here shortly after it opened. To get to the tower, enter the fairgrounds from Masuren Allee.
www.funkturmrestaurant.de 🅰 Map p. 189 D4 ✉ Hammarskjöldplatz ☎ 030 30 38 29 00 💲 $ 🅱 U-Bahn: Kaiserdamm

INSIDER TIP:

In the historic Kolk district, the oldest area of Spandau, Brauhaus Spandau (*Neuendorfer Strasse 1*) **serves a changing cast of excellent house beers.**

—GABRIELLA LE BRETON
National Geographic author

Georg-Kolbe-Museum

One of Germany's leading 20th-century sculptors, Georg Kolbe (1877–1947) was a controversial figure, an artist on the edge who managed to garner Nazi approval. The museum is located in the brick studio he had built in 1928. Next door, constructed in the same stark, cubical style, was his house (now a café). Kolbe's statues are scattered about the gardens and in the main first-floor room. Some rooms host temporary exhibitions.

If you think Kolbe's house and studio are harsh in their design, continue down Sensburger Allee to Heilsberger Allee. Atop the wooded rise before you stands a stark housing complex concocted by the Swiss architect Le Corbusier (1887–1965) in 1957. The **Corbusierhaus** (*Flatowallee 16, www.corbusierhaus.de, S-Bahn: Olympiastadion*) was the precursor to the wave of characterless high-rise apartments that

swept the West from the 1960s on.
www.georg-kolbe-museum.de 🅰 Map p. 189 C5 ✉ Sensburger Allee 25 ☎ 030 304 21 44 🕐 Closed Mon. 💲 $$ 🅱 S-Bahn: Heerstrasse

Museumsdorf Düppel

The Museumsdorf Düppel, a self-proclaimed center for "experimental archaeology," is a short bus ride south of the Grunewald. This medieval village has been re-created on the site of a 12th-century settlement. At its core is a huddle of towering thatched houses, where costumed volunteers make crafts, breed near-extinct species of sheep and pigs, and grow long-forgotten plants. The traditional farming tools are copies of ones used in the Middle Ages. Despite their dedication to self-sufficiency, the original settlers stayed only 30 years; chances are they moved on to greener pastures in the village of **Zehlendorf.** Every Sunday at 11 a.m., a tour is given of the village, and at 2 p.m., a workshop demonstrates how you can make tar from wood. You can easily combine the visit with a couple of hours of sunbathing at the Schlachtensee.
www.dueppel.de 🅰 Map p. 189 C1 ✉ Clauertstrasse 11 ☎ 030 802 66 71 🕐 Open Thurs. & Sun. 💲 $ 🅱 S-Bahn: Zehlendorf, then bus 115

Teufelsberg

About a third of a mile (0.5 km) south of the Georg-Kolbe-Museum stretches a peaceful wooded hill, one of the highest in Berlin at 377 feet (115 m). Known as the Teufelsberg (Devil's Mountain), it is entirely artificial, made from rubble carted here in the wake of World War II. The hill is topped by a decommissioned Cold War listening station, now in a state of peaceful decay. The surrounding woods are laced with walking tracks, and the western slope is a good spot for tobogganing in winter.
🅰 Map p. 189 C4 ✉ Teufelsee Strasse 🅱 S-Bahn: Heerstrasse

History both scenic and somber at Potsdam, Sachsenhausen, Dresden, and other destinations not far from Berlin's city limits

Excursions

Introduction & Map   208–209

Potsdam   210–216

Sachsenhausen   217

Mecklenburg Lake District Drive   218–219

Dresden   220–224

Experience: Saxony's Paddle Steamers   221

Leipzig   225–228

Spreewald   229

Lutherstadt Wittenberg   230

More Excursions from Berlin   231–232

Hotels & Restaurants   254–255

A bust of Johann Sebastian Bach honors the man who was choirmaster of Leipzig's Thomaskirche for 27 years.

Excursions

Berlin is not the only exciting destination in northeastern Germany. The capital is ringed by significant sites: Some are cultural, while others offer wonderful ways to lose yourself in the countryside.

Dresden is booming after the horrors of World War II and long years of GDR stagnation.

The satellite town of Potsdam, for instance, southwest of Berlin, is the capital of Brandenburg state. The old town was devastated by World War II bombings, but the sprawling parade of palaces and parks to its west and north was left intact, presenting a fairy-tale escape hatch for Berliners.

An altogether different trip leads to Sachsenhausen. An hour-long S-Bahn ride through the northern suburbs of Berlin brings the visitor to this former concentration camp, one of the first established by the Nazis in the 1930s. Hundreds of thousands of Jews, homosexuals, communists, and others considered dangerous to Hitler's regime suffered and, in many cases, died here. It is a potently moving place to visit.

Farther from the capital, a wealth of possibilities opens up. The two main cities of the former kingdom of Saxony, Dresden and Leipzig, are magnets to the south. Both have put themselves back on the map since the German Democratic Republic collapsed in 1990. Dresden is perhaps best remembered for the horrific Allied bombings in 1945 that wiped out much of its old center. Its greatest symbol, the baroque Frauenkirche (Church of Our Lady) is only the latest of its historic monuments to rise from the ashes. Leipzig, 44 miles (115 km) to the west, is an equally attractive town, once home to the likes of Bach and Felix Mendelssohn. Its compact historic center holds churches, art collections, and history museums.

Between Leipzig and Berlin lies a key town in the history of modern Christianity. For it was in pretty Lutherstadt Wittenberg that the Reformation, which would split Europe into Catholic and Protestant camps, was born. The churches and other buildings associated with Martin Luther and his contemporaries are a UNESCO World Heritage site.

Escapes into the countryside can be launched in the Spreewald, southeast of Berlin, or among the lakes of southern Mecklenburg, north of the capital. A host of other small towns, typically not much more than an hour by train from Berlin, round out the options for exploration. ∎

NOT TO BE MISSED:

Taking in the royal pleasure dome of Potsdam **210–216**

Making a pilgrimage to the memorial of Sachsenhausen **217**

A treasure trove of Saxon riches in Dresden **220–224**

Enjoying the elegant arcades and musical traditions of historic Leipzig **225–228**

The birthplace of the Reformation at Lutherstadt Wittenberg **230**

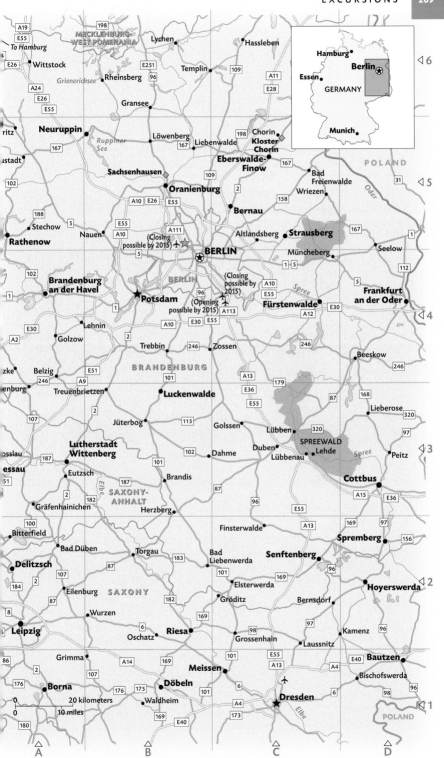

Potsdam

Not overly enamored of Berlin, Friedrich II created for himself a majestic bucolic getaway in the nearby town of Potsdam, 15 miles (24 km) southwest of the city, complete with gardens and a pair of palaces. His successors took up where he left off. By the end of World War I, the town boasted three parks dotted by palaces, mansions, and other whimsical buildings, along with the pleasantly planned baroque quarters gathered around the Old Town core.

The elaborate Neues Palais was built by Friedrich II in 1770.

Potsdam

🅜 209 B4

Visitor Information

✉ Brandenburger Strasse 3

 0331 27 55 80

 Car: A115 from Charlottenburg to the Babelsberg exit. Follow Nuthestrasse W to Potsdam. S-Bahn: Potsdam Hauptbahnhof

www.potsdam tourismus.de

On the night of April 15, 1945, a hail of British bombs rained down on this royal vacation spot, wreaking havoc on the old center but leaving the surrounding parks and palaces largely untouched. Easily reached from central Berlin, Potsdam today is a relatively well-to-do residential satellite of Berlin. It offers more than enough sightseeing to fill a couple of days.

If you come by S-Bahn from Berlin, your first impressions may

prompt you to turn around and catch the first train back. Don't! Having crossed the Lange Brücke (Long Bridge), you have before you a strange mix. The dome and neoclassic facade of the Karl Friedrich Schinkel–designed **Nikolaikirche** fronts a somewhat desolate square, still known as the Alter Markt (Old Market). Facing the square are the **Altes Rathaus** (Old City Hall), the 18th-century manor **Knobelsdorffhaus,** and an awful GDR-era college building (earmarked for demolition). This is the core of old Potsdam, and it bore the brunt of the bombing.

The church and former city hall (the latter now a local history museum and cultural center) were mostly rebuilt after the war, but something was missing: the **Stadtschloss** (City Palace). The 17th-century royal residence was damaged and subsequently demolished by the GDR. The government is now building a new state parliament, whose exterior will be a duplicate of the Stadtschloss, on this spot. Completion is scheduled for fall 2014.

The nearby **Marstall** is a long, low, fire-red, 18th-century orangerie designed by Georg Wenzeslaus von Knobelsdorff. It was turned into stables under Friedrich Wilhelm I and restored in the 1960s. Today it houses the **Filmmuseum Potsdam,** a look at the history of cinema.

A block north of the museum, the Neuer Markt (New Market) square boasts pretty renovated houses and the rather pompous facade of the Kutschstall (Coach Stable), which houses the **Haus der Brandenburgisch-Preussischen Geschichte** (House of Brandenburg-Prussian History), with displays on 900 years of Brandenburg history.

The aptly named Breite Strasse (Broad Street) is lined by mostly GDR-period buildings, but in coming years another key Potsdam building will reappear. The 18th-century baroque **Garnisonkirche** was heavily damaged in 1945, but its 1735 bell tower survived. The ideologues of the GDR, however,

decided it was representative of nasty imperial German tendencies and demolished it in 1968. With private funding, it is being rebuilt bit by bit. A temporary chapel has been raised, and a reconstructed bell tower will follow in 2017.

Baroque District

A few blocks north, the streets around Brandenburger Strasse make up Potsdam's baroque district, consisting mostly of pedestrian-only streets with two-story houses. Friedrich Wilhelm I ordered the district built from 1732 to 1742. Its prettiest

---

Fritz Fever

These days, the face of Frederick the Great ("Old Fritz" to his affectionate subjects) seems to be everywhere in Berlin and neighboring Brandenburg, apparently eclipsing the chancellor and even Germany's Next Top Model in popularity. In 2012, celebrations of the monarch's 300th birthday prompted an extra buffing of his equestrian statue on Unter den Linden. Sales boomed for Fritz postage stamps, special-issue coins, and bottles of Rex pilsener, brewed in Potsdam. Somewhat oddly, his majesty's mug does not peer from his gravestone at Schloss Sanssouci (see pp. 214–215), where admirers still leave potatoes to honor Frederick, who introduced the tuber to Prussia.

Nikolaikirche
- ✉ Alter Markt
- ☎ 0331 289 68 21
- 💲 Dome $$

www.nikolai-pots dam.de

Altes Rathaus
- ✉ Alter Markt
- ☎ 0331 289 68 21
- 🕐 Closed Mon.
- 💲 Potsdam Museum $

Filmmuseum Potsdam
- ✉ Marstall am Lustgarten, Breite Strasse 1a
- ☎ 0331 271 81 12
- 💲 $

www.filmmuseum potsdam.de

Haus der Brandenburgisch-Preussischen Geschichte
- ✉ Kutschstall, Am Neuer Markt 9
- ☎ 0331 620 85 50
- 🕐 Closed Mon.
- 💲 $

www.hbpg.de

part, just north of Bassinplatz, is the **Holländisches Viertel** (Dutch Quarter), with more than 130 gabled houses that Dutch workers called home. The core lies between Kurfürstenstrasse and Gutenberg Strasse.

A sobering excursion into Potsdam's darker history can be made at the **Gedenkstätte Lindenstrasse 54,** used by the Nazis as an *Erbgesundheitsgericht* (hereditary health court). Decisions on compulsory sterilization were made here; later it was used as a prison. Under the GDR, the Stasi (secret police) expanded it as a political prison. The cells have been left as they were in 1989.

The Nauener Tor (Nauen Gate) and Jägertor (Hunter's Gate) mark the northern boundary

Park Sanssouci

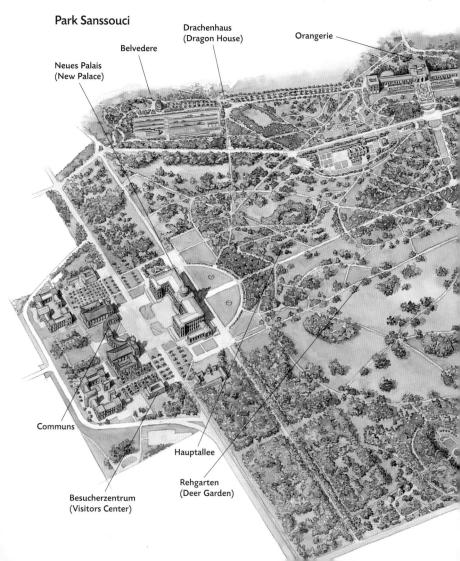

Neues Palais (New Palace)

Belvedere

Drachenhaus (Dragon House)

Orangerie

Communs

Besucherzentrum (Visitors Center)

Hauptallee

Rehgarten (Deer Garden)

of the baroque quarter. A brisk walk a few hundred yards (0.5 km) north of either gate leads to the **Alexandrowka,** also known as the Russian Colony, a group of Siberian-style chalets built in 1826 in memory of the Prusso-Russian alliance that helped defeat Napoleon. A delightful Orthodox church tops a nearby hill.

Park Sanssouci

To the west is Park Sanssouci, Friedrich II's fairy-tale creation,

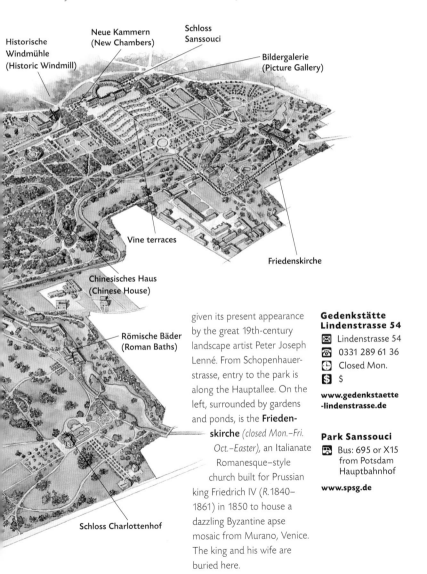

Historische Windmühle (Historic Windmill)

Neue Kammern (New Chambers)

Schloss Sanssouci

Bildergalerie (Picture Gallery)

Vine terraces

Friedenskirche

Chinesisches Haus (Chinese House)

Römische Bäder (Roman Baths)

Schloss Charlottenhof

given its present appearance by the great 19th-century landscape artist Peter Joseph Lenné. From Schopenhauerstrasse, entry to the park is along the Hauptallee. On the left, surrounded by gardens and ponds, is the **Friedenskirche** (closed Mon.–Fri. Oct.–Easter), an Italianate Romanesque–style church built for Prussian king Friedrich IV (R.1840–1861) in 1850 to house a dazzling Byzantine apse mosaic from Murano, Venice. The king and his wife are buried here.

Gedenkstätte Lindenstrasse 54

✉ Lindenstrasse 54
☎ 0331 289 61 36
🕐 Closed Mon.
💲 $

www.gedenkstaette
-lindenstrasse.de

Park Sanssouci

🚌 Bus: 695 or X15 from Potsdam Hauptbahnhof

www.spsg.de

Schloss Sanssouci

✉ Maulbeerallee

☎ 0331 969 42 00

🕐 Closed Mon.

💲 $$$ (incl. audio guide)

www.spsg.de

Schloss Sanssouci

At the **Grosse Fontäne** (Big Fountain), turn right for Schloss Sanssouci, Friedrich II's favorite summer residence. A sweeping stairway leads past vine terraces to this prime example of Prussian rococo. The king appointed Knobelsdorff to build the palace, but had the last word on all details. He wanted a place where he could be "without care" *(sans souci),* to play music, talk philosophy with friends, and relax.

The guided tour inside starts on the north flank in the vestibule, which features a statue of Mars, the god of war, at rest (as Friedrich wanted to be here). The king's private rooms follow. In the **Kleine Galerie,** the twisting, floral motifs of rococo decor are in full evidence. Among the paintings are some by Antoine Watteau, underlining the king's preference for all things French. His library, next up, contains many of the volumes in his original collection of books, all in French.

Friedrich Wilhelm II, who loathed the rococo giddiness, later changed the decoration in Friedrich's study and bedroom. After the Seven Years' War, the gout-plagued king retired to Sanssouci and died of old age in a pale green armchair that remains in his study.

The **Konzertzimmer** (Music Room) is where Friedrich II would regale guests with flute performances of his own composition. Then comes the **Marmorsaal** (Marble Room), an oval room made largely of Carrara marble shipped from Italy. Here the king and his friends (including French philosopher Voltaire, who lived at Sanssouci from 1750 to 1753) conducted round-table chats late into the night.

A series of guest rooms follows, of which the last is the most curious. Painted in yellow Chinese lacquer, its walls drip with reliefs of flora and fauna. It is said the

Vine terraces bisected by sweeping stairs lead to Frederick the Great's favorite retreat, Schloss Sanssouci.

Spy Swap

The iron Glienicker Bridge that links Berlin and Potsdam over the Havel River was rebuilt by the East Germans and named the Brücke der Einheit (Unity Bridge), in what must have been a moment of black humor, in the 1950s. From 1961, only authorized military personnel of the four occupying powers could cross this bridge. On three occasions between 1962 and 1986, it was the stage for international spy swaps, starting on February 10, 1962, with U.S. Capt. Gary Powers (1929–1977), who had been shot down in his U-2 spy plane over the Soviet Union two years earlier. The last swap took place on February 11, 1986, when Russian dissident Anatoly Sharansky (born 1948), accompanied by three Allied spies, was exchanged for two busloads of Eastern-bloc spooks. (See www.glienicker-bruecke.de.)

king had this special decoration made for Voltaire, but that it was finished only after the fiery French thinker had left Prussia in a huff, never to return.

Around the Palace

Just east of the palace, the sober baroque **Bildergalerie** (Picture Gallery) was built to house the king's art collection, much of it lost after World War II. On the other side of the palace is a similar building, the **Neue Kammern** (New Chambers), which houses more guest rooms. The **Historische Windmühle** (Historic Windmill) stands just behind it. The original windmill, built in the 18th century, was destroyed in World War II. Rebuilt in 2003, it is a functioning museum-mill and home to the Prussian castles and gardens foundation.

Perhaps the most self-indulgent structure of all is the **Ruinenberg** (Ruin Mountain), set on a rise directly north of the palace. A series of classical "ruins" hide a complex pumping system for fountains in the park that, sadly, did not work.

The **Orangerie** west of Schloss Sanssouci is an enormous Italianate building with paintings in the style of Italian Renaissance artist Raphael. In late fall and winter, you can stroll underneath hundreds of palms, agaves, laurels, and orange trees of the **plant hall** on a guided tour (Sat. 10:30 a.m., reserve at tel 0331 969 42 00, $$). Beyond it are the pagodalike **Drachenhaus** (Dragon House), now a restaurant, and the **Belvedere,** which has views across the park.

Neues Palais

The Neues Palais (New Palace) stretches to the south. It was built by Friedrich II in 1770 to reflect Prussia's growing self-confidence as a great power. The most striking room is the **Grottensaal** (Grotto Room) on the first floor, with an over-the-top decoration of mineral fragments, shells, and semiprecious stones. Above it, on the second floor, are two enormous ballrooms, the most stunning of them the **Marmorsaal** (Marble Room). Behind the palace stand more ostentatious buildings, the **Communs.** Now used by Potsdam university,

Bildergalerie
- ✉ Im Park Sanssouci 4
- ☎ 0331 969 41 81
- 🕐 Closed Nov.–April & Mon. May–Oct.
- 💲 $

www.spsg.de

Neue Kammern
- ✉ Im Park Sanssouci
- ☎ 0331 969 42 06
- 🕐 Closed Tues.
- 💲 $

www.spsg.de

Orangerie
- ✉ An der Orangerie 3–5
- ☎ 0331 969 42 80
- 🕐 Closed Mon. May–Oct., Nov.–March, & Mon.–Fri in April
- 💲 $ guided tour

www.spsg.de

Neues Palais
- ✉ Am Neuen Palais
- ☎ 0331 969 43 61
- 🕐 Closed Fri.
- 💲 $$ guided or audio tour

www.spsg.de

Chinesisches Haus

✉ Am Grünen Gitter

☎ 0331 969 42 22

🕐 Closed Mon. & Nov.–April

💲 $

www.spsg.de

Schloss Cecilienhof

✉ Im Neuen Garten 11

☎ 0331 969 42 00

🕐 Closed Mon.

💲 $$

🚊 Tram: 92 from Potsdam Hauptbahnhof & bus 603

www.spsg.de

Marmorpalais

✉ Im Neuen Garten 10

☎ 0331 969 45 56

🕐 Closed Mon. May–Oct. & Mon.–Fri. Nov.– April

💲 $$ guided tour only

🚊 Tram: 92 from Potsdam Hauptbahnhof & bus 603

www.spsg.de

Filmpark Babelsberg

✉ Grossbeeren- strasse

☎ 0331 721 27 50

🕐 Closed Nov.– March & Mon. in Sept.

💲 $$$$

🚊 S-Bahn: Griebnitzsee

www.filmpark.de

they served as servants' quarters and kitchens.

The **Rehgarten** (Deer Garden), once hunting grounds, rolls east of the Neues Palais. At its eastern end stands the **Chinesisches Haus** (Chinese House), a fantasy pavilion that expresses perfectly the fad for Chinese art that swept European courts in the late 18th century.

The modest **Schloss Charlottenhof** (tel 0331 969 42 28, closed Mon., $), southwest in the park, is a palace in neoclassical style backed by a rose garden. The building was planned in the 1820s by Schinkel and Lenné for Friedrich Wilhelm IV when he was still crown prince.

Neuer Garten

You can find another Lenné park, the **Neuer Garten** (New Garden), northeast of central Potsdam. Within sight of the Jungfernsee, a lake that branches off the Havel River, is the enchanting **Schloss Cecilienhof.** Kaiser Wilhelm II had this palace built in 1913–1917 for his son, Crown Prince Wilhelm. The palace is best known as the location of the Potsdam Conference, held by the Allies from July 17 to August 2, 1945. Fateful decisions, such as the division of Berlin into four occupation sectors, were made here.

Much of this historic palace has been a hotel since 1960 (see Travelwise pp. 254–255). Built over a series of inner courtyards, the place has the air of a rustic country mansion. Its modest layout belies the fact that it has 176 rooms. The palace—including the conference rooms where Allied delegations

met—can be visited on a guided or audio tour (closed Mon., $$).

The **Marmorpalais** overlooks another lake, the Heiliger See, on the east edge of the park. Originally built in 1787–1799 from designs by Carl Gotthard Langhans and Carl von Gontard under the command of Friedrich Wilhelm II, the palace did not have a complete interior until 1845. Damaged in World War II, the building wound up as the GDR's Army Museum. Its 40 rooms and neoclassical facade were recently restored.

Potsdam extends east across the Havel into the Babelsberg district. Its northwestern corner holds the Lenné-designed **Park Babelsberg,** dotted by several

INSIDER TIP:

Order a traditional German meal with a house-brewed beer at Krongut Bornstedt, an Italianate complex in Sanssouci gardens.

—LARRY PORGES
National Geographic travel books editor

19th-century caprices, including **Schloss Babelsberg**—built in 1833 and currently closed for restoration—and the odd-looking neo-Gothic **Flatowturm** (Flatow Tower; *Park Babelsberg 12*) built in the 1850s. To the east of the district lies the **Filmpark Babelsberg,** a U.S.-style movie theme park on the grounds of the Babelsberg film studios, still in action. ■

Sachsenhausen

The Sachsenhausen concentration camp 21 miles (34 km) northwest of Berlin was built by prison labor in 1936. From then until 1945, more than 200,000 people (Jews, communists, opponents of the regime, and later foreign prisoners) were incarcerated and tormented here, and tens of thousands died. Today, with some of its barracks restored and lorded over by watchtowers, it is a chilling place.

An empty watchtower stands guard over Sachsenhausen's bleak grounds.

Gedenkstätte Sachsenhausen

🅰 209 B5

✉ Strasse der Nationen 22, Oranienburg

☎ 03301 20 02 00

🕐 Museum closed Mon.

🚗 Car: A111 (toward Hamburg), then A10 (Berlin ring road) at Oranienburger Kreuz toward Prenzlau. Exit at Birkenwerder, take the B96 to Oranienburg and follow signs for Sachsenhausen. S-Bahn: (line 1) from Berlin to Oranienburg, then bus 804 (heading for Malz) or 20-min. walk.

www.stiftung-bg.de

After picking up a map (*$*) or audio guide (*$*), go down the street to the camp entrance. You pass a museum on the history of the camp as a memorial site and then through the main gate, adorned with the taunting phrase: *Arbeit Macht Frei* (Freedom Through Work). A permanent exhibition on the everyday organization of the camp is due to open in 2014 and will be split between the gatehouse at Tower A and the commandant's quarters.

Inside is the Appellplatz, where prisoners would be called for daily muster and often left to stand for hours, no matter what the weather. To the right of the Appellplatz, two of the barracks have been reconstructed, mostly with original materials. The crowded triple bunks and common toilet and shower areas are on display. Exhibitions in the two barracks explore Nazi persecution of the Jews and the horrors of daily life (and death) in the concentration camp.

Nearby is a remaining wing of the former cell block. On the camp's west flank are factories where prisoners toiled, along with mass-execution ditches and the remains of crematoriums. Here the visitor will find an exhibition on murder in Sachsenhausen. The southwest corner holds the hospital barracks, where prisoners were subjected to vile medical experiments.

Sachsenhausen was transformed into a Soviet prison from 1945 to 1950. Some 60,000 people were held in those years, and thousands of them died. ∎

Mecklenburg Lake District Drive

Glorious Müritzsee, Germany's second biggest lake, lies at the heart of a national park encompassing lakes and waterways about 80 miles (130 km) northwest of Berlin in the state of Mecklenburg-Vorpommern (Mecklenburg-West Pomerania). The Mecklenburg Lake District makes a delightful drive, and if you add some miles, you can carve out a two-day route finishing up in Schwerin, the region's beautiful capital.

Schweriner Schloss, once home to nobility, is now the seat of the state parliament.

Head north out of Berlin along the A111 toward Oranienburg, continuing for another 35 miles/57 km (west on 167 at Löwenberg and north on L19 after Herzberg) for **Rheinsberg ❶**, where you can find a lakeside palace (see p. 232). The road north leads past a string of lakes to Wesenberg and on to Neustrelitz. Skip this town to proceed north along the Tollensesee lake on E251/96 to **Neubrandenburg ❷**. Although much of the old town was devastated in the final days of World War II, its 1.5-mile-long (2.5 km) medieval defensive wall was left intact. Punctuated by four city gates, the wall is dotted by restored *Wiekhäuser*, or fortlets.

From Neubrandenburg, the 192 road leads west via Penzlin to **Waren ❸**, a pretty town

NOT TO BE MISSED:

Neubrandenburg • Müritzsee • Güstrow • Schwerin

on the north flank of **Müritzsee** and a pleasant spot to spend the night. Those with more time might prolong their stay and take advantage of the lake, which is 18 miles (29 km) long. Yachts and canoes are available for rent. The latter are a great way to discover the waterways of the **Müritz-Nationalpark** (*www.nationalpark-mueritz.de*), a patchwork of more than a hundred lakes created by receding glaciers. Cycling is another option, with some 125 miles (200 km) of marked riding paths in the park.

Animals, especially birds, abound in the area, including cranes, storks, and sea eagles.

From Waren, take the 192 road south along the west side of the lake, and veer west via Malchow to the A19, which you follow north. Take the Güstrow exit and drive west on 104 to **Güstrow ④**. In one of the most charming of the lake district towns, the compact *Altstadt* (old town) rewards a stroll. Its heart is the Marktplatz square, lined by tightly knit houses and a dazzling *Rathaus* (city hall). Also worth visiting is the Renaissance-era *Schloss (Franz-Parr-Platz 1, tel 03843 75 20 12, closed Mon., $$)*; the 16th-century palace set in beautiful gardens is a mix of French, German, and Italian models. The Gothic *Dom* (cathedral) is a towering medieval structure.

Although it is another 31 miles (50 km) west on 104, it would be a shame to miss out on **Schwerin ⑤**. Set on a hill amid seven lakes, the old town's narrow alleys are a joy to wander. The highlight is the Schloss *(Lennéstrasse 1, tel 0385 525 29 20, www.museum-schwerin.de, closed Mon., $$)*, located on its own island and rebuilt in the 19th century in the style of a Loire château. The Altstadt is dominated by the 19th-century tower of the Gothic brick Dom. You can climb the tower for sweeping views.

🅰 See also area map p. 209
► Berlin
🕐 2 days
↔ 197 miles (317 km)
► Schwerin

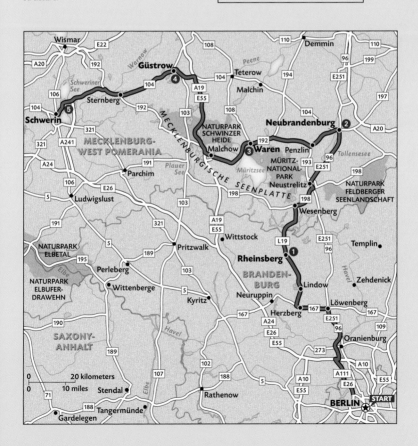

Dresden

Hailed as "Florence on the Elbe," the capital of Saxony (125 miles/200 km south of Berlin) has doggedly rebuilt much of its glorious architecture since February 1945, when Allied bombs destroyed its historic center. A pinnacle, but by no means the finish line, was reached with the opening of the rebuilt baroque Frauenkirche in 2005. The city is richly stocked with world-class museums, and the nearby pretty Elbe Valley scenery is a draw for those with wheels.

The medieval splendor of Dresden, as seen in the Residenzschloss, is being lovingly restored.

Dresden's partially rebuilt **Altstadt** (Old Town) lies on the left bank of the Elbe, but the silhouette is best viewed from the Neustadt (New Town) on the north side of the river. The skyline is dominated by the monumental dome of the **Frauenkirche** (Church of Our Lady, see sidebar p. 222), completed in 1743 as the city's surprisingly opulent central place of Protestant worship, destroyed in 1945, and rebuilt and opened again in 2005.

In the last months of the war, refugees fleeing the advance of the Red Army crowded into Dresden, where they and the local populace thought they would be safe from Allied bombing. Dresden had no industry to speak of and was not a military target. Germans also hoped that the western Allies would spare a city of such artistic and cultural importance.

They were wrong. Massed bomber fleets unleashed a deadly firestorm in the heart of Dresden on the night of February 13, destroying three-quarters of the city and killing an unknown number of locals and refugees.

Marking the western end of the Altstadt is the **Zwinger**. Intended as a magnificent backdrop for courtly ceremonies and festivals, the fabulous architectural fancy is now a museum complex. Architect Matthäus Daniel Pöppelmann (1662–1736) built it on the orders of the most colorful of Saxony's kings, August der Starke (Augustus the Strong, 1670–1733), who came to the throne in 1694. Consisting of a series of lavish, low-slung buildings arranged around a spacious, grassy courtyard with pools and fountains, the Zwinger is the supreme expression of German baroque architecture and the repository of Dresden's collection of old-master paintings.

Touring the Zwinger

Approach the Zwinger through the gateway of the **Glockenspielpavillon,** with its carillon of bells made from Meissen porcelain. In the center of the left wing is the **Kronentor** (Crown Gate), topped by sculptures of eagles guarding the crown of Poland (Augustus also ruled Saxony's eastern neighbor for a time). To the right is the massive **Sempergalerie** (Semper Gallery), designed by

Gottfried Semper (1803–1879) and added to the complex in 1855. The structure that commands the most attention, though, is the **Wallpavillon,** on the far side of the courtyard. This is Pöppelmann's masterpiece, enhanced by the lively sculptures carved by his collaborator, Baltasar Permoser (1651–1732). Even greater exuberance appears in the adjoining **Nymphenbad,** a sunken grotto in which stone nymphs disport themselves.

Inside the Zwinger are a wide variety of treasures. The **Mathematisch-Physikalischer Salon** (Mathematics-Physics Salon; $$) displays an array of scientific instruments from the 16th century on, while the extensive **Porzellansammlung** (Porcelain Collection; $$) presents superb examples of porcelain from the royal collections. Augustus the Strong was fascinated by porcelain. By experimenting in the vitrification of clays with heat, his alchemist, Johann Friedrich Böttger (1682–1719), discovered how to make fine china, thereby laying

Dresden
🅰 209 C1
Visitor Information
✉ Schössergasse 23 & Hauptbahnhof, & Wiener Platz 4
☎ 0351 50 16 01 60
🚗 Car: The A113 to the A13, which runs to Dresden. Train: From Berlin Hauptbahnhof (2–3 hours)
www.dresden.de

Frauenkirche
✉ An der Frauenkirche
☎ 0351 65 60 61 00
🕐 Services closed to tourists
💲 Dome $$
www.frauenkirche-dresden.de

Zwinger
✉ Sophienstrasse
☎ 0351 49 14 20 00
🕐 Closed Mon.
www.skd-dresden.de

EXPERIENCE: Saxony's Paddle Steamers

As Mark Twain would surely agree, a trip on a vintage paddlewheel steamer run by **Sächsische Dampffahrt** (Saxon Steamship Company; *www.saechsischedampfschiffahrt.de*) is an unforgettable experience. Nine lovingly restored vessels, the oldest dating from 1879, ply the waters of the Elbe between Diesbar-Seusslitz by Meissen and Bad Schandau near the Czech border,

affording a gorgeous view of royal castles, ice age rock towers, and gently sloping vineyards. Popular with day-tripping German families, the *Elbtal Express* wends its way from Dresden to Schloss Pillnitz, a comely baroque pile commissioned by Saxon king Augustus the Strong. Every August, the fleet turns into a floating stage for music and dancing during the **Dampfschiff-Fest** (Steamship Festival).

The Fall & Rise of the Frauenkirche

Before 1945, Dresden's skyline was dominated by the monumental dome of the baroque Frauenkirche, completed in 1743 as the opulent central place of Protestant worship. Amazingly, the dome survived the 1945 firestorm, but collapsed after a few days as the stonework cooled. For decades, the heap of blackened rubble lay hardly disturbed, a memorial to the wanton destruction of war. In 1994, the decision was made to rebuild. The surviving stonework, each piece carefully numbered, was stored in an on-site depot ready for reuse. Fragments were turned into souvenirs—they appeared in watch faces, for example—all helping to finance the largely private operation. The reconstructed church was unveiled in 2005, in time for the city's 800th anniversary a year later.

The magnificence of the new-old church is testimony to the determination of Dresden's population to resurrect the city's past charms. How little remains of the original soaring baroque beauty is clear from the color of the stone. The sparse darker patches are original—like the chunk of old dome now on display behind the church. Inside, soft pinks, blues, and ochers dominate. The altar bursts with decoration, while three galleries line the high walls above. Be sure to climb into the dome, admire the religious frescoes, and explore the viewing platform atop the church, which affords a stunning panorama over Dresden's old town.

Gemäldegalerie Alter Meister

- 🕐 Closed Mon.
- 💲 $$$ with Porzellansammlung & special exhibitions

Semperoper

- ✉ Theaterplatz
- ☎ 0351 491 17 05
- 💲 Guided tours $$

www.semperoper.de

the foundation of an industry that is inseparable from the names of Dresden and Meissen.

The main attraction in the Zwinger is the **Gemäldegalerie Alter Meister** (Old Masters Gallery), a collection of some 750 paintings assembled by Augustus the Strong and his successor, Augustus III (R. 1734–1763). The gallery's most celebrated painting (in **Room 117** on the second floor) is the "Sixtinische Madonna" ("Sistine Madonna," 1512–1513) by Raphael, admired not only for its exquisite representation of the Mother and Child but also for the delightful pair of bored cherubs at the base of the picture. Another renowned painting from the Italian Renaissance is Giorgione's "Schlummernde Venus" ("Sleeping Venus"), which Titian (ca 1490–1576) completed after the artist died in 1510. Works

by many of the great names of Western European art abound; Rembrandt, Vermeer, Claude Lorrain, Nicholas Poussin, El Greco, Velázquez, Lucas Cranach the Elder, and Dürer are among the stars. The gallery also contains a series of six paintings of Dresden (in **Room 102**) by Canaletto (Bernardo Bellotto, 1722–1780), nephew of the more famous painter of the same name.

The northeast facade of the Gemäldegalerie looks out over **Theaterplatz,** an imposing square bounded by some of Dresden's outstanding landmarks. Even the visitor information center is a neoclassical temple, a guardhouse (Schinkelwache) designed by Berlin's star architect, Karl Friedrich Schinkel, in 1830–1832.

Also on Theaterplatz is the grandiose **Semperoper** (Semper Opera House), home to the

Saxon State Opera and the State Orchestra. Named after the architects Gottfried Semper and his son, Manfred, the theater's sumptuous interior was the backdrop for premieres of operas by Richard Wagner and Richard Strauss (1864–1949). The building was reduced to a shell in 1945; the complex task of rebuilding it was completed on the 40th anniversary of its destruction. It is usually possible to join a guided 45-minute tour (in English or German) of the lavish interior at least once a day. Times are posted outside, although it's a good idea to reserve tickets online.

Residenzschloss

The nearby Residenzschloss (Residential Palace) is where the rulers of Saxony lived for centuries until 1918. Construction of the palace began on the site of an earlier castle in 1530 and has constantly been meddled with since. Heavily damaged in World War II, the fully restored *Schloss* was presented in 2013.

The steep-roofed **Georgenbau** serves as a dazzling entrance tower. Examine the extraordinary frieze on the long wall facing Augustusstrasse. Made of Meissen tiles, it depicts the *Fürstenzug* (princely procession), glorifying key figures from the dynasty's 800-year rule. That they appear on horseback is no coincidence, for within the building was the **Stallhof** (Royal Stables).

Inside the palace are the restored **Grünes Gewölbe** (Green Vaults), which house a dazzling treasure of jewelry and gold.

Tickets must be bought in advance for a specific time slot (*www.skd .museum, tel 0351 49 14 20 00*). Don't miss the wildly extravagant porcelain piece known as the "Hofstaat des Grossmoguls" ("The Court of Delhi on the Birthday of the Great Moghul"). Augustus the Strong's court jeweler, Johann Melchior Dinglinger (1664–1731), worked with his brothers for seven years to make this thinly veiled glorification of the Saxon king's own ostentatious court.

One of the world's greatest collections of arms and armory, the **Rüstkammer,** returned to its original chamber in the renovated Schloss in 2013. Focusing on knighthood from the 15th to 18th centuries, the exhibition includes parade weapons, jousting equipment, and lavish ceremonial garb. Among the highlights is a sumptuous golden suit of armor, forged in the mid-16th century by Antwerp goldsmith Eliseus Liaerts. A related collection, the **Türckische Cammer** (Turkish Chamber), is

Residenzschloss

- ✉ Taschenberg 2
- ☎ 0351 49 14 20 00
- 🕐 Closed Tues.
- 💲 $$; $$ Grünes Gewölbe; $$ Rüstkammer

www.skd-dresden.de

Dresden's Semperoper, built in the late 19th century, is one of the world's finest opera houses.

Hofkirche

✉ Schlossstrasse 24

☎ 0351 484 47 12

www.bistum-dres den-meissen.de

Albertinum

✉ Tzschirnerplatz- Neumarkt

☎ 0351 49 14 97 41

🕐 Closed Mon.

💲 $$

www.skd.museum.de

devoted to weaponry and artisans' wares from the Ottoman Empire. Most items were acquired as diplomatic gifts, purchases, or booty. Most impressive are eight life-size, hand-carved wooden horses decked out in Arabian-style decorations, and a gorgeous three-masted tent made of satin, cotton, and gilted leather.

Other collections in the palace

INSIDER TIP:

In July or August, go to Dresden's fabulous Filmnächte, an open-air movie and concert festival held on the banks of the Elbe.

—ULRICH VAN STIPRIAAN
Freelance journalist

include the **Kupferstichkabinett** (Engravings Cabinet) and the **Münzkabinett** (Coin Cabinet). You can also climb the 330-foot-high (100 m) **Hausmannsturm** tower *(closed Nov.–March).*

Along the Elbe

Linked to the Residential Palace by a bridge, the Roman Catholic **Hofkirche** caused a stir in this ultra-Protestant city when Catholic convert Augustus the Strong ordered it built in 1738. The king's architect was Italian Gaetano Chiaveri (1689–1770), who brought in a team of his countrymen to carry out the work. They were housed on the Elbe embankment in what is still called the **Italienisches**

Dörfchen (Little Italian Village), now home to several restaurants. Sandstone statues of saints parade on the balustrade of Chiaveri's lovely church, and the interior has fine baroque furnishings. The remains of Saxon rulers lie buried in the church's crypt.

The classic view of the mighty Elbe River is from the **Brühlsche Terrasse,** a promenade laid out over the riverside fortifications in the 18th century by Count Heinrich von Brühl (1700–1763). You reach the terrace by a magnificent flight of steps that begin near the Hofkirche and are decorated with sculptures representing the seasons.

The stairs also lead to the **Albertinum,** which once served as the royal arsenal and now houses a number of museums. Floods in 2002 badly damaged the museum, which was given a waterproof depository (dubbed "the Ark") and reopened in 2010. Its treasures include antique (mostly Roman) sculptures and the **Gemäldegalerie Neuer Meister** (New Masters Gallery), a major collection of German 19th- and 20th-century paintings, with a few works by such foreigners as Gauguin, van Gogh, and Manet thrown in.

On the far bank of the river, reached via the Augustusbrücke of 1910, is the **Neustadt** (New Town), laid out in the 18th century. It was barely touched by the 1945 bombing and, with its shops and cafés on and around Königstrasse and Rähnitzgasse, makes for a pleasant wander. ∎

Leipzig

Saxony's second city (population 497,500) is known for its musical and intellectual traditions and trade fairs. Since the overthrow of the GDR regime in 1990, in which Leipzig's citizens played a leading role—Leipzig came to be known as the "City of Heroes" for its antiregime demonstrations in 1989—the city *(100 miles/160 km southwest of Berlin)* has moved swiftly to recover its place as one of Germany's stars.

Locals treat themselves to some shopping in the elegant art nouveau Mädler-Passage.

Leipzig makes a grand first impression for travelers by train. The city's main station, the **Hauptbahnhof** (originally completed in 1915 and rebuilt after World War II), is one of Europe's great rail terminals, its vastness tempered by tasteful ornament.

Southwest across Willy-Brandt-Platz and the ring road, Leipzig's historic core, the **Innenstadt,** is compact and easily explored on foot. Occupying much of wide-open Sachsenplatz is the **Museum der Bildenden Künste** (Fine Arts Museum). What looks like a giant glass-and-cement cube from the outside is an impressive new temple to the city's top art collections. Inside, interlocking planes of glass, cement, and wood paneling form the framework for a broad range of art, covering centuries of German painting from the Middle Ages to a swath of GDR artists. Thrown into the mix are collections of mostly minor French, Italian, Spanish, and Dutch works from the 15th to 18th centuries.

On the same square is the new building that houses temporary exhibitions of the

Leipzig

🅰 209 A2

Visitor Information

✉ Katharinen-strasse 8

☎ 0341 710 42 60

🚗 Car: A9 toward Nuremberg. Train: From Berlin Ostbahnhof (1.25 hours)

www.leipzig.de
www.lts-leipzig.de

Museum der Bildenden Künste

✉ Katharinenstrasse 10

☎ 0341 21 69 90

🕐 Closed Mon.

💲 $$

www.mdbk.de

Stadtgeschichtliches Museum

✉ Altes Rathaus, Markt 1

☎ 0341 96 51 30

🕐 Closed Mon.

💲 $

www.stadtgeschicht lichesmuseum-leipzig .de

Zeitgeschichtliches Forum Leipzig

✉ Grimmaische Strasse 6

☎ 0341 222 00

🕐 Closed Mon.

www.hdg.de/zfl

Stadtgeschichtliches Museum (Municipal History Museum). Included in the ticket is a visit to the permanent display on the city's history in the **Altes Rathaus** (Old Town Hall), a block south in the old city center. Built in 1556, it is one of the earliest and finest examples of Germany's Renaissance town halls, with a high roof, tall tower, stepped gables, and arcaded first floor facing the marketplace. Its imposing reception hall is hung with portraits of princes and city fathers.

In the adjacent **Naschmarkt** square stands a statue of Johann Wolfgang von Goethe, one of Germany's greatest poets and playwrights. The small baroque building behind it, the **Alte Börse,** was a produce exchange and now serves as a concert hall.

Germany's recent history is explored in the town's

Zeitgeschichtliches Forum Leipzig (Contemporary History Forum), south across Grimmaische Strasse from Naschmarkt. Its displays, an engaging mix of audio, video, photos, documents, newspapers, and artifacts, start with the Allied occupation of Germany in 1945 and the country's subsequent division. The sections on life in the GDR and the events that led to its collapse in 1989–1990 are fascinating.

Stretching south from Grimmaische Strasse is the **Mädler-Passage,** the most splendid of Leipzig's *Passagen* (shopping arcades). It is three stories high and an attractive combination of art nouveau and neo-Renaissance.

Another early 20th-century arcade, the tastefully modernized **Specks Hof,** can be found diagonally north of the Mädler-Passage. Opposite it stands the

The centuries-old Nikolaikirche was a rallying point for opponents of the GDR regime in 1989.

Nikolaikirche *(Nikolaikirchhof, tel 0341 124 53 80)*, or St. Nicholas's Church. Regular Monday prayer meetings for peace began to be held here in 1982, and in 1989 the meetings were a rallying point for demonstrators against the East German government. The somber exterior of what was originally a Romanesque church belies the glittering 18th-century interior.

Music History

About 1,300 feet (400 m) west along Grimmaische Strasse and its continuation, Thomasgasse, is Leipzig's second great church, the **Thomaskirche** *(Thomas-kirchhof 18, tel 0341 22 22 40)*. Founded in 1212, St. Thomas's was rebuilt in Gothic style at the end of the 15th century. It is best known as the home of the Thomaner, a celebrated boys' choir that has been around since the church was founded.

From 1723 until his death in 1750, Johann Sebastian Bach (1685–1750) was cantor (choir-master) of St. Thomas's and also Leipzig's director of music. He is now buried in the church, and a statue of him stands outside. Bach had a big family and always seemed to be short of cash, which is why the left pocket in the statue is turned out.

Opposite, the **Bachmuseum** *(Thomaskirchhof 16, tel 0341 913 72 00, www.bach-leipzig.de)* has documents on the composer's life and musical instruments. The best way to honor the musician and the choir he led, however, is to attend one of the regular services at which the Thomaner choir

performs *(see www.thomaskirche.org for details)*.

If the Thomaskirche represents one pole of Leipzig's musical life, the other is the vast **Augustus-platz,** on the far east side of the Innenstadt. At the north end of the square is the **Opernhaus** (Opera House) of 1960, and on the south the **Neues Gewand-haus** (New Concert Hall), home to the city's orchestra, whose origins go back to the mid-18th century. Felix Mendelssohn was appointed its director in 1835 at the age of 26.

The present building is a far cry from the clothmakers' guildhall *(Gewandhaus)* where a concert hall was initially improvised in 1781. One of the prestige projects of the GDR, this concert hall was built in 1981.

On the square's southwest flank, the university's new campus buildings emulate the Paulinerkirche (St. Paul's Church),

---

Over a Barrel

When you visit Leipzig, follow in Goethe's footsteps by visiting **Auerbachs Keller** *(Grimmaische Strasse 2–3, tel 0341 21 61 00, www.auerbachs-keller-leipzig.de, guided tours 11 a.m. & 3 p.m. in German, book ahead for English, $$–$$$)*, a historic restaurant that owes its fame to the diabolical drama *Faust*. A frequent guest, the German poet spent long evenings here gleaning inspiration from glasses of Saxon wine. On a tour of the *Fasskeller* (barrel cellar), you can admire an impressively carved tree trunk depicting Faust and Mephistopheles flying off on a wine barrel. To find the entrance, look for two devilish statues in the stylish Mädler-Passage (see p. 226).

Grassi-Museum

✉ Johannisplatz
5–11

☎ 0341 222 91 00

🕐 Closed Mon.

💲 Ethnology
museum $

**www.grassimuseum
.de**

**Museum in der
Runden Ecke**

✉ Dittrichring 24

☎ 0341 961 24 43

**www.runde-ecke
-leipzig.de/cms**

blown up in GDR times because the government did not want a church on a socialist square.

Museums & Memorials

A block east and built in the Bauhaus style in the late 1920s, the **Grassi-Museum** contains three separate areas: **Völkerkunde** (Ethnology), **Musikinstrumente** (Musical Instruments), and **Angewandte Kunst** (Applied Arts). The ethnology section has more than 100,000 objects from all over the world, ranging from Aboriginal Australian art to traditional North African jewelry. The musical instrument section is rich in instruments, mostly

INSIDER TIP:

A historic cotton mill, the Leipziger Spinnerei [www.spinnerei .de, S-Bahn: Plagwitz], is now home to galleries and studios of the famous Leipziger Schule of artists.

—JEREMY GRAY
National Geographic author

European, dating from the 14th century. The applied arts collection is equally diverse, spanning the continents and a couple of millennia. Ceramics, glassware, furniture, woodwork, costumes, jewelry, and textiles are (or will be) on display.

Dominating the southwest

edge of the Innenstadt is the **Neues Rathaus** (New City Hall), a monumental affair raised in 1905 and dominated by its stout 376-foot (115 m) **tower** *(open 11 p.m. weekdays for climbing & 2 p.m. for guided tour, $)*. To its north along the ring road is the **Museum in der Runden Ecke** (Museum in the Round Corner), installed in the Stasi secret police's former local headquarters. Its permanent display, "Stasi–Macht und Banalität" ("Stasi–Power and Banality"), documents the lengths to which the GDR's rulers went to control their subjects.

In October 1813, Napoleon suffered a crushing defeat on the outskirts of Leipzig at the hands of the armies of Prussia, Austria, and Russia. The clash, known in German as the Völkerschlacht (Battle of the Peoples), involved half a million troops and cost about 85,000 lives. On October 18, 1913, Kaiser Wilhelm II opened the enormous **Völkerschlachtdenkmal memorial** *(Prager Strasse, tel 0341 961 85 38, www.voelkerschlachtdenkmal.de, $$)* just south of Leipzig's city center. Inside the giant crypt, titanic statues look down upon you, their tiny visitors. Climb the steps (or take an elevator) to the viewing platforms at 223 feet (68 m) and 299 feet (91 m) for grand views over Leipzig.

Businesspeople often head for the **Neue Messe,** the modern trade fair on the city's northern outskirts. The complex of five exhibition halls is the latest incarnation of Leipzig's 800-year-old trade-fair tradition. ∎

Spreewald

About an hour's drive southeast of Berlin, the Spree River splits into slow-moving channels, a kind of inland delta shaded by alder, poplar, and ash trees. This watery forest is the 295-square-mile (475 sq km) Spreewald. For centuries, local people, mostly of the Sorbian minority, got around by flat-bottomed punt *(Kahn).* Berliners started visiting in the 19th century.

A chauffeur-driven punt is the best way to get around the wooded waterways of the Spreewald.

Spreewald

- 209 C3
- 50 miles (80 km) SE of Berlin
- Car: A113 to the A13 and exit at Duben. Train: From Berlin Hauptbahnhof to Lübben or Lübbenau

Visitor Information

- Ehm-Welk-Strasse 15, Lübbenau
- 03542 36 68

www.spreewald -online.de

Lübben

- 209 C3

Visitor Information

- Ernst-von-Houwald-Damm 15
- 03546 30 90

www.luebben.com

Today more than two million visitors a year pour into the forest, declared a UNESCO biosphere in 1991. Apart from taking rides in a punt, there are endless options for walking, cycling, and canoeing.

The most popular gateway to the Spreewald is **Lübbenau** (Lubnjow in Sorbian). The **Spreewald-Museum** *(Topfmarkt 12, tel 03542 24 72, closed Mon., $$)* is housed in the 1850 Torhaus, a three-story building that in GDR times was used as a prison. The museum is a curious mix, where displays on Sorbian culture rub shoulders with others on local GDR history.

The Sorbians (also known in German as Wenden) were the original Slavic inhabitants of much of the Mark Brandenburg before the Germans arrived in force

in the Middle Ages. They have maintained their cultural identity (and refer to the Spreewald as Blota), but few Sorbians still speak the language. You can find more about them at the **Freilandmuseum** *(tel 03542 24 72, closed Nov.–March, $$),* where traditional buildings have been reassembled. The museum is in **Lehde** (Ledy in Sorbian), a short punt trip or 1.2-mile (2 km) stroll from Lübbenau.

You will become aware that one of the Spreewald's biggest claims to fame is the gherkin, once a popular local product and now a slightly silly regional symbol. It is the subject of tours in Lübbenau.

Just 8 miles (13 km) from Lübbenau is 12th-century **Lübben** (Lubin), with a castle and beautiful gardens by the Spree River. It is accessible by bus or train. ■

Lutherstadt Wittenberg

One of the greatest upheavals in Western society began in this attractive Saxon town 60 miles (100 km) southwest of Berlin. On October 31, 1517, Catholic scholar Martin Luther (1483–1546) hammered his 95 Theses against abuses in the Church to the main door of the Schlosskirche—or so the legend goes. What is indisputable is that he launched the Reformation that split the Christian Church in Western Europe.

Lutherstadt Wittenberg

🅰 209 A3

Visitor Information

✉ Schlossplatz 2

☎ 03491 49 86 10

🚗 Car: A9 toward Leipzig. Train: From Berlin Hauptbahnhof

www.lutherstadt-wittenberg.de

Today a bronze door with the theses inscribed in it, erected by Prussian king Friedrich Wilhelm IV, stands in place of the original wooden door, which was destroyed with much of the church in a fire in 1760.

Four years after Luther attracted the wrath of Rome for his 95 impertinent theses, the world's first Protestant service took place in the **Stadtkirche St. Marien** in the center of the compact old town. Luther gave lectures here and later married an ex-nun in the church. His friend, artist Lucas Cranach the Elder (1472–1553), who once lived in Wittenberg, painted the altar.

To gain a perspective on all this upheaval, visit the whitewashed **Lutherhaus** (*Collegienstrasse 54, tel 03491 420 30, www.martinluther.de, closed Mon. & Nov.–March, $$*). This museum in the house where Luther lived from 1508 contains artifacts, furniture, and multimedia displays. There is an extensive collection of portraits of Luther, not all of them particularly flattering. Another section, the *Schatzkammer* (treasury), holds religious relics.

A brisk walk from the Lutherhaus toward the town center takes you to the restored Renaissance **Melanchthon Haus** (*Collegienstrasse 60, tel 03491 420 30, www.martinluther.de, closed Mon. & Nov.–March, $$*), where Luther's supporter Philipp Melanchthon (1497–1560) lived. It now contains a museum on his life and times. A bronze memorial to Luther's theses, as well as his tombstone, can be found in the **Schlosskirche** on the western edge of town, near the imposing Schlossturm. ∎

Statues of Luther and his ally Melanchthon stand amid the cobblestones of Lutherstadt Wittenberg.

More Excursions from Berlin

Brandenburg an der Havel

This ancient town, whose historic center is split into three parts intersected by the Havel River, Beetzsee lake, and canals, has gone through some ups and downs. Mostly destroyed in the Thirty Years' War and badly damaged in World War II, today it makes a pretty excursion about one hour southwest of Berlin. The oldest building is the **Dom St. Peter und Paul** (Burghof, tel 03381 211 22 21, museum $) on the Dominsel (Cathedral Island) in the heart of the old town. The 12th-century cathedral was expanded in Gothic style in the following two centuries and renovated several times thereafter. Inside are some precious medieval altars, the pretty **Bunte Kapelle** (Colorful Chapel), and a museum. From here, a stroll around the Dominsel, across to **Neustadt** and then **Altstadt,** is a pleasant way to spend a few hours. Of the half dozen other churches, the most engaging is the early 15th-century brick **St. Katharinenkirche** (Katharinenkirch-platz 2, tel 03381 52 11 62) in Neustadt. On the Neustadt side of the Havel River, when approaching from the Dominsel, is the medi-eval **Mühlentorturm** (Mill Gate Tower), once a customs checkpoint and prison. www.stg-brandenburg.de ⛰ Map p. 209 A4 **Visitor Information** ✉ Neustädtischer Markt 3 ☎ 03381 796 36 29

Chorin

The village of Chorin is dominated by its redbrick *Kloster*, or monastery, and for once it is not just another example of the late 19th-century North German predilection for neo-Gothic building, but the real McCoy. Cistercian monks started building the mon-astery in 1273. Although it fell into disuse in the 16th century and was half-heartedly meddled with in subsequent centuries, this handsome complex is surprisingly intact. At its heart is the early Gothic Klosterkirche,

which was much restored in the 19th century. Also well preserved are the central cloister and ambulatory, which you reach through the imposing western facade. The monastery is the setting for the **Choriner Musiksommer** series of concerts on most weekends from June to August. www.kloster-chorin.org ⛰ Map p. 209 C5 ✉ Amt Chorin 11 ☎ 033366 703 77 💲 $

Cottbus

The main reason for heading southeast to Cottbus (population 102,000), which lies by the Spree River, is the magnificent **Schloss Branitz** (Robinienweg 5, tel 0355 751 50, www .pueckler-museum.de, closed Mon. Nov.–March, $$). In the von Pückler family since 1696, the property became subject to the garden-

INSIDER TIP:

For a fine day trip outside Berlin, take your bike on the train to Waren and cycle south to the Boek windmill on the shore of Müritzsee.

—ROLAND WEBER
Müritz National Park ranger

ing craze of Hermann von Pückler-Muskau (1785–1871) when he moved here in 1845. The 1,500 acres (600 ha) of planned gardens that he created offer delightful walks. The *Schloss,* a dignified mansion, is home to a museum on the gardener-prince's life and times as well as local art. The town is also proud of its art nouveau theater, for the architecture as well as the productions. Cottbus considers itself a bicultural town, with its German and Sorbian history woven together (see p. 229). Find out more about this ancient minority at the **Wendisches**

Museum *(Mühlenstrasse 12, tel 0355 79 49 30, www.wendisches-museum.de, closed Mon.–Tues., $).*
www.cottbus.de  Map p. 209 D3 **Visitor Information** ✉ Berliner Platz 6
☎ 0355 754 20

Neuruppin

Almost completely enclosed by its 15th-century walls, the old town core of Neuruppin, about 90 minutes by train northwest from Berlin's main station, makes for a pleasant stroll. Located on the 9-mile-long (14 km) **Ruppiner See** (lake), it is best known as the birthplace of Theodor Fontane (1819–1898), one of Germany's greatest novelists. The grand, late 18th-century **Gymnasium** *(Schulplatz),* or high school, hosts exhibitions and a Fontane research center. Not far away is Fontane's 18th-century **birthplace** *(Karl-Marx-Strasse 84, closed to the public),* where his father ran a pharmacy. The **Klosterkirche St. Trinitatis** *(Niemöller-platz)* was begun in the 13th century, but most of what you see today was redesigned by Karl Friedrich Schinkel (who was born in Neuruppin) in the mid-19th century.

www.neuruppin.de  Map p. 209 B5 **Visitor Information** ✉ Rheinsberger Tor, Karl-Marx-Strasse 1 ☎ 03391 454 60

Rheinsberg

The future Friedrich II, tired of the thrashings meted out by his soldier-king father, Friedrich Wilhelm I, may well have considered the four years he spent as a young man in Rheinsberg the happiest of his life. His father bought the Renaissance residence, which itself had replaced an earlier medieval moated castle, in 1734. Young Friedrich oversaw much of its transformation into a baroque palace overlooking **Grienericksee,** a pretty lake. Today you can see the sparsely furnished but impressive **Schloss Rheinsberg** *(Mühlenstrasse 1, tel 033931 72 60, closed Mon., $$)* and wander through its romantic gardens. Inside, the broad **Spiegelsaal** (Hall of Mirrors) is one of the most attractive rooms in the palace, although today short of mirrors. The **Muschelsaal's** (Shell Room) ceiling is festooned with mussel and snail shells.
www.rheinsberg.de  Map p. 209 B6 **Visitor Information** ✉ Rhinpassage, Rhinstrasse 19 ☎ 03393 13 49 40

Schloss Branitz in Cottbus is as remarkable for its gardens as for the building itself.

Travelwise

Travelwise Information 234–240

Planning Your Trip 234–236

How to Get to Berlin 236

Getting Around 237

Practical Advice 238–240

Emergencies 240

Hotels & Restaurants 241–255

Shopping 256–259

Entertainment 260–264

Language Guide & Menu Reader 265

Trams, trains, and buses will get you anywhere you need to go in Berlin.

TRAVELWISE

PLANNING YOUR TRIP
When to Go

Try as you will, there's no bad time to visit Berlin. The warm seasons are the obvious favorites for exploring the city on foot—spring, summer, and early fall. That said, the colder months offer many of the same world-class attractions. In December, the Christmas markets spread a special magic, and some say you haven't lived until you pop the bubbly on New Year's Eve at the Brandenburg Gate.

To avoid the biggest crowds, enjoy an outdoor festival, and have a shot at decent weather, try visiting in the spring shoulder season from April through early June, or in the fall from September to October. Berlin's hectic pace slows a beat, hotels are cheaper, and lines shrink at the popular museums. In the high-season months of July and August, Berlin crawls with tourists but on the upside, reliably balmy temperatures, beach bars, and a multitude of outdoor events will keep you smiling.

Climate

Berlin's relatively cool, temperate climate has more in common with Moscow than Paris. Seasons are more extreme than the German average, with hot summers and fairly harsh winters. Cold fronts roll in from central Russia, bringing freezing temperatures and moderate, but usually not paralyzing, amounts of snow.

In summer from June to late August, the mercury can soar into the low 90s°F (low 30s°C). Indian summer into late October can be delightful, with blue skies, fluffy clouds, and trees turning to gold.

Average Daytime Temperatures

Spring: mid-March to mid-May 50°F (10°C)
Summer: mid-May to the end of August 65°F (18°C)
Fall: September to mid-November 52°F (11°C)
Winter: mid-November to mid-March 35°F (2°C)

Festivals & Events

Berlin's annual calendar is packed with cultural events, festivals, and trade fairs. Some highlights include:

January

Bread & Butter, Berlin's premier fashion extravaganza, mid-Jan., www.breadandbutter.com
Grüne Woche, consumer fair for food, agriculture, and gardening, 2nd–3rd weeks, www.gruene-woche.de
Transmediale, digital and media art festival, late Jan.–early Feb., www.transmediale.de

February

Berlin International Film Festival, stars and premieres at dozens of cinemas, 2nd–3rd weeks, www.berlinale.de
Tanzolymp, international dance-fest, five days in mid-Feb., www.tanzolymp.com

March

International Tourism Fair, around 120 countries woo visitors, 1st–2nd weeks, www.itb-berlin.com
Maerzmusik, contemporary music festival, nine days in mid-March, www.berlinerfestspiele.de
Festival Days (Festtage), gala concerts and operas, ten days in late March—early April, www.staatsoper-berlin.org

April

Berlin Biennale, contemporary arts festival, next events 2014 and 2016, late April—early July, www.berlinbiennale.de.
Gallery Weekend Berlin, art spaces gang up in late April, www.gallery-weekend-berlin.de
Tanz in den Mai, boogie and booze on the witches' sabbath, April 30, www.kulturbrauerei.de

May

Carnival of Cultures, vibrant Kreuzberg carnival and parade, four days in mid-May, www.karneval-berlin.de
Berlin Summer Rave, ravers shake Tempelhof's old hangars in mid-May, www.berlin-summer-rave.de
DFB Soccer Final, rivalry for Germany's second-tier trophy at the Olympiastadion, late May—early June, www.tickets1a.de

June

Potsdam Music Festival, classical concerts and plays at the Sanssouci gardens, two weeks in mid-June, www.musikfestspiele-potsdam.de
48 Stunden Neukölln, performing and visual arts for two days in mid-June, www.48-stunden-neukoelln.de
Fete de la Musique, free music on stages across the city, late June, www.fetedelamusique.de
Christopher Street Day, Germany's biggest gay pride parade, late June, www.csd-berlin.de

July

German-American Volksfest, a sauerkraut-to-Stetsons fun fair, late July—mid-Aug, www.deutsch-amerikanisches-volksfest.de
Classic Open Air, all-star concerts on Gendarmenmarkt, one week early July, www.classicopenair.de

Berlin Fashion Week, catwalks galore, one week early July, www .fashion-week-berlin.de

August

Tanz im August, major dance do with international talent, two weeks mid-Aug., www.tanzim august.de

Tag der offenen Ministerien, Chancellor Merkel and ministries roll out the welcome mat, third Saturday in Aug., www.bundes -regierung.de

Judische Kulturtage, Jewish cultural and dance festival, ten days late Aug., www.juedische -kulturtage.org

Long Museum Night, cultural institutions burn the midnight oil, late Aug., www.lange-nacht-der-museen.de

September

International Consumer Electronics Fair, megashow of the latest gadgetry, one week early Sept., www .ifa-berlin.de

Popkomm/Berlin Music Week, pop trade fair and concerts, early Sept., www.berlin-music-week.de

Musikfest Berlin, classical music at the Berliner Philharmonie, three weeks early Sept., www.berlinerfestspiele.de

Berlin Marathon, 26.2-mile (42 km) jaunt to the Brandenburg Gate, late Sept., www.berlin -marathon.com

October

Tag der deutschen Einheit, German Unity Day, concerts and events around the government quarter, Oct. 3.

Festival of Lights, landmarks illuminated with projected images, two weeks mid-Oct., http:// festival-of-lights.de

Berlin Music Days, electronic musicfest in nightclubs, late Oct.– early Nov., http://bermuda-ber lin.de

November

JazzFest Berlin, cool cats blow for three days in early Nov., www.jazzfest-berlin.de

Berlin Tattoo, military bands, dancers, and choirs, early Nov., www.berlintattoo.eu

December

Christmas Markets, gingerbread, mulled wine, and gifts (see pp. 146–147), late Nov.–Dec. 23.

Silvester, mammoth New Year's Eve bash at the Brandenburg Gate, Dec. 31, www.silvester-ber lin.de

What to Take

If you plan to explore the city's parks, gardens, and historic districts, remember to bring comfortable footwear. Berlin's weather is changeable, so even in summer pack a waterproof jacket and layers of clothing. Hats and sunscreen are advised if you're going to be outdoors for any length of time. Don't forget any prescription drugs and a second pair of glasses. Just about everything else can easily be purchased in Berlin.

Insurance

It pays to take out a travel insurance policy that offers coverage for medical treatment and expenses, including repatriation, baggage, and money loss. Make photocopies of important documents and keep them separate from the originals, in case the latter are stolen.

Entry Formalities

Visitors from the United States, Canada, Australia, New Zealand, Israel, Hong Kong, Japan, South Korea, and most European countries can visit Germany for three months without a visa. Residents of other countries need to apply in advance at their German Embassy. For stays of more

than three months, apply for a residence permit; you will need to prove you have the means to support yourself and have a legitimate reason for living in Germany.

Further Reading

Aimée & Jaguar by Erica Fischer, 1995. Tender wartime memoir of two women, one the wife of a German soldier and the other a Jew, who pick the wrong time to fall in love.

Berlin: The Downfall, 1945 by Antony Beevor, 2003. Superb account of the last days of World War II, seen through the eyes of city dwellers and advancing Russian and American troops.

Berlin Rising: The Biography of a City by Anthony Read and David Fisher, 1994. Excellent social history told by colorful characters, including the often bizarre Hohenzollern princes who ruled before 1918.

A Dance Between Flames: Berlin Between the Wars by Anton Gill, 1994. Evocative description of Berlin's creative frenzy between the world wars, with terrific portraits of café society, criminals, and the theater.

Goodbye to Berlin by Christopher Isherwood, 1939. A hilarious, semiautobiographical tale of a young man lost in the Berlin of the 1920s. It inspired the classic 1972 film *Cabaret*.

Man Without a Face by Markus Wolf and Anne McElvoy, 1999. Fascinating autobiography of Wolf, the wily chief of East Germany's loathsome Stasi secret police.

The Rise and Fall of the Third Reich by William L. Shirer, 1960. Classic, very readable history of Adolf

Hitler's "thousand-year" empire written by CBS's wartime correspondent in Berlin.

Spies Beneath Berlin by David Stafford, 2003. Gripping real-life account of MI6 and the CIA tunneling under the Soviet sector of Cold War Berlin.

The Wall: The People's Story by Christopher Hilton, 2001. Based on the lives of those affected by the Wall on both sides.

Weimar Germany: Promise and Tragedy by Eric Weitz, 2009. This rollicking history of 1920s Berlin delves into its liberal mores, avant-garde arts scene, and Weimar-era personalities.

HOW TO GET TO BERLIN
By Plane
There are surprisingly few direct flights to Berlin from abroad. Most arrivals are routed through larger European hubs in London, Amsterdam, or Frankfurt to board a connecting flight.

Until the new, much-delayed regional Berlin-Brandenburg Airport (BER) opens, possibly in 2014, flights will go in and out of two other airports, Tegel and Schönefeld. Some 5 miles (8 km) northwest of the center, Tegel links destinations within Germany and western Europe, while 11 miles (18 km) to the southeast, Schönefeld serves pretty much the rest of the globe. After BER goes online, Tegel will be mothballed and Schönefeld absorbed.

For details of connections, contact the flight information desk (tel 01805 00 01 86) or see the full schedule under Flight Planning at www.berlin-airport.de.

Both Schöneberg and Tegel are an easy train, bus, or taxi ride to/ from downtown. Tegel is linked to the Hauptbahnhof (main train

station, about 20 minutes) and Alexanderplatz (30 minutes) by the express TXL bus, and to Zoologischer Garten station (15 minutes) by Bus X9 or 109. Schönefeld is 30 to 45 minutes removed from Alexanderplatz by RE AirportExpress trains or by slower S-Bahn commuter rail.

For an overview of the local transportation network, see the foldout Berlin Metro System map in the rear sleeve of this book.

A taxi from Tegel to Alexanderplatz will cost about €20 ($26); from Schönefeld it will run €30–35 ($40–$45).

Airlines Serving Berlin
Air Berlin tel 030 34 34 34 34, www.airberlin.com
American Airlines tel 01805 11 37 09, www.aa.com
British Airways tel 01805 26 65 22, www.britishairways.com
Delta tel 01805 80 58 72, www.delta.com
EasyJet tel 01805 66 60 00, www.easyjet.com
Germanwings tel 0900 19 19 100, www.germanwings.com
KLM-Royal Dutch tel 01805 25 47 50, www.klm.com
Lufthansa tel 01805 80 58 05, www.lufthansa.com
Ryanair tel 0900 116 06 00, www.ryanair.com
Swiss tel 01805 11 00 36, www.swiss.com
United Airlines tel 069 50 98 50 51, www.united.com

By Train
Germany's efficient national railway network is run by Deutsche Bahn (DB, www.bahn.de). Long-distance IntercityExpress (ICE), InterCity (IC), and EuroCity (EC) trains stop at both the main Hauptbahnhof and Ostbahnhof stations. RegionalExpress (RE) trains link Berlin to centers in the surrounding state of Brandenburg and beyond.

Every large station has a *Rei-*

sezentrum (travel service center) with timetables and connections posted in the main hall. (For timetable details in English, you can also call tel 11861 from anywhere in Germany.) Train tickets are available at the service center, from DB vending machines, or online. If you wait to purchase your ticket on DB trains, you'll pay a surcharge (but not on the private Interconnex line, see p. 237). Foreign visitors are eligible for special vacation passes.

The Euraide information center (www.euraide.de) has an office in the first lower level of the Hauptbahnhof. Its English-speaking staff can handle complicated queries about train travel and itineraries.

By Bus
Slow but tolerably comfortable long-distance buses link Berlin to the rest of Europe. Most arrive at the ZOB (Zentraler Omnibusbahnhof, www.iob-berlin.de), the central bus station in Charlottenburg opposite the Funkturm (radio tower).

By Car
If you've got wheels, the A10 ring road around Berlin links you up with other German and foreign cities. Drivers from Britain can bring their car on ferry services via Denmark, France, and the Netherlands. P&O North Sea Ferries (www.poferries.com), Stenaline (www.stenaline.com), and DFDS Scandinavian Seaways (www.dfdsseaways.co.uk) all take vehicles. The Eurotunnel (www .eurotunnel.com) runs under the English Channel between Dover, England, and Calais, France. From there, you can expect eight to ten hours' driving time to Berlin.

Popular car services include Mitfahrgelegenheit (www.mit fahrgelegenheit.de), which matches drivers to passengers for a fee.

GETTING AROUND

By Subway, Bus, & Tram

Berlin's tightly woven network of buses, trams (Strassenbahn), subways (U-Bahn), and commuter rail (S-Bahn) is run by the Berlin Transport Authority BVG (tel 030 194 49, www.bvg.de). U- and S-Bahns run from around 4 a.m. till 12:30–1:30 a.m., when night buses take over. On Fridays and Saturdays, U- and S-Bahns run all night.

Combined local transportation tickets are valid on buses, trams, and commuter rail. Buy tickets from ticket machines at U- or S-Bahn stops or, in the case of buses and trams, from the conductor or onboard ticket machine. Then validate your ticket in a time-stamping machine—found inside buses and trams and on the platforms of U- and S-Bahn stations.

Berlin is divided into three public transportation zones: A and B for the central urban area, and C for outer districts, including Potsdam and Schönefeld Airport. Most destinations in town can be reached with a single A-plus-B ticket.

Available at ticket offices and many Berlin hotels, the Welcome Card is a public transportation ticket valid for up to 72 hours on all buses, trams, and trains. Holders are entitled to free admission or reductions of up to 50 percent on guided tours or walks, boat trips, museums, theaters, and other leisure facilities in Berlin and Potsdam.

By Bicycle

Berlin's growing network of cycle paths is a serious alternative to road transportation and arguably the most pleasant and convenient way to get around.

The city has around 390 miles (620 km) of routes snaking through town and out into the lush Brandenburg countryside. The route map published by German cycling association ADFC (Brunnenstrasse 28, tel 030 448 47 24, www.adfc.de) is a good investment. You can plan urban journeys online at BBBike (www.bbbike.de), allowing you to set preferences for road type, greenery, and traffic lights.

If you take your bike on the train, buy an extra *Fahrradkarte* (bicycle ticket) and board carriages marked with a bicycle logo. You're not supposed to do so during peak times (6 a.m.–9 a.m. and 2 p.m.–5 p.m. on weekdays), but officials turn a blind eye unless it's crowded.

Reliable bicycle agencies include Prenzlberger Orange Bikes (Kolle 37, tel 030 44 35 68 52, www.kolle37.de) and Fat Tire (under the Fernsehturm/TV Tower, tel 030 24 04 79 91, www.berlinfahradverleih.com). An innovative rival is Call-a-Bike (www.callabike-interaktiv.de), whose fleet, available by the hour, day, or week, is positioned at nearly 100 stations in Mitte and Prenzlauer Berg.

By Train

For excursions farther afield, you'll need to take regional or national trains run by Deutsche Bahn (www.bahn.de). A private rail operator, Interconnex (www.interconnex.de), serves Leipzig and Schwerin and is usually cheaper than DB.

By Car

Germany is blanketed by toll-free expressways *(Autobahnen)*, which can get you where you're going in a hurry. Contrary to popular belief, a speed limit of 130 kph (81 mph) normally applies. Stretches without speed limits are few and far between. If you're on one, you'll know immediately: the fast lane becomes a blur of vehicles moving at speeds of 200 kph (124 mph) or more. Secondary highways (*Landstrassen* or *Bundesstrassen*) are slower but serene, and often picturesque. The roads network in the former East is modernizing rapidly, though you'll still encounter the occasional bumpy cobblestone surface.

In central Berlin, all vehicles are required to display an *Umweltplakette* (emissions sticker) costing €5 to €15. If you bring your own car, order a sticker at www.tuev-sued.de or pick one up on the Berlin outskirts at a certified testing center (see www.berlin.de/umweltzone for details).

Leading car rental agencies with offices in Berlin include Alamo, Avis, Budget, Enterprise, Europcar, Hertz, National, Sixt, and Thrifty. Some of the best deals can be found through local operators such as Robben & Wientjes (tel 030 61 67 70, www.robben-wientjes.de) or Buchbinder (tel 0180 282 42 46, www.buchbinder.de). Special offers are common from Friday afternoon to Monday morning.

By Taxi

Taxi stands are located at airports, at train and subway stations, and throughout the city, but you can also hail taxis in the street. Flag fall is €3.20 ($4.16), then €1.65 ($2.15) per km for the first 7 kilometers, then €1.28 ($1.66) per km after that. A tip for nightclubbers: a *Kurzstrecke* (short trip) up to 2 km (1.2 mi) costs €4 ($5.20)—inform the driver you want this fare before you set off. Also, check whether the driver accepts credit cards beforehand.

Main Taxi Companies

City-Funk 030 21 02 02
Funk Taxi 030 26 10 26
Taxi-Funk 030 44 33 22
Würfel-Funk 030 21 01 01 or 0800 222 22 55 (toll-free)

PRACTICAL ADVICE

Communications

Post Offices

Post offices run by Deutsche Post, the national mail service, run like clockwork but are few and far between. Opening hours are generally 8 a.m. to 6 p.m. Monday to Friday and till noon on Saturday. Branches in airports and larger train stations are open seven days a week. Buy stamps at the post office counter or from vending machines outside. To find a post office branch near you, go to www.deutschepost.de and search under *Filiale*.

Telephones

Public telephones are available in ever-dwindling numbers. The rate from telephone booths run by national provider Deutsche Telekom is about 23 cents a minute. Most public telephones are card operated, although some also take coins. Phone cards (*Telefonkarten*) are sold at post offices, convenience stores, and supermarkets for €10, €15, and €20. Note that numbers prefixed with 0900, 0180, or 0190 are toll numbers.

If you bring your cell phone to Germany, make sure it is compatible with Europe's GSM network. To keep costs down, sign up for an international roaming plan with your mobile provider. Or, once in Berlin you can a buy a local SIM card or inexpensive mobile with prepaid airtime. Check the offers at electronics warehouses like MediaMarkt or Saturn on Alexanderplatz.

To make an international call from Germany, dial 00 followed by the country code and the rest of the number, deleting the initial 0 if there is one. Country codes include: Australia 61, Canada 1, U.K. 44, United States 1. International information is 11834 and national information, 11837 (in English).

Wireless Internet

Berlin is planning to provide citywide Wi-Fi (WLAN) for free, eventually. Until then, you can surf on your mobile device at many hotels, cafés, and restaurants for little or no charge. The Sony Center on Potsdamer Platz has a popular free Wi-Fi zone. Kabel Deutschland operates a few dozen hotspots that cost nothing for the first 30 minutes (search for locations at www.hotspot.kabeldeutschland.de).

Conversions

1 kilo = 2.2 lb
1 liter = 0.2642 U.S gallons
1 kilometer = 0.62 mile

Women's clothing

U.S.	8	10	12	14	16	18
European	36	38	40	42	44	46

Men's clothing

U.S.	36	38	40	42	44	46
European	46	48	50	52	54	56

Women's shoes

U.S.	6/6.5	7/7.5	8/8.5	9/9.5
European	37	38	39	40

Men's shoes

U.S.	8	8.5	9.5	10.5	11.5	12
European	41	42	43	44	45	46

Electricity

German sockets are of the round, European continental, two-pin variety, so you'll need an adapter to use equipment with U.S. or U.K. plugs. The current of 220V, 50 Hz is fine for British gear, but Americans will need a converter. Airport shops carry them.

Etiquette & Local Customs

Berlin is a useful corrective to Germany's reputation for formality. The capital city is a fairly casual, elbow-rubbing kind of place. Apart from fancy restaurants, the opera, and some nightclubs, you needn't dress up. That's not to say Berliners aren't fashion conscious, as the chic attire of those pencil-thin models might suggest. Business attire is smart casual.

Shaking hands is common among both men and women, at least at first meeting. Friends and acquaintances, especially among younger people, will hug and peck on both cheeks.

Do not use first names or the informal *Du* unless invited to do so. However, many young people will dispense with the formal *Sie* more or less immediately. People who introduce themselves as *Herr* or *Frau* (perhaps even *Frau Doktor*), want to be addressed that way.

If you're invited to someone's home, take along a little something like flowers or a bottle of wine. A polite thank-you card or call the next day is appreciated.

Berliners are renowned for their *Schnauze* (big mouth) and won't hesitate to sound off on any imaginable topic. It is okay to bring up the Third Reich as long as you do it with tact.

Holidays

Banks, post offices, and many museums, art galleries, and stores close in Berlin on the following holidays. Stores and businesses also shut on Christmas Eve and New Year's Eve.

January 1–New Year's Day
March/April–Good Friday
March/April–Easter Monday
May 1–Labor Day
May/June–Ascension Day
May/June–Pentecost (Whit) Monday
October 3–Day of German Unity
December 25 & 26–Christmas

Media, Newspapers, & Magazines

The main broadsheets are the left-leaning *Berliner Zeitung*, the center-right *Tagesspiegel,* and the more moderate *BerlinerMorgenpost.* The largest circulation belongs to the sensationalist *BZ,* the rough equivalent of the U.S. *National Enquirer* or Britain's *Sun.* Another saucy tabloid is the *Berliner Kurier.*

Berlin doesn't have a heavyweight national daily, so serious readers resort to newspapers published elsewhere in Germany. These include the liberal *Sueddeutsche Zeitung (SZ),* the conservative *Frankfurter Allgemeine Zeitung (FAZ),* and the conservative *Die Welt.* Popular national tabloids are *Bildzeitung* and *Express.* All of them publish editions online.

Weekly periodicals play an important role. On Monday, the hard-hitting magazines *Der Spiegel* and *Focus* are published; on Thursday, the sophisticated *Die Zeit* and the entertaining, gossipy magazines *Stern* and *Bunte.* American and British newspapers are available in airports, major railroad stations, and large hotels.

Entertainment Listings

The twice-monthly *Zitty, TiP,* and *Prinz* and their websites publish the best listings of entertainment and cultural events. The free event guide *030* is available in cafés and nightclubs. A slender English-language monthly, *The Ex-Berliner,* has some listings. A good rolling calendar of party and nightclub events is *Beatstreet* (http://unlike.net/berlin/afterdark/beatstreet).

Radio

If you take a taxi, you'll probably hear *Radio Eins,* the rock-pop broadcaster. For English-language programs, tune in to BBC World Service at 94.8 and National Public Radio Berlin at 104.1.

Television

German television relies heavily on national broadcasters ARD and ZDF, the parent networks for a host of regional public channels. RBB and TV Berlin are the main networks for Berlin and Brandenburg. Arte is a respected German-French public channel with a variety of culture and documentary programs. Stiff competition comes from the private broadcasters such as RTL, ProSieben, and SAT 1. Channels available in English include CNN, NBC, and BBC World.

Money Matters

In 2002, the euro (€) replaced the beloved Deutsche Mark as Germany's official currency. There are 100 cents to 1 euro. Euro banknotes come in denominations of 5, 10, 20, 50, and 100, as well as the rare 200 and 500 bills. Coins come in €1 and €2 as well as 1, 2, 5, 10, 20, and 50 cents.

Most major banks have ATMs for bank cards and credit cards with instructions in several languages. Cash and traveler's checks can be exchanged in banks and currency booths at railroad stations and airports.

Opening Times

Banks 8 a.m.–4 p.m. (around 5:30 p.m. on Thurs.); some in outlying areas close for lunch between 1 p.m. and 2 p.m. All banks are closed Saturday and Sunday.
Museums Generally 9 a.m.–6 p.m. Many museums are closed on Monday but stay open late on Thursday evenings.
Pharmacies Open during normal store hours and on a rotation schedule to cover nights and weekends.
Post Offices Generally 8 a.m.–6 p.m. weekdays and until noon on Saturday.
Retailers Weekdays 8:30 a.m.–6:30 p.m. (till 8 p.m. or 10 p.m. for many department stores and on Thursdays). On Saturday,

hours are 8:30 a.m.–8 p.m., although smaller shops close between noon and 2 p.m. Stores are generally closed on Sunday, except in airports and large train stations.

Restrooms

Train stations, tourist attractions, and many public buildings have accessible restrooms. In department stores, you can use them for a small fee (around 25 cents). In bars, cafés, and restaurants, they're normally for customers only, although a look of urgency will work wonders. Look for signs saying *Toilette* or WC and doors marked *Herren* (men) and *Damen* (women). Modern, self-cleaning pay cabins can be found in some busy areas. *Café Achteck* is a Berlin term for the old-fashioned public urinals still found in parts of town.

Time Differences

Germany is on Central European Time (CET), one hour ahead of Greenwich Mean Time and six hours ahead of Eastern Standard Time. Noon in Germany is 6 a.m. in New York. Clocks move ahead one hour in the summer. Remember that Germans use the 24-hour clock, so that 8 p.m. becomes *20 Uhr* in German.

Travelers With Disabilities

Germany is fairly well equipped for the needs of the mobility impaired. There are access ramps and elevators in many public buildings, including train stations, museums, and theaters. Most buses and trams carry a blue wheelchair symbol and have special ramps. Most S- and U-Bahn stations downtown have ramps or elevators; exactly which ones do is displayed on the BVG network map.

For information and support,

contact the Berlin Disabled Association at Jägerstrasse 63d (tel 030 204 38 47, www.bbv-ev.de). The free online database of activist group Mobidat (www .mobidat.net) lists over 34,000 buildings in Berlin, including hotels, restaurants, and cinemas, with details of their accessibility.

Visitor Information

The city's tourist authority, Berlin Tourism and Marketing (BTM, tel 030 25 00 23 33, www.visitberlin .de), is helpful and well organized. A large Infostore is located in the Hauptbahnhof (main train station, open 8 a.m.–10 p.m. daily). Branches can be found in the south wing of the Brandenburg Gate, at the Alexa shopping mall on Alexanderplatz, in the Reichstag Pavilion, and at the airport.

EMERGENCIES
Crime & Police

Berlin is a remarkably safe place, and big-city common sense will steer you clear of most trouble. Some U- and S-Bahn stations in parts of Kreuzberg and Friedrichshain—Kottbusser Tor, Görlitzer Bahnhof, and Warschauer Strasse, for instance—may look rough, but the hang-abouts are generally harmless and looking for handouts. More care is urged in the outer suburbs of Lichtenberg, Marzahn, Neukölln, and Wedding, where muggings and street assaults do sometimes occur.

If you need help for any reason, dial emergency number 110 to contact the police. There are police stations in every district, including ones at Jägerstrasse 48 near Gendarmenmarkt and Joachimstaler Strasse 14–19 just south of Zoologischer Garten station. The police will take a statement, cancel your credit cards, let you use the telephone, and help contact your embassy. If

you encounter trouble on trains, the Bahnpolizei have offices at major stations.

German police officers can be identified by their solid blue uniforms (marked POLIZEI on the back) and blue-and-silver squad cars. Motorized police known as the Verkehrspolizei patrol the streets, roads, and motorways. Many German police officers speak English and are easy to find in busy areas.

Be sure to carry proof of identification, such as a passport, driver's license, or ID card, with you at all times—it's the law.

Embassies & Consulates

Australian Embassy, Wallstrasse 76–79, 10179 Berlin, tel 030 880 08 80, www.germany.embassy .gov.au
British Embassy, Wilhelmstrasse 70–71, 10117 Berlin, tel 030 20 45 70, http://ukingermany.fco .gov.uk
Canadian Embassy, Leipziger Platz 17, 10117 Berlin, tel 030 20 31 20, www.berlin.gc.ca
Irish Embassy, Jägerstrasse 51, 10117 Berlin, tel 030 22 07 20, www.embassyofireland.de
New Zealand Embassy, Friedrichstrasse 60, 10117 Berlin, tel 030 20 62 10, www.nzembassy .com
South African Embassy, Tiergartenstrasse 18, 10785 Berlin, tel 030 22 07 30, www.suedafrika .org
U.S. Embassy, American Citizen Services Section, Clayallee 170, 14191 Berlin, tel 030 830 50, http://germany.usembassy.gov

Emergency Phone Numbers

Fire department & ambulance (*Feuerwehr*) 112
Police (*Polizeinotruf*) 110
Medical emergency (*Notarzt,* for house calls) 030 31 00 31

Dental emergency 030 89 00 43 33
Poison Control 030 192 40

Health

Apart from party fatigue, there are few health risks involved in visiting Berlin. For minor ailments, qualified staff at pharmacies offer expert advice. Doctors' consulting hours are normally 9 a.m. to noon and 3 to 5 p.m., except weekends. For urgent attention outside consulting hours, go to a hospital (*Krankenhaus*). German medical treatment and facilities are generally very good. The best known hospital in Berlin is the Charité (Schumann Strasse 20–21, tel 030 450 50), which has a 24-hour emergency ward.

Lost Property

Your travel insurance should cover the loss or theft of your property if you are not already covered by your home insurance. Theft must be reported to the police so you can obtain a certificate confirming that the crime has been reported. The national rail service Deutsche Bahn has its own lost property office (tel 0900 199 05 99), as does the Berlin urban transportation network BVG (tel 030 194 49). For items lost elsewhere, try the municipal lost property office (Fundbüro, Potsdamer Strasse 180/182, tel 030 194 49).

Lost or Stolen Credit Cards

American Express (AE) tel 069 97 97 20 00, www.american express.com
Diners Club (DC) tel 07531 363 31 11, www.dinersclub.com
MasterCard (MC) tel 0800 819 10 40, www.mastercard.com
Visa (V) tel 0800 811 84 40, www.visa.com

Hotels & Restaurants

Travelers who have wined, dined, and slumbered in other European capitals will find their pocket money goes a long way in Berlin. Since reunification, the hotel and restaurant trade has grown by leaps and bounds.

Hotels

Berlin has plenty of guest beds: over 130,000 at last count, enough for the entire population of Waco, Texas, to throw a slumber party. This is an investment in the future and good news for visitors. The excess capacity translates into rates well below those in, say, Amsterdam, London, or Paris. Even during popular events and trade fairs, it's a cinch to find an affordable place to sleep.

A spree of hotel-building has brought eastern Berlin largely up to standards in the west. The central Mitte district boasts the lion's share of main draws such as the Museum Island art collections, and naturally it's the most popular area to stay. The old West can feel a bit staid, but there's refined charm in the squares and boutique-lined streets that feed into Kurfürstendamm (Ku'damm).

Before you book a room, it helps to make a personal checklist of must-have items such as elevators, air-conditioning, or a quiet location. Many hotels overlook busy streets, and not all have decent soundproofing.

If you're driving, know that many central hotels do not have their own parking and may direct you to a paid lot or garage nearby. Street parking may be a little tricky in built-up areas, although some establishments issue parking permits.

In our listings, unless otherwise stated:
• Breakfast is not included in the price.
• All rooms have a telephone and television. Many hotels also provide Internet access, and Wi-Fi is increasingly standard in mid- to top-end establishments.
• Room prices are a rough indicator and do not take seasonal variations or special offers into account.

Online Resources

A good starting point is www .visitberlin.de, run by the city's capable tourist authority, Berlin Tourismus Marketing. The search-and-book pages show availability, special offers, location, features, and photos for over 400 hotels, hostels, and B&Bs.

Restaurants

Once a gastronomic backwater, Berlin is emerging as a hub of creative cuisine for ambitious, up-and-coming chefs. Options among the 6,000-odd eateries range from simple kebab stands to "secret" supper clubs and Michelin-starred gourmet temples. Competition is fierce and prices are reasonable on a European scale.

German and Brandenburg specialties prepared with local ingredients are definitely worth exploring. In an expert chef's hands, even rib-sticking fare like traditional *Kassler Rippen* (smoked pork chops) can be terrific (see Food & Drink, pp. 38–39). Foreign influences are led by the Mediterranean rim and Asia, although more fusion fare is available than ever before.

Dishes from eastern Europe such as borscht or blini are more common east of the Brandenburg Gate. Spicy Mexican, Szechuan, or Indian is likely to be toned down to German tastes. Purely vegetarian eateries are few and far between, but most menus will have a list of meatless dishes.

Once you have a table, no one will hassle you to eat up and move on. Remember to ask for the bill at the end of the meal; it is considered rude for the server to bring it before you're ready. The flip side is that service can be glacial.

Smoking is still popular in many bars, cafés, and restaurants. Against the national trend, puff-happy Berlin overturned an EU-initiated smoking ban in such establishments. All the same, nonsmoking areas are now more or less standard wherever food is consumed. Patrons will slip outside to light up unless the place is signposted as a *Raucherlokal* (smoker's locale).

Tips are included in the bill, but most patrons still round up by 5 to 10 percent. Give the server the tip upon payment, rather than leaving it on the table. If your bill is €14, you might hand the server a €20 and say "15." Waiters are happy to split group bills for individuals.

Organization & Abbreviations

Hotels and restaurants have been organized by location, price, and then alphabetical order.

Abbreviations used are:

L = Lunch
D = Dinner
S = S-Bahn
U = U-Bahn

▦ UNTER DEN LINDEN & POTSDAMER PLATZ

HOTELS

▦ ADLON
▮ KEMPINSKI
$$$$$
UNTER DEN LINDEN 77, MITTE
TEL 030 22 61 11 11
www.hotel-adlon.de
British club meets art deco at this portal of German history, where Marlene Dietrich was discovered and Joseph Goebbels chased his mistress down the corridor. The grand dame of Berlin hotels has been restored to its pre-WWII splendor, complete with grandstand views of the Brandenburg Gate. The elegant Lorenz restaurant boasts three Michelin stars. All rooms have flat-screen TVs and Wi-Fi.

🛈 382 + suites 🚇 U55, S1, S2 Brandenburger Tor 🅿 ⬆ ⊘ ⊘ ☎ 📺 ⬥ All major cards

▦ GRAND HYATT
$$$$$
MARLENE-DIETRICH-PLATZ 2, TIERGARTEN
TEL 030 25 53 12 34
www.berlin.hyatt.com
A haunt of movie stars, celebrities, and the merely moneyed, this temple of luxury has matte black surfaces and carved cedarwood that exude a Euro-Japanese elegance. Rooms boast superior amenities such as heated bathroom floors and Bauhaus art, and on the rooftop you'll find a gym, pool, and beauty center.

🛈 342 🚇 S1, S2, U2 Potsdamer Platz 🅿 ⬆ ⊘ ☎ 📺 ⬥ All major cards

▦ RITZ-CARLTON BERLIN
$$$$$
POTSDAMER PLATZ 3, TIERGARTEN
TEL 030 33 77 77
www.ritzcarlton.com
One of Berlin's premier luxury hotels, housed in a retro U.S.-style skyscraper with a hushed, columned lobby and sweeping staircase that harks back to the Prussian Empire. Rooms gleam with polished cherrywood, marble, and brass fittings. The Curtain Club resembles a British gentlemen's club with fireplace; the bar curtains are ceremoniously raised every night by a genuine Beefeater.

🛈 341 + suites 🚇 S1, S2, U2 Potsdamer Platz 🅿 ⬆ ⊘ ☎ ⬥ All major cards

▦ DORINT SOFITEL AM
▮ GENDARMENMARKT
$$$$
CHARLOTTENSTRASSE 50–52, MITTE
TEL 030 20 37 50
www.dorint.com
A major facelift turned this ex-communist hotel on Gendarmenmarkt, a gorgeous church-studded square, into a cozy retreat. Light floods into the atrium restaurant, the rooftop gym, and even the ballroom via translucent floor tiles. Rooms are on the snug side but comfortable, and the upper-floor balconies are level with the stunning belfry of the Französicher Dom.

🛈 114 🚇 U2 Stadtmitte, U6 Französiche Strasse 🅿 ⬆ ⊘ ⊘ 📺 ⬥ All major cards

▦ MANDALA
SUITES
$$$–$$$$
FRIEDRICHSTRASSE 185–190, MITTE
TEL 030 20 29 20
www.themandala.de
All manner of sophisticates frequent this luxurious, ultra-discreet hideaway on Berlin's swanky Friedrichstrasse. If you want room service, bellboys, and concierges, go someplace else, but you'll miss pamperings in five categories of suite

<table>
<tr><th colspan="2">PRICES</th></tr>
<tr><td colspan="2">HOTELS
An indication of the cost of a double room in the high season is given by $ signs.</td></tr>
<tr><td>$$$$$</td><td>Over $270</td></tr>
<tr><td>$$$$</td><td>$200–$270</td></tr>
<tr><td>$$$</td><td>$130–$200</td></tr>
<tr><td>$$</td><td>$80–$130</td></tr>
<tr><td>$</td><td>Under $80</td></tr>
<tr><td colspan="2">RESTAURANTS
An indication of the cost of a three-course meal without drinks is given by $ signs.</td></tr>
<tr><td>$$$$$</td><td>Over $80</td></tr>
<tr><td>$$$$</td><td>$50–$80</td></tr>
<tr><td>$$$</td><td>$35–$50</td></tr>
<tr><td>$$</td><td>$20–$35</td></tr>
<tr><td>$</td><td>Under $20</td></tr>
</table>

ranging from 430 to 1,100 square feet (40–100 sq m). Quarters have marble baths, walk-in closets, kitchen, and modern workspaces with Wi-Fi.

🛈 82 suites 🚇 U2, U6 Stadtmitte 🅿 ⬆ ⊘ 📺 ⬥ All major cards

RESTAURANTS

▮ MARGAUX
$$$$–$$$$$
UNTER DEN LINDEN 78, MITTE
TEL 030 22 65 26 11
www.margaux-berlin.de
A stone's throw from the Brandenburg Gate, the vaunted Michelin-starred kitchen of Michael Hoffmann is at the forefront of Berlin's gourmet elite. The interior is a princely robe of black onyx, marble, and gold. The changing six- to eight-course meals are intensely flavorful and light as a feather. The extensive wine list bristles with top European and New World vintages.

✦ 74 ⬥ Closed L & Sun. – Mon. 🚇 U55, S1, S2 Brandenburger Tor ⬥ All major cards

---

▦ Hotel ▮ Restaurant 🛈 No. of Guest Rooms ✦ No. of Seats ⬥ Closed 🚇 U- or S-Bahn 🅿 Parking ⬆ Elevator

SOMETHING SPECIAL

🍽 VAU
$$$$–$$$$$
JÄGERSTRASSE 54–55, MITTE
TEL 030 202 97 30
www.vau-berlin.de
Chef Kolja Kleeberg once aspired to acting, and this Michelin-starred restaurant near Gendarmenmarkt is something of a movie set, with screaming orange walls, walnut floors, and halogen spots. The menu is at once sophisticated and down-to-earth. You might start with the chestnut soup before moving on to breast of pigeon with black root and a dusting of cocoa, polishing it off with braised pineapple and a lemongrass-chili sherbet. Business lunch is an incredible treat, especially on balmy summer days in the attractive courtyard. Reserve ahead.
🪑 115 🕐 Closed Sun.
🚇 U6 Französische Strasse
🏧 All major cards

🍽 DESBROSSES
$$–$$$
POTSDAMER PLATZ 3
TEL 030 337 77 64 00
www.desbrosses.de
The 1875 interior of this traditional brasserie was transplanted, piece by historic piece, to Potsdamer Platz from a ladies' hat boutique in Mâcon, Burgundy. Guests of the Ritz-Carlton hotel stream in to dine on a changing cast of seasonal French specialties, prepared before your very eyes in the open kitchen and bakery. The lunch specials are a great value. For good luck, rub the snout of the porcelain pig on display.
🪑 220 🚇 U2, S1, S2 Potsdamer Platz 🏧 All major cards

🍽 SUPPENBÖRSE
$
DOROTHEENSTRASSE 43, MITTE
TEL 030 20 64 95 98

www.suppenboerse.de
This nice little soup bar is a welcome alternative to the fast-food joints on nearby Friedrichstrasse. The changing cast of vegan and vegetarian fare might include creamed French celery with orange juice, honey, and cayenne pepper, or Thai chicken-peanut with coconut milk and rice. All ingredients are shockingly fresh and free of preservatives and flavor enhancers.
🪑 25 🕐 L. only. Closed Sun. & (on very hot days in summer) Sat. 🚇 S1, S2, S5, S7, U6 Friedrichstrasse 🏧 No credit cards

■ CENTRAL BERLIN

HOTELS

🏨 ART'OTEL BERLIN
🍽 MITTE
$$$$
WALLSTRASSE 70–73, MITTE
TEL 030 24 06 20
www.artotels.de
This rococo mansion, a onetime haunt of Berlin's intellectual elite, has been transformed into a plush hotel cum art gallery. Spread over its six floors is a collection of works by modernist painter Georg Baselitz. You can dine in the glass-roofed Factory restaurant or outside on the banks of the Spree.
🛏 105 🚇 U2 Märkisches Museum 🅿 🔄 🚭 🔆
🏧 All major cards

🏨 RADISSON SAS
$$$–$$$$
KARL-LIEBKNECHT-STRASSE 3, MITTE
TEL 030 23 82 80
www.radissonsas.com
The Radisson claims the world's largest cylindrical aquarium (82 ft/25 m high) and most guests fall under its Jules Verne spell right away. The most impressive rooms face either the towering tank in the atrium-style lobby or

overlook the Spree River and majestic Berlin Cathedral. Flatscreen TVs and free Wi-Fi are standard. All guests get a free riverboat tour, and for those with energy to burn, the fitness room is open 24 hours.
🛏 427 🚇 S5, S7, U2, U5, U8 Alexanderplatz 🅿 🔄
🚭 🔆 🚾 🚩 🏧 All major cards

🏨 ALEXANDER PLAZA
🍽 BERLIN
$$$
ROSENSTRASSE 1
TEL 030 24 00 17 63
www.hotel-alexander-plaza.de
Housed in a stolid Bismarck-era monument that was once a furrier's studio, this hotel bristles with period details. There are vintage glazed tiles and a "floating" staircase apparently held up by stucco. The ergonomically designed rooms have soothing color schemes and panoramas of the historic quarter. Breakfast is served in the glass-covered *Wintergarten*.
🛏 92 🚇 S5, S7, U2, U5, U8 Alexanderplatz 🅿 🔄
🚭 🚩 🏧 All major cards

🏨 ARCOTEL VELVET
🍽 $$$
ORANIENBURGER STRASSE 52, MITTE
TEL 030 278 75 30
www.arcotel.at
This stylish member of the Arcotel chain occupies a plum spot in Mitte, close to the Neue Synagoge and Friedrichstrasse. Furnishings are sleek contemporary with dark hardwoods, red leather, and floor-to-ceiling windows. Flat-screen TVs and free room Wi-Fi are standard. Rooms on the upper floors offer fabulous views over the historic district. Breakfast is served in the fine Lutter & Wegner restaurant downstairs.
🛏 85 🚇 U6 Oranienburger Tor 🅿 🔄 🚭 🔆 🏧 All major cards

🚭 Nonsmoking 🔆 Air-conditioning 🚊 Indoor Pool 🏊 Outdoor Pool 🚩 Health Club 🏧 Credit Cards

⌂ ARTIST RIVERSIDE
🍴 HOTEL & SPA
$$$

FRIEDRICHSTRASSE 106
TEL 030 28 49 00
www.great-hotel.de

Behind its bland communist-era facade, you'll be surprised by the quirky blend of art nouveau décor and spa facilities. Rooms range from basic budget to the pleasure-filled spa suite with waterbed and a claw-footed tub. Vegas-style highlight: a shell-shaped saltwater tub. Windows in many rooms, as well as the downstairs café and restaurant, have arresting views over the Spree.

ⓘ 40 🚇 S1, S2, S5, S7, U6 Friedrichstrasse 🅿 🔁 ⓢ 🍸
◈ All major cards

⌂ AUGUSTINEN
HOF
$$$

AUGUSTSTRASSE 82, MITTE
TEL 030 30 88 60
www.hotel-augustinenhof.de

Run by a Christian charity, this small hotel dating from 1868 has a hip location in Auguststrasse, with many bars and art galleries nearby. Decoration is all about the Mediterranean with gleaming wooden floors, some intriguing art, and all the mod cons. Barrier-free facilities for the disabled are outstanding. Ask for rooms overlooking the tranquil courtyards. Breakfast is included.

ⓘ 63 + 3 apts. 🚇 S1, S2 Oranienburger Strasse 🅿
🔁 ◈ All major cards

⌂ HACKESCHER MARKT
$$$

GROSSE PRÄSIDENTENSTRASSE 8
TEL 030 28 00 30
www.hotel-hackescher-markt.com

In a nicely renovated 19th-century town house, this urbane hotel is perfectly situated for tapping the nightlife around Hackescher Markt.

The rooms and suites have pleasant country-style furnishings and floor heating in the bathrooms. Most quarters face a peaceful green courtyard, and some even have balconies. The English-speaking staff are eager to help. Although some rooms are snug, you can't quibble with the location.

ⓘ 31 + 3 suites 🚇 S5, S7, Hackescher Markt 🅿 🔁 ⓢ
◈ All major cards

⌂ HONIGMOND GARDEN
$$$

INVALIDENSTRASSE 122, MITTE
TEL 030 28 44 55 77
www.honigmond.de

This romantic, family-run hotel transports you to 19th-century Berlin with original antiques, stucco ceilings, and polished wood floors. The rear chambers and kitchen-equipped cottages face an idyllic, shady garden with Japanese fishpond and century-old trees. Breakfast is included.

ⓘ 20 🚇 S1, S2 Nordbahnhof 🅿 ⓢ ◈ No credit cards

⌂ INDIGO
🍴 ALEXANDERPLATZ
$$$

BERNHARD-WEISS-STRASSE 5
TEL 030 505 08 60
www.hotelindigoberlin.com

Located just a few minutes' walk north of Alexanderplatz, this new and affordable hotel is a good home base for exploring central Berlin. The rooms are small but crisply clean and modern, and excellent service is provided by a friendly, youthful staff. Other amenities include a large and welcoming bar, free Wi-Fi, in-room coffee machines, and a well-appointed gym.

ⓘ 153 🚇 S5, S7, U2, U5, U8 Alexanderplatz 🅿 (in vicinity) 🔁 ⓢ 🍸 ◈ All major cards

SOMETHING SPECIAL

⌂ KÜNSTLERHEIM LUISE
$$$

LUISENSTRASSE 19, MITTE
TEL 030 28 44 80
www.kuenstlerheim-luise.de

Bedroom fantasy, you say? Each of the 50 rooms at this wacky art hotel is an installation designed by young artists. Some play with your head (one has a ridiculously huge four-poster bed), draw on sci-fi (a Jetsons shower), or are chilled (Japanese screens and Zen music). The location is convenient to the Reichstag, Unter den Linden, and the sights along Oranienburger Strasse. Rooms are tastefully appointed and quiet, apart from a few beds next to the S-Bahn tracks.

ⓘ 50 🚇 U6 Oranienburger Tor; S1, S2, S5, S7, U6 Friedrichstrasse 🔁 ⓢ ♿ 🍸
◈ All major cards

⌂ LUX ELEVEN
$$$

ROSA-LUXEMBURG-STRASSE 9–13, MITTE
TEL 030 936 28 00
www.lux-eleven.com

A haunt of pencil-thin fashion models and media types, these spacious apartments were once used by visitors to the dreaded Ministry of State Security. They are now done up in a minimalist Far Eastern style. Soft cuddly things abound—pillows, comfy chairs, piles of towels—to make spaces plush and inviting. Rooms boast Wi-Fi and flatscreen TVs. Guests here can plug into the gallery scene of Mitte or just retreat to their personal cocoons.

ⓘ 72 apts. 🚇 S5, S7, U2, U5, U8 Alexanderplatz 🅿 🔁 ⓢ 🍸 ◈ All major cards

CIRCUS
$$–$$$
ROSENTHALER STRASSE 1, MITTE
TEL 030 20 00 39 39
www.circus-berlin.de
Handily situated on Rosenthaler Platz in the hub of the Mitte district, the Circus is like a luxury youth hostel for grown-ups. The garden courtyard (and rear quarters overlooking it) are a great place to relax, and there are hip little amenities such as iPods loaded with Berlin music. Rooms are clean, stylish, and sport imaginative touches—look for the quotes engraved in windows. There's Wi-Fi throughout and breakfast is included.
🛏 60 🚇 U8 Rosenthaler Platz 🔄 🚭 🏧 All major cards

BERLIN APARTMENT
$$
VETERANENSTRASSE 10, MITTE
TEL 030 70 22 13 58
www.midi-inn.de
This stylish boutique hotel has an enviable location—overlooking the rolling Weinbergspark, on the cusp of sight-filled Mitte and hip Prenzlauer Berg. Though on the cozy side, the double rooms have huge windows, smart designs, and attractive canvases by a London artist. Management rents out several fine apartments close by. Breakfast is served in the Mediterranean restaurant-bar.
🛏 3 + 4 apts. 🚇 U8 Rosenthaler Platz 🔄 🚭 🏧 AE, MC, V

WOMBAT'S CITY
HOSTEL
$
ALTE SCHÖNHAUSERSTRASSE 2
TEL 030 84 71 08 20
www.wombats-hostels.com
Run by a young, go-ahead staff of expats in a vibrant neighborhood, the Wombat nicely combines a kicking party hostel with hotel amenities. Rates

in the spotless, three- to six-bed dorms include bedsheets, kitchen use, and Web access in the downstairs lounge. Double rooms are available—a real deal in this category. The popular rooftop bar affords a stunning view over Mitte, and several nightclubs are within walking distance.
🛏 84 🚇 U2 Rosa-Luxemburg-Platz 🔄 🚭 🏧 AE, MC, V

RESTAURANTS

AIGNER
$$$
FRANZÖSISCHE STRASSE 25
TEL 030 203 75 18 50
www.aigner-gendarmenmarkt.de
On a corner of Berlin's prestigious Gendarmenmarkt, the Aigner was a historic café in Vienna before being dismantled and moved to the German capital. This is a prime spot for a business lunch or dinner, with tasty Austro-German dishes such as braised shoulder of young bull with pureed olives or pan-fried Brandenburg duck. Try Aigner's warm chocolate-laced pear with vanilla ice cream.
🍴 150 🚇 U6 Französische Strasse, Stadtmitte 🏧 All major cards

GANYMED
$$$
SCHIFFBAUER DAMM 5, MITTE
TEL 030 28 59 90 46
www.ganymed-brasserie.de
A visit to this cozy riverside brasserie is like going on vacation in la belle France. The forté of chef Vincent Garcia is seafood: locally harvested mussels, shrimp, crabs, and oysters flown in from the coast and prepared in a bewildering number of ways. The candlelit dining room with checkered tablecloths and art deco globes is a treat, but on summery days the riverside terrace is the place to be.
🍴 75 🚇 S1, S2, S5, S7, U6

Friedrichstrasse 🏧 All major cards

WEINBAR RUTZ
$$$
CHAUSSEESTRASSE 8, MITTE
TEL 030 24 62 87 60
www.rutz-weinbar.de
An oenophile's dream, the Rutz cellars boast over a thousand different European wines, including an impressive spread of German and Austrian vintages. For a reasonable €18 surcharge, you can have a bottle brought up from the downstairs shop and uncorked. The contemporary Michelin-starred cuisine is terrific across the board. The showstopper is entrecôte from milk-fed Kobe cattle served in truffle gravy.
🍴 110 🕐 Closed L & Mon. 🚇 U6 Oranienburger Tor 🏧 All major cards

LAS OLAS
$$
KARL-LIEBKNECHT-STRASSE 29, MITTE
TEL 030 241 54 72
www.lasolas.de
Berlin's best Spanish food is served in what's got to be the ugliest spot on Alexanderplatz. Jammed under a socialist-era tower block, this hidden gem surprises with its relaxed atmosphere, friendly servers, and authentic Iberian dishes. The array of tapas and paellas is superb. Reserve ahead.
🍴 120 🕐 Closed L & Sun. 🚇 S5, S7, U2, U5, U8 Alexanderplatz 🏧 AE, MC, V

NOLA'S AM WEINBERG
$$
VETERANENSTRASSE 9, MITTE
TEL 030 44 04 07 66
www.nola.de
This Swiss-style restaurant in a postwar pavilion overlooks the sweet little Weinbergspark. The relaxed ambience draws the occasional Hollywood star—Brad Pitt and Angelina

Jolie were spotted here. Expect a patchwork of Alpine cuisine from cheese fondue to baked river trout. In summer, a broad mix of students and families flake out on the terrace deck chairs.

🏃 100 🚇 U8 Rosenthaler Platz 💳 All major cards

🍴 SCHWARZWALD-STUBEN
$$
TUCHOLSKYSTRASSE 48, MITTE
TEL 030 28 09 80 84
www.schwarzwaldstuben
-berlin.com
A humorous nod to the Swabian region in Germany's southwest corner. The jumble of living room furniture, brewing equipment, antlers, and hunting gear is more than a tad bizarre and puts a question mark over Hemingway's view that the Black Forest was too prim. Try a *Flammkuchen* (thin-crust pizza) with pear and gorgonzola topping while savoring a Tannenzäpfle pils.

🏃 50 🚇 S1, S2 Oranienburger Strasse 💳 No credit cards

🍴 KELLERRESTAURANT IM BRECHT-HAUS
$
CHAUSSEESTRASSE 125, MITTE
TEL 030 282 38 43
www.brechtkeller.de
The onetime home of author Bertolt Brecht and next door to the cemetery where he is buried, this cellar eatery has heaps of atmosphere and German specialties such as *Fleischlabberln* (spicy meat patties) and Wiener schnitzel. All dishes are from Brecht's wife Helene Weigel's handwritten cookbook, based on recipes from Bohemia. In summer, the lovely garden is thrown open to diners.

🏃 65 🕐 Closed L 🚇 U6 Oranienburger Tor 💳 AE, MC, V

🍴 MUTTER HOPPE
$
RATHAUSSTRASSE 21, MITTE
TEL 030 24 72 06 03
www.prostmahlzeit.de
/mutterhoppe
This wood-paneled restaurant in the Nikolai quarter is named for Mother Hoppe, a formidable cook who used to whip up mountains of food for her family and friends. Photos and knickknacks recall the world of yesteryear. Sit down to a hearty serving of *Eisbein* (pork knuckle) or an oversized schnitzel and enjoy golden oldies from the '20s and '30s. Live bands play on weekends.

🏃 90 🚇 U2, U8, S5, S7 Alexanderplatz 💳 MC, V

■ TIERGARTEN & AROUND

HOTELS

🏨 BERLIN, BERLIN
🍴 $$-$$$
LÜTZOWPLATZ 17, TIERGARTEN
TEL 030 260 50
www.hotel-berlin-berlin.com
Host to many a business conference, this cavernous hotel has over 700 rooms yet manages to feel warm and personal. During the Cold War, visiting celebrities and politicians often stayed here, and staff are full of anecdotes of the era. The rooms are immense, modern, and spotless. Wi-Fi is free throughout the hotel, and breakfast is included.

ⓘ 710 🚇 U1, U3, U4 Nollendorfplatz 🅿 🔄 📺 💳 All major cards

RESTAURANTS

🍴 PARIS-MOSKAU
$$$$
ALT-MOABIT 141, TIERGARTEN
www.paris-moskau.de
Once a signalman's home, this pretty wood-frame restaurant

is renowned for its flawless service and excellent wines. The cuisine aims halfway between the French and Russian capitals, with nuances coming out in hearty dishes such as fresh pike perch in fried blood sausage with red wine and shallots. Reservations are a good idea. Ask for an al fresco table in summer.

🏃 60 🕐 Closed L 🚇 S5, S7, U55 💳 No credit cards

🍴 ANGKOR WAT
$$-$$$
PAULSTRASSE 22, TIERGARTEN
TEL 030 393 39 22
http://angkorwat.kambod
schareise.de
Palms, bright flowers, and a beach-hut bar set the tone of this Cambodian fondue restaurant. The house specialty is served with beef, shrimp, chicken, octopus, or shark filet. The food arrives uncooked in earthy wire baskets, ready for dunking in a bubbling cauldron right at your table. What sets it apart from European fondues are the spicy sauces, lemongrass, and bamboo sprouts. If you've still got room, try a

sugar palm fruit with sweet rice and coconut milk.
🍴 220 🕐 Closed L Mon.–Fri.
🚇 S5, S7 Bellevue 💳 MC, V

🍴 CAFE EINSTEIN STAMMHAUS

$$–$$$

KURFÜRSTENSTRASSE 58,
TIERGARTEN

TEL 030 261 50 96

www.cafeeinstein.com

Red leather banquettes, parquet flooring, and carved wooden chairs re-create old Vienna in this opulent villa from 1878. The Einstein serves traditional Wiener schnitzel and apple strudel as well as Austrian nouvelle cuisine. The garden is wonderful for breakfast, or coffee and cake. At one time, the villa belonged to actress Henny Porten, a mistress of Nazi propaganda chief Joseph Goebbels; a painting of Porten hangs in the upstairs bar.

🍴 300 🚇 U1 Kurfürsten-strasse 💳 DC, MC, V

■ CHARLOTTEN-BURG

HOTELS

🏨 BRANDENBURGER 🍴 HOF

$$$$$

EISLEBENER STRASSE 14,
CHARLOTTENBURG

TEL 030 21 40 50

www.brandenburger-hof.com

Bauhaus and modern design come together in this elegant villa dating from the early 1900s. The hotel is supremely atmospheric and quiet, featuring stylish but livable rooms with 13-foot ceilings. The house restaurant Die Quadriga is considered one of the city's finest and serves only fine German wines.

🛏 58 🚇 U3 Augsburger Strasse 🅿 ⬌ 🚭 ❄ 💪 💳 All major cards

🏨 Q!

$$$–$$$$

KNESEBECKSTRASSE 67,
CHARLOTTENBURG

TEL 030 810 06 60

www.loock-hotels.com

A cool gray facade signals your arrival at the Q, an ultrachic retreat named for the nearby Ku'damm. This hotel smoothes out the rough edges by eliminating corners. Hardwood floors curve up the walls in the rooms, where you can literally slide from the tub into bed. The spa has its own self-contained beach with heated sand, aromatherapy, and sound and light effects.

🛏 77 🚇 S5, S7 Savignyplatz 🅿 🚭 ❄ 💳 All major cards

🏨 SAVOY 🍴 $$$–$$$$

FASANENSTRASSE 9–10,
CHARLOTTENBURG

TEL 030 31 10 30

www.hotel-savoy.com

A Berlin institution, this hotel oozes old-world charm of bowler hats and rustling petticoats. Standard rooms are a little generic, but the suites named after regular guests like Henry Miller or Greta Garbo have heaps of character on the 6th floor (the only level with air-conditioning). The Times Bar has a walk-in humidor.

🛏 125 🚇 S5, S7, U2 Zoolo-gischer Garten, U9 ⬌ 🚭 ❄ 💳 All major cards

🏨 BLEIBTREU 🍴 $$$

BLEIBTREUSTRASSE 31,
CHARLOTTENBURG

TEL 030 88 47 40

www.bleibtreu.com

The cheery, ecofriendly materials and minimalist Italian furniture of this boutique hotel are completely in step with the fancy apparel shops along Bleibtreustrasse. Some rooms are on the tight side, but the in-house bar and Restaurant 31 are quite elegant.

🛏 59 🚇 S5, S7, S9 Savigny-platz; U1 Uhlandstrasse, U9 ⬌ 🚭 💪 💳 All major cards

🏨 CASA

$$$

SCHLÜTERSTRASSE 40,
CHARLOTTENBURG

TEL 030 280 30 00

www.hotel-casa.de

This slick hotel caters to savvy urbanites who value practical but chic décor. The color schemes meld designer cool and welcoming hospitality. The sleek Philippe Starck furniture is offset by warm Mediter-ranean hues in the roomy apartments. Breakfast is served till noon.

🛏 29 🚇 S5, S7, S9 Savigny-platz; U1 Uhlandstrasse, U9 ⬌ 🚭 💳 All major cards

🏨 HECKER'S 🍴 $$$

GROLMANSTRASSE 35,
CHARLOTTENBURG

TEL 030 889 00

www.heckers-hotel.de

Just a few steps off busy Ku'damm, this renowned boutique hotel prides itself on the personal service it heaps on celebrities such as Michael Douglas, Valéry Giscard d'Estaing, and Austrian rock star Udo Jürgens. The huge, elegant quarters range from Bauhaus to Italo-chic. The lobby has a striking ice blue backlit bar.

🛏 72 🚇 U1 Uhlandstrasse 🅿 ⬌ 🚭 ❄ 💳 All major cards

🏨 KU'DAMM 101

$$$

KURFÜRSTENDAMM 101,
CHARLOTTENBURG

TEL 030 520 05 50

www.kudamm101.com

A bit removed from the action, this hotel is fascinating viewing for anyone with an eye for minimalist design. The lobby combines '60s design with New Age–column lamps, curvy banquettes, and recessed ceilings. The rooms are a clever blend of light and shadow. There's high-speed Internet and retro touches like a wood-grain console that hides the TV.

ℹ 170 🚇 S41, S42, S47 Halensee 🅿 🛗 ⚙ 🅰 All major cards

🏨 ASKANISCHER HOF
$$–$$$
KURFÜRSTENDAMM 53,
CHARLOTTENBURG
TEL 030 881 80 33
www.askanischer-hof.de
For a dose of Berlin history, check into this intimate hotel on the city's most famous shopping avenue. The Askanischer Hof was raised in the early 1900s and furnished in Golden '20s style. The rooms are all individually designed and boast high-tech features. Rock star David Bowie was a regular guest in the 1970s.

ℹ 16 🚇 S5, S7 Savignyplatz 🅿 🎦 🅰 All major cards

🏨 PENSION DITTBERNER
$$–$$$
WIELANDSTRASSE 26,
CHARLOTTENBURG
TEL 030 884 69 50
www.hotel-dittberner.de
This friendly third-floor pension has been in the Lange family for generations. This is old Berlin in spades: soaring ceilings, adorned with stucco and aging lithographs, and a bright breakfast room with antique sideboard. Breakfast is included.

ℹ 22 🚇 S5, S7, S9 Savignyplatz 🅿 🛗 ⚙ No credit cards

SOMETHING SPECIAL
🏨 PROPELLER ISLAND CITY LODGE
$$–$$$
ALBRECHT-ACHILLES-STRASSE 58,

CHARLOTTENBURG
TEL 030 891 90 16
www.propeller-island.com
Get ready for a surprise—nothing about this place can be described as ordinary. This 19th-century apartment block has been rewired as an eccentric hotel where every room is an inhabitable work of art. Beds can be found in coffins, hovering in the air, or hidden in a fortress. The Two Lions sports a pair of caged mattresses 5 feet (1.5 m) above the ground. Every stick of furniture was designed and crafted by the owner-artist himself.

ℹ 45 🚇 U7 Adenauerplatz 🅰 All major cards

RESTAURANTS

🍴 FLORIAN
$$$
GROLMANSTRASSE 52,
CHARLOTTENBURG
TEL 030 313 91 84
www.restaurant-florian.de
Actors, gallery owners, and celebrities hang out at this stylish Savignyplatz café. The kitchen canters between down-home German and refined international dishes, served in elegant bistro surroundings. Owners Gerti and Ute mingle happily with their guests. A long-standing ritual is the Nuremberg bratwurst with sauerkraut, served only after 11 p.m.

🪑 70 🚇 S5, S7 Savignyplatz 🅰 AE, MC, V

🍴 MAROOUSH
$$$
KNESEBECKSTRASSE 48,
CHARLOTTENBURG
TEL 030 887 11 83 35
www.marooush.de
Arabian Nights décor (white chiffon curtains and metal lanterns) gets you in the mood for the tasty mezes (starters) and regional gems such as Asian barbeque or lamb with

couscous, pomegranate, and mint yogurt sauce. Pastries, chais (teas), and water pipes are served in the lounge. Reserve ahead for the belly dancing shows on Friday and Saturday nights.

🪑 90 🕐 Closed L 🚇 U1 Uhlandstrasse; U3 Hohenzollernplatz 🅰 AE, MC, V

🍴 BORRIQUITO
$$
WIELANDSTRASSE 6,
CHARLOTTENBURG
TEL 030 312 99 29
www.el-borriquito.de
After dark, things really get hopping in the "Little Donkey" near Savignyplatz. Night owls converge for Rioja and classic Spanish dishes like paella with giant *gambas*. Someone's always singing or playing the guitar.

🪑 125 🕐 Closed L 🚇 S5, S7 Savignyplatz ⚙ No credit cards

🍴 BREL
$$
SAVIGNYPLATZ 1,
CHARLOTTENBURG
TEL 030 31 80 00 20
www.cafebrel.de
Named for chanson singer Jacques Brel, this hair-down café is perfect for seeing and being seen among west-side artistic types. Belgian classics of onion soup, rump steak with *frites* (fries), and steamed mussels are worth the inevitable wait.

🪑 95 🚇 S5, S7 Savignyplatz 🅰 AE, MC, V

SOMETHING SPECIAL
🍴 CAFE IM LITERATURHAUS
$$
FASANENSTRASSE 23,
CHARLOTTENBURG
TEL 030 882 54 14
www.literaturhaus-berlin.de
Nestled in an old villa a heartbeat from the Kurfürstendamm, this café-

restaurant exudes the kind of worldly sophistication that comes from generations of intellectual debate over coffee. In the basement is a well-stocked bookshop, while the salon and glassed-in Wintergarten are renowned for tasty seasonal dishes such as roast rosemary lamb or trout with new potatoes.

🚻 100 🚇 U1, U9 Uhlandstrasse 🚫 No credit cards

🍽 JULEP'S
$$
GIESEBRECHTSTRASSE 3, CHARLOTTENBURG
TEL 030 881 88 23
www.juleps-berlin.de
In a quiet side street off the Ku'damm, Julep's is a clone of a New York speakeasy. Juicy steaks, quarter-pound burgers, and Manhattan clam chowder share the menu with Tex-Mex and the Pacific Rim. Patrons come to cheer American football on the big screen or just to linger over a mint julep, one of 120 cocktails on offer.
🚻 100 🚇 U7 Adenauerplatz 🚫 AE, MC

🍽 SACHIKO SUSHI BAR
$$
GROLMANSTRASSE 47, CHARLOTTENBURG
TEL 030 313 22 82
www.sachikosushi.com
Tucked into an alleyway by the railway line on Savignyplatz, this intimate little sushi bar could scarcely have a better hiding place. Shockingly fresh sushi floats to you in a river built right into the oval bar.
🚻 25 🚇 S5, S7 Savignyplatz 🚫 AE, MC, V

🍽 ZWÖLF APOSTEL
$$
BLEIBTREUSTRASSE 49, CHARLOTTENBURG
TEL 030 312 14 33
www.12-apostel.de
The tireless staff of the 12 Apostles serves stone-oven

pizzas, mouth-watering pastas, and homemade breads round-the-clock. The pseudo-Roman dining rooms make even the most exhausted clubber look great. Reservations are recommended.
🚻 200 🚇 S5, S7 Savignyplatz 🚫 No credit cards

🍽 ROGACKI
$–$$
WILMERSDORFER STRASSE 145–146, CHARLOTTENBURG
TEL 030 343 82 50
This rambling, well-stocked deli has been serving locals for over 80 years. The bewildering choice includes 200-plus varieties of meats, breads, and poultry as well as 150 kinds of cheese. Pride of place goes to the ice-filled seafood counters. For a quintessential experience, head to the gourmet serving stations and dine at the traditional standing tables. Saturday lunch is the best time to go.
🚻 35 + 80 standing 🚇 U2, U7 Bismarckstrasse 🚫 MC, V

🍽 ASHOKA
$
GROLMANSTRASSE 51, CHARLOTTENBURG
TEL 030 313 20 66
http://myashoka.de
Just off Savignyplatz, this hole-in-the-wall Indian eatery whips up its delectable meat and vegetarian dishes an arm's length from your well-worn table. On balmy evenings, the sidewalk tables are perfect for people-watching.
🚻 25 🚇 S7, S5 🚫 No credit cards

▪ PRENZLAUER BERG, FRIEDRICHSHAIN, & THE EAST

HOTELS

🏨 NHOW BERLIN
$$$–$$$$
STRALAUER ALLEE 3

TEL 030 290 29 90
www.nhow-hotels.com
Flash Gordon meets Barbie at this "music lifestyle hotel" lodged in a converted riverside granary. Futuristic shapes and bubblegum colors dominate. Rooms are equipped with Wi-Fi, iPod dock, and flat-screen IP-TVs that double as mirrors. The stainless steel tower has music studios for rent; room service will send up a Gibson guitar with headphones. 🛏 304 🚇 S5, S7, U1 Warschauer Strasse 🅿 🛗 🚫 ❄ 🏋 🚫 All major cards

🏨 🍽 ADELE
$$$
GREIFSWALDER STRASSE 227
TEL 030 44 32 43 10
www.adele-hotel.de
From the street, this lounge hotel is cleverly camouflaged by a row of coffee and wine shops. Rooms look like something out of *Wallpaper* magazine, with dark hardwoods and leathers set off by cream and pastel hues. There's a fine Mediterranean-inspired restaurant.
🛏 14 🚇 U2 Senefelderplatz 🅿 🛗 🚫 🚫 All major cards

🏨 KASTANIENHOF
$$$
KASTANIENALLEE 65
TEL 030 44 30 50
www.kastanienhof.biz
This guesthouse has a great location on Kastanienallee, a hip nightlife strip in Prenzlauer Berg. The historic building hosted a butcher shop, Russian military post, and tenements before being turned into one of East Berlin's first hotels after reunification. The furnishings are simple, but the historic maps and photos in the rooms ooze atmosphere.
🛏 35 🚇 U8 Rosenthaler Platz 🅿 🛗 🚫 🚫 All major cards

MICHELBERGER
$$–$$$

WARSCHAUER STRASSE 39
TEL 030 29 77 85 90
www.michelbergerhotel.com
An old warehouse reborn as a
hotel, the Michelberger pitches
affordable charms for night
owls in buzzing Friedrichshain.
The interiors are kept raw with
exposed wiring, feature playful
touches like raised beds, and
have free Wi-Fi. The laid-back
bar area has comfy sofas and
a travel library. Easy walking
distance from nightclubs like
Berghain.
🛈 119 🚇 S5, S7, U1 Warschauer Strasse 🔄 🚫 💳 MC, V

EAST SIDE
$$

MÜHLENSTRASSE 6,
FRIEDRICHSHAIN
TEL 030 29 38 34 00
www.eastsidehotel.de
A stone's throw from the
East Side Gallery—the longest
remaining section of the Berlin
Wall—this friendly, supermod-
ern hotel has a minimalist
decor featuring art and photos
devoted to the former barrier.
Front rooms have views of
the gallery and the river, but
are noisier than those to the
rear. Breakfast is included and
served 24 hours.
🛈 36 🚇 S5, S7, U1 Warschau-
er Strasse 🅿 🔄 💳 All major
cards

26 BERLIN
$$

GRÜNBERGER STRASSE 26,
FRIEDRICHSHAIN
TEL 030 297 77 80
www.hotel26-berlin.de
For no-nonsense digs a cut
above a hostel, try this small,
eco-friendly hotel in the go-
ahead Friedrichshain district.
Breakfast (included) is a magnificent organic spread of cheeses,
fresh juices, and cold cuts. You
can chill in the pleasant café or
catch some rays on the lounge
chairs in the rear garden.

🛈 19 🚇 S5, S7, U1 Warschauer Strasse 🅿 🚫 💳 All major
cards

UPSTALSBOOM
$$

GUBENER STRASSE 42
TEL 030 293 750
www.upstalsboom-berlin.de
An oddity in landlocked Berlin,
this perky hotel is part of a
chain of seaside resorts. The
sleek rooms come in four sizes,
some with kitchens, and the
Friesendeel restaurant serves
wonderful fish specialties. The
rooftop garden has sweeping
views over the Friedrichshain
district. Rates include bicycle
rentals and use of the sauna
and gym.
🛈 170 🚇 S5, S7, U1
Warschauer Strasse
🅿 🔄 🚫 🛗 💳 All major
cards

GREIFSWALD
$–$$

GREIFSWALDER STRASSE 211,
PRENZLAUER BERG
TEL 030 442 78 88
www.hotel-greifswald.de
Tucked into a historic building,
this little hotel is something
of a rock shrine. Guests have
included members of Step-
penwolf and guitarist Albert
Lee. Dozens of autographed
photos adorn the reception
area and breakfast room. The
comfy albeit generic rooms
and small apartments with
kitchen are popular with
families.
🛈 30 🚇 Tram M4 or Bus 200
🅿 🚫 💳 All major cards

JUNCKER'S
$–$$

GRÜNBERGER STRASSE 21
TEL 030 293 35 50
www.junckers-hotel.de
This family-run hotel is one of
Berlin's best kept secrets. The
simple rooms are cut a little
close but are bright and spotless. Free Wi-Fi, coffee, and
mineral water make you feel

PRICES

HOTELS

An indication of the cost of
a double room in the high
season is given by **$** signs.

$$$$$	Over $270
$$$$	$200–$270
$$$	$130–$200
$$	$80–$130
$	Under $80

RESTAURANTS

An indication of the cost of
a three-course meal without
drinks is given by **$** signs.

$$$$$	Over $80
$$$$	$50–$80
$$$	$35–$50
$$	$20–$35
$	Under $20

right at home. The gracious
owner, Herr Juncker, is a font
of local knowledge and speaks
fluent English.
🛈 30 🚇 S5, S7, S9,
U1 Warschauer Strasse
🅿 🔄 💳 MC, V

RESTAURANTS

GUGELHOF
$$$

KNAACKSTRASSE 37,
PRENZLAUER BERG
TEL 030 442 92 29
www.gugelhof.de
This lively Franco-German
eatery was once the scene of a
dinner with President Clinton
and Chancellor Schröder.
Alsatian delights such as
Flammkuchen and *choucroute*
(meats and sausages on a bed
of sauerkraut) are typical, as
are the delicate Riesling wines.
In summer, the terrace affords
views of pretty Kollwitzplatz.
🪑 90 🚇 U2 Senefelderplatz
💳 All major cards

NOCTI VAGUS
$$$

SAARBRÜCKER STRASSE 36–38
TEL 030 74 74 91 23

🏨 Hotel 🍴 Restaurant 🛈 No. of Guest Rooms 🪑 No. of Seats 🔄 Closed 🚇 U- or S-Bahn 🅿 Parking 🛗 Elevator

www.noctivagus.com
If you've never had the pleasure, Berlin's first "darkness restaurant" will open up new sensory worlds. You're led to your table in utter blackness by blind waiters. For many, it's a disconcerting but enriching experience as taste, smell, and hearing are heightened. Reservations, for set meals only, are required.
🛏 52 🕐 Closed L 🚇 U2 Senefelderplatz 💳 MC, V

SOMETHING SPECIAL

🍴 ODERQUELLE
$$$
ODERBERGER STRASSE 27
TEL 030 44 00 80 80
www.oderquelle.de
This hidden gem lends German classics a Franco-Italian accent. The seasonal menu changes daily and might include lamb filet served with Sicilian eggplant and pastry or tender braised beef on parsley potatoes. Service is impeccable and the laid-back staff speaks English. You can dine in paneled chambers with antique fittings and a gorgeous wooden bar or on the shady front terrace. Save room for the homemade chocolate-pear cake.
🛏 120 🕐 Closed L 🚇 U2 Eberswalder Strasse 💳 MC, V

🍴 BABEL
$$
GABRIEL MAX STRASSE 16 &
KASTANIENALLEE 33
TEL 030 29 36 87 84
Diners squat on padded poufs for cozy conversation in soft red lighting at this Middle Eastern eatery. Enjoy tasty Lebanese specialties like *kafta* (grilled lamb kabobs), hummus (spicy pureed chickpeas), or the bulging Babel Platter for two to three people, paired with a Lebanese wine. Also popular are the potent cocktails and water pipes stoked with fruity tobaccos.

Locations are in Friedrichshain and Prenzlauer Berg.
🛏 85 🕐 Closed L 🚇 U5 Frankfurter Tor, U2 Eberswalder Strasse 💳 No credit cards

🍴 GORKI PARK
$$
WEINBERGSWEG 25
TEL 030 448 72 86
http://gorki-park.de
Past the small bar serving glasses of vodka and Russian beer, the down-at-heel dining rooms exude an air of pleasant decline. Specialties include lightly peppered *pelmeni* (dumplings) with sour cream and hearty borscht. The Sunday brunch is legendary.
🛏 40 🚇 U8 Rosenthaler Platz 💳 No credit cards

🍴 UMSPANNWERK OST
$$
PALISADENSTRASSE 48
TEL 030 42 80 94 97
www.umspannwerk-ost.de
Housed in a 19th-century power plant, this is Friedrichshain's largest restaurant and one of its most atmospheric. Starters include razor-thin beef carpaccio and orange-carrot soup, while main dishes like thyme-crusted lamb don't skimp on quality or quantity. It's tough to decide where to sit—the spacious terrace, the old transformer hall, or right at the bar.
🛏 160 🚇 U5 Weberwiese 💳 MC, V

🍴 WEINSTEIN
$$
LYCHENER STRASSE 33,
PRENZLAUER BERG
TEL 030 441 18 42
www.weinstein.eu
Wine dealer Roy Metzger and his brother Marc serve up an eclectic mix at this cozy wine bar–restaurant. Mixed salad with Brandenburg veal, dumplings stuffed with goat cheese, and marinated tuna are typical of the fare, influenced by the

French Alsace region.
🛏 65 🕐 Closed Sun. L 🚇 U2 Eberswalder Strasse 💳 MC, V

🍴 I DUE FORNI
$–$$
SCHÖNHAUSER ALLEE 12
TEL 030 44 01 73 33
The punk rock waiters in this unusual Italian eatery serve some of Berlin's greatest thin-crust pizza. Engrossed couples, families, and students share communal tables in an atmosphere of barely contained chaos. Reserve ahead, as the cavernous hall gets packed. Grunge bands play later on.
🛏 150 🚇 U2 Senefelderplatz 💳 No credit cards

🍴 CONMUX
$
SIMON DACH STRASSE 35,
FRIEDRICHSHAIN
TEL 030 291 38 63
www.conmux.de
In the thick of café-filled Friedrichshain, Conmux is a fixture for its industrial décor and gargantuan breakfasts. Only organic ingredients make it onto your plate. Sit on the shady terrace and watch the ebb and flow of hipsters along Simon Dach Strasse.
🛏 85 🚇 S5, S7, U1 Warschauer Strasse; U5 Frankfurter Tor 💳 No credit cards

🍴 HABBA HABBA
$
KASTANIENALLEE 15,
PRENZLAUER BERG
TEL 030 36 74 57 26
www.habba-habba.de
Authentic Middle Eastern street food: deep-fried halloumi cheese speckled with sesame, fresh falafel, and kafta with pomegranate sauce. Grab one of the two tables on the poop deck overlooking hip Kastanienallee.
🛏 20 🚇 U2 Eberswalder Strasse 💳 No credit cards

🍴 KONNOPKE

$

SCHÖNHAUSER ALLEE 440,
PRENZLAUER BERG

TEL 030 442 77 65

www.konnopke-imbiss.de

This venerable snack bar under Eberswalder Strasse station (the U2 line) claims to have invented *Currywurst* (curried sausage) back in 1960. Celebrities frequent the joint, and even Angela Merkel lined up and dined with the locals at the standing tables. The secret is in the ketchup-curry sauce.

🕐 Closes 8 p.m. 🚇 U2 Eberswalder Strasse 🚫 No credit cards

🍴 TRANSIT THAI

$

SONNTAGSTRASSE 48,
FRIEDRICHSHAIN

TEL 030 26 94 84 157

www.transit-restaurants.com

Colorful birdcages hang over diners in this perky purveyor of Asian tapas. Choose from dishes like Duck in Pajamas (wrapped in pancake) or Party Girl (a spicy papaya salad), to be combined with side orders of rice or noodles. It gets crowded with merrymakers late at night, so try to reserve a table.

🔁 70 🚇 S5, S7, S3 Ostkreuz 🚫 No credit cards

■ SCHÖNEBERG TO KREUZBERG

HOTELS

🏨 HÜTTENPALAST BERLIN
🍴 $$$

HOBRECHTSTRASSE 66,
NEUKÖLLN

TEL 030 37 30 58 06

www.huettenpalast.de

Indoor "glamping" is the draw at this old vacuum cleaner factory. Artists have redesigned three vintage camping trailers and three huts for guests.

Relax in the garden under fake trees. An organic breakfast (included) is served in the courtyard café. Regular rooms with en suite bathrooms are available in the rear wing.

🛏 12 🚇 U7, U8 Hermannplatz

🏨 MÖVENPICK BERLIN
🍴 $$$

SCHÖNEBERGER STRASSE 3,
KREUZBERG

TEL 030 23 00 60

www.moevenpickhotels.com

Once the headquarters of electronics giant Siemens, this hotel south of Potsdamer Platz offers funky design in a historic shell. The lounge bar is made of high-voltage equipment, and old turbines are displayed in the halls. Other highlights are the glass-bricked bathrooms, olivewood, and perky colors recalling Mövenpick ice cream.

🛏 243 🚇 S1, S2 Anhalter Bahnhof 🅿 🔃 🚭 🚭 🎎 All major cards

🏨 RIEHMERS
🍴 HOFGARTEN
$$$

YORCKSTRASSE 83, KREUZBERG

TEL 030 78 09 88 00

www.riehmers-hofgarten.de

This romantic small hotel near Viktoriapark was designed by Wilhelm Riehmers, a talented 19th-century architect. French double doors open into spacious rooms with stucco ceilings and contemporary décor. The in-house restaurant, named for writer E. T. A. Hoffmann, serves meals in a quiet cobblestone courtyard.

🛏 22 🚇 U6, U7 Mehringdamm 🅿 🔃 🚭 🎎 All major cards

🏨 PARK PLAZA WALL STREET
$$–$$$

WALLSTRASSE 23–24,
KREUZBERG

TEL 030 847 11 70

www.parkplaza.com

This deluxe four-star hotel near Checkpoint Charlie is something of a capitalist send-up, with dollar bills and stock-ticker symbols printed on carpets and drapes. The quarters are plush, roomy, and state of the art. The well-appointed rooms are packed with quality woods, textiles, and perks like free Wi-Fi, a flatscreen TV, and a laptop safe.

🛏 80 🚇 U2 Märkisches Museum 🅿 🔃 🚭 🚭 🎎 🎎 All major cards

RESTAURANTS

SOMETHING SPECIAL

🍴 TIM RAUE

$$$–$$$$

RUDI-DUTSCHKE-STRASSE 26,
KREUZBERG

TEL 030 25 93 79 30

www.tim-raue.com

A stellar talent, Kreuzberg-born chef Raue turned heads in 2012 by racking up a second Michelin star. The house specialty is Asian fusion, and Raue's dim sum has few equals. Blue lobster, jasmine pigeon on figs, and diamond-label, Cantonese-peppered beef grace the four- to six-course tasting menus, all free of white sugar, gluten, and dairy. The action revolves around a heavy oak table with views of the open kitchen. Reservations are essential.

🔁 50 🕐 Closed Mon. 🚇 U6 Kochstrasse 🎎 All major cards

🍴 ALTES ZOLLHAUS

$$$

CARL-HERZ-UFER 30, KREUZBERG

TEL 030 692 33 00

www.altes-zollhaus-berlin.de

Enjoy some fine German-international dining in this picturesque half-timbered house, a former customs post. Try the roast rabbit and venison with chanterelles, or the house specialty, roast duck on Savoy cabbage. In summer, you can

sit in the garden at the edge of the pretty Landwehr canal.
🛏 180 🕐 Closed Sun.–Mon. 🚇 U1 Prinzenstrasse 🅿 💳 DC, MC, V

🍴 LE COCHON BOURGEOIS

$$$

FICHTESTRASSE 24, KREUZBERG
TEL 030 693 01 01
www.lecochon.de

The "Bourgeois Pig" is one of the best French restaurants in Berlin. Chef and owner Hannes Behrmann has made a career of pork dishes like jugged wild boar on candied licorice. He also works miracles with game and seafood dishes like monkfish in bacon sauce on green lentils. Every night, a pianist tickles the ivories in the stylish interior—formerly the showroom of a colonial-goods dealer.
🛏 55 🕐 Closed Mon. 🚇 U7 Südstern 💳 No credit cards

🍴 AROMA

$$–$$$

HOCHKIRCHSTRASSE 8, KREUZBERG
TEL 030 782 58 21
www.cafe-aroma.de

Nestled in a quiet side street east of Kleistpark, Aroma parades the passion of two chefs from Lombardy and southern Tirol. Seasonal ingredients loom large from the Brandenburg countryside, and a local hunter provides the wild boar and venison. The café doubles as a gallery, concert hall, and a sort of Italian cultural center. 🛏 60 🕐 Closed Mon.–Fri. L 🚇 S1, S2 Yorckstrasse, U7 💳 No credit cards

🍴 DER GOLDENE HAHN

$$–$$$

PÜCKLERSTRASSE 20, KREUZBERG
TEL 030 618 80 98
www.goldenerhahn.de

This gem of a Tuscan restaurant has old farm implements and an apothecary's cabinet behind the bar. Stuffed pearl hen with anise sauce, giant grilled calamari, or pumpkin gnocchi in Parma butter are some highlights. The owner will pair your food with an excellent Italian wine. In the evening, a DJ will spin a disc of your choice.
🛏 110 🕐 Closed L 🚇 U1 Görlitzer Bahnhof 💳 MC, V

🍴 KADEWE

$$–$$$

TAUENTZIENSTRASSE 21, SCHÖNEBERG
TEL 030 212 10
www.kadewe.de

Berlin's most famous department store has a legendary food hall on the sixth floor, known locally as the *Fress-Etage* (glutton's floor). Wander goggle-eyed past gourmet counters selling roast bison, fresh octopus quiche, gooey French cheeses, and filled chocolates. The top-level cafeteria with atrium has fine views over Wittenbergplatz.
🕐 Closed Sun. 🚇 U1, U2, U3 Wittenbergplatz 💳 AE, MC, V

🍴 SAUVAGE

$$–$$$

PFLÜGERSTRASSE 25, NEUKÖLLN
TEL 030 53 16 75 47
www.sauvageberlin.com

Berlin's first restaurant for Paleolithic cuisine. Only natural, unprocessed foodstuffs from the Stone Age are allowed—lots of meat and fish and even wine, but no sugar, pasta, rice, or legumes. The benefits of eating "paleo," according to the English-speaking team, include clearer skin, a stronger immune system, and detoxification. Screamingly popular, so reserve ahead.
🛏 50 🕐 Closed Mon. & L 🚇 U8 Schönleinstrasse 🚭 💳 No credit cards

🍴 AMRIT

$$

WINTERFELDTSTRASSE 40, SCHÖNEBERG
TEL 030 21 01 46 40
www.amrit.de

Everything about Amrit is big, from the giant Buddha to the lurid wall mirrors and ringed chandeliers. Try the Indian dishes prepared in the tandoori ovens—heaping portions of spicy shrimp fried in basmati rice, nuts, vegetables and raisins, or the spicy marinated duck in honey sauce. It goes down best with a mango *lassi* or yogi tea.
🛏 100 🚇 U1, U3, U4 Nollendorfplatz 💳 All major cards

🍴 OUSIES

$$

GRUNEWALDSTRASSE 16, SCHÖNEBERG
TEL 030 216 79 57
www.taverna-ousies.de

In old Greece, tavernas served hot and cold appetizers instead of main dishes. Ousies enthusiastically pursues this tradition with tasty tapas like hamburger balls filled with spinach and cheese, mussels baked in lemon-oregano juice, or morsels of tsatsiki chicken. Wash it all down with jugs of Greek wine or ouzo shots. Reservations are advised.
🛏 65 🕐 Closed L 🚇 U7 Eisenacher Strasse 💳 MC, V

🍴 PRANZO E CENA

$–$$

GOLTZSTRASSE 32, SCHÖNEBERG
TEL 030 216 35 14

Authentic is the term for this cute little Italian eatery near Winterfeldtplatz. The stone-oven-cooked pizza may get top billing, but the lasagnas and spaghettis from freshly made pasta are just as good. The friendly chef takes requests for off-menu items. A great spot for a bargain lunch or dinner before hitting the bars and clubs.

🚭 Nonsmoking 🌀 Air-conditioning 🏊 Indoor Pool 🏊 Outdoor Pool 💪 Health Club 💳 Credit Cards

🍴 70 🚇 U2, U3, U4 Nollendorfplatz 💳 AE, MC, V

🍴 BURGERMEISTER

$

OBERBAUMSTRASSE 8,
KREUZBERG

TEL 030 22 43 64 93

http://burger-meister.de

A public-relations nightmare, this popular hamburger joint lives in a former public toilet below an elevated section of the S-Bahn, traffic speeding by on both sides—but somehow it's always buzzing. The *bio* (organic) beef and chili-cheese fries are done to perfection. Popular with nightowls taking a time-out from clubbing.

🍴 40 🕐 Closed Sun. L 🚇 U1 Schlesisches Tor 💳 No credit cards

🍴 HUDSON'S

$

BOPPSTRASSE 1, KREUZBERG

TEL 01577 682 78 29

www.hudsonscakes.com

If you think English cuisine stops at beans on toast, think again. The adventurous owners pour more than her Her Majesty's pride into their scrumptious cakes; the dark chocolate is made with porter. Delicious, too, are the ploughman's lunches, soups, salads, and genuine scones with clotted cream. Gets packed for English breakfast on weekends.

🍴 30 🚇 U8 Schönleinstrasse 💳 No credit cards

🍴 KNOFI

$

BERGMANNSTRASSE 98,
KREUZBERG

www.knofi.de

The tantalizing aroma of garlic wafts out of this café specializing in Greek-style sandwich spreads, juicy olives, and delicious cakes. Eat on the terrace and study the locals ambling down lively Bergmannstrasse, or stock up for a picnic.

🍴 40 🚇 U7 Gneisenaustrasse 💳 No credit cards

🍴 YELLOW SUNSHINE

$

WIENERSTRASSE 19

TEL 030 69 59 87 20

This vegetarian fast-food cafe in Kreuzberg sells dozens of types of veggie burgers, country-style fries, and salads, plus soy-milk ice cream and a potpourri of other vegan delights, topped off with organic juices or beer. It's enough to convert the most stubborn of carnivores to the other side. The staff speaks English fluently.

🍴 40 🚇 U1 Görlitzer Bahnhof 💳 No credit cards

🍴 ZUR HENNE

$

LEUSCHNERDAMM 25

TEL 030 614 77 30

Just off Kreuzberg's vibrant Oranienstrasse, this earthy bar-cafe is where dyed-in-the-wool Berliners meet to eat, drink, and trade gossip. Back in '63, the Henne sent John F. Kennedy an invitation to stop by. JFK couldn't make it, but sent a letter of apology which is still framed over the bar. The menu is easy to get your head around: roast chicken, sauerkraut, and bread. But the roast birds are so juicy, you'll want nothing else. Reserve ahead.

🍴 80 🕐 Closed L *&* Mon. 🚇 U1, U8 Kottbusser Tor 💳 No credit cards

▥ SPANDAU, DAHLEM, *&* THE WEST

🍴 ZITADELLENSCHÄNKE

$$$

AM JULIUSTURM, SPANDAU

TEL 030 334 21 06

Located in Spandau's 16th-century fortress, this is the place to live out your medieval fantasy—if it involves consuming a leg of boar to the strains of authentic minstrel song.

PRICES

HOTELS

An indication of the cost of a double room in the high season is given by $ signs.

$$$$$	Over $270
$$$$	$200–$270
$$$	$130–$200
$$	$80–$130
$	Under $80

RESTAURANTS

An indication of the cost of a three-course meal without drinks is given by $ signs.

$$$$$	Over $80
$$$$	$50–$80
$$$	$35–$50
$$	$20–$35
$	Under $20

Try to book ahead, as the vaulted, candlelit banquet hall is popular with groups.

🍴 220 🕐 Closed Mon. *&* L Tues.–Fri. 🚇 U7 Rathaus Spandau 💳 DC, MC, V

🍴 ALTER KRUG

$$

KÖNIGIN-LUISE-STRASSE 52,
DAHLEM

TEL 030 84 31 95 40

This half-timbered eatery just south of the Botanical Gardens retains a village feel, going back to an era before Berlin's tram lines reached Dahlem. It's known for hearty standards like *boulette* (spicy hamburger patties) and Swabian fare such as *Maultaschen* (ravioli). There's a lovely beer garden that's inevitably packed in summer.

🍴 125 🚇 U3 Dahlem-Dorf 💳 No credit cards

▥ EXCURSIONS

POTSDAM

🏨 SCHLOSSHOTEL CECILIENHOF

$$$

NEUER GARTEN

TEL 0331 370 50

FAX 0331 29 24 98

www.relexa-hotel.de

Situated in a park on the shore of the Wannsee, this grand mansion was the setting for the Potsdam Conference, where Truman, Churchill, and Stalin met in 1945 to discuss the fate of a defeated Germany. Furnished in classic Tudor style, the hotel is close to Potsdam but has a tranquil country atmosphere.

🛈 41 🚊 S1 Potsdam or RE train 🅿 🅢 All major cards

🍴 SPECKERS GASTSTÄTTE ZUR RATSWAAGE

$$$

AM NEUEN MARKT 10

TEL 0331 280 43 11

Enjoy country food such as hearty eel soup or roast rabbit filled with black pudding at this elegant restaurant in historic surroundings. Much of the produce is from local farmers. The old well in the romantic courtyard is a much loved feature.

🍴 70 🕐 Closed Sun. D 🚊 S1 Potsdam or RE train 🅢 AE, MC, V

🍴 BLOCKHAUS NIKOLSKOE

$$–$$$

NIKOLSKOER WEG 15

TEL 030 805 29 14

About 2.5 miles (4 km) east of Potsdam and boasting a fine view of the Wannsee lake, this sprawling wooden lodge was built by Prussian king Frederick Wilhelm III for his daughter and her husband, Tsar Nicholas I. Game dishes are the menu's strength, but the selection runs the gamut, as do the prices. In good weather, dining is popular on the riverside terrace.

🍴 260 🚊 S1, S7 Wannsee or RE train 🅢 All major cards

DRESDEN

🏨 ART'OTEL DRESDEN

$$–$$$

OSTRAALLEE 33, 01067

TEL 0351 492 20

FAX 0351 492 27 77

www.artotels.de

Situated a ten-minute walk from the Semperoper and the historic Old Town. Expect a voguish allure in these large, snazzy rooms where form scores highly over function. The stylish interior is the product of a Milan designer; the in-house gallery features some challenging works by Dresden artist A. R. Penck. The staff speaks English.

🛈 183 🅿 🖢 🅢 🕃 🖤 🅢 All major cards

🍴 KUPPEL

$$

WEISSERITZSTRASSE 3

TEL 0351 490 59 90

Located in the former Yenidze cigarette factory, this restaurant serves Middle Eastern and Saxon specialties under a terrific stained-glass dome. The building is fairly surreal, styled after an Oriental mosque with a smokestack disguised as a minaret. In warm weather, you can dine on the rooftop terrace and admire the twinkling lights of Dresden.

🍴 130 🅢 MC, V

🍴 OPERNRESTAURANT

$$

THEATERPLATZ 2

TEL 0351 491 15 21

In a posh modern building behind the Semperoper, this sophisticated place offers cuisine from Italian to German. Opera lovers flock here before and after performances. Guests can enjoy the terrace in fine weather.

🍴 80 🕐 Closed Mon.–Sat. L 🅢 All major cards

LEIPZIG

🏨 LEIPZIGER HOF

🍴 $$

HEDWIGSTRASSE 1–3

TEL 0341 697 40

FAX 0341 697 41 50

www.leipziger-hof.de

This protected building may have been built in Bismarck's day, but rooms are equipped with the latest technology. Paintings of historic Leipzig adorn the walls, giving the place a documentary feel. Breakfast is included, and there's a beer garden that teems with socialites after local art shows.

🛈 68 + 4 apts. 🅿 🅢 🖀 🖤 🅢 All major cards

🍴 AUERBACHS KELLER

$$

MÄDLER-PASSAGE, GRIMMAISCHE STRASSE 2–4

TEL 0341 21 61 00

One of Germany's classic restaurants, founded in 1525, Auerbachs Keller has earned plenty of acclaim for its contemporary European cuisine. Whatever you do, sneak a peek at the historical section, which depicts a scene from Goethe's *Faust*. In it, Mephistopheles and Faust carouse with students before riding off on a barrel—a scene often reenacted at night.

🍴 250 🅢 All major cards

🍴 BARTHELS HOF

$$

HAINSTRASSE 1

TEL 0341 141 31 13

This sprawling, historic eatery—Leipzig's oldest—has a bar, wine cellar, and restaurant serving Saxon dishes such as *Heubraten* (marinated lamb roasted on hay). Waitresses wear traditional costume, but the rooms are contemporary. The courtyard is nestled among Leipzig's oldest Renaissance buildings.

🍴 180 🅢 All major cards

🅢 Nonsmoking 🅢 Air-conditioning 🖀 Indoor Pool 🚊 Outdoor Pool 🖤 Health Club 🅢 Credit Cards

Shopping

Berlin's shopping scene is scattered but comprehensive. You'll find those high-tech designer goods Germany is famous for, plus quality jewelry, traditional handicrafts, and GDR memorabilia. What really sets the capital apart are its hole-in-the-wall fashion boutiques whose creations may not be haute couture, but bristle with post-Wall attitude.

The eastern districts are a petri dish of the latest streetwear. To see what's hot in Mitte, start with the upscale fashion shops around Hackescher Markt and browse the local designers along Alte Schönhauser Allee. In Prenzlauer Berg, hip Kastanienallee teems with pocket-size boutiques selling indie and retro garb.

Test your credit limits at the glittering passages of Quartier 206 on Friedrichstrasse. Potsdamer Arkaden and Alexa are American-style malls on Potsdamer Platz and Alexanderplatz.

In western Berlin, the Kurfürstendamm (Ku'damm) is the domain of top-end brands like Versace, Gucci, and Jil Sander. Chains such as H&M and Urban Outfitters cater to young fashionistas. In the side streets around the Ku'damm, the boutiques of Bleibtreustrasse and Fasanenstrasse are more upscale. Nearby is Berlin's legendary department store, KaDeWe (Kaufhaus des Westens, see p. 138).

For alternative and wickedly individual items, hit the lively shopping strips of Oranienstrasse and Bergmannstrasse in Kreuzberg, or Wühlischstrasse in Friedrichshain. You'll find bookshops, esoterica, clothing, and household gear with Berlin's offbeat flair.

Opening Hours

Since 2008, German retailers are allowed to open 24 hours a day from Monday to Saturday, but few do so. Small shops tend to start business between 9.30 and 11 a.m. and close around 6:30 p.m. Department stores keep going till 10 p.m. On Sunday, only bakeries and stores in train stations, airports, and filling stations may operate. *Spätkaufs* (convenience stores) seem never to take a break.

Sunday shopping is allowed several times a year in each district, and during the run-up to Christmas, many retailers open seven days a week.

Payment & Taxes

Cash remains king in Germany. Department stores take debit and credit cards, but smaller shops often do not; check the door stickers. Most Germans pay by cash or direct debit. Except for EU citizens, visitors to Germany are entitled to a refund on value-added (or sales) tax for all nonedible goods bought in German stores. The usual minimum is €50 in a single store. Ask to fill out a form at stores displaying the tax-free sign. When you leave the country, the form will be stamped by customs after you present goods in original packaging. Tax can be refunded on the spot or sent to you by mail.

Art Galleries

Berlin has 600-plus private art galleries in a colorful variety of venues—anything from backroom studios to vast industrial spaces and stately villas. To find out what's on, pick up the bimonthly magazine *Artery Berlin* (www .artery-berlin.de), the free listings brochure *Berliner Galerien* (www .berliner-galerien), or the "Gallery Guide Berlin" smartphone app.

Blain/Southern, Potsdamer Strasse 77–87, Schöneberg, tel 030 644 93 15 10, www.blain southern.com. An offshoot of a famous New York–London art axis, the cavernous ex-premises of the *Tagesspiegel* newspaper form the backdrop for its large-scale contemporary statements.

Camera Work, Kantstrasse 149, Charlottenburg, tel 030 31 50 47 83, www.camerawork.de. A Bauhaus-inspired courtyard building is the setting for this renowned photography gallery. Entry is always free.

C/O Berlin, Amerika Haus, Hardenbergstrasse 22–24, Charlottenburg, tel 030 28 44 41 60, www.co-berlin.info. A showcase of classy imagery, this comely old postal depot promotes emerging photographic talent and household names such as Henri Cartier-Bresson, Annie Leibovitz, and Martin Parr. Its series of meet-the-photographers lectures is very popular.

Galerie Sprüth Magers, Oranienburger Strasse 18, Mitte, tel 030 288 88 40 30, www .spruethmagers.com. Once a dance hall, this important commercial gallery is half of a Berlin–London axis of cutting-edge contemporary art, video, and film work. Big-name artists it represents include Peter Fischli, Cyprien Gaillard, Cindy Sherman, and Rosemarie Trockel. The same complex hosts **ImageMovement**, an arts movie store.

KW Institute for Contemporary Art, Auguststrasse 69, Mitte, tel 030 243 45 90, www .kw-berlin.de. Lodged in a former margarine factory, KW is a major art events hub despite having no collection of its own. During the Berlin Biennale, artists and prospective buyers congregate in the pretty courtyard café.

Sammlung Boros, Reinhardstrasse 20, Mitte, www.sammlung-boros.de. An imposing World War II bunker was reborn as a contemporary art gallery, run by advertising mogul Christian Boros. Book private tours via the website.

VW Berlin, Rudi-Dutschke-Strasse 26, Kreuzberg, tel 030 816 16 04 18, www.vwberlin.com. Leading gallerist Michael Werner teamed up with Gordon Veneklasen to open this progressive space near Checkpoint Charlie. Werner's contacts with key artists like Jörg Immendorf, A. R. Penck, and Sigmar Polke translate into a wealth of exciting paintings, sculptures, and drawings.

Books

Berlin has more volume sellers than a dog has fleas. Enter, browse, and notice (not) how entire afternoons evaporate. Among them:

Berlin Story, Unter den Linden 40, Mitte, tel 030 20 45 38 42, www.berlinstory.de. The largest bookstore devoted to Berlin has 3,000 volumes in 12 languages, with 250 titles in English alone.

Bücherbogen, Stadtbahnbogen, Savignyplatz 593, Charlottenburg, tel 030 31 86 95 11, www .buecherbogen.de. Set underneath the S-Bahn arches, this enormous selection is strong on painting, sculpture, design, photography, and architecture, with many tomes in English.

Bücherstube Marga Schöller, Knesebeckstrasse 33, Charlottenburg, tel 030 881 11 12, www .margaschoeller.de. Bertolt Brecht frequented this literary institution, going strong for nearly 80 years. Good English-language section.

Dussmann, Friedrichstrasse 90, Mitte, tel 030 20 25 11 11, www .kulturkaufhaus.de. Padded armchairs invite you to sit and read at this "cultural department store" on three spacious floors. Sections include a huge CD display and a separate English bookstore.

Department Stores & Malls

Galeria Kaufhof, Alexanderplatz 9, Mitte, tel 030 24 74 30, www .galeria-kaufhof.de. All-around retailer with a soaring, Bauhaus-influenced central atrium. At ground level, you can peruse fancy perfumes, watches, and a gourmet supermarket, while midrange fashion, gifts, and household goods are among the draws on the upper floors.

Galeries Lafayette, Französische Strasse 23, Mitte, tel 030 20 94 80, www.lafayette-berlin.de. This upscale French emporium has a stunning funnel-shaped atrium. Besides designer apparel, cosmetics, and accessories, there's an excellent supermarket and a swish delicatessen serving oysters and champagne.

KaDeWe, Tauentzienstrasse 21–24, Schöneberg, tel 030 212 20, www.kadewe.de. The German opposite number of London's Harrods, the imposing Kaufhaus des Westens is the country's largest department store. In the sixth-floor food hall, you can sample delicacies from around the globe at 34 cooking stations.

Manufactum, Hardenbergstrasse 4–5, Charlottenburg, tel 030 24 03 38 44, www.manu factum.de. This treasure trove of design classics harks back to yesteryear. Samples from the catalog: handcrafted straight razors from Solingen, a 1924 Desny desk lamp, and a Porsche pepper mill.

Stilwerk, Kantstrasse 17, Charlottenburg, tel 030 315 11, www.stilwerk.de. This fancy design mall has 60 stores on five floors, all bristling with the latest must-haves for house and home. Pick up a stylish Rolf Benz couch, Artimide reading lamp, or Bechstein grand piano.

Fashion

In the early 20th century, Berlin was an international center of fashion, and today its designers are busy restoring that past glory. Numerous events throughout the year (see p. 164) are a must for professional buyers. Shops to check out include:

Barfuss oder Lackschuh, Oranienburger Strasse 89, Mitte, tel 030 28 39 19 91. One look at the designer sneakers, shiny boots, and towering pumps and you couldn't possibly leave *barfuss* (barefooted). Expect to pay top dollar in this minimalist boutique.

Birkenstock, Georgenstrasse 24, Mitte, tel 030 20 45 43 29, www.birkenstock.de. Basic Roman footwear elevated to an icon of alternative lifestyle. Their trendy designs grace the feet of Tom Cruise, Madonna, and German supermodel Heidi Klum. Offers shipping to your home address.

Budapester Schuhe, Kurfürstendamm 43, 199, & 204, Charlottenburg, tel 030 88 62 42 06, www.budapester.eu. Timeless footwear for the well-heeled. Ladies' brands include Prada, Miu Miu, and Jimmy Choo, while gentlemen can choose from English brogues, Gucci loafers, or handcrafted shoes from Hungary.

Crème Fresh, Kastanienallee 221, Mitte, tel 030 48 62 58 27. Things often aren't what they seem in Berlin, and this shop isn't about dairy products. Cult European labels like Fornaria or Gsus can be snapped up at reasonable prices.

Eisdieler, Kastanienallee 12, Prenzlauer Berg, tel 030 28 39 12 91, www.eisdieler.de. Run by five well-known Berlin designers, each managing their own label, this former ice-cream parlor spins urban wear into a collective art form. The trend-setting shop has a busy little studio in the back.

Fiona Bennett, Potsdamer Strasse 81, Mitte, tel 030 28 09 63 30, www.fionabennett.com. Celebs like Vivienne Westwood,

Brad Pitt, and Christina Aguilera can be spotted wearing Fiona's exquisite hats. The Berlin-born owner trained at a traditional millinery, but her creations of feathers, straw, and felt are anything but stuffy.

F95 Fashion Store, Luckenwalder Strasse 4-6, Kreuzberg, tel 030 42 08 33 58, www.f95store .com. Ready-to-market garments from the Premium fashion show appear at this spacious, gritty-chic store in an old train depot. Markdowns are frequent.

Hut Up, Heckmann Höfe, Oranienburger Strasse 32, Mitte, tel 030 28 38 61 05, www.hutup .de. Elegant hats, dresses, and home accessories for self-assured females. Christine Birkle's handmade pieces blend felt with materials like organza or chiffon. Nestled in the handsome Heckmann Höfe courtyards.

Killerbeast, Schlesische Strasse 31, Kreuzberg, tel 030 99 26 03 19, www.killerbeast.de. Killing uniformity is the credo, recyclable materials are the means at this hub of new urban street and kids' wear. Kooky designs roll out almost every week. Bring in an old garment and they'll rejuvenate it.

Schmucksalon Krüger, Falckensteinstrasse 45, Kreuzberg, tel 030 69 56 42 19, www .schmucksalon-krueger.de. Jeweler Sigrid Widmoser dreams up dazzling amorphous shapes in attractive colors. Her elegant brooches, earrings, and necklaces have an eye-catching meld of raw and smooth facets. Couples can sign up to make their own silver wedding rings.

Penthesileia, Tucholskystrasse 31, Mitte, tel 030 282 11 52, www.ankerunge-taschen.de. This tempting trove of hand-crafted leather goods and jewelry is named for an Amazonian queen in Greek mythology, and judging by the twice-yearly collections, she was dressed to kill.

Thatchers, Hackesche Höfe, Rosenthaler Strasse 40–41, Mitte, tel 030 27 58 22 10, www .thatchers.de. Thatchers unveils three trendy lines a year for both men and women, inspired by music, digital art, and architecture. Designs are playfully tongue-in-cheek—don a translucent Heartache blouse, an airline-themed Take Off dress, or snakeskin Alien boxer shorts.

Trippen Shoes, Hackesche Höfe, Rosenthaler Strasse 40–41, Mitte, tel 030 28 39 13 37, www .trippen.com. Shapely, medieval-influenced, highly individual footwear in quality calf leather and wood. Materials and production are 100 percent ecofriendly. There's a cheaper factory outlet at Köpenicker Strasse 187.

Flea Markets

Berlin's many flea markets are stuffed to the gills with antiques, GDR memorabilia, and vintage clothing. With a little perseverance, you can unearth some bargains at the following locations, and haggling often pays off.

Antik & Buchmarkt, Am Kupfergraben, Mitte, www .antik-buchmarkt.de. Opposite the Bode-Museum, this row of tented stalls is a gold mine of antiques, old books, and Russian *ushankas* (furry ear hats), albeit touristy. Saturday and Sunday 11 a.m.–5 p.m.

Boxhagener Platz, Friedrichshain, www.boxhagenerplatz.de. Every Sunday, this square buzzes with residents hawking their dearest attic treasures. Keep an eye out for the stalls of artists and T-shirt designers. On Saturday, local chefs stock up at the excellent organic farmers' market. 10 a.m.–5 p.m.

Kunst & Trödelmarkt, Strasse des 17. Juni, Tiergarten, www .berliner-troedelmarkt.de. Oil paintings, antiques, and early 20th-century doodads crowd this busy market just west of Tiergarten S-Bahn stop. Head north of Charlottenburg Gate to peruse the arts and crafts section. 10 a.m.–5 p.m. Saturday and Sunday.

Mauerpark, Prenzlauer Berg, www.mauerparkmarkt.de. This onetime spur of no-man's-land is now the scene of a bustling flea market, the city's largest. Vintage clothing, bicycle parts, and cartons of black-market CDs wink at you from hundreds of stalls. Sunday 8 a.m.–6 p.m.

Food & Spirits

Absinth Depot, Weinmeisterstrasse 4, Mitte, tel 030 281 67 89, www.erstesabsinthdepotber lin.de. Absinthe was the bad boys' drink of bohemian Paris. On offer are more than 100 varieties, plus elaborate fountains, spoons, and glasses. The Canadian owner serves samples.

Berlin Bonbonmacherei, Heckmann Höfe, Oranienburger Strasse 32, Mitte, tel 030 44 05 52 43, www.bonbonmacherei .de. Scents of sweet nostalgia waft out of this basement store. Old-fashioned sour drops, blueberry mints, and leaf-shaped May leaves pop out from hand-operated equipment in the open kitchen.

Fassbender & Rausch, Charlottenstrasse 60, Mitte, tel 030 20 45 84 43, www.fassbender -rausch.com. Cocoa nuts flock to this traditional chocolatemaker's shop on Gendarmenmarkt. A syrup fountain gurgles next to the edible sculptures of the Brandenburg Gate, Reichstag, and Kaiser Wilhelm Memorial Church.

Königsberger Marzipan Wald, Pestalozzistrasse 54a, Charlottenburg, tel 030 323 82 54, www .wald-koenigsberger-marzipan.de. Irmgard Wald's incredible marzipan cakes and cookies are still made with a family recipe from the former German province of Königsberg, now part of Russia.

Food Markets

So enticing are the regional meats, cheeses, and produce sold at the many farmers' markets that locals may never set foot in a supermarket. Look for steep markdowns around closing time.

Kollwitzplatz, Prenzlauer Berg. A wonderful place to stock up on artisanal breads, gourmet cheeses, and organic sausage. A nexus of gentrification, the square has a playground for the small fry. Saturday 9.30 a.m.–4 p.m.

Turkish Market, Maybachufer, Neukölln, www.tuerkenmarkt .de. This bustling market caters to Berlin's large Turkish community, with vendors shouting prices over barrels of olives and rolls of textiles. Prices are very competitive. Tuesday to Friday 11 a.m.–6:30 p.m.

Winterfeldt Markt, Winterfeldtplatz, Schöneberg, http:// winterfeldt-markt.de. This beautiful array of foodstuffs is arguably Berlin's most delightful. Handmade designer clothing can be found at the rear by St. Michael's Church. Wednesday and Saturday 8 a.m.–2 p.m.

Gifts & Souvenirs

Ampelmann Galerie Shop, Hackesche Höfe, Mitte, tel 030 44 04 88 01, http://ampelmann.de. A wave of Ostalgie–nostalgia for East German stuff–brings you the crosswalk man (see sidebar p. 98), who graces everything from fridge magnets to beach shoes and bath towels.

Aus Berlin, Karl-Liebknecht-Strasse 17, Mitte, tel 030 41 99 78 96, www.ausberlin.de. Items made exclusively in the German capital. Cool local apparel from Andrea van Reimerdahl or EastBerlin rubs shoulders with Adler schnapps, Berlin Wall bookends, and Brandenburg Gate cookie cutters.

Berliner Zinnfiguren, Knesebeckstrasse 88, Charlottenburg, tel 030 315 70 00, www.zinnfigur

.com. Home to medieval knights, ancient Chinese warriors, and vast garrisons of Prussian cavalry, painted in meticulous detail. Take-home molds for the pewter or resin figures are available.

Erzgebirgskunst Original, Sophienstrasse 9, Mitte, tel 030 28 26 75 44, www.erzgebirge-in -berlin.de. Traditional wooden handicrafts from the Ore Mountains of Saxony–incense-puffing "smoking men," Christmas pyramids, nutcrackers, and angels.

Gipsformerei, Sophie-Charlotten-Strasse 17–18, Charlottenburg, tel 030 321 70 11, www.smb-spk-berlin.de. This fascinating workshop near Schloss Charlottenburg stocks over 7,000 replicas of sculptures from Berlin's state museums. The bust of Queen Nefertiti is a favorite.

Museum Shop at Checkpoint Charlie, Friedrichstrasse 43–45, Kreuzberg, tel 030 253 72 50, www.mauermuseum.de. Chunks of the Berlin Wall, T-shirts saying you're leaving the American sector, and posters of Brezhnev and Honecker kissing make popular souvenirs.

Neurotitan, Rosenthaler Strasse 39, Mitte, tel 030 30 87 25 76, www.neurotitan.de. Underground books, comics, posters, and an achingly good selection of Berlin electronic music. Artworks by Danielle de Picciotto, cofounder of the Love Parade, pop up in the rear gallery. The entrance is behind the Anne Frank Zentrum.

Ostpaket, Karl-Liebknecht-Strasse 13, Mitte, tel 030 71 55 39 06, www.ostpaket.de. This dimly lit store in a sad little mall carries near-forgotten brands once available everywhere in the GDR. Choice gems are Trabant towels, modular eggcups, and schnapps bearing the face of premier Erich Honecker.

Porcelain

Monarchs Prussian and Saxon

were entranced by the "white gold" of china. Berlin has boutiques and factory showrooms.

Königliche Porzellan-Manufaktur, Wegelystrasse 1, Tiergarten, tel 030 39 00 90, https://kpm-berlin.com. Founded by Frederick the Great in 1763, the working factory, shop, and museum exude three centuries of porcelainmaking. On factory tours, you can watch the painters applying the delicate historical designs.

Meissener Porzellan, Unter den Linden 39, Mitte, tel 030 22 67 90 28, www.meissen.de. Fine plates, sculptures, and chandeliers from the royal porcelainmaker. Prices reach from a few euros for a teaspoon into the thousands for a hand-fashioned vase.

Toys

Hase Weiss, Windscheidstrasse 25, Charlottenburg, tel 030 31 99 67 37, www.haseweiss.de. Wooden toys, dolls, and children's furniture that change as the little ones grow up. A high chair becomes a set of shelves, and a dollhouse turns into a satchel.

Onkel Philipp's Toy Store, Chorinerstrasse 35, Prenzlauer Berg, tel 030 449 04 91, www. onkel-philipp.de. This rambling shop keeps the stuff of childhood alive, even if it's your second one. Look out for classic Folkmanis puppets, Darda racing cars, and wooden Werdauer dump trucks from East Germany. In the basement is a small remote-controlled cemetery of GDR toys.

Steiff Concept Store, Kurfürstendamm 38–39, Charlottenburg, tel 030 88 62 50 06, www .steiff.com. Richard Steiff claimed to have invented the teddy bear in 1902, before the Americans thought of it. A vast zoo of creatures is now manufactured with Steiff's trademark button in the ear.

Entertainment

No other city in Germany celebrates with more energy or abandon than its nonstop capital. There's something for everyone, usually at any time of day or night, and chances are you'll find yourself staying out a tad later than usual.

Excellent opera, dance, and theater productions thrive alongside hundreds of music and dance venues of every conceivable ilk. The scene in the West is well established, with classical and upscale venues in Charlottenburg, gay-friendly clubs and bars around Winterfeldplatz in Schöneberg, and pleasantly grungy joints along Kreuzberg's Oranienstrasse and Bergmannstrasse.

The western theater district is centered around Savignyplatz and the streets leading off the Kurfürstendamm (Ku'damm), while the former East focuses on Friedrichstrasse north of the Spree and Rosa-Luxemburg-Platz.

Mitte, Prenzlauer Berg, and Friedrichshain are a bellwether of the latest bar and nightclub trends. Hackescher Markt, Oranienburger Strasse, and choice bits of Friedrichstrasse are touristy but fun. The avenue Kastanienallee and streets around Kollwitzplatz and Helmholtzplatz draw the painfully hip in P-Berg. For the alternative scene, head east to Friedrichshain.

Bars & Beach Fun

Even since Berlin became a slacker's heaven, the bar scene keeps widening and deepening. East Berlin innovates with living room furniture and GDR leftovers, often with an art gallery or stage tacked on. For its part, the West continues to flash old-money connections and a touch of time warp. Both have their charms, depending on your mood and movements.

Anna Koschke, Krausnickstrasse 11, Mitte, tel 030 283 55 38, www.anna-koschke.de.

Decorated with old lamps and faded photographs, this smoky, traditional pub dates back to the early 20th century. Perfect for deep conversation over a pilsner or three. Theater shows are held in the rear garden.

Aufsturz, Oranienburger Strasse 67, Mitte, tel 030 28 04 74 07, www.aufsturz.de. This eclectic bar-club carries more than 100 kinds of bottled beer and a changing cast of weekly brews. The guest area doubles as an art gallery, while live jazz, indie, and chansons shake the basement stage.

Beckett's Kopf, Pappelallee 64, Prenzlauer Berg, tel 0162 237 94 18, www.becketts-kopf.de. Steeped in tradition and heavy velvet curtains, this is one of Berlin's finest cocktail bars. The drinks list is extensive and includes literary references. The barkeepers will mix their creations around your preferred ingredients.

Billard House Friedrichshain, Rudolfstrasse 4, tel 030 20 05 68 56, www.billardhouse.com. Spread over two floors, this cavernous pool hall offers 18 pool and 3 snooker tables, darts, and poker, available any time of day or night. Tuesday evenings you can join a house tournament.

Cafe Schwarzsauer, Kastanienallee 13–14, Prenzlauer Berg, tel 030 448 56 33. The huge windows of this insomniac's hangout are ideal for seeing and being seen. The sidewalk tables usually teem with hipsters primed for a night out. Open 24/7.

Dr Pong, Eberswalder Strasse 21, Prenzlauer Berg, www.drpong.net. Berlin's table tennis craze goes indoors at this bare-bones

bar. The first rounds of rotating, multiplayer killer pong usually start by 10 p.m. The eliminated drink and cheer from the sidelines.

Green Door, Winterfeldtstrasse 50, Schöneberg, tel 030 215 25 15, http://greendoor.de. Mecca for lovers of retro interiors and fine expensive cocktails. The wavy bar, glowing dog lamp, and garish wallpaper invite partiers to take a break from the frenzy around Nollendorfplatz. To enter, buzz at the green padded door.

Hops and Barley, Wühlischstrasse 22, Friedrichshain, tel 030 29 36 75 34, www.hopsandbarley-berlin.de. This dyed-in-the-wool brewpub serves excellent pils, dark, and wheat beers. Sunday night is popular for *Tatort*, a TV detective series.

Joseph Roth Diele, Potsdamer Strasse 75, Schöneberg, tel 030 26 36 98 84, http://joseph-roth-diele.de, closed weekends. Named for the prolific Jewish writer whose quotes and book covers dot the walls of this pub-café. The bistro furniture, aged wainscoting, and gilt-edged crockery take you back to the Berlin of yesteryear.

Kumpelnest 3000, Lützowstrasse 23, Tiergarten, tel 030 261 69 18, www.kumpelnest3000.com. Lodged in a onetime brothel, this cramped, smoky, fur-lined bar-club is noted for its lack of inhibition. Expect a colorful crowd of transvestites, tipsy businessmen, and wide-eyed tourists, and check the schedule for karaoke night—it's a hoot.

Lindenbräu, Sony Center am Potsdamer Platz, tel 030 25 75 12 80, www.linden-hopfinger-braeu.de. Bavarian brewpub with fabulous *Weissbier* served in giant beveled mugs. Kind of touristy, but with excellent views from the second-floor deck outside.

Madame Claude, Lübbener Strasse 19, Kreuzberg, tel 0177 621 65 62, www.madameclaude .de. Everything's topsy-turvy at this former cathouse with furniture nailed to the ceiling. The labyrinth of small rooms and corridors leads to several bars and Ping-Pong, as well as a stage for acoustic music acts.

Newton Bar, Charlottenstrasse 57, Mitte, tel 030 20 61 29 99, www.newton-bar.de A magnet for high-society types around Gendarmenmarkt, this sexy watering hole was inspired by Berlin-born photographer Helmut Newton, a frequent guest. Prints of his Big Nudes (see p. 151) grace the interior. Upstairs are a walk-in humidor and lounge with gold-leaf ceiling.

BeachMitte, Caroline Michaelis Strasse 8, Mitte, tel 0177 280 68 61, www.beachmitte.de. Far from the clubbing crowd, this popular outdoor bar and volleyball club lures Berlin's poor-but-sexy set with wicker beach baskets, energy drinks, and 54 sandy courts.

Ständige Vertretung, Schiffbauerdamm 8, Mitte, tel 030 282 39 65, www.staev.de. "Permanent representation" was the Cold War term for West Germany's quasi-embassy in East Berlin. A sea of photos and political doodads set the scene for rounds of *Kölsch* (Cologne beer) and Rhineland dishes like sauerbraten.

Strandbar Mitte, Montbijoustrasse 3, Mitte, tel 030 28 38 55 88, www.strandbar-mitte.de. Berlin's most central beach bar is an urban send-up of holiday culture. Grab a brew and a deck chair, and wave to the passing tourist boats from under the palm trees. Thursday is tango night on the makeshift dance floor.

Weinerei Forum, Fehrbelliner Strasse 57, Prenzlauer Berg, tel 030 60 05 30 72, www.weinerei .com. This wine bar runs on the honor system: Serve yourself and pay as much as you think it's worth.

Wohnzimmer, Lettestrasse 6, Prenzlauer Berg, tel 030 445 54 58, www.wohnzimmer-bar.de. Vintage lounge lizard territory with laid-back music and killer caipirinhas. The Sunday brunch is legendary.

Beer Gardens

Classic German (read: Bavarian) beer gardens are few and far between in Berlin. Pale imitations are more like clubs or beach bars. The best approximations have picnic tables under chestnut trees.

Cafe am Neuen See, Lichtensteinallee 2, Tiergarten, tel 030 254 49 30. This leafy, open-air beer garden is the closest Berlin gets to the genuine article. Tables are spread under shady chestnuts overlooking a glittering pond. Line up for half liters of wheat beer, *Leberkäse* (spicy meatloaf), and pretzels. There's a sandbox for the kiddies, and you can paddle a rented boat.

Eschenbräu, Triftstrasse 67, Wedding, tel 030 462 68 37, www.eschenbraeu.de. This delightful brewpub and garden are famously hard to find, in a leafy courtyard between student dorms. Brewmaster Eschenbrenner serves big mugs of fabulous suds—*Weizen* (wheat beer), seasonal *Bock* (a strong amber), and unfiltered pilsners.

Golgatha, Viktoriapark, Kreuzberg, tel 030 785 24 53, www.golgatha-berlin.de. Aromas of grilled sausage lead you to this quirky dance club and garden, hidden behind the hill in Viktoriapark. Grab a brew and head for the upper deck next to the athletics field.

Prater, Kastanienallee 7–9, Mitte, tel 030 448 56 88, www .pratergarten.de. Berlin's oldest beer garden, founded in 1837. Shaded by towering chestnuts, its 600 seats at traditional picnic tables are popular in summer. On offer are foaming mugs of beer, steak sandwiches, and bratwurst. The wood-paneled restaurant serves pike perch fresh from the Havel.

Schleusenkrug, Müller-Breslau-Strasse 1, Tiergarten, tel 030 313 99 09, www .schleusenkrug.de. Overlooking the pretty Landwehrkanal, this traditional drinking hole is a beloved stop in the Tiergarten. Grab a wooden bench and watch the pleasure boats line up at the lock.

Cinema

The plush décor in some of Berlin's 100-plus *Kinos* (cinemas) evokes the hopes and dreams of the 1920s, when Germany rivaled the U.S. in movie production. Arthouse and a few mainstream theaters show films in the original language (OV, for *Originalversion*) or with subtitles (OMU, for *Original mit Untertiteln*). Tickets cost a little more from Thursday to Sunday.

Arsenal, Potsdamer Platz, Potsdamer Strasse 21, tel 030 26 95 51 00, www.arsenal-berlin.de. Run by the Filmmuseum next door, this comfy duplex theater shows independent and classic movies that figure prominently in the history of cinema. The archive numbers 9,000 films.

Babylon Mitte, Rosa-Luxemburg-Strasse 30, Mitte, tel 030 24 72 78 01, www.babylon-berlin.de. Berlin's finest 1930s art deco movie house is a tour de force of live entertainment: film screenings, cabaret, concerts, and literature readings. Monday is devoted to Spanish film, Thursday to New German Cinema, and Sunday to Italian CinemAperitivo.

Central Kino, Rosenthaler Strasse 39, Mitte, tel 030 28 59 99 73, www.kino-central .de. A main venue of the future BerlinBeta Media Festival, this former squat shows indie films and obscure oldies. Many selections are in English with German subtitles.

CineStar Event, Potsdamer Strasse 4, Tiergarten, tel 030 26 06 64 00, www.cinestar.de. This plush eight-screen multiplex shows movies in their original languages without subtitles—a rarity in Berlin, where foreign films are usually subtitled or dubbed. Hosts premieres during the Berlinale.

Hackesche Höfe Cinema, Rosenthaler Strasse 40–41, Mitte, tel 030 283 46 03, www .hoefekino.de. International arthouse with subtitles at this five-screen art deco cinema. Filmmakers turn up for preview chats in the upstairs lounge.

Zeughauskino, Unter den Linden 2, Mitte, tel 030 920 30 44 20, www.dhm.de. An offshoot of the Deutsches Historisches Museum, this theater screens masterpieces such as Fritz Lang's *Metropolis* or Sergei Eisenstein's *Battleship Potemkin*. A special treat are the silent-film nights with live piano.

Classical Music & Theater

Ever since Mozart swung a baton during his European tour, Berlin has been a hub of the performing arts. After World War I, cabaret added a string to its frazzled bow. Both traditions live on with a vengeance.

Bar jeder Vernunft, Schaperstrasse 24, Wilmersdorf, tel 030 883 15 82, www.bar-jeder-ver nunft.de. A mixture of classical theater and old-style cabaret, mostly in German. The venue alone is worth the admission, with art deco mirrors, theater

boxes lined in red velvet, and hand-carved paneling. You can relax in the bar or beer garden.

Berliner Ensemble, Bertolt-Brecht-Platz 1, Mitte, tel 030 28 40 81 55, www.berliner-ensemble .de. Esteemed theater company established by legendary dramatist Brecht after he returned from exile in the U.S. His most famous piece, *The Threepenny Opera*, is occasionally performed here. The gorgeous multigallery theater plays host to works by leading European playwrights.

Berliner Philharmoniker, Herbert-von-Karajan-Strasse 1, Tiergarten, tel 030 25 48 80, www.berliner-philharmoniker .de. The first-rate performances conducted by Sir Simon Rattle enjoy world renown. Alumni include Claudio Abbado and the charismatic Herbert von Karajan, musical director from 1955 to 1988. The angular 1960s design of the building was revolutionary, and fine views and acoustics can be enjoyed from anywhere in the main hall. Free lunchtime concerts are held at 1:30 p.m. September to June—show up at the performers' entrance a half hour earlier. For other events, call or book tickets online. In July and August, the Philharmoniker performs a popular series of concerts at the open-air Waldbühne near the Olympiastadion (see pp. 190–191).

Chamäleon, Hackesche Höfe, Rosenthaler Strasse 40–41, Mitte, tel 030 40 00 59 30, www .chamaeleonberlin.de, closed Mon. Plush, 300-seat variety theater with a quality program of gala nights, concerts, acrobatics, and plays. Order dinner and drinks while you watch.

Deutsche Oper, Bismarckstrasse 35, Charlottenburg, tel 030 34 38 43 43, www.deutscheoper berlin.de. Established in 1912, the German Opera is known for its artistic chutzpah and lavish stage

sets. Classic ballet and opera share the billing with avant-garde productions.

Deutsches Theater, Schumannstrasse 13a, Mitte, tel 030 28 44 12 25, www .deutschestheater.de. Built in 1850 as a vehicle for operettas, this stage with the beautiful neoclassical facade became famous under legendary director Max Reinhardt. The theater hosts chamber theater and one of Berlin's most progressive dance companies.

Komische Oper, Behrensstrasse 55–57, Mitte, tel 030 47 99 74 00, www.komische-oper -berlin.com. Imaginative blend of light opera, musicals, modern dance, and orchestral concerts. Children's events and workshops are quite popular. The exterior was destroyed in World War II, but the dazzling 19th-century theater survived.

Konzerthaus, Gendarmenmarkt, Mitte, tel 030 203 09 21 01, www.konzerthaus.de. Home to the Konzerthaus Orchester, this handsome restored concert hall is drenched in tradition. Weber's *Der Freischütz* premiered and Wagner directed his *Fliegender Holländer* here. Every year, there are more than 550 concerts and events such as Classic Open Air.

Piano Salon Christophori, Uferstrasse 8, Wedding, tel 0176 39 00 77 53, www.konzertfluegel .com. Tucked away in a defunct tram hall, this atmospheric venue is known for intimate recitals of classical and jazz music. The salon also restores, sells, and rents out historic grand pianos. Reserve by 4 p.m. and your seat will be marked by name.

Schaubühne, Leniner Platz, Kurfürstendamm 153, Charlottenburg, tel 030 89 00 23, www .schaubuehne.de. Drawing on a wellspring of original material, the stage productions feature some of the country's most accomplished actors.

Staatsoper, Unter den Linden 5–7, Mitte, tel 030 20 35 45 55, www.staatsoper.de. The oldest and best of Berlin's three opera houses, the State Opera occupies a stunning 18th-century neoclassical building, the first major project commissioned by Frederick the Great. During renovation work through 2015, performances will be held in Charlottenburg's Schillertheater (Bismarckstrasse 110, same tel). Renowned musical director Daniel Barenboim draws top talent to the annual Festival Days.

Volksbühne, Linienstrasse 227, Mitte, tel 030 24 06 55, www .volksbuehne-berlin.de. A hub of dissidence during the GDR, this marvelous old stage is known for polarizing dramas directed by Frank Castorf. Rock concerts, movies, and literature readings share the program. An attached ballroom, the Grüner Salon, hosts everything from Jewish blues and Dixieland to salsa dancing.

Cultural Complexes

Because art can't always decide where to put everything, these all-in-one cultural venues are full of surprises.

Acud, Beteranenstrasse 21, Mitte, tel 030 449 10 67, www.acud.de. This higgledy-piggledy complex is a full-service nod to underground culture, with an art gallery, café, cinema, theater, music stages, and in summer a sandy beer garden. Every weekend, the Calabash Club raises the roof with indie grooves.

Admiralspalast, Friedrichstrasse 101–102, Mitte, tel 030 47 99 74 99, www.admiralspalast .de. In the Roaring '20s, the Admiralspalast was the focus of Friedrichstrasse's entertainment mile, comprising a sauna, grand café, theater, concert halls, and an ice rink. Restored and reopened in 2006, the art deco Grosser

Saal and several other stages host high-profile performances of cabaret, music, and contemporary dance.

Cassiopeia, Revalerstrasse 99, Friedrichshain, tel 030 27 38 59 49, www.cassiopeia-berlin .de. In the bowels of a ramshackle train depot, you'll find the indie music club RAW-Tempel as well as a beer garden, skating hall, and freaky climbing wall, set on the sides of a World War II bunker. Movies are shown in the courtyard.

Kulturbrauerei, Knaackstrasse 97, Prenzlauer Berg, tel 030 44 31 51 52, http://kulturbrauerei.de. The old Schultheiss brewery is the scene of 20-odd venues for parties, movies, and dining sprinkled around a heritage-protected courtyard. Options include the Franzz nightclub, music venues Kesselhaus, Maschinenhaus, and Palais, and atmospheric billiard hall Pool & Cigars.

Radialsystem V, Holzmarktstrasse 33, Friedrichshain, tel 030 28 87 88 50, www.radialsystem .de. Best known for experimental dance led by choreographer Sasha Waltz, this handsome old pumping station stages events in cooperation with concert halls, orchestras, opera houses, and galleries from around the globe. The riverside bar is a delight.

Urania, An der Urania 17, Schöneberg, tel 030 218 90 91, www.urania.de. A scientific society founded in 1888, the Urania has grown into a nexus of Berlin culture. The hodgepodge agenda covers two arthouse cinemas, theater, stand-up comedy, academic lectures, and workshops.

Jazz Venues

While the Cold War put a dent in Berlin's jazz scene, in recent years some venues are pulling in top-notch talent.

A-Trane, Bleibtreustrasse 1, Charlottenburg, tel 030 313 25

50, www.a-trane.de. Jazz giants Billy Cobham, Wynton Marsalis, and Lee Konitz have graced the tiny stage of this west Berlin club. Special Afro-Cuban nights are a regular feature. Book ahead.

Badenscher Hof, Badensche Strasse 29, Wilmersdorf, tel 030 861 00 80, www.badenscher-hof .de. One of Berlin's oldest and coziest jazz clubs is covered in memorabilia. Features African-American bands, modern jazz, and a garden open in summer.

B Flat, Rosenthaler Strasse 13, Mitte, tel 030 283 31 23, www .b-flat-berlin.de. Behind the tall, steamed-up windows lies Mitte's best jazz club, run by a pair of Greek musician brothers. The mongrel program ranges from blues and mainstream jazz to tango dance nights. Book ahead.

Kunstfabrik Schlot, Chausseestrasse 18, Mitte, tel 030 448 21 60, www.kunstfabrik -schlot.de. The iron-and-stone fittings recall the origins of this factory space, now one of Berlin's quirkier spots for live jazz. Beer flows magically from a saxophone over the bar.

Quasimodo, Kantstrasse 12a, Charlottenburg, tel 030 312 80 86, www.quasimodo.de. This club under the historic Delphi cinema is a magnet for visiting jazz, rock, and blues artists, many from the U.S. Recent guests have included Mike Stern, Bob Mintzer, and Robben Ford.

Nightclubs

Euroravers from Barcelona and London don't bother to book accommodations in this 24/7 hub. Though less edgy than in the heady 1990s, the party spirit has imbued a new generation.

Badeschiff, Eichenstrasse 4, Treptow, tel 030 533 20 30, www .arena-berlin.de. This retired barge has been reborn as a swimming pool, linked to a beach club via a wooden boardwalk. In winter, a tent is pulled over an indoor pool, saunas, and lounge area with DJs.

CCCP Club, Rosenthaler Strasse 71, Mitte, tel 0151 23 60 76 05. The joke here is morose Russian décor: heavy velvet curtains, rickety lamps, and flowery wallpaper. DJs spin house music to lava-lamp images and cult films. It's standing room only at the monthly burlesque shows.

Clärchens Ballhaus, Auguststrasse 24, Mitte, tel 030 282 92 95, www.ballhaus.de. A GDR-era dance hall reincarnated for Mitte's insatiable party set. Its split personality sees pizzas and *Bouletten* (spicy Berlin meatballs) during the day and a diet of tango to funk after sunset. There's a free introduction to salsa on Thursday nights.

Club der Visionäre, Am Flutgraben 1, Treptow, tel 030 69 51 89 42, www.clubdervisionaere .com. Neatly hidden in a Spree inlet, this old boathouse hosts a cool dockside bar and dance floor for all-night jolts of elektro. The MS *Klaus* can be chartered for parties.

Kaffee Burger, Torstrasse 60, Mitte, tel 030 28 04 64 95, www .kaffeeburger.de. In the GDR, this club was a meeting place for aspiring émigrés. The dissidents have moved on, but a giant Soviet star was left for posterity. Eastern European bands such as the Rotfront Kollektiv are a fixture.

Kater Holzig, Michaelkirchstrasse 22, Friedrichshain, tel 01577 252 52 77, www.katerholzig.de. This faux-alternative playground for pseudo-grungers is housed in an abandoned soap factory with a theater/cinema, dance floor, restaurant, and sauna. The courtyard is the scene of bonfires and concerts under a giant painted skeleton.

Lido, Cuvrystrasse 7, Kreuzberg, tel 030 69 56 68 40, www .lido-berlin.de. For no-nonsense rock and ethnic grooves, this former ballroom takes some beating. Buy tickets in advance online for popular acts like Balkan Beats or Tinariwen (founded in a Libyan rebel camp during the Qaddafi era).

MIKZ, Revalerstrasse 99, Friedrichshain, tel 030 95 60 33 51, www.mikz-berlin.de. This totally untouristed cultural center, based in a derelict railway site, turns into a kicking club on Wednesday nights and weekends. Tech house DJs help promote emerging local artists.

Ritter Butzke, Ritterstrasse 24, Kreuzberg, tel 030 902 77 31 01, www.ritterbutzke.de. Kreuzberg's tireless bohos rock at postindustrial clubs like Butzke, a backstreet bastion of elektro, trance, and house music that is distinctly Berlin. The organizers stage offbeat events like Möbelrücken ("rearranging furniture"), poetry slams, and the annual shoeless night.

Sage Club, Köpenicker Strasse 76, Mitte, tel 030 278 98 30, www.sage-club.de. One of Berlin's trendiest clubs, the Sage seethes with house music on three dance floors. High-profile DJs host charity party nights with proceeds going to the Sage Hospital in Senegal. Outdoor swimming pool for cooling off.

Spindler & Klatt, Köpenicker Strasse 16–17, Kreuzberg, tel 030 319 88 18 60, www.spindlerklatt .com. This Spreeside club-restaurant always makes the A-list of Berlin's dinner-and-dance spots. Beautiful people recline on white dining futons while nibbling pan-Asian specialties. Music runs the gamut from hip-hop to jazz.

Tresor, Köpenicker Strasse 70, Kreuzberg, tel 030 62 90 87 50, www.tresorberlin.com. In the roaring '90s, the Safe was the motherlode of underground techno. This smooth successor spins elektro in an old power station cum art gallery.

Trompete, Lützowplatz 9, Tiergarten, tel 030 23 00 47 94, www.trompete-berlin.de, closed Sun.–Tues. Far from the madding crowd of Mitte, this relaxed bar and concert lounge run by actor Ben Becker wanders the charts from soul and disco to hip-hop and jazz. Garden action in summer.

Watergate, Falckensteinstrasse 49, Kreuzberg, tel 030 61 28 03 96, www.water-gate.de. Bone-rattling techno, ceiling LED shows, and a superb riverside terrace next to the gorgeous Oberbaum Bridge keep this club in the world's top 20—a prominent DJ mag says so.

Weekend, Alexanderplatz 5, Mitte, tel 030 24 63 16 76, www .week-end-berlin.de. On the 12th floor of GDR-era tower Haus des Reisens, this glitzy joint affords stunning views of the city and nocturnal workouts to house and techno.

White Trash Fast Food, Schönhauser Allee 6–7, Prenzlauer Berg, tel 030 50 34 86 68, www.whitetrashfastfood.com. Madonna, Mick Jagger, and Kid Rock all gyrated at this wildly alternative club-restaurant. The décor is somewhere between Irish pub and Chinatown—touristy but irresistible. The basement has a tattoo parlor, a smokers' cinema, and a second stage in the Diamond Lounge.

Language Guide

Useful Words & Phrases

Yes *Ja*
No *Nein*
Please *Bitte*
Thank you *Danke*
Excuse me *Entschuldigen Sie bitte*
Sorry *Entschuldigung*
Goodbye *Auf Wiedersehen*
Goodbye (informal) *Tschüs*
Good morning *Guten Morgen*
Good day (afternoon) *Guten Tag*
Good evening *Guten Abend*
Good night *Guten Nacht*

here *hier*
there *dort*
today *heute*
yesterday *gestern*
tomorrow *morgen*
now *jetzt*
later *später*

large *gross*
small *klein*
hot *heiss*
cold *kalt*
good *gut*
bad *schlecht*
left *links*
right *rechts*
straight ahead *geradeaus*

Do you speak English? *Sprechen Sie Englisch?*
I am American *Ich bin Amerikaner (m)/Amerikanerin (f)*
I don't understand *Ich verstehe Sie nicht*
Please speak more slowly *Bitte sprechen Sie langsamer*
Where is/are...? *Wo ist/sind...?*
I don't know *Ich weiss nicht*
My name is... *Ich heisse...*
At what time? *Wann?*
What time is it? *Wieviel Uhr ist es?*

Numbers

one *eins*
two *zwei*
three *drei*
four *vier*
five *fünf*
six *sechs*
seven *sieben*
eight *acht*
nine *neun*
ten *zehn*
twenty *zwanzig*

Days of the Week

Monday *Montag*
Tuesday *Dienstag*
Wednesday *Mittwoch*
Thursday *Donnerstag*
Friday *Freitag*
Saturday *Samstag/Sonnabend*
Sunday *Sonntag*

In the Hotel

Do you have a vacancy? *Haben Sie noch ein Zimmer frei?*
a single room *ein Einzelzimmer*
a double room *ein Doppelzimmer*
with/without bathroom/shower *mit/ohne Bad/Dusche*

Emergencies

Help *Hilfe*
I need a doctor/dentist *Bitte rufen Sie einen Arzt/Zahnarzt*
Can you help me? *Können Sie mir helfen?*
Where is the hospital?/police station?/telephone? *Wo finde ich das Krankenhaus?/die Polizeiwache?/das Telefon?*

Shopping

Do you have...? *Haben Sie...?*
How much is it? *Wieviel kostet es?*
Do you take credit cards *Akzeptieren Sie Kreditkarten?*
When do you open/close? *Wann machen Sie auf/zu?*
size (clothes) *Kleidergrösse*
size (shoes) *Schuhgrösse*
brown *braun*
black *schwarz*
red *rot*
blue *blau*
green *grün*
yellow *gelb*
cheap *billig*
expensive *teuer*

Sightseeing

visitor information *Touristen-Information*
exhibition *Ausstellung*
open *geöffnet*
closed *geschlossen*
entry fee *Eintrittspreis*
free *frei/umsonst*
cathedral *Kathedrale*
church *Kirche*
castle *Schloss*
old town *Altstadt*
town hall *Rathaus*

MENU READER

I'd like to order *Ich möchte bestellen*
I am a vegetarian *Ich bin Vegetarier (m) Vegetarierin (f)*
The check, please *Die Rechnung, bitte*
dinner *Abendessen*
menu *Speisekarte*
sugar *Zucker*
bread *Brot*
cheese *Käse*
wine list *Weinkarte*

Drinks/*Getränke*

Apfelsaft apple juice
Bier beer
Kaffee coffee
Orangensaft orange juice
Rotwein red wine
Weisswein white wine

Breakfast/*Frühstück*

Brötchen bread roll
Eier eggs
Speck bacon

Meat & Fish/*Fleisch & Fisch*

Bockwurst large frankfurter
Forelle trout
Krabben shrimp
Lachs salmon
Leberknödel liver dumplings
Rinderbraten roast beef
Sauerbraten marinated beef
Schinken ham

Fruit & Vegetables/*Obst & Gemüse*

Apfel apple
Apfelsine/Orange orange
Erdbeeren strawberries
Kartoffeln potatoes
Kohl cabbage
Reis rice
Spargel asparagus
Weintrauben grapes
Zitrone lemon
Zwiebeln onions

Desserts/*Nachspeisen*

Apfelkuchen apple cake
Gebäck pastry
Krapfen/Berliner doughnuts
Obstkuchen fruit tart
Sachertorte chocolate cake

INDEX

Boldface indicates illustrations.
CAPS indicates thematic categories.

A

Abguss-Sammlung Antiker Plastik
    Berlin 153
Ahmadiyya-Moschee 153, **154**
Air travel 92, 185, 236
Akademie der Künste 59
Alexanderplatz & around **81, 102,**
    102–104, 123, 147
Alliierten-Museum 200–201
Alte Nationalgalerie 65, **87,** 90–92,
    91
Alter Jüdischer Friedhof 109
Altes Museum **87, 95,** 95–96
Ampelmännchen (pedestrian lights) 98
Anne Frank Zentrum 108
AquaDom & Sea Life Center **81,**
    102, 104
Archenhold Observatory 168
Architecture 40–42, **122,** 122–123
Art galleries & museums *see*
    MUSEUMS
Arts 40–50, 45, 256–257
Arts Bunker 111
ATMs 239
Auerbachs Keller, Leipzig 227, 255

B

Bach, Johann Sebastian **207,** 227
Balloon rides 72
Banks 239
Bars & beaches 20, **20–21,** 203, **203,**
    260–261
Bats 193
Bauhaus Archiv 131, **131**
Beaches 20, **20–21,** 203, **203,**
    260–261
Beer 39, 106, 261
Berlin Airlift 34, **34,** 176, 185
Berlin Wall **78,** 78–79
    artwork **20–21, 155,** 167, **167**
    bicycling 79
    Checkpoint Charlie 77, **77**
    fall of 36, 59
    memorials 100, 114
    Palace of Tears Exhibition 80
Berliner Dom 97, **97**
Berliner Medizinhistorisches Museum
    111
Berliner Unterwelten 166
Berlinische Galerie **18, 178,** 178–179
Bicycling 79, 237
Bismarck, Otto von 25–26, 121
Boat rentals & tours 143, **143,** 221
Bode-Museum **86,** 90
Books & literature 45–46, 128,
    235–236, 257
Botanical gardens *see* GARDENS
Bowie, David 50
Brandenburg an der Havel 231
Brandenburger Tor **6, 22–23, 58,**
    58–59, 147
Brecht, Bertolt 29, 34, 46, 110–111,
    246, 262

Brecht-Weigel-Gedenkstätte
    110–111
Breweries 106
Bröhan-Museum 150, **150**
Brücke Museum 201–202
Bücher-Sonderverkauf (book sale) 128
Bus travel 8–9, 10, 236, 237

C

Camera Work 154, 256
Car rentals and driving **218,** 218–
    219, 236, 237
Cell phones 238
Central Berlin 9, 81–114
    Alexanderplatz & around **81,**
        102, 102–104, 123, 147
    Berliner Dom & Lustgarten
        97, **97**
    DDR Museum 99, **99**
    Gedenkstätte Berliner Mauer 114
    Hackescher Markt & around
        107, 107–109, 244
    Historischer Hafen 114
    hotels & restaurants 243–246
    maps 82–83, 100–101
    Märkisches Museum 114, **114**
    Museum Island 16, 82, **84,**
        84–96, **86–87, 88, 91, 93, 95**
    Nikolaiviertel **105,** 105–106
    Oranienburger Tor **110,**
        110–111
    Red Berlin walk 100–101
    Schlossplatz & around 98
Centrum Judaicum 109
Charlottenburg 133–154
    Abguss-Sammlung Antiker Plastik
        Berlin 153
    Ahmadiyya-Moschee 153, **154**
    Bröhan-Museum 150, **150**
    Camera Work 154, 256
    Gedenkstätte Plötzensee 152,
        152
    hotels & restaurants 247–249
    Kaiser-Wilhelm-Gedächtniskirche
        26, 136, **136,** 138
    Käthe-Kollwitz-Museum 137,
        137, 138
    Kurfürstendamm walk **138,**
        138–139
    Ludwig-Erhard-Haus 123, **133,**
        139
    maps 134–135, 139
    Museum Berggruen & Sammlung
        Scharf-Gerstenberg **148,**
        148–149
    Museum Charlottenburg-
        Wilmersdorf 154
    Museum für Fotografie 139,
        151, **151**
    Rathaus Charlottenburg 154
    Schloss Charlottenburg **2–3,**
        140, 140–142, **144,** 144–145
Checkpoint Charlie 77, **77**
Chorin 231
Christmas markets 146–147, 235

CHURCHES
    Berliner Dom 97, **97**
    Deutscher Dom 69
    Dom St. Peter und Paul,
        Brandenburg an der Havel 231
    Dorfkirche St. Annen 205
    Französischer Dom **68,** 68–69
    Frauenkirche, Dresden 220, 222
    Friedrichstadt Kirche 68, **68**
    Friedrichswerdersche Kirche
        65, **65**
    Gethsemanekirche 173
    Heilig-Geist-Kapelle 104
    Kaiser-Wilhelm-Gedächtniskirche
        26, 136, **136,** 138
    Marienkirche 103
    Matthäuskirche 124
    Nikolaikirche **12,** 105, **105**
    Nikolaikirche, Leipzig **226,** 227
    Nikolaikirche, Spandau 193
    Sophienkirche 108
    St.-Hedwigs-Kathedrale 64
    Stadtkirche St. Marien,
        Lutherstadt Wittenberg 230
    Thomaskirche, Leipzig **207,** 227
    Zionskirche 158
Cinema 46–49, **47**
    Deutsche Kinemathek **42–43,**
        74–75
    film festival 234
    Marlene Dietrich 47–48, 182,
        182
    silent films 48
    venues 261–262
    Zeughauskino 67
City Hall 103–104
Classical music & theater 49–50,
    262–263
Climate 234
Clothing 164, **164,** 235, 238,
    257–258
Concentration camps 32, 208,
    217, **217**
Consulates 240
Conversions (measurement) 238
Corbusierhaus **205,** 206
Cottbus 231–232, **232**
Credit cards 240, 256
Crime 240
Cultural complexes 263
Currency 239
Currywurst 38, 153
Customs (etiquette) 238

D

Dahlem *see* Spandau, Dahlem &
    the West
Daimler Contemporary 76
Dalí—The Exhibition 80
Dance 29
DDR Museum 99, **99**
Department stores 138, **138,** 253,
    257
Deutsch-Russisches-Museum 169
Deutsche Kinemathek **42–43,** 74–75
Deutscher Dom 69

Deutsches Historisches Museum **66**, 66–67
Deutsches Technikmuseum Berlin 184, **184**
Dietrich, Marlene 47–48, 182, **182**
Diplomatenviertel 131
Disabilities, travelers with 239–240
Discount cards 10, 85
Dom St. Peter und Paul, Brandenburg an der Havel 231
Domäne Dahlem 197
Dorfkirche St. Annen 205
Dorotheenstädtischer Friedhof 110
Dresden 208, **208, 220,** 220–224, **223,** 255
DRIVES
    driving and car rental 236, 237
    Mecklenburg Lake District **218,** 218–219

E
The East see Prenzlauer Berg, Friedrichshain, & the East
East Side Gallery **20–21,** 167, **167**
Electricity 238
Embassies & consulates 240
Emergencies 240, 265
Entertainment 239, 260–264
Ephraim-Palais 105–106
Ernst-Thälmann-Park 173, **174**
Etiquette & customs 238
Excursions 207–232
    Brandenburg an der Havel 231
    Chorin 231
    Cottbus 231–232, **232**
    Dresden 208, **208, 220,** 220–224, **223,** 255
    hotels & restaurants 254–255
    Leipzig **207,** 208, **225,** 225–228, **226,** 255
    Lutherstadt Wittenberg 208, 230, **230**
    maps 209, 219
    Mecklenburg Lake District drive **218,** 218–219
    Neuruppin 232
    Potsdam 208, **210,** 210–216, **212–213, 214,** 234, 254–255
    Rheinsberg 218, 232
    Sachsenhausen 32, 208, 217, **217**
    Spreewald 229, **229**
EXPERIENCES
    art gallery hopping 179
    beach bar craze 20
    bicycling the Berlin Wall 79
    boat trips 143, **143,** 221
    breweries 106
    chocolate 64
    dance scene 29
    Domäne Dahlem 197
    Festival of Lights 147
    ice rave 202
    long museum nights 90, 235
    M10 (party tram) 160
    paddle steamers 221
    Photoautomats 109
    secret supper clubs 39
    silent cinema 48

trippy tours 92
    underground tours 166, **166**

F
Fashion 164, **164,** 235, 257–258
Faust (Goethe) 227
Fernsehturm 101, 102, 103
Festival of Lights 147, 235
Festivals & events 147, 234–235
Film see Cinema
Flea markets 193, 258
Fledermauskeller 193
Food & drink **38,** 38–39
    beer 39, 106, 261
    Currywurst 38, 153
    menu reader 265
    secret supper clubs 39
    shopping for **38,** 258–259
    see also HOTELS & RESTAURANTS
Französischer Dom **68,** 68–69
Frauenkirche, Dresden 220, 222
Frederick the Great 24, **25,** 211
Friedrichshain see Prenzlauer Berg, Friedrichshain, & the East
Friedrichstadt Kirche 68, **68**
Friedrichstadtpassagen 69
Friedrichswerdersche Kirche 65, **65**
Funkturm 205–206

G
GARDENS
    Botanischer Garten 205
    Kleistpark 186
    Pfaueninsel 204
    Schloss Branitz, Cottbus 231
    Schloss Schönhausen 165
    Schlossgarten Charlottenburg 145
Gaslaternenmuseum 121
Gedenkstätte Berlin Hohenschönhausen 162–163
Gedenkstätte Berliner Mauer 114
Gedenkstätte Deutscher Widerstand 132
Gedenkstätte Normannenstrasse (Stasi Museum) **161,** 161–162
Gedenkstätte Plötzensee 152, **152**
Gedenkstätte Sachsenhausen 208, 217, **217**
Gemäldegalerie 116, **126,** 126–128
Gendarmenmarkt & around **68,** 68–69, 147
Georg-Kolbe-Museum 206
Gethsemanekirche 173
Graffiti 108
Grassi-Museum, Leipzig 228
Grosser Müggelsee 172, **172**
Grünau 172
Grunewald **200,** 200–202
Güstrow 219

H
Hackescher Markt & around **107,** 107–109, 244
Hamburger Bahnhof/Museum für Gegenwart–Berlin 111

Handwerkervereinshaus 108
Hanf Museum 106
Hansa Studios 50
Haus der Kulturen der Welt 119
Haus der Wannsee-Konferenz **187,** 204
Haus Huth 76
Heilig-Geist-Kapelle 104
Heinrich Zille Museum 106
Hess, Rudolf 192, **194,** 194–195, **195**
Heuwer, Herta 153
Hinterhöfe (courtyards) 26
Historische Ausstellung 69
Historischer Hafen 114
History 22–37
Hitler, Adolf **30,** 31–32, 55, 71–72, 132, 152, 191, 194, **194**
Hohenschönhausen Memorial 162–163
Holidays 234–235, 238
Holocaust 31, 113, 165, 204
Holocaust Monument **60,** 60–61, 123
Hot-air balloons 72
HOTELS & RESTAURANTS 38–39, 241–255
    Central Berlin 243–246
    Charlottenburg 247–249
    excursions 254–255
    language guide 265
    Prenzlauer Berg, Friedrichshain, & the East 249–252
    Schöneberg to Kreuzberg 252–254
    Spandau, Dahlem, & the West 254
    Tiergarten & around 246–247
    tipping 11, 241
    Unter den Linden & Potsdamer Platz 76, 242–243
Hugenottenmuseum 68–69
Das Humboldt-Forum 98

I
Ice raves 202
Information, tourist 9, 240
Insurance 235
Internet 238
Invalidenfriedhof 111

J
Jagdschloss Grunewald 202
Jewish Academy 181
Jewish community **112,** 112–113, 235
    Nazi persecution 31–32, 107, 109, 112–113, **113**
    see also Holocaust
Jüdischer Friedhof Weissensee 165, **165**
Jüdisches Gemeindehaus 139
Jüdisches Museum Berlin 123, **180,** 180–181

K
KaDeWe 138, **138,** 253, 257
Kaiser-Wilhelm-Gedächtniskirche 26, 136, **136,** 138
Karl-Marx-Allee 173–174
Karlshorst 169, **169**

Käthe-Kollwitz-Museum 137, **137**, 138
Kennedy, John F. 59, 176, 186
Kleistpark 186
Kollwitz, Käthe 137
Komische Oper 62–63, 262
Konzerthaus 69, 262
Köpenick **170**, 170–171
Kreuzberg **40–41**, 177, 183, **183**
Ku'damm (Kurfürstendamm) 134–135, **138**, 138–139
Kulturforum 16, 116, **124**, 124–125
Kunstgewerbemuseum 116, 125, 171
Kupferstichkabinett 128

L

Language guide 265
Leipzig **207**, 208, **225**, 225–228, **226**, 255
Lichtenberg **161**, 161–163
Liebermann-Villa am Wannsee 203–204
Long Museum Night 90, 235
Lost property 240
Ludwig-Erhard-Haus 123, **133**, 139
Luftwaffenmuseum 193
Lutherstadt Wittenberg 208, 230, **230**

M

M10 (party tram) 160
Maps
    central Berlin 82–83, 100–101
    Charlottenburg 134–135, 139
    excursions 209, 219
    Mecklenburg Lake District 219
    Prenzlauer Berg, Friedrichshain, & the East 156–157, 159
    Schöneberg to Kreuzberg 176–177
    Spandau, Dahlem, & the West 188–189
    Tiergarten & around 116–117
    Unter den Linden & Potsdamer Platz 52–53, 71
Marie-Elisabeth-Lüders-Haus 118–119
Marienkirche 103
Markets 174, 193, 199, 258
Märkisches Museum 114, **114**
Marmorpalais, Potsdam 216
Martin-Gropius-Bau 80
Matthäuskirche 124
Mauermuseum 77
Mauerpark 174, 258
Mecklenburg Lake District drive **218**, 218–219
Mediaspree 123
Medical care 240
Mielke, Erich 161–162, 163
Mitte *see* Central Berlin
Mobile phones 238
Money matters 239
Mosques 153, **154**
Movies *see* Cinema
Museum Island 16, 82, 84–96, **86–87**
    Alte Nationalgalerie 65, 90–92, **91**
    Altes Museum **95**, 95–96
    Bode-Museum 90
    Museum für Byzantinische Kunst 90
    Museum für Islamische Kunst 89

Neues Museum 92–94, **93**
Pergamonmuseum **84**, 85–86
Vorderasiatisches Museum 87–89, **88**
MUSEUMS
    art gallery hopping 179
    long museum nights 90, 235
    opening times 239
    tickets and passes 10, 85
    Abguss-Sammlung Antiker Plastik Berlin 153
    Akademie der Künste 59
    Alliierten-Museum 200–201
    Alte Nationalgalerie 65, **87**, 90–92, **91**
    Altes Museum **87**, **95**, 95–96
    Anne Frank Zentrum 108
    Arts Bunker 111
    Bachmuseum, Leipzig 227
    Bauhaus Archiv 131, **131**
    Beate Uhse Erotikmuseum 138
    Berliner Medizinhistorisches Museum 111
    Berlinische Galerie **18**, **178**, 178–179
    Bode-Museum **86**, 90
    Bröhan-Museum 150, **150**
    Brücke Museum 201–202
    Camera Work 154, 256
    Daimler Contemporary 76
    Dalí—The Exhibition 80
    DDR Museum 99, **99**
    Deutsch-Russisches-Museum 169
    Deutsche Kinemathek **42–43**, 74–75
    Deutsches Historisches Museum **66**, 66–67
    Deutsches Technikmuseum Berlin 184, **184**
    Domäne Dahlem 197
    East Side Gallery **20–21**, 167, **167**
    Gaslaternenmuseum 121
    Gedenkstätte Deutscher Widerstand (Bendlerblock) 132
    Gedenkstätte Normannenstrasse (Stasi Museum) **161**, 161–162
    Gemäldegalerie 116, **126**, 126–128
    Georg-Kolbe-Museum 206
    Grassi-Museum, Leipzig 228
    Grünauer Wassersportmuseum 172
    Hamburger Bahnhof/Museum für Gegenwart–Berlin 111
    Hanf Museum 106
    Heinrich Zille Museum 106
    Historische Ausstellung 79
    Holocaust Monument **60**, 60–61, 123
    Hugenottenmuseum 68–69
    Jüdisches Museum Berlin 123, **180**, 180–181
    Käthe-Kollwitz-Museum 137, **137**, 138
    Kunstgewerbemuseum 116, 125, 171
    Kupferstichkabinett 128
    Luftwaffenmuseum 193

Lutherhaus, Lutherstadt Wittenberg 230
Märkisches Museum 114, **114**
Martin-Gropius-Bau 80
Mauermuseum 77
Museen Dahlem—Kunst und Kulturen der Welt **196**, 196–199, **198**
Museum Berggruen & Sammlung Scharf-Gerstenberg **148**, 148–149
Museum Blindenwerkstatt Otto Weidt 108
Museum Charlottenburg-Wilmersdorf 154
Museum der Bildenden Künste, Leipzig 225
Museum für Byzantinische Kunst 90
Museum für Fotografie 139, 151, **151**
Museum für Islamische Kunst 89
Museum für Kommunikation 80
Museum für Naturkunde 111
Museum Haus am Checkpoint Charlie 77
Museum in der Runden Ecke, Leipzig 228
Museum Island 16, 65, 82, **84**, 84–96, **86–87**, **88**, **91**, **93**, **95**
Museumsdorf Düppel 206
Musikinstrumenten-Museum 125
Neue Nationalgalerie 116–117, **129**, 129–130
Neues Museum **86–87**, 92–94, **93**
Nikolaikirchemuseum 105
Palace of Tears Exhibition 80
Pergamonmuseum **84**, 85–86, **86–87**
Plattenbau Museum, Hellersdorf 104
Schwules Museum 132
Spreewald-Museum 229
Stasi Bildungszentrum 72
The Story of Berlin 138–139
Topographie des Terrors 73, **73**
Vorderasiatisches Museum 87–89, **88**
Zeitgeschichtliches Forum Leipzig 226
Zeughaus **66**, 66–67
Zwinger, Dresden 220–222
Music 49–50, 262–263
Musikinstrumenten-Museum 125

N

National debt clock 69
Nazis
    arts 48, 50, 63
    historical sites 17, 70–73
    history 31–32, 55, 108, 191
    persecution of Jews 31–32, 107, 109, 112–113, **113**
    war crimes trials 194
    see also Hitler, Adolf; Holocaust
Neue Nationalgalerie 116–117, **129**, 129–130
Neue Synagoge 109

Neue Wache 64–65, 100
Neuer Garten, Potsdam 216
Neues Museum **86–87,** 92–94, **93**
Neues Palais, Potsdam **210,** 215–216
Neuruppin 232
Newton, Helmut 151
Nightclubs **17, 110,** 263–264
Nikolaikirche **12,** 105, **105**
Nikolaikirche, Leipzig **226,** 227
Nikolaikirche, Spandau 193
Nikolaiviertel **105,** 105–106
Nuremberg war crimes trials 194

O
Oberbaumbrücke 167, **175**
Ökowerk 202
Old Regierungsviertel **70,** 70–73, **73**
Olympiastadion **190,** 190–191
Opernpalais 64
Oranienburger Tor **110,** 110–111

P
Palace of Tears Exhibition 80
PALACES
    Marmorpalais, Potsdam 216
    Neues Palais, Potsdam **210,**
        215–216
    Residenzschloss, Dresden **220,**
        223–224
    Schloss Bellevue 119
    Schloss Branitz, Cottbus 231
    Schloss Cecilienhof, Potsdam 216
    Schloss Charlottenburg **2–3,**
        140, 140–142, **144,** 144–145
    Schloss Friedrichsfelde 163
    Schloss Köpenick **170,** 170–171
    Schloss Sanssouci, Potsdam 211,
        214, 214–215
    Schloss Schönhausen 165
Pankow 165
Panoramapunkt 76
Pariser Platz **13, 58,** 58–59
PARKS
    Ernst-Thälmann-Park 173, **174**
    Kleistpark 186
    Lustgarten 97
    Mauerpark 174, 258
    Müritz-Nationalpark 218–219
    Neuer Garten, Potsdam 216
    Opernpalais 64
    Park Sanssouci, Potsdam **212–**
        213, 213
    Spreewald 229, **229**
    Tempelhof Park 185
    Tiergarten **115,** 116, **120,**
        120–121
    Treptower Park 168
    Viktoriapark 176–177, 183, **183**
    Volkspark Friedrichshain **4,** 160
Passports & visas 235
Paul-Löbe-Haus **118,** 118–119
Pergamonmuseum **84,** 85–86, **86–87**
Pfaueninsel 204
Philharmonie 124, **124**
Phones 238
Photoautomats 109
Plattenbau Museum, Hellersdorf 104
Plötzensee 152, **152**

Police 240
Post offices 238, 239
Potsdam 208, 210–216
    baroque district 211–213
    Filmpark Babelsberg 216
    Garnisonkirche 211
    hotels & restaurants 254–255
    Marmorpalais 216
    music festival 234
    Neuer Garten 216
    Neues Palais 210, 215–216
    Park Sanssouci **212–213,** 213
    Schloss Cecilienhof 216
    Schloss Sanssouci 211, **214,**
        214–215
Potsdamer Platz **14–15, 74,** 74–76,
    122, **122,** 147
Prenzlauer Berg, Friedrichshain, & the
    East 155–174
    Berlin Wall **155**
    East Side Gallery **20–21,** 167, **167**
    Ernst-Thälmann-Park 173, **174**
    Gethsemanekirche 173
    Grosser Müggelsee & Grünau
        172, **172**
    hotels & restaurants 249–252
    Karl-Marx-Allee 173–174
    Karlshorst 169, **169**
    Köpenick **170,** 170–171
    Lichtenberg **161,** 161–163
    maps 156–157, 159
    Mauerpark 174, 258
    Pankow & Weissensee 165, **165**
    Prenzlauer Berg promenade **158,**
        158–159
    Treptower Park 168
    Volkspark Friedrichshain **4,** 160
Priam's gold 94

Q
Quartier Potsdamer Platz 75–76

R
Radio 239
Rathaus Charlottenburg 154
Rathaus Schöneberg 186
Reagan, Ronald 59
Regierungsviertel (new) **118,** 118–
    119, 122–123
Regierungsviertel (old) **70,** 70–73, **73**
Reichstag Building **33, 54,** 54–57,
    56–57, 118
Residenzschloss, Dresden **220,**
    223–224
Restaurants see HOTELS &
    RESTAURANTS
Restrooms 239
Rheinsberg 218, 232
Riehmers Hofgarten 183, 252
Rotes Rathaus 103–104
Russian Embassy 62

S
Sachsenhausen 32, 208, 217, **217**
St.-Hedwigs-Kathedrale 64
Sammlung Scharf-Gerstenberg
    148, 149

Scheunenviertel **107,** 113
Schloss Bellevue 119
Schloss Branitz, Cottbus 231
Schloss Cecilienhof, Potsdam 216
Schloss Charlottenburg **2–3, 140,**
    140–142, **144,** 144–145
Schloss Friedrichsfelde 163
Schloss Köpenick **170,** 170–171
Schloss Sanssouci, Potsdam 211, **214,**
    214–215
Schloss Schönhausen 165
Schlossgarten Charlottenburg 145
Schlossplatz & around 98
Schöneberg to Kreuzberg 175–186
    Berlinische Galerie **18, 178,**
        178–179
    Deutsches Technikmuseum
        Berlin 184, **184**
    hotels & restaurants 252–254
    Jüdisches Museum Berlin 123,
        180, 180–181
    Kleistpark 186
    Kreuzberg & Viktoriapark
        40–41, 176–177, 183, **183**
    map 176–177
    Oberbaumbrücke 167, **175**
    Rathaus Schöneberg 186
    Tempelhof Park 185
Schwerin 219
Schwules Museum 132
Sea Life Center **81, 102,** 104
Segway tours 92
Semperoper, Dresden 222–223, **223**
Shopping 256–259
    department stores & malls 138,
        138, 253, 257
    fashion 164, 257–258
    flea markets 193, 258
    language guide 265
    opening hours 239, 256
Sony Center **14–15, 42–43,** 74, **74**
Sophienkirche 108
Sophiensäle 108
Sophienstrasse 108–109
Sowjetisches Ehrenmal, Tiergarten
    100, 120, **120**
Sowjetisches Ehrenmal, Treptower
    Park 168
Spandau, Dahlem, & the West
    187–206
    Botanischer Garten 205
    Dorfkirche St. Annen 205
    Funkturm 205–206
    Georg-Kolbe-Museum 206
    Grunewald **200,** 200–202
    map 188–189
    Museen Dahlem–Kunst und
        Kulturen der Welt **196,**
        196–199, **198**
    Museumsdorf Düppel 206
    Olympiastadion **190,** 190–191
    restaurants 254
    Spandau 146–147, **192,** 192–193
    Teufelsberg 206
    Wannsee **187, 203,** 203–204
Spreepark 168
Spreewald 229, **229**
Spreewald-Museum 229

Spy swaps 215
Staatsbibliothek 63, 100
Staatsoper **51**, 64, 262
Stadtkirche St. Marien, Lutherstadt Wittenberg 230
Stasi Bildungszentrum 72
Stasi Museum **161**, 161–162
Stauffenberg, Claus Schenk Graf von 132
Stolpersteine (memorial plaques) 31
The Story of Berlin 138–139
Strandbad Wannsee 203, **203**
Subway 9, 237
Synagogues 109, 159

T

Taxes 256
Taxis 9, 11, 237
Telephones 238
Television 239
Tempelhof Park 185
Teufelsberg 206
Thälmann, Ernst 173
Theater 262–263
Thomaskirche, Leipzig **207**, 227
Tiergarten & around 115–132
    Bauhaus Archiv 131, **131**
    Diplomatenviertel 131
    Gedenkstätte Deutscher Widerstand 132
    Gemäldegalerie & Kupferstichkabinett 116, **126**, 126–128
    hotels & restaurants 246–247
    Kulturforum 16, 116, **124**, 124–125
    map 116–117
    Neue Nationalgalerie 116–117, **129**, 129–130
    Regierungsviertel **118**, 118–119, 122–123
    Schwules Museum 132

Tiergarten **115**, 116, **120**, 120–121
Tierpark Berlin 163
Time differences 239
Tipping 11, 241
Topographie des Terrors 73, **73**
Tourist information 9, 240
Tours, guided 92, 166, **166**
Transportation 8–9, 10, 160, **233**, 236, 237
Travel insurance 235
Treptower Park 168

U

Underground tours 166, **166**
Unter den Linden & Potsdamer Platz 51–80
    Berlin Wall **78**, 78–79
    Brandenburger Tor & Pariser Platz **6**, **13**, **22–23**, **58**, 58–59, 147
    Checkpoint Charlie 77, **77**
    Dalí–The Exhibition 80
    Gendarmenmarkt **68**, 68–69, 147
    Holocaust Monument **60**, 60–61, 123
    hotels & restaurants 76, 242–243
    maps 52–53, 71
    Martin-Gropius-Bau 80
    Museum für Kommunikation 80
    Palace of Tears Exhibition 80
    Potsdamer Platz **14–15**, **74**, 74–76, 122, **122**, 147
    Reichstag Building **33**, **54**, 54–57, **56–57**, 118
    Staatsoper **51**, 64, 262
    Unter den Linden **62**, 62–65, **65**
    Wilhelmstrasse & Old Regierungsviertel walk **70**, 70–73, **73**
    Zeughaus & Deutsches Historisches Museum **66**, 66–67

V

Viktoriapark 176–177, 183, **183**
Visas & passports 235
Visitor information 9, 240
Vistas 76
Voigt, Friedrich Wilhelm 171
Volkspark Friedrichshain **4**, 160
Vorderasiatisches Museum 87–89, **88**

W

Waldbühne 125
WALKS
    Kurfürstendamm **138**, 138–139
    Prenzlauer Berg **158**, 158–159
    Red Berlin 100–101
    Wilhelmstrasse & Old Regierungsviertel **70**, 70–73, **73**
Wannsee **187**, **203**, 203–204
Weather 234
Weihnachtsmarkt (Christmas market) 146–147
Weissensee 165, **165**
The West *see* Spandau, Dahlem, & the West
Wi-Fi 238
Wild boar 201
Wilhelm II, Kaiser 26–28, **27**, 44
Wilhelmstrasse **70**, 70–73, **73**

Z

Zeitgeschichtliches Forum Leipzig 226
Zentralfriedhof Friedrichsfelde 162
Zeughaus **66**, 66–67
Zionskirche 158
Zitadelle, Spandau **192**, 192–193
Zoos 121, 163
Zwinger, Dresden 220–222

ILLUSTRATIONS CREDITS

National Geographic

TRAVELER

Berlin

Published by the National Geographic Society
John M. Fahey, *Chairman of the Board and Chief Executive Officer*
Declan Moore, *Executive Vice President; President, Publishing and Travel*
Melina Gerosa Bellows, *Executive Vice President; Chief Creative Officer, Books, Kids, and Family*
Lynn Cutter, *Executive Vice President, Travel*
Keith Bellows, *Senior Vice President and Editor in Chief, National Geographic Travel Media*

Prepared by the Book Division
Hector Sierra, *Senior Vice President and General Manager*
Janet Goldstein, *Senior Vice President and Editorial Director*
Jonathan Halling, *Design Director, Books and Children's Publishing*
Marianne R. Koszorus, *Design Director, Books*
Barbara A. Noe, *Senior Editor, National Geographic Travel Books*
R. Gary Colbert, *Production Director*
Jennifer A. Thornton, *Director of Managing Editorial*
Susan S. Blair, *Director of Photography*
Meredith C. Wilcox, *Director, Administration and Rights Clearance*

Staff for This Book
Lawrence M. Porges, *Editor*
Karen Carmichael, *Project Editor*
Patricia Daniels, *Text Editor*
Linda Makarov, *Designer*
Carl Mehler, *Director of Maps*
Michael McNey and Mapping Specialists, *Map Research and Production*
Marshall Kiker, *Associate Managing Editor*
Galen Young, *Rights Clearance Specialist*
Katie Olsen, *Production Design Assistant*

Production Services
Christopher A. Liedel, *Chief Financial Officer*
Phillip L. Schlosser, *Vice President*
Chris Brown, *Technical Director*
Nicole Elliott, *Manager*
Monika D. Lynde, *Manager*
Rachel Faulise, *Manager*

First edition: Edited and designed by AA Publishing (a trading name of Automobile Association Developments Limited, whose registered office is Norfolk House, Priestley Road, Basingstoke, Hampshire, England RG24 9NY. Registered number: 1878835).

Area maps drawn by Chris Orr Associates, Southampton, England

The information in this book has been carefully checked and to the best of our knowledge is accurate. However, details are subject to change, and the National Geographic Society cannot be responsible for such changes, or for errors or omissions.140

The National Geographic Society is one of the world's largest nonprofit scientific and educational organizations. Founded in 1888 to "increase and diffuse geographic knowledge," the member-supported Society works to inspire people to care about the planet. Through its online community, members can get closer to explorers and photographers, connect with other members around the world, and help make a difference. National Geographic reflects the world through its magazines, television programs, films, music and radio, books, DVDs, maps, exhibitions, live events, school publishing programs, interactive media, and merchandise. National Geographic magazine, the Society's official journal, published in English and 38 local-language editions, is read by more than 60 million people each month. The National Geographic Channel reaches 440 million households in 171 countries in 38 languages. National Geographic Digital Media receives more than 25 million visitors a month. National Geographic has funded more than 10,000 scientific research, conservation, and exploration projects and supports an education program promoting geography literacy. For more information, visit www.nationalgeographic.com.

For more information, please call 1-800-NGS LINE (647-5463) or write to the following address:

National Geographic Society
1145 17th Street N.W.
Washington, D.C. 20036-4688 U.S.A.

For information about special discounts for bulk purchases, please contact National Geographic Books Special Sales: ngspecsales@ngs.org

For rights or permissions inquiries, please contact National Geographic Books Subsidiary Rights: ngbookrights@ngs.org

Copyright © 2006, 2014
All rights reserved. Reproduction of the whole or any part of the contents without written permission from the publisher is prohibited.

National Geographic Traveler: Berlin
(Second Edition)
ISBN: 978-1-4262-1267-3

Printed in Hong Kong
13/THK/1